Managing Innovation and Change

Managing Innovation and Change

Second Edition

Edited by Jane Henry and David Mayle

The Open University

BUSINESS SCHOOL

in association with

SAGE Publications

London • Thousand Oaks • New Delhi

This publication is the prescribed MBA Course Reader for the Creativity, Innovation and Change Module (B822) at The Open University Business School. Details of this and other Open University courses can be obtained from the Call Centre, PO Box 724, The Open University, Milton Keynes MK7 6ZS. United Kingdom: tel. +44 (0)1908 653231: e-mail ces-gen@open.ac.uk

Alternatively, you may visit The Open University Business School website at http://oubs.open.ac.uk or The Open University website at http://www/open.ac.uk

 SAGE Publications Ltd
6 Bonhill Street
London EC2A 4PU

SAGE Publications Inc
2455 Teller Road
Thousand Oaks, California 91320

SAGE Publications India Pvt Ltd
32, M-Block Market
Greater Kailash – I
New Delhi 110 048

British Library Cataloguing in Publication data

A catalogue record for this book is available from the British Library

ISBN 0-7619-6608-0
ISBN 0-7619-6609-9 (pbk)

Library of Congress Control Number: 200113590

Typeset by Keystroke, Jacaranda Lodge, Wolverhampton
Printed in Great Britain by Biddles Ltd, Guildford, Surrey

Contents

The authors

Philip Anderson, Associate Professor of Business Administration, School of Business, Dartmouth College.

Mahlon Apgar IV, Consultant, previously with McKinsey.

Michael B. Arthur, Professor of Management, Frank Sawyer School of Management, Suffolk University, Boston.

Jordan J. Baruch, Consultant, previously Assistant Secretary, Commerce for Science and Technology, USA.

John Bessant, Professor, Centre for Innovation Management, University of Brighton, Sussex.

David E. Bowen, Associate Professor of Management, Business Programs, Arizona State University.

Ivan Briscoe, Journalist and former researcher, DEMOS.

Philip Bromiley, Professor, Carlson School of Management, Minnesota.

Robert Brown, Professor, Cultural Studies, University of Minnesota.

James C. Collins, Management educator and author, runs a management learning laboratory, Boulder, Colorado.

Robert J. DeFillippi, Director, Entrepreneurial Studies, Frank Sawyer School of Management, Suffolk University, Boston.

Jeffrey H. Dyer, Assistant Professor of Management, Wharton School, University of Pennsylvania.

James Dyson, CEO, Dyson.

Göran Ekvall, Research Fellow, FA Institute, Stockholm and Visiting Professor, Center for Studies in Creativity, State University College, Buffalo.

Sydney Finkelstein, Professor of Strategy and Leadership, Tuck School of Business, Dartmouth College.

Gary Hamel, Chairman, Strategos, Visiting Professor, London Business School.

Michael Hammer, Consultant, author, previously Professor of Computer Science, MIT.

Jane Henry, Co-chair, Creativity, Innovation and Change Programme, Open University Business School, Milton Keynes, UK.

Robert D. Hof, *Business Week*, California.

Daniel T. Jones, Professor of Management, Cardiff Business School, University of Wales.

John Kay, Director, London Economics, Professor LSE, previously Director Said Business School, Oxford University, Institute of Fiscal Studies and Professor, London Business School, *Financial Times* columnist.

Edward E. Lawler III, Director, Center for Effective Organizations, Graduate School of Business Administration, University of Southern California.

Richard K. Lester, Director, Industrial Performance Center, Massachusetts Institute of Technology (MIT).

Roger Levett, CAG Consultants, London, UK.

Ken Lewis, Managing Director, Dutton Engineering, Bedfordshire.

Steve Lytton, Co-ordinator, CLASP, Bedfordshire and N. Bucks Supply Chain and Best Practice Network, Bedfordshire.

Kamal M. Malek, Researcher, Industrial Performance Center, MIT.

David Mayle, Co-chair, Creativity, Innovation and Change Programme, Open University Business School, Milton Keynes, UK.

Gary McWilliams, Staff reporter, *Wall Street Journal*, Houston.

Geoff Mulgan, Director, DEMOS, London.

William G. Ouchi, Professor of Management, Anderson Graduate School of Management, UCLA.

Keith Pavitt, Science Policy Research Unit, University of Sussex, Brighton.

Jeffrey Pfeffer, Professor of Organizational Behaviour, Graduate School of Business, Stanford University.

Michael J. Piore, Professor of Economics, MIT.

Jerry I. Porras, Lane Professor of Organizational Behaviour and Change, Stanford University Graduate School of Business.

C. K. Prahalad, Harvey C. Fruehauf Professor of Business Administration and Professor of Corporate Strategy and International Business, University of Michigan Business School, Ann Arbor.

James B. Quinn, Professor, Dartmouth College, Hanover, New Hampshire.

Alan G. Robinson, Professor of Operations Management, Eugene M. Isenberg School of Management, University of Massachusetts, Amherst.

Roy Rothwell, Professor, Science Policy Research Unit, University of Sussex.

Gabrielle Saveri, *Business Week*, San Francisco.

Dean M. Schroeder, Schulz Professor of Management, College of Business Administration, Valparaiso University, Indiana.

Gordon Shaw, Executive Director of Planning, 3M, St Paul, Minnesota.

Joe Tidd, Management School, Imperial College of Science and Technology, London University, London

James P. Womack, Consultant and Research Affiliate, Japan Programme, MIT.

Katherine A. Zein, Creativity and Innovation Lab, Polaroid Corporation, Cambridge, Massachusetts.

Acknowledgements

The authors would like to thank the Creativity, innovation and change critical readers, in particular Ros Bell and Ian Williams for their comments on an earlier draft of this manuscript, also Roger Summers for alerting them to Chapter 9, and Geoff Jones to Chapter 22 and to Paul Gardiner for suggesting Chapter 8.

Chapter 1: J. B. Quinn, J. J. Baruch and K. A. Zein: Edited extract from Chapter 1 of J. B. Quinn, J. J. Baruch and K. A. Zein, *The Innovation Explosion*, Free Press, NY, 1997.

Chapter 2: G. Hamel and C. K. Prahalad: Competing for the future. *Harvard Business Review*, Jul/Aug 1994, pp. 122–128.

Chapter 3: R. K. Lester, M. J. Piore and K. M. Malek: Interpretive management. *Harvard Business Review*, Mar/Apr 1998.

Chapter 4: R. Levett: edited chapter from *The Earthscan Reader in Business and the Environment* by Richard Welford and Richard Starkey (eds), pp. 251–268, Earthscan Publications Ltd, London: © Richard Welford, 1996.

Chapter 5: J. Pfeffer: Edited excerpt from 'Competitive advantage through people' *California Management Review*. Copyright © 1994 by Jeffrey Pfeffer; all rights reserved. Reprinted by permission of Harvard Business School Press.

Chapter 6: J. Collins and J. Porras: Extracted from *California Management Review*, 37, 2, Winter 1995, pp. 80–100. Copyright 1994 J. C. Collins and J. I. Porras. HarperCollins authorized reprint in CMR from their 1994 book.

Chapter 7: J. B Quinn, P. Anderson and S. Finkelstein: Managing professional intellect. *Harvard Business Review*, Mar/Apr 1996, pp. 71–80.

Chapter 8: G. Ekvall: Conditions and levels of creativity. Edited from *Creativity and Innovation Management*, 6, 4, December 1997, pp. 195–205. Blackwell Publishers Ltd.

Chapter 9: R. Rothwell: 5th generation. Edited article from *International Marketing Review*, 11, 1, 1994, pp. 7–30.

Chapter 10: J. Kay: *Financial Times*, 13 May 1998.

Chapter 11: J. P. Womack and D. T. Jones: Lean enterprise. Extract from *Harvard Business Review*, Mar/Apr 1994, pp. 93–103.

Chapter 12: J. Dyson: A new philosophy of business. Chapter from *Against the Odds*, Orion, 1997.

Chapter 13: G. Shaw, R. Brown and P. Bromiley: Strategic stories: How 3M is writing business planning. *Harvard Business Review*, May/June 1998.

Chapter 14: J. Tidd, J. Bessant and K. Pavitt: Learning through alliances. Edited extract from chapter 8 in *Managing Innovation*, John Wiley, 1997.

Chapter 15: R. J DeFillippi and M. B. Arthur: Paradox in project-based enterprise. Edited from *California Management Review*, 10, 2, Winter 1998.

Chapter 16: J. H. Dyer and W. G. Ouchi: Japanese-style partnerships. Extracted from *Sloan Management Review*, Fall 1993, pp. 51–63.

Chapter 17: K. Lewis and S. Lytton: Partnership sourcing. Extract from Chapter 5 in K. Lewis and S. Lytton, *How to transform your company – and enjoy it*, Management Books 2000, 1995 Didcot, Oxford.

Chapter 18: D. M. Schroeder and A. G. Robinson: Edited extract from *Sloan Management Review*, Spring 1991, pp. 67–79.

Chapter 19: D. E Bowen and E. E. Lawler: Edited extract from *Sloan Management Review*, Spring 1992, pp. 31–39.

Chapter 20: M. Hammer: Extracted from *Harvard Business Review*, Jul/Aug 1990.

Chapter 21: M. Apgar: Alternative workplace. Extract from *Harvard Business Review* 1998.

Chapter 22: G. Mulgan and I. Briscoe: Societies of networks. From *Demos* 8, 1996, pp. 29–30.

Chapter 23: R. Hof, G. McWilliams and G. Saveri: The 'click here' economy. Edited extract from *Business Week*, 22 June 1998.

Preface

Innovation and change are becoming increasing central parts of business life as organizations struggle to keep up with changing tastes, global competition and faster product life cycles. It has never been easy to predict which product and services will prove popular with customers and users. Neither is it a simple task to get the balance right between the need to allow staff sufficient freedom to be creative and innovative and to coordinate business objectives, standardize certain product specifications and conform to legal regulations. While some aspects of managing innovation are perennial, new technology, the global marketplace and deregulation are forcing new organizational forms and ways of working upon businesses which aspire to be innovative. This text aims to illustrate some of the strategies now available to manage innovation in a changing environment.

This book comprises three parts: management, innovation and change. The first part, Management, looks at the current business environment and its implications for the innovative management style now needed. The second part, Innovation, examines the importance of innovation in today's environment and some of the different strategies that can be adopted to manage innovation within and across organizations and business networks. The third part, Change, illustrates some of the different ways in which organizations have attempted to restructure themselves and the effects of new information and communications technology.

Part 1, Management, has two sections: section A looks at certain new approaches to management and section B looks at ways of developing people in innovative organizations.

Section A, Management context, examines the role of innovation in the current business environment. In chapter 1 Quinn highlights the prominence of intellectually based services in today's global marketplace. In chapter 2 Hamel and Prahalad make a plea for a more proactive approach to the future (rather than the more usual downsizing, reengineering or quality initiatives) as the best bet for securing future market share. In chapter 3 Lester offers the idea of improvisation as a modern metaphor for research and development, one he considers more appropriate in a changing environment than the traditional engineering metaphor of problem solving. In chapter 4 Levett discusses some of the factors a public sector organization needs to bear in mind when aiming for environmental innovation.

Section B, Managing people, looks at the key role of people in today's organization, the characteristics of leaders of organizations that retain their innovative qualities in the long term, ways of managing professionals and impact of organizational climate. In chapter 5 Pfeffer argues that staff and organizational culture are the critical differentiating factors between more and less successful firms. In chapter 6 Collins and Porras argue that the successful companies are often built by leaders who deliberately set up a self-sufficient and self-perpetuating innovative organization. In chapter 7 Quinn et al. explore ways of managing professionals and providing incentives that invite knowledge sharing. In chapter 8 Ekvall outlines the characteristics associated with an innovative organizational climate, highlighting the difference between such open climates and those strategies better suited to organizations practising incremental or adaptive creativity.

Part 2, Innovation, has two sections: on policy and management and on partnerships and networks.

Section C deals with innovation policy and innovation management. In chapter 9 Rothwell explains how ideas about the cause of innovation have changed over time and their consequences for innovation policy. In chapter 10 Kay illustrates the dangers of being a first mover and the merits of being a fast follower. In chapter 11 Womack and Jones develop their lean enterprise thesis to argue for an organizational form that places greater emphasis on skill development. Chapter 12 gives Dyson the opportunity to advocate a diligent approach to product and market development. Chapter 13 offers Shaw and colleagues' description of the development of storytelling in place of bullet points at that doyen of innovative organizations, 3M.

Section D addresses the question of partnerships across organizational boundaries. In chapter 14 Tidd, Bessant and Pavitt examine the role of interorganizational collaboration in the development and transfer of innovation. In chapter 15 DeFillippi and Arthur look at project-based enterprise in the film industry and the successive alliances of people loosely linked through social and business networks. In chapter 16 Dyer and Ouchi advocate the merits of long-term relationships with fewer preferred suppliers as a more productive use of organizational energy. In chapter 17 Lewis and Lytton describe the benefits of outsourcing in a small business.

Part 3, Change, comprises two sections. Section E examines some well-known but contrasting ways of developing organizational capability (continuous improvement, empowerment and reengineering). Section F looks at some of the ways in which technology is transforming business life.

Section E begins, in chapter 18, with Schroeder and Robinson's historical account of continuous improvement from suggestion schemes through to kaizen. In chapter 19 Bowen and Lawler examine whether the appropriate degree of empowerment is contingent on the nature of the business. In chapter 20 Hammer's classic article illustrates the case for reengineering processes around identifiable business outcomes.

In section F, on technology, chapter 21 by Apgar describes how organizations are managing a shift to home-based working and remote management. In chapter 22 Mulgan and Briscoe illustrate the very different form of organizational structure adopted by certain highly successful information age organizations. In chapter 23 Hof et al. outline some of the potential offered by e-commerce.

Readers familiar with Jane Henry and David Walker's 1991 Sage publication *Managing Innovation* will notice some changes of emphasis in this second edition, notably the critical place given to people, intellect, partnerships, networks and devolved structures. Some themes, however, are unaltered – open cultures still have a role to play and both innovation and change are still presented as long-term rather than short-term enterprises. The emphasis on project-based management, present in the previous text, is reinforced in this edition.

Managing Innovation and Change is part of the Open University Masters course in Creativity, Innovation and Change. It complements the *Organising for Innovation* textbook by Jane Henry et al. (Open University Press, 2002). Sage publishes an associated reader on *Creative Management* (2nd edition, 2001) also by Jane Henry.

The editors would like to thank Ros Bell and the Creativity, innovation and change critical readers for their comments on an earlier version of this draft.

Jane Henry and David Mayle
Open University Business School
2002
j.a.henry@open.ac.uk
d.t.mayle@open.ac.uk

Part 1

Management

Section A Management Context

Innovation and change are now central to today's business environment and this in turn has led to new management practices. The first four chapters highlight the nature of some of these changes. Quinn et al. explain how ill suited current economic models are to the business environment we now face and outline the key role of intellect, innovation and services in today's economy. Hamel and Prahalad argue for the importance of taking account of longer timescales and a wider perspective. Lester and colleagues illustrate the increase in flexibility now needed in product development and the implications for management. Levett outlines some of the factors facing local government when they try to be innovative.

Quinn et al. outline the consequences of the radically changed business environment facing industry today, highlighting the role of intellectually based services, world over-capacity, the centrality of software to innovation, the new disaggregated forms of organization and global outsourcing. They point out the importance of intellect, innovation and technology to economic growth and the need for new forms of organization and more appropriate forms of performance measures and incentives.

Hamel and Prahalad make an elegant plea for a continuous process of company foresight, involving managers from different parts of the organization. With a series of telling figures, they point out that downsizing may make the performance ratio look good in the short term, but it alienates staff and risks losing market share. Think of the UK in the 1970s and 1980s: it cut the manufacturing workforce by half but increased income by only about 10%, effectively losing market share. Hamel and Prahalad are no kinder to reengineering and quality initiatives; making the company better, they argue, is not enough to guarantee market share in the future. Leaders need to make a point of continuously gathering together collective wisdom to develop their corporate foresight and prepare the company for the future. They describe a case where market discontinuities, corporate competencies, benchmarking competitors and considering future opportunities were used as aids to developing company strategy.

Lester illustrates how a similar paradigm change is affecting work in product development and R&D. He calls this a switch from analytical to interpretative management. The thrust of this chapter is that an engineering approach to design and development, which aims to identify the problem and allocate resources to sort the problem only works in environments that are more stable than the present one. He illustrates how research needs to be rethought as a process that emerges from conversation, that values a willingness to improvise and requires an ability to orchestrate the outcome in the manner of jazz musician. He uses the fashion industry to illustrate the ever changing and fluid nature of new product development and argue the case for flexibility.

Levett discusses some of the factors entailed in public sector innovation. Specifically, he outlines the part a UK local authority (the local level of government) can play in assisting businesses in their area to innovate environmentally. He also points out where central government is better placed to do this and how certain central government innovations disrupt local environmental initiatives.

1 Intellect, Innovation, and Growth

James B. Quinn, J. J. Baruch and K. A. Zein

With rare exceptions, the economic and producing power of a modern corporation or nation lies more in its intellectual and systems capabilities than in its hard assets of raw materials, land, plant, and equipment. This is especially true for the large services industries – software, medical care, communications, education, entertainment, accounting, law, publishing, consulting, advertising, retailing, wholesaling, and transportation – that provide 79% of all jobs and 76% of the gross national product (GNP) in the United States today.[1] (See Table 1.1.)

In manufacturing as well, intellectual activities – such as research and development (R&D), process design, product design, logistics, marketing, market research, systems management, and technological innovation – generate the preponderance of value-added. By the year 2000 McKinsey & Company estimates, 85% of all jobs in the United States and 80% of those in Europe will be knowledge,

Table 1.1 US national income: contribution and employment by industry, 1996

	National income ($ billions)	Employment (millions)
Total economy	6,153.9	121.6
Goods sector		
Agriculture, forestry, fisheries	114.1	1.9*
Mining and construction	325.9	6.1
Manufacturing	1,069.1	18.2
Total goods sector	1,509.1 (24.5%)	26.2 (21.2%)
Services sector		
Finance, insurance, real estate	1,037.0	7.0
Retail trade	506.6	21.6
Wholesale trade	351.2	6.6
Transportation and public utilities	322.9	6.3
Communications	148.5	}34.4
Other services	1,444.1	
Total private services	3,810.3	75.9
Government+government enterprises	843.1	19.5
Total services sector	4,653.4 (75.6%)	95.4 (78.5%)

Source: Survey of Current Business (April–May 1997)
*1995 data
The services industries are large, technologically orientated and capital intensive

software, or technology based. Germany's Ministry of Labor estimates that by 2010 only 10% of all German jobs will be in manufacturing trade skills.[2]

The results of this changing economic landscape are profound for both corporate and national policymakers for the next two decades.

Intellectually based services will account for almost all the job growth in the world's advanced and rapidly emerging countries, in both the services industries and manufacturing. Managing intellect and services effectively in world-wide competition will pose some of the decade's most serious management challenges.

Over-capacity will exist world-wide for virtually all raw materials, foods, manufactures and physical goods, holding average returns on these items close to cost of capital. The exceptions – other than a smattering of cartels and cyclicalities – will be those companies and countries that can add value through unique development of their intellectual, innovation, or services capabilities.

Software will emerge as the core element in innovating, managing effectively and creating competitive edge in the new economy. It will decrease innovation times, costs, and risks by factors of ten while increasing value in customers' hands even more. Managing innovation and software will be the two most critical management skills of the new decade, yet few companies know how to exploit this interface to achieve its full potentials.

New highly disaggregated organizational forms, flexible innovation structures, and fast-response intellect-leveraging capabilities – enabled by software – provide benefits well beyond those that "teams" can offer. Much advanced innovation will be done through "independent collaborative" approaches featuring virtual laboratories, virtual skunk works, and software-modelling techniques that will allow companies to leverage their human and fiscal resources in ways never before imagined.

Global outsourcing and services trade will occur on a scale dwarfing past practice. Intellectually based services dominate the value chains of virtually all companies. And new technologies have decreased traditional scale and location advantages for everyone. Disaggregation, global sourcing, and dealing with the lateral competition of best-in-world specialist service suppliers have become strategic imperatives of the new era.

Nations and enterprises that hope to be successful in world competition need to understand, integrate, and manage their intellectual, technological, and innovation resources in a dramatically different fashion.

Strategic forces in the new economy

Certain powerful forces are compelling enterprises and governments to change the ways they conceptualize and implement their technology and growth strategies.

Intellectually based services

Services are a dominant and growing economic activity in the United States and all other major advanced economies (see Figures 1.1 and 1.2). The most useful

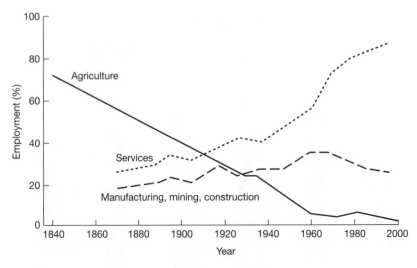

Figure 1.1 Employment as a percentage of total labour force

Source: Bureau of Census, *Historical Statistics of the U.S.: Colonial Times to 1970* and *Survey of Current Business 1971–1997*
Services jobs have always exceeded those in manufacturing and have provided virtually all job growth in this century

definition of services is that used by the *Economist*: "Services are anything sold in trade that could not be dropped on your foot."

Globally, services trade expanded 56% faster than merchandise trade from 1980 to 1992. In addition to the services industries, intellectually based services like R&D, product design, process design logistics, management information systems (MIS) marketing, sales, distribution, accounting, and human resources development dominate the value chains of product producers.

Virtually all new product innovations are made in software and embody intellectual intangibles. None of the official trade figures on services reflects either these values or the huge transaction volumes of asset exchanges handled by software and services entities world-wide (see Table 1.2).

Software usually provides the most valued functionalities for information technology (IT) hardware or other heavy investments (e.g. computer and communication infrastructures, print or copy generation, materials handling, and transportation facilities) that support services outputs. Service innovations have certain unique characteristics. They tend to be continually and interactively developed between the producing and using parties. Rapid diffusion and limited proprietary protection are common in service innovations. Both service innovations and service outputs move across borders and boundaries easily. Most service outputs are customized in some way for each user. And in a competitive services environment, most output benefits accrue to the using, not the innovating, country or enterprise.

Developing intellect, innovation, technology, and services – not managing physical resources – is the key to growth for most companies, as well as industries

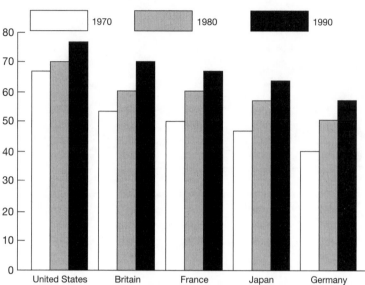

Employment in services as % of total employment

Figure 1.2 Employment in services: competitor nations

Sources: OECD: national statistics. Reproduced by special permission from "Schools Brief: The Manufacturing Myth," *Economist*, March 19, 1994, p. 91
Major advanced countries economies depend increasingly on services

Table 1.2 Transaction values in services

	Value ($ trillions)
Foreign exchange	320
FedWire	220
Treasury bonds	65
Custodial accounts	14
Swaps and derivatives	13
Mutual funds	3
US credit card volume	0.7

Transaction volumes in financial services exceed GNP and trade volumes by factors of 30 to 50 times

and nations. A major management shift is necessary at the enterprise level from a focus on managing ROA (return on physical assets) to managing a new form of ROI (return on intellect). At the enterprise level, this means that recruiting, developing, challenging, capturing, and measuring intellect need as much – or more – attention than buying, maintaining, improving, or exploiting physical assets and products.

Both business managers and national policymakers need to shift their thought processes away from traditional hard product and manufacturing concepts and toward a software, innovation, and services focus. Traditional modes of stimulating innovation and protecting intellectual property often break down in this environment.

For nations, it means first providing meaningful, accessible, and challenging educational opportunities and, second, strengthening the knowledge, skill base, and information infrastructures of the society. At the policy level it means a decreased focus on massive capital expenditure programs and an increased emphasis on creating incentives, new technological and work opportunities, market-driven demand systems and public support infrastructures that encourage people to learn, to apply their skills, and to excel in useful activities.

Sadly, few nations or enterprises have handled this shift well. Nevertheless, companies like Sun Microsystems, GE, IBM, Ford, Orbital Engines, Nintendo, Argyle Diamonds, AF&T, and all surviving publishers suggest the benefits of doing so.

World-wide over-capacity

For the next several decades, over-capacity world-wide will exist for virtually all physical goods, raw materials, foods, and manufactures. For over a century, almost all raw materials and manufactures have dropped in cost relative to real wages, and food production per capita has increased for decades (see Figures 1.3 and 1.4). If latent demand (where need exists) could be converted into effective demand (where purchasing power exists), producing sufficient goods would now present few problems with available technologies. Ultimately, unchecked population growth could destroy all possibilities of raising average wealth. For the near term, however – both world-wide and within the United States – the key issue is likely to be more one of distribution than production. The resulting problems are tragically large.

Figure 1.3 Trends and cycles in prices of commodities and manufactured goods

Source: International Monetary Fund, World Economic Outlook, Washington, D.C. (October 1995).
a Derived from the Hodrick-Prescott filter.
b Commodity prices deflated by the price of the manufacturers.
Manufacturer and commodity prices continue to drop indicating technological advances and greater availability.

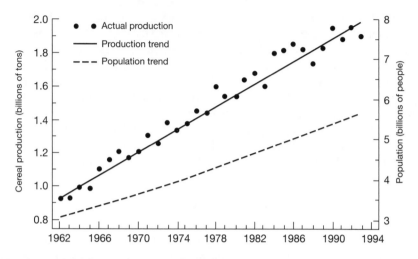

Figure 1.4 World food production and world population trends

Source: United Nations, *Statistical Yearbook*, relevant years

For over three decades, per capita food supplies have grown. Advanced countries could produce much more if wealth were distributed differently worldwide

Goods now pile up and are thrown away in mountainous heaps by the rich, while the poor suffer devastating shortages; greater world-wide wealth distribution and help decrease population growth.

For the next several decades, however, where adequate incentives exist the primary economic problems world-wide will be managing production overabundance, wealth distribution, and the impacts of overpopulation on natural systems. From an input viewpoint, not only are materials abundant; today's electronic capabilities can also convert world-wide intellect into an essentially infinite resource. If intellect is the dominant value-producing component of capital, there is no shortage of such capital, except in the sense of stimulating it to work on future versus current consumption projects. Since intellectual capital can constantly be generated or amplified through learning, the key element in capital for productive purposes is infinitely expandable. The real problem is in creating incentives and mechanisms to *generate* intellect and *connect* it to present and future market demands. Hence the pre-eminent economic resource issue from a national viewpoint is how to create maximum useful learning and distribution of knowledge. Paradigms focused on allocating limited capital and physical resources are increasingly questionable. Unfortunately, all our development and economic concepts are based on scarcity, emphasizing efficient resource use. We need new paradigms at both national and corporate level that move from efficiency in resource use and toward effectiveness in value creation.

Only as people become more affluent and better educated will they stop the population pressures that could become world destroying. This shift in issues calls for radical changes in traditional economic, social, and management approaches focused on exploiting physical assets. We will outline some important approaches emphasizing management of intellect, conservation, and innovation that are both feasible and most promising.

Software

Software is central to virtually all sophisticated innovation and management activities. It facilitates all stages of value creation and innovation processes, from initial problem identification and basic research stages to product design, process design, prototyping, flexible production, market analysis, new product presentation. Effective marketing and distribution, logistics management, iterative adaptation of products and services to customer needs, and post-sale service. Needs are often first sensed in software from system models or online customer databases. Most basic and applied research is performed using electronic databases and electronic models. Most major products and constructions – ships, aircraft, automobiles, machine tools, tunnels, buildings, resource exploitation systems, roads, city designs, circuits, molecule designs, industrial processes – are now first conceived, rendered, and prototyped in software. Frequently designs move directly from software to production through the media of CAE/CAD/CAM.[3]

Often the end product itself or the highest value component in that product is software – as in computer entertainment, communications, advertising, logistics, and financial services outputs. This is true in many of the fastest growing industries. Increasingly, financial services, product design, entertainment, publishing, marketing, databases, scientific discoveries, network services, and software create many millionaires, while hardware production generates only a few. Microsoft has a gross margin of 85%; Compaq, the leading hardware manufacturer, makes 23%. As many of the intermediate steps in innovation become compressed into software, the structures, risks, costs, time delays, leverage points, organizations, and research systems for innovation in both software and hardware all change dramatically. Improved management of software and its utilization to support new innovation and organizational capabilities will be the crucial factors in almost all future corporate and national growth strategies.[4] Both corporations and nations now need genuine strategies for these purposes. Few have them.

Beyond teams: Radically disaggregated organizations

To compete successfully in this vastly changed economy, management styles and organizations must change radically. Staying ahead requires that enterprises have both greater depth in intellectual resources and greater capacity to integrate these resources for rapidly changing customer needs. This calls for personnel with T-shaped skills – deep vertical knowledge and strong lateral associative skills – and for highly disaggregated, interactive, yet strategically focused organizations. Adhocracy is not enough. Disaggregated groups must be stimulated to outperform the world's best competitors toward focused strategic goals. Creative groups cannot be driven to such ends: they must be led. They must see themselves as active participants in the company's vision, genuine resources in its strategy, and drivers toward "figure of merit" targets that *define winning* – not just "benchmarks", which mean *competitive equality* and eventual mediocrity. Strategies need to focus resources on those few intellectually based core competencies that will ensure best-in-world capabilities.

Radically disaggregated organizations are not just teams in a new guise. Market and technological complexities often force innovative structures beyond the limits where teams can operate effectively. Software-based innovation sometimes demands "non-organizations", independent collaborations, virtual labs and skunk works, where experts and customers can work independently, asynchronously and with urgency toward goals of compelling interest to all. In other cases, it permits decentralized, market-focused groups to innovate separately but effectively with highly centralized technical experts, production facilities or resource bases that must stay together for efficiency or strategic reasons. Software creates permeable boundaries for organizations and allows experts to work together in new modes that do not require expensive organizational reconfigurations or co-location. Knowledge, not people or things, moves across boundaries. Software-based innovation cuts cycle times, investments and risks by factors of ten and increases impacts even more by providing software "hooks" – open interfaces and capabilities through which customers (and their customers) can further modify the service or product output for their own purposes. These outsiders voluntarily become contributors to the enterprise's innovative success.

The software system becomes an integral part, and often the essence, of these enterprises' organization and culture. It determines the language, rules, feasibility, and limits of communication. In companies like Kao, Merrill Lynch. Boeing, NovaCare, Wal-Mart, Sharp, Ford, American Airlines, Silicon Graphics, Sun Microsystems, Microsoft, and Bechtel, it allows unending possibilities for fast responsive future innovations. Over time, organizations often migrate toward a circular "three-level" form that best represents and accommodates the swirling interactiveness such innovation requires. Totally new inverted, infinitely flat, lattice, starburst and weblike structures come into being and call for new leadership, coordination, incentive, and performance measurement techniques. Practical adaptations of these organizational forms and their supporting management structures have forever changed innovation practice.

Globalization, outsourcing, and knowledge diffusion

Globalization and knowledge diffusion affect all markets, raw materials, parts, and services competition and sourcing. Because the dominant competitive resource is intellect – and intellect can be shipped across borders instantly and tariff free – remote locations no longer imply remoteness from marketplaces. Research, design, advertising, financial, software, data entry, and other services can be produced anywhere. And through software, innovations are instantly available and accessible anywhere else in the world. (See Figure 1.5.) Large distribution chains, the Internet, and global outsourcing allow innovators to link their concepts immediately to international needs and to leverage their innovations quickly into the most advanced markets in the world. Each company is now in competition with all the world's inventors trying to subvert, replace, or improve each element in its value chain anywhere in the world. Innovation is forever foreshortened and changed.

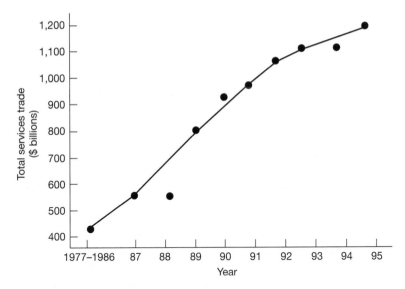

Figure 1.5 World trade in services

Sources: Coalition of Service Industries, *The Service Economy*, Vol. 10, No. 3, 1996. Washington, D.C. based on data from U.S. Department of Commerce, Bureau of Economic Analysis: U.S. Department of Labor, Bureau of the Census.
Even with the limitations of current measurements, services trade has grown 300% in ten years – 56% faster than merchandise trade – and may help stimulate wealth re-distribution.

By exploiting intellect as the dominant resource for economic development, it is possible for less developed countries (and innovators in them) to vault over or shorten – as Japan, Israel, Korea, Singapore, and parts of India have – many of the heavy investment or basic industry building steps that were long considered essential for technological exploitation or development. By concentrating on intellectual and services trade (domestically and internationally) individual innovators, corporations, and societies can also leverage the value of their resources much more extensively than traditional models have suggested. Technologies now enable and demand such leveraging on a much wider geographical scale to achieve their full efficiencies. Information technologies are not the sole enablers in this respect. Improved transportation, materials handling, storage, producing, farming, communication, and management technologies enhance the potential production and sale of virtually all products and services anywhere in the world. Research, design, agricultural, logistics, environmental, biotechnology, financial, entertainment, and education technologies can also be easily produced, diffused, and exploited globally, expanding growth potentials everywhere.

Such technology diffusion tends to generate far greater economic benefits than the original innovation. Extensions into international markets, and the future potential intellectual and product sources this diffusion taps, can create gigantic benefit multiples beyond those of the domestic markets toward which innovations are usually initially targeted. Corporate or national policies that do not concentrate on such diffusion leverages, as most do not, forgo the most promising rewards from knowledge and innovation. Through associated technological multipliers, the benefits of diffusion usually vastly overwhelm the profits made on the original innovation, as did the world-wide sales of TVs, camcorders, tapes, movie rentals, audio-visual systems, and myriad software and service enhancements that sprang off Sony's videotape recorder (VTR) innovation or MITS's (Altair) and Apple's (personal computer) innovations. Corporate and national strategies should reflect this reality.

Chaos and hyper-competition

Market chaos and hyper-competition are the result of these new forces.[5] Since any element in a company's value chain can be produced by an independent external party specializing in that activity, companies no longer compete just with other companies in their "industries." They must compete laterally with the best-in-world producer of that activity, wherever that producer may be. Everyone is competing with everyone else: for example, banks, airlines, telecommunications, retailers, overnight delivery services, and auto companies all compete in the financial services and transportation businesses. Thus innovations that appear in one sector or country constantly affect many others. To deal with this, wholly new strategies – focusing on core competencies, strategic outsourcing, alliances, and highly disaggregated organizations – now link enterprises and nations in new ways. All center on developing, managing, and leveraging intellectual capabilities much more effectively.

These forces have created a much faster-moving, more chaotic, and more competitive environment than ever before. Both corporate executives and national policymakers have found that highly centralized, command-driven systems no longer work well. More interactive, incremental, and decentralized strategies are replacing them. But most institutions need to move much more radically and quickly than they have. The rapid replacement and customization potentials that software-based innovation imposes make this an urgent imperative. At both the national and enterprise level, the problem for managers is how to maintain the clear benefits of careful analysis and choice in guiding their enterprises, while at the same time dealing with the essential chaos, irrationalities, and unknowns that technological innovation and diffusion processes entail. A rapid, proactive, targeted, but flexible innovation system – designed around a few intellectually based core competencies developed in great depth – may be the only strategy that can continually win in this tumultuous hyper-competitive world.

Changing traditional economic paradigms

It now seems clear that intellect, innovation, and technology are central to economic growth. Yet, for years, economists did not acknowledge the special role of these factors in economic growth. Technology was considered "a residual," providing only 0.1 to 0.5% of all growth.[6] Innovation and the intellectual assets supporting it were largely ignored or subsumed as mere components in the capital and labor factors of economic equations. Today, neither intellect, innovation, nor technology is explicitly included in most macroeconomic models or clearly measured in the elaborate output statistics collected by the US Department of Commerce, Census Bureau, Organization for Economic Co-operation and Development (OECD), United Nations and other macroeconomic measurers.

Breaking with tradition

Determining the impact of technology and innovation on growth is very difficult.[7] Schumpeter was perhaps the first major economist to break with the historic tradition and focus on entrepreneurial forces.[8] But his work had little initial impact on the macroeconomic measuring community. In the mid-1950s, studies by Abramovitz, Kendrik, Solow, Kindelberger, and Dewhurst began to accord technology its proper role: not just as one aspect of growth but the central one for many societies.[9] Kuznet's and Solow's studies suggested that some 70% of all growth in the mid-1900s was due to technological innovation, and perhaps 80 to 90% of all productivity gains were technologically based, under the broad definition of technology used here.[10] Finally, Robert Solow won the 1987 Nobel Prize for his work on the interactions of technology as a factor in economic growth. On close analysis, technology turns out to be the vital growth component in each of the four more traditional economic input factors: land, labor, capital, and education (see Box 1.1).

Box 1.1 Technology in traditional economic factors for growth

Land, and the natural resources it represents, can contribute little to growth unless technology is applied to unlock its riches. The great 'heavy crude' reserves of Venezuela or the Athabasca Tar Sands of Canada are worthless without technologies to exploit them but immensely valuable with technology.[11] Technology can convert the desert wastes of Israel or the minerals in Siberia's frozen interior into a great growth stimulus. Properly applied, it can allow the world's arable land to support a population of 30 billion people or convert a worthless grain of sand into a powerful computer.[12]

Labor's contribution to growth is limited without the application of intellect and technology. Over two-thirds of all labor income derives from investments in these factors.[13] Social reorganizations can, of course, increase the percentage of people usefully employed, and transferring labor from less to more productive sectors can add a further increment. Once usefully employed, however, workers' physical capacities quickly limit to about 30% the increased output they can achieve by more rapid performance of the same task. Once workers have learned their tasks and are motivated to perform them, technology and innovation become the critical factors in providing an estimated 80 to 90% of all increased output value per person-hour and hence workers' real contributions to wealth, as well as workers' capacities to earn higher real wages.[14] Intellect and innovation, not more physical effort by workers, are the critical factors in achieving higher output from work processes. Together they provide both the real impetus for higher standards of living and the knowledge bases that create wealth for the next generation.

Capital makes several important contributions to growth. It provides the resources that allow higher level technological choices. It helps create and maintain desired aggregate demand levels. It provides a basis for aggregating and allocating outputs for future versus present consumption. But it is the utilizable technology in a capital investment, and not the fact of the investment, that makes the major contribution to growth. Capital investment in political or religious monuments or in unused military hardware does not offer nations continuing economic gains. It is the capital invested in expanding technological intellect the systematic knowledge and skills to satisfy needs that creates human capital's most important economic contributions.[15] Once a nation's savings level drops to just equal the capital it consumes, its growth is limited almost completely to the technology and knowledge improvements it can absorb. How capital is invested is as important as the level of investment. Japan saves (invests) far more per capita than the United States and Germany invests 40% more on plant and equipment, but because the capital is less efficiently used, their GDP per person is lower than America's.[16]

Capital provides its greatest growth stimulus when invested in technological or intellectual infrastructures such as education and training, information or auto highways, communications or healthcare systems, or intellect-incorporating software and machines that increase productivity or the value-added to raw materials.[17] Effective investments continue to produce useful outputs year after year for many people. Increasingly, the embodiments of capital expenditures do not need to be physical things. Databases, educational systems, legal structures, software, and human know-how have similar effects. Software often is critical to the output of both physical and intellectual systems, makes new output options possible, or (as in financial service products, advertisements, TV programs, movies, or games) becomes the value-creating output itself. In many cases, without software, hard asset investments would be useless. But most of our corporate or national capital accounts do not even show software investments as assets.

Education and training are critical input factors for growth. Many economists are now studying the relationship between human capital and growth.[18] It turns out that education too has a technological component. Increasing students' capacities to understand human or physical relationships and apply such knowledge to human–technical systems can help society create, produce, and distribute all its products and services much more effectively. These are the elements of education that relate most directly to economic growth, although other aspects of academic training (like the arts) may offer important benefits in terms of creativity or quality of life. A recent study showed that raising the average level of employee education by even one year correlated with improved productivity of 8.5% in manufacturing and 13% in services.[19]

There was almost no growth in living standards or per capita wealth until technology enabled the Industrial Revolution. Prior to that time, the situation of most people living on farms or in cities had changed little for centuries. Suddenly the application of technology enabled the value of people's outputs to significantly exceed their living cost. Earnings could fulfil more than bare necessities. Wealth could be *accumulated*, providing the capital for future investment, growth, and efficiency improvements. Now the information revolution may, for the first time – without coercion – allow the effective *distribution* of wealth, which is essential to inure a humane and peaceful world.

Technology for quality of life, not just productivity

Technology is now the greatest single driver of quality of life for most of the world. It enhances quality and choice in foods, housing, transportation, jobs, entertainment, healthcare, water quality, and so on. Most societies would like to exploit these benefits further. But, ever more urgently, new and stronger policy and social concepts are needed to deal with technological change's negative by-products, like job displacement, pollution, new human health problems, ageing populations, terrorism, alienation, or misuses of the technologies themselves.

Progress on these issues is rapidly becoming the limiting factor in how quickly nations and private companies can apply technology to improve life quality – hence our focus on national policy issues as well as private innovation.

Despite the enormous and demonstrable contributions technology makes in all these respects, the economic models used to generate and test policy at the national level neither measure nor separate the special contributions of technology. As a result, technology receives a much lower priority in political and economic discussions than it generally warrants.

Technology multipliers

One major failure is that the powerful multipliers technology creates never enter into discussions. The Keynesian multipliers that capital investment produces are widely recognized. These operate by creating higher levels of demand through the multiple expenditures caused by an incremental investment infusion; capital goods producers pay monies to employees, suppliers, and shareholders, who then purchase more goods and services from retailers, who distribute the sums to their employees and suppliers, who then purchase more products and services, employing more retailers, wholesalers, and producers, and so on. Such infusions are at the heart of deficit spending policies in recessions. Under proper conditions, Keynesian multipliers of three to six are not uncommon.

But there are classes of technological innovation (like Edison's light bulbs or power generators) that can induce a matrix of change and progress in other sectors that are thousands of times the Keynesian multipliers of the investment in the original innovation. For example, when installed and diffused in a regional power network (like the Tennessee Valley Authority or Rural Electrification Agency), these innovations essentially create a whole new economy. They permit new manufacturing and service enterprises that otherwise could not exist, allow the use of modern technology and equipment in these facilities, widen the service areas available to achieve scale economies for support industries, raise expectations and hence latent demand levels, and ultimately create home appliance, light fixture, communication, electrical equipment, component, entertainment, and service demands that otherwise could never exist. More dramatically, relatively tiny investments in innovating the first microprocessors, radios, spreadsheets, hybrid corns, personal computers (PCs), antibiotics, the Internet, and scientific selective breeding have created economic multipliers millions of times greater than their original investments.

Direct and indirect multipliers

A single innovation may directly affect an entire industry's concept of that product's use by customers (as Intel's development of the microprocessor did) and cause sales, profitability, employment, and value-added growth out all of proportion to the innovator's initial expenditure. Ted Hof's almost intuitive initial innovation of the microprocessor directly enabled others to create today's $156 billion PC and software support markets. In addition, such innovations can have even greater "indirect multiplier" effects on other enterprises and sectors. The Nations Aeronautics and Space Administration officially estimates the effects of these indirect multipliers as 15 times its programs' actual cost, probably low in terms of their computer and satellite contributions alone.[20] Silicon Graphics customers have made thousands of times its profits by exploiting its products. As microprocessors, biotechnology, and cellular phones have, new technologies often enable other innovations to create cost savings, new industries, new services, or quality improvements that were previously unimaginable. In addition to the profits that microprocessors make for semiconductor and PC manufacturers, whole segments of the $3.6 trillion service and $1 trillion manufacturing industries depend on this technology. Many derivative industries, including the robust software, smart components, and work-at-home industries, have sprung up. For example:

> As an adjunct of the microprocessors development, Nintendo (with the largest installed base of microcomputers in the world) largely created the video games industry and became the highest volume user of chips and producer of creative interactive software in Japan. Its suppliers then utilized these new capacities to provide both more sophisticated hardware components and other software at higher quality and lower cost for customers, opening totally new options for the suppliers themselves and a secondary wave of entire new industries (based on 32-bit and 64-bit systems) in Japan and abroad. Nintendo's software suppliers in Hokkaido, Russia and India quickly became important pockets of economic growth and progress in their societies.

In stimulating long-term growth through innovation, policymakers need to understand that the primary driving force is neither the initial investment nor innovation itself but the technological multipliers that technological innovation and diffusion achieve. An incremental $1 billion invested in an effective technology could create $100 billion each year over many years in employment opportunities and profits, plus the Keynesian multipliers the supporting investments achieve.

Rationally picking winners?

All this appears terribly rational. Why not just pick those technologies which have the highest technological, economic, and sociological multipliers and support those? In part, this became the command and control model of early national R&D, and later technology strategies.[21] Business managers also attempted a similar approach in their strategies: analyze and identify markets with the greatest potentials and allocate resources toward those. Such approaches worked reasonably well at both the national and corporate level when there were shortages in most markets, as was the case during the Great Depression and after World War II. Several examples will make the point at the national level.

In the post-World War II era the French National Plan successfully stimulated basic industries' technologies and quickly rebuilt public infrastructures destroyed during the war.[22] Israel successfully targeted its education and technology strategies toward the problems of military survival and absorption of a huge inflow of immigrants – many from devastated or relatively underdeveloped countries – with neither savings nor particular skills. And Japan focused on high-investment, labor-intensive, mass production industries, with high export potentials and possibilities for great technological leverage. Japan supported this strategy through financial policy mechanisms that discriminated against current consumption, encouraged savings, and lowered capital costs.[23] The combination enabled Japan to employ its huge displaced labor force after World War II, export in sufficient volume to meet its needs for raw materials and energy imports, and develop the high technologies that could use its superb educational system in the second generation of its growth strategies.

Although it is now popular to deride such policies as non-productive, the United States successfully stimulated growth through similar approaches for many decades. For 200 years, the government invested heavily in canal, dam, railroad, highway, and airline infrastructures, developing and linking the nation's geographically dispersed markets. It created the Rural Electrification Agency to bring electricity to all farm homes, provided tax incentives for oil, gas and natural resource development, and diverted a massive percentage of many rivers' flows for urban and agricultural development. And it developed education and health systems.

The impacts of scale and affluence

But all such strategies broke down as shortages disappeared, affluence grew, over-capacity became manifest, and customization of products became important. Many national programs and laboratories became bureaucratized, inefficient, corrupted, or irrelevant.[24] Even private enterprises found that the rules appropriate for management and policymaking changed as economies moved from eras of shortages to those of plenty. Managers discovered that command-and-control allocation techniques – which had been very useful for R&D in the post-World War II era when the main problem was to apply available technologies to demonstrable customer demands – grew increasingly slow and ineffective as customers became more specialized, fragmented, demanding, and custom oriented. Market research often did not predict customer responses well in new concept or upscale markets as new products front xerography, to microcomputers, to Zap Mail, automatic teller machines (ATMs), video games, Post-it Notes, or the Internet clearly demonstrated. Corporate executives also made large errors. They found that products which seemed highly beneficial when used in niche markets could become enterprise destroying when unanticipated (and unintended) counter-forces began to interact in larger scale uses or in mass markets. Asbestos, DDT, interuterine devices, supersonic transports, silicone breast implants, chlorofluorocarbons, Thalidomide, fission power reactors, and consumer packages that allowed cyanide inserts provided some of the more bizarre interactions and consequences. All of these have led to new approaches to public intervention and private innovation.

Outmoded economic measures and models

National policies also faltered as outmoded economic constructs, measures, and incentives began to distort reality and lead to wrong conclusions.[25] Most experts agree that services' $4.4 trillion output and $770 billion world-wide trade figures are massively understated, especially when one considers the value of embedded software and design, informational, financial transaction, and intra-company intellectual exchanges not captured.[26] Services especially require new measures reflecting changes in service quality and the benefits captured by customers.

While significantly understating services contributions, the national accounts identify as additions to GNP the extra taxi fares and gasoline usage of people caught in automobile-induced traffic jams, as well as the "new sales" value of appliances, houses, component parts, and service incomes required to repair or replace things that fail because of poor quality. Simultaneously, the increased asset values of better educational systems, more highly trained people, more extensive access to libraries or databases, and better quality healthcare or environmental systems appear nowhere. The national accounts distort these public economic values at three levels: (1) the real costs of existing environmental or lifestyle degradation (from pollution, inadequate education, police protection, or healthcare) are not recognized in public accounts, (2) the positive values (cleaner rivers, higher land prices, better trained people, and longer lives) generated by public expenditures to correct these degradations are never credited to the activities that created them; and (3) the market values (of the outputs, jobs, and supplier industries) created by these expenditures are perversely considered solely as costs in national analyses and in the public mind. The results are poor policy, wasted national resources, a less efficient market economy, and fewer growth opportunities for jobs and entrepreneurship.

Major changes in our conceptual structures, approaches, and outcome measures are needed to improve both the efficiency of resource use and the total benefits society achieves from their deployment. Key among these is developing a framework of efficient "public markets" for goods and services people desire, but whose markets cannot be created directly by individuals or private firms. The aggregate of individual decisions and individual wealth does not determine the aggregate wealth of a country. Public wealth – including parks, water resources, information bases, educational, waste handling, legal, and defense institutions – goes well beyond the sum of individuals' wealth and is crucial to future quality of life. These assets also determine much of the nation's future wealth-generating potential. Developing and measuring these real wealth capabilities need much higher priority than they have been accorded in most economic constructs and public discussions. Public markets are natural extensions and facilitators of private markets. The challenge is great. So are the opportunities.

Summary

Intellect, science, technology, innovation, and knowledge diffusion are the crucial growth forces in any modern economy or corporation. Intellectually based services provide 79% of all jobs, 76% of GNP, and almost all the value-added in the economy and in individual companies, including manufacturers. Meanwhile over-capacity in virtually all product and commodity markets is decreasing their prices and profits relative to real wages and forcing average returns toward cost-of-capital levels. Unfortunately, many of our corporate practices, economic and accounting measurements, and national policies reflect an earlier materials- and product-based economy and waste inordinate resources.

Software has enabled disaggregation of organizations and outsourcing on a scale never seen before. These forces have created a hyper-competitive world, where each enterprise must compete against best-in-world competitors on each element in its value chain. The key factors for corporate success and economic growth, with few exceptions, have shifted from managing physical resources toward managing knowledge creation, innovation, and diffusion. Software has become the key element in managing and leveraging intellect. It is revolutionizing all steps in the innovation process, creating totally new strategies and organizational options for corporations and forcing a review of all past concepts for stimulating national economic growth. Nations and companies that win will be those that use the new capabilities to implement new knowledge-based growth strategies, disaggregated yet focused organizational structures, software-based innovation techniques, and more appropriate performance and incentive measures in this new era.

References

1 Bureau of Economic Analysis. 'The national income and product accounts of the United States', series in the *Survey of Current Business*.
2 *Economist*, 28 September 1996, p. 25.
3 K. Sabbagh, *The Twenty First Century Let* (New York: Scribner's, 1996).
4 J Quinn, J. Baruch, and K. A. Zein, 'Software-based innovation', *Sloan Management Review*, Summer 1996.
5 R. D'Aveni, *Hypercompetition* (New York: Free Press, 1994).
6 'How does your economy grow?' *Economist*, 30 September 1995.
7 M. Boskin and L. Lan, 'Capital, technology and economic growth', in N. Rosenberg, R. Landau, and D. Mowery (eds) *Technology and the Wealth of Nations* (Stanford, CA: Stanford University Press, 1992) analyze the key elements in this calculus.
8 J. Schumpeter, *The Theory of Economic Development* (Cambridge, MA: Harvard University Press, 1949) is his principal statement of these theories.
9 M. Abramovitz, 'Resource and output trends in the U.S. since 1870', *American Economic Review Papers and Proceedings*, May 1956; J. Kendrick, 'Productivity trends: capital and labor', *Review of Economics and Statistics*, August 1956; R. Solow, 'A contribution to the theory of economic growth', *Quarterly Journal of Economics*, February 1956; J. Kindelberger, *Economic Development* (New York: McGraw-Hill, 1965); J. Dewhurst, *America's Needs and Resources: A New Survey* (New York: Twentieth Century Fund, 1965).

10   S. Kuznets, *Economic Growth of Nations* (Cambridge, MA: Harvard University Press; 1971); R. Solow, 'A contribution to the theory of economic growth'; same author, 'Technological change and the aggregate production function', *Review of Economics and Statistics* 39, August 1957; same author, *Growth Theory. An Exposition* (Cambridge: Oxford University Press, 1988).

11   US Department of Energy, Energy Information Administration, *International Energy Annual* (Washington, DC: Government Printing Office, 1984).

12   R. Revelle, 'The resources available for agriculture', *Food and Agriculture* (San Francisco: Freeman, 1976).

13   G. Mankiw, 'The growth of nations', *Brookings Papers on Economic Activities* (Washington, DC: Brookings Institution, September 1995).

14   Ibid.

15   P. Romer, 'Endogenous technological change', *Journal of Political Economy* 98, 5, 1990.

16   *Economist*, 8 June 1996, p. 19.

17   D. Jorgensen and R. Landau (eds) *Technology and Capital Formation* (Cambridge, MA: MIT Press, 1989).

18   P. Romer and R. Barro, 'Human capital and growth: theory and evidence', *Carnegie-Rochester Conference Series on Public Policy* (Spring 1990), develops the evidence rigorously and shows the influence of different government policies.

19   *Economist*, 14 September 1996, p. 26.

20   Interview by J. Quinn with G. Carr, former astronaut, now Senior VP, Camus, September 1996.

21   D. Price, 'The scientific establishment', in W. Nelson (ed.) *The Politics of Science* (New York: Oxford University Press, 1968).

22   J. Quinn, 'National planning of science and technology in France', *Science* 19, November 1965.

23   See National Academy of Engineering, *Time Horizons and Technology Investments* (Washington, DC: National Academy Press, 1992); E. Hatsoupolis, P. Krugman, and L. Summers, 'U.S. competitiveness beyond the trade deficit', *Science*, 15 July 1988; J. Poterba, 'Comparing the cost of capital in the U.S. and Japan', *Federal Reserve Board of New York, Quarterly Review*, Winter 1991.

24   M. Reisner, *Cadillac Desert. The American West and its Disappearing Water* (New York: Penguin Books, 1987) cites numerous specific examples of such misallocations.

25   P. Romer et al. have a series of papers on how technology and human capital affect growth: 'Implementing a national technological strategy with self-organizing industry', *Breakout Papers on Economic Activity*, 1993, pp. 345–399; 'Idea gaps and object gaps in economic development', *Journal of Monetary Economics* 32, 1994 and 'Increasing return and long-run growth', *Journal of Political Economy* 94, 5, 1986, 1002–1037. Also note National Research Council, Computer Science and Telecommunications Board, *Information Technology in the Services Society* (Washington, DC: National Academy Press, 1994).

26   M. Baily and R. Gordon, 'The productivity slowdown: measurement issues and the explosion of computer power', *Brookings Papers on Economic Activity* (Washington, DC: Brookings Institution, 1988).

2 Competing for the Future

Gary Hamel and C. K. Prahalad

Look around your company. Look at the high-profile initiatives that have recently been launched, the issues preoccupying senior management, the criteria and benchmarks by which progress is measured, your track record of new-business creation. Look into the faces of your colleagues, and consider their ambitions and fears. Look toward the future, and ponder your company's ability to shape that future in the years and decades to come.

Now ask yourself: Do senior managers in my company have a clear and shared understanding of how the industry may be different ten years from now? Is my company's point of view about the future unique among competitors?

These are not rhetorical questions. Get a pencil and score your company.

How does senior management's point of view about the future compare with that of your competitors?
Conventional and reactive   *Distinctive and far sighted*

Which business issue absorbs more senior-management attention?
Reengineering core processes   *Regenerating core strategies*

How do competitors view your company?
Mostly as a rule maker   *Mostly as a rule follower*

What is your company's strength?
Operational efficiency   *Innovation and growth*

What is the focus of your company's advantage-building efforts?
Mostly catching up   *Mostly getting out in front*

What has set your transformation agenda?
Our competitors   *Our foresight*

Do you spend the bulk of your time as a maintenance engineer preserving the status quo or as an architect designing the future?
Mostly as an engineer   *Mostly as an architect*

If your scores fall somewhere in the middle or off to the left, your company may be devoting too much energy to preserving the past and not enough to creating the future.

When we talk to senior managers about competing for the future, we ask them three questions. First, what percentage of your time is spent on external rather than internal issues – on understanding, for example, the implications of a particular new technology instead of debating corporate overhead allocations? Second, of this time spent looking outward, how much do you spend considering how the world may change in five or ten years rather than worrying about winning the next big contract or responding to a competitor's pricing move? Third, of the time devoted to looking outward *and* forward, how much do you spend working with colleagues to build a deeply shared, well-tested perspective on the future as opposed to a personal and idiosyncratic view?

The answers to these questions typically conform to what we call the '40/30/20 rule'. In our experience, about 40% of a senior executive's time is devoted to looking outward and, of this time, about 30% is spent peering three, four, five or more years into the future. Of that time spent looking forward, no more than 20% is devoted to building a collective view of the future (the other 80% is spent considering the future of the manager's particular business). Thus, on average, senior managers devote less than 3% (40% $\times$ 30% $\times$ 20%) of their time to building a *corporate* perspective on the future. In some companies, the figure is less than 1%. Our experience suggests that to develop a distinctive point of view about the future, senior managers must be willing to devote considerably more of their time. And after the initial burst of energy that they must expend to develop a distinct view of the future, managers must be willing to adjust that perspective as the future unfolds.

Such commitment as well as substantial and sustained intellectual energy is required to answer such questions as: What new core competencies will we need to build? What new product concepts should we pioneer? What alliances will we need to form? What nascent development programs should we protect? What long-term regulatory initiatives should we pursue?

We believe such questions have received far too little attention in many companies, not because senior managers are lazy – most are working harder than ever – but because they won't admit, to themselves or to their employees, that they are less than fully in control of their companies' future. Difficult questions go unanswered because they challenge the assumption that top management really is in control, really does have more accurate foresight than anyone else in the corporation and already has a clear and compelling view of the company's future. Senior managers are often unwilling to confront these illusions. So the urgent drives out the important; the future is left largely unexplored; and the capacity to act, rather than to think and imagine, becomes the sole measure of leadership.

Beyond restructuring

The painful upheavals in so many companies in recent years reflect the failure of one-time industry leaders to keep up with the accelerating pace of industry change. For decades, the changes undertaken at Sears, General Motors, IBM, Westinghouse, Volkswagen, and other incumbents were, if not exactly glacial in speed, more or less linear extrapolations of the past. Those companies were run by managers, not leaders, by maintenance engineers, not architects.

If the future is not occupying senior managers, what is? Restructuring and reengineering. While both are legitimate and important tasks, they have more to do with shoring up today's business than with building tomorrow's industries. Any company that is a bystander on the road to the future will watch its structure, values, and skills become progressively less attuned to industry realities. Such a discrepancy between the pace of industrial change and the pace of company change gives rise to the need for organizational transformation.

A company's organizational transformation agenda typically includes downsizing, overhead reduction, employee empowerment, process redesign, and portfolio rationalization. When a competitiveness problem (stagnant growth, declining margins, and falling market share, for example) can no longer be ignored, most executives pick up a knife and begin the painful work of restructuring. The goal is to carve away layers of corporate fat and amputate underperforming businesses. Executives who don't have the stomach for emergency-room surgery, like John Akers at IBM or Robert Stempel at GM, soon find themselves out of a job.

Masquerading behind terms like refocusing, delayering, decluttering, and right-sizing (Why is the "right" size always smaller?), restructuring always results in fewer employees. In 1993, large US companies announced nearly 600,000 layoffs – 25% more than were announced in 1992 and nearly 10% more than in 1991, the year in which the US recession hit its lowest point. While European companies have long tried to put off their own day of reckoning, bloated payrolls and out-of-control employment costs have made downsizing as inevitable in the old world as it is in the new. Despite excuses about global competition and the impact of productivity-enhancing technology, most layoffs at large US companies have been the fault of senior managers who fell asleep at the wheel and missed the turnoff for the future.

With no growth or slow growth, companies soon find it impossible to support their burgeoning employment rosters and traditional R&D budgets and investment programs. The problems of low growth are often compounded by inattentiveness to ballooning overheads (IBM's problem), diversification into unrelated businesses (Xerox's foray into financial services), and the paralysis imposed by an unfailingly conservative staff. It is not surprising that shareholders are giving moribund companies unequivocal marching orders: "Make this company lean and mean;" "Make the assets sweat;" "Get back to basics." In most companies, return on capital employed, shareholder value, and revenue per employee have become the primary arbiters of top-management performance.

Although perhaps inescapable and in many cases commendable, restructuring has destroyed lives, homes, and communities in the name of efficiency and productivity. While it is impossible to argue with such objectives, pursuing them single-mindedly does the cause of competitiveness as much harm as good. Let us explain.

Imagine a CEO who is fully aware that if he or she doesn't make effective use of corporate resources, someone else will be given the chance. So the chief executive launches a tough program to improve return on investment. Now, ROI (or return on net assets or return on capital employed) has two components: a numerator – net income – and a denominator – investment, net assets, or capital employed. (In a service industry, a more appropriate denominator may be head count.) Managers know that raising net income is likely to be harder than cutting assets and head count. To increase the numerator, top management must have a sense of where new opportunities lie, must be able to anticipate changing customer needs, must have invested in building new competencies, and so on. So under intense pressure for a quick ROI improvement, executives reach for the lever that will bring the fastest, surest result: the denominator.

The United States and Britain have produced an entire generation of managers obsessed with denominators. They can downsize, declutter, delayer, and divest better than any other managers. Even before the current wave of downsizing, US and British companies had, on average, the highest asset-productivity ratios of any companies in the world. Denominator management is an accountant's shortcut to asset productivity.

Don't misunderstand. A company must get to the future not only first but also for less. But there is more than one route to productivity improvement. Just as any company that cuts the denominator and maintains revenues will reap productivity gains, so too will any company that succeeds in increasing its revenue stream atop a slower-growing or constant capital and employment base. Although the first approach may be necessary, we believe the second is usually more desirable.

In a world in which competitors are capable of achieving 5%, 10% or 15% real growth in revenues, aggressive denominator reduction under a flat revenue stream is simply a way to sell market share and the future of the company. Marketing strategists term this a *harvest strategy* and consider it a no-brainer. Between 1969 and 1991, for example, Britain's manufacturing output (the numerator) went up by only 10% in real terms. Yet over this same period, the number of people employed in British manufacturing (the denominator) was nearly halved. The result was that during the early and mid-1980s (the Thatcher years), British manufacturing productivity increased faster than that of any other major industrialized country except Japan. Although Britain's financial press and Conservative ministers trumpeted this as a "success," it was, of course, bittersweet. While new legislation limited the power of trade unions and the liberalization of statutory impediments to workforce reduction enabled management to excise inefficient and outmoded work practices, British companies demonstrated scant ability to create new markets at home and abroad. In effect, British companies surrendered global market share. One almost expected to pick up the *Financial Times* and find that Britain had finally matched Japan's manufacturing productivity – and that the last remaining person at work in British manufacturing was the most productive son of a gun on the planet.

The social costs of such denominator-driven job losses are high. Although an individual company may be able to avoid some of those costs, society cannot. In Britain, the service sector could not absorb all the displaced manufacturing workers and underwent its own vicious downsizing in the recession that began in 1989. Downsizing also causes employee morale to plummet. What employees hear is that "people are our most important asset." What they see is that people are the most expendable asset.

Moreover, restructuring seldom results in fundamental business improvements. At best, it buys time. One study of 16 large US companies with at least three years of restructuring experience found that while restructuring usually did raise a company's share price, such improvement was almost always temporary. Three years into restructuring, the share prices of the companies surveyed were, on average, lagging even further behind index growth rates than they had been when the restructuring effort began.

Beyond reengineering

Downsizing attempts to correct the mistakes of the past, not to create the markets of the future. But getting smaller is not enough. Recognizing that restructuring is a dead end, smart companies move on to reengineering. The difference between restructuring and reengineering is that the latter offers at least the hope, if not always the reality, of getting better as well as getting leaner. Yet in many companies, reengineering is more about catching up than getting out in front.

For example, Detroit automakers are catching up with Japanese rivals on quality and cost. Supplier networks have been reconstituted, product development processes redesigned, and manufacturing processes reengineered. However, the cheerful headlines heralding Detroit's comeback miss the deeper story – among the losses have been hundreds of thousands of jobs, 20-some percentage points of market share in the United States, and any hope of US automakers beating Japanese rivals in the booming Asian markets anytime soon.

Catching up is not enough. In a survey taken at the end of the 1980s, nearly 80% of US managers polled believed that quality would be a fundamental source of competitive advantage in the year 2000, but barely half of Japanese managers agreed. Their primary goal was to create new products and businesses. Does that mean Japanese managers will turn their backs on quality? Of course not. It merely indicates that by the year 2000 quality will be the price of market entry, not a competitive differentiator. Japanese managers realize that tomorrow's competitive advantages will be different from today's. It remains to be seen whether Detroit will set the pace in the next round of competition and produce vehicles as exciting as they are fuel efficient and reliable or will once again rest on its laurels.

We come across far too many top managers whose advantage-building agenda is still dominated by quality, time-to-market, and customer responsiveness. While such advantages are prerequisites for survival, they are hardly a testimony to management foresight. Although managers often try to make a virtue out of imitation, dressing it up in the fashionable colors of "adaptiveness", what they are adapting to all too often are the preemptive strategies of more imaginative competitors.

Consider Xerox: During the 1970s and 1980s, Xerox surrendered a substantial amount of market share to Japanese competitors, such as Canon and Sharp. Recognizing that the company was on the slippery slope to oblivion, Xerox benchmarked its competitors and fundamentally reengineered its processes. By the early 1990s, the company had become a textbook example of how to reduce costs, improve quality, and satisfy customers. But amid all the talk of the new "American Samurai," two issues were overlooked. First, although Xerox halted the erosion of its market share, it has not fully recaptured share lost to its Japanese competitors:

Canon remains one of the largest copier manufacturers in the world. Second, despite pioneering research in laser printing, networking, icon-based computing, and the laptop computer, Xerox has not created any substantial new businesses outside its copier core. Although Xerox may have invented the office as we know it today and as it's likely to be, the company has actually profited very little from its creation.

In fact, Xerox has probably left more money on the table, in the form of underexploited innovation, than any other company in history. Why? Because to create new businesses, Xerox would have had to regenerate its core strategy: the way it defined its market, its distribution channels, its customers, its competitors, the criteria for promoting managers, the metrics used to measure success and so on. A company surrenders today's businesses when it gets smaller faster than it gets better. A company surrenders tomorrow's businesses when it gets better without changing.

We meet many managers who describe their companies as "market leaders". (With enough creativity in delimiting market boundaries, almost any company can claim to be a market leader.) But market leadership today certainly doesn't equal market leadership tomorrow. Think about two sets of questions:

Today	*In the future*
Which customers do you serve today?	Which customers will you serve in the future?
Through what channels do you reach customers today?	Through what channels will you reach customers in the future?
Who are your competitors today?	Who will your competitors be in the future?
What is the basis for your competitive advantage today?	What will be the basis for your competitive advantage in the future?
Where do your margins come from today?	Where will your margins come from in the future?
What skills or capabilities make you unique today?	What skills or capabilities will make you unique in the future?

If senior executives don't have reasonably detailed answers to the "future" questions, and if the answers they have are not significantly different from the "today" answers, there is little chance that their companies will remain market leaders. The market a company dominates today is likely to change substantially over the next ten years. There's no such thing as "sustaining" leadership; it must be regenerated again and again.

Creating the future

Organizational transformation must be driven by a point of view about the future of the industry: How do we want this industry to be shaped in five or ten years? What must we do to ensure that the industry evolves in a way that is maximally advantageous for us? What skills and capabilities must we begin building now if we are to occupy the industry high ground in the future? How should we organize for opportunities that may not fit neatly within the boundaries of current business units and divisions? Since most companies don't start with a shared view of the future, seniors managers' first task is to develop a process for pulling together the collective wisdom within an organization. Concern for the future, a sense of where opportunities lie, and an understanding of organizational change are not the province of any group; people from all levels of a company can help define the future.

One company that developed a process for establishing a point of view about the future is Electronic Data Systems (EDS), based in Plano, Texas. In 1992, EDS's position seemed unassailable. With $8.2 billion in sales, EDS had recorded its thirtieth consecutive year of record earnings and looked forward to the ever-growing demand for computer-services outsourcing. EDS expected to become at least a $25 billion company by the year 2000.

But some top executives, including chairman Lester Alberthal, foresaw problems. Margins were under intense pressure from new competitors, such as Andersen Consulting. Customers were demanding hefty discounts in their long-term service contracts. Fewer new customers could be found among leading-edge IT users in the United States. And future business needs would focus on the home, not the office.

The company's top officers, known as the Leadership Council, concluded that EDS was no more immune from "great company disease" than any other successful enterprise. Council members committed themselves to rebuilding industry leadership for the 1990s and beyond.

As it happened, others in the company were already thinking along similar lines. Back in 1990, a small band of EDS managers, none of them yet corporate officers, had created a Corporate Change Team. Despite their lack of an official charter, team members believed EDS needed to rethink its direction and its deepest assumptions. They soon realized this would require far more resources, both temporal and intellectual, than could be mustered by one small team.

After talking with the Leadership Council about its goals, the Corporate Change Team developed a unique approach to company renewal. From across the company and around the world, 150 EDS managers – key resource holders as well as less senior managers who were known to be challenging, bright, and unconventional – gathered in Dallas, 30 at a time, to begin creating the future. Each of the five "waves" considered in detail the economic threats to EDS and the opportunities afforded by the digital revolution. Each wave was given an assignment. The first wave studied the discontinuities that EDS could use to change the shape of the industry. The second and third waves tried to develop a view of the company's competencies that was substantially independent from current definitions of EDS's served markets. They then benchmarked those competencies against EDS's strongest competitors. Drawing on the work of the previous waves, wave four explored opportunities on the horizon. And wave five considered how to devote more company resources to building competencies and developing opportunities.

Each wave's output was thoroughly debated by the other waves and with the Leadership Council. Finally, a team composed of members from all the waves produced a draft corporate strategy, which, again, was debated throughout the company.

EDS's new strategy is captured in three words: globalize, informationalize, and individualize. The strategy is based on the company's ability to use information technology to span geographical, cultural, and organizational boundaries; to help customers convert data into information, information into knowledge, and knowledge into action; and to mass customize and enable individuals to mass customize information services and products.

The process of developing this strategy for the future was full of frustrations, surprises, unexpected insights and missed deadlines. More than 2000 people participated in the creation of EDS's new strategy, and nearly 30,000 person-hours were devoted to the exercise. (More than one-third of the time investment was made outside the company's normal business hours.)

EDS emerged from the process with a view of its industry and its role that was substantially broader, more creative, and more prescient than it had been 12 months earlier. This view was held not only by a few technical gurus or corporate visionaries but by every senior EDS manager. Indeed, those who participated in the process thought it contributed as much to leadership development as it did to strategy development.

The quest for foresight

To create the future as EDS has done requires industry foresight. Why do we talk of foresight rather than vision? Vision connotes a dream or an apparition, and there is more to industry foresight than a blinding flash of insight. Industry foresight is based on deep insights into trends in technology, demographics, regulations, and lifestyles, which can be harnessed to rewrite industry rules and create new competitive space. While understanding the potential implications of such trends requires creativity and imagination, any "vision" that is not based on a solid foundation is likely to be fantastical.

For this reason, industry foresight is a synthesis of many people's visions. Often, journalists or sycophantic employees have described foresight as the "vision" of one person. Much of the credit for NEC's visionary concept of "computers and communication" may have gone to Akira Kobayashi, but the idea of exploiting the convergence between the two industries synthesized the thinking of many in the company. Senior executives are not the only ones with industry foresight. In fact, their primary role is to capture and exploit the foresight that exists throughout the organization.

Given that change is inevitable, the real issue for managers is whether that change will happen belatedly, in a crisis atmosphere, or with foresight, in a calm and considered manner; whether the transformation agenda will be set by a company's more prescient competitors or by its own point of view; whether transformation will be spasmodic and brutal or continuous and peaceful. Palace coups make great press copy, but the real objective is a transformation that is revolutionary in result and evolutionary in execution.

Developing a point of view about the future should be an ongoing project sustained by continuous debate within a company, not a massive one-time effort. Unfortunately, most companies consider the need to regenerate their strategies and reinvent their industries only when restructuring and reengineering fail to halt the process of corporate decline. To get ahead of the industry change curve, to have the chance of conducting a bloodless revolution, top managers must recognize that the real focus for their companies is the opportunity to compete for the future.

Note

Donald Hambrick, *Reinventing the CEO: 21st Century Report* (New York: Korn Ferry International and the Columbia University Graduate School of Business, 1989).

3 Interpretive Management: What General Managers can Learn from Design

Richard K. Lester, Michael J. Piore and Kamal M. Malek

As the pace of marketplace change has accelerated over the past two decades we have seen a dramatic shift in the nature of business organizations. Companies have abandoned the old hierarchical model, with its clean functional divisions and clear lines of authority, and adopted flatter, less bureaucratic structures. The watchword of these new organizations is flexibility. The goal is to adapt quickly to changes while ensuring that all the pieces of the organization are able to work together effectively, without the need for a long chain of command.

But if most organizations have begun to adapt to uncertainty, most managers have not. They remain locked into the mechanical, engineering mindset of the industrial age. They set fixed, quantified goals – a 5% reduction in manufacturing costs, a 99.5% accuracy rate in order fulfilment, a 15-point gain in customer satisfaction – and they "engineer" the organizational structures and processes required to achieve those goals in the most efficient manner possible. They assume, in other words, that any management challenge can be translated into a clearly defined problem for which an optimal solution can be designed.

This management approach works well in markets that are stable and even in those that change in predictable ways. Today's markets, however, are increasingly unstable and unpredictable. They evolve in unforeseeable ways with unforeseeable consequences. Confronted with this kind of radical uncertainty, managers can never know precisely what they're trying to achieve or how best to achieve it. They can't even define the problem, much less engineer a solution. A company may successfully hit its targets for reducing manufacturing costs, improving order-fulfilment accuracy, or boosting customer satisfaction only to discover that a new technology or a new competitor has rendered its entire business obsolete.

The challenge facing the general manager under these circumstances begins to resemble the challenge that the manager of new-product development has always confronted. In the unpredictable world of research and design, neither the flow of the development process nor its end point can be defined at the outset. The shape of the new product changes, often dramatically, as the effort to create it proceeds. A strictly mechanical approach to management, with its stress on clearly defined objectives, roles, and structures, would kill the creativity that lies at the heart of design. Success in new-product development requires a different kind of management and a different kind of manager.

Two approaches to management

Does the experience of design managers hold practical lessons for general managers who are facing increasing uncertainty in their own businesses? With that question in mind, we studied the product development activities of companies in a number of rapidly changing industries, such as cellular telephones, medical devices, automobiles, and apparel. We found two sharply contrasting approaches to management, which we term *analytical* and *interpretive*. While the analytical approach reflects the traditional managerial perspective, the interpretive approach involves a new perspective, one highly suited to rapidly changing, unpredictable markets. Both approaches are valid, but each serves very different purposes and calls for very different organizational strategies and managerial skills.

Under the analytical approach, the design of a new product is viewed as essentially an engineering challenge – as a problem that must be solved. The analytical manager seeks to define a clear objective, usually based on research into customer needs, and he identifies the resources – human, financial and technical – available to meet that goal, as well as the constraints on those resources. The manager then divides the problem into a series of discrete components and assigns each one to a knowledgeable specialist. A dishwasher manufacturer, for example, may have market research indicating that customers are placing an increasingly high premium on low water consumption and quiet operation. In response, the company will set strict goals for reducing water usage and noise in its next generation of products. The product development leader will then assign different elements of the design problem to experts in materials, chemistry, industrial design, acoustics, and other relevant disciplines. The solution is ultimately obtained by integrating all the components in some optimal combination. The entire development effort is viewed as a single project, which must be brought to closure as quickly and efficiently as possible.

But not all the activity that takes place in product development can be accommodated within such a tightly structured analytical framework. Frequently, for example, the customer doesn't really know what he wants or needs – as the case today in everything from electronic commerce to biotechnology to home entertainment. Indeed, it is often more accurate to think of the customer as having no pre-existing needs at all. Those needs instead emerge out of a series of inter-actions, or conversations, during which the customer and the designer together discover something about the customer's life and how the new product might fit into it. The features of the product emerge in the same way – through an ongoing give-and-take between the customer and the company, and among the various members of the product development team, including manufacturing and marketing. Nothing is fixed at the outset: not the customer's needs, not the product itself, not even the product's components or the elements of the manufacturing system.

When there is such a high degree of uncertainty, the development effort is better understood as an open-ended *process* rather than as a project in which a specific problem is solved. The role of the design organization is not so much one of analysis or problem solving as it is of *interpreting* the new situation – listening to and talking with customers and technical experts and discerning the new possibilities that open up through those interactions. Interpretation, no less than invention, is a highly creative process. To encourage and harness that creativity, the manager of the interpretive organization needs to act less like an engineer and more like the leader of a jazz combo. Diverse components need to be brought together – musicians, instruments, solos, themes, tempos, an audience – but their roles and their relationships are changing all the time. The goal is not to arrive at a fixed and final shape but to channel the work in a way that both influences and fulfils the listener's – the customer's – expectations. The interpretive manager, unlike the analytical manager, embraces ambiguity and improvisation as essential to innovation. She seeks openings, not endings. (See Box 3.1.)

Box 3.1 The view through the interpretive lens

From the perspective of the interpretive manager, many traditional business practices and institutions take on a very different look. Consider, for example, how the interpretive lens might change our view of management education, corporate research and development and the research university.

Management education
Management education is frequently criticized for failing to imbue students with the creativity required for effective leadership and strategic thinking. Some critics go so far as to claim that the current stress on analytical problem solving "breeds out" the creative dimensions of management – the dimensions that successful leaders tend to describe not in analytical terms but in terms of vision, inspiration and instinct. The *common* response to this critique is that creativity cannot be taught. Creative managers are born, not made.

The interpretive perspective challenges that view. It shifts attention away from individualistic notions of creativity, from "isolated genius" theories of innovation; toward an understanding of creativity as a social process. It suggests a way of thinking about the creativity of organizations – of communities – rather than the creativity of individuals, and it places a new stress on orchestration and interpretation as leadership styles. The implication for education is clear: to train interpretive leaders, management teaching would need to be broadened, focusing on developing not only problem-solving skills but also the humanistic skills traditionally associated with the more interpretive fields of literature, history, and anthropology. Management would need to be viewed as much as a liberal art as a science.

Corporate research and development
The ongoing debate over the role of corporate R&D, and especially that of central research laboratories, is marked by two contradictory trends. Most US companies that own central labs have been shrinking or dismantling them, redirecting much of their remaining R&D activity toward the shorter term product development needs of their business units. Meanwhile, many Japanese companies are moving in the opposite

direction, seeking to build up their central labs. They have come to view their traditional reliance on other countries to make fundamental discoveries as a disadvantageous, unsustainable strategy. It is easy to view these events as reflecting competing views of the relative merits of centralization and decentralization in the organization of in-house research. The interpretive approach, however, would lead us to focus less on the organizational structure per se and more on the role of the in-house R&D unit in orchestrating conversations between the company's business units on the one hand and the outside research community on the other.

From the interpretive perspective, the oft-told tale of Xerox's Palo Alto Research Center (PARC) takes on a different aspect. Xerox's inability to capitalize on PARC's technological breakthroughs, including its pioneering research into the graphical user interface, is often used as a lesson in the failure of central research laboratories. The blame is typically placed on PARC's close ties to Silicon Valley, which surrounded the lab and ultimately came to commercialize many of its innovations. PARC, according to this view, gave away the store. But from the interpretive perspective, PARC's relationships with outside researchers may have been not a weakness but a strength – the relationships actually underpinned the lab's breakthroughs. The failure might lie instead in the parent company's inability to integrate the lab with its business units. The interpretive manager would have sought ways to link corporate R&D more closely to the product divisions without weakening its relationships with the larger technical community. The lesson for the Japanese companies now investing in central laboratories, the interpretive manager would argue, is that if these labs are isolated from the broader research community they will be much less likely to succeed.

The research university
The interpretive view also places academic research in a different light. As the federal government slashes its research funding, US research universities are wrestling with their future role. They are, in particular, looking to industry to make up for the loss in government dollars. They are finding, however, that many companies will provide funding only under proprietary research agreements.

As universities negotiate their future with government and industry sponsors, they should never lose sight of the role they are best suited to play in research and development. Once again, the interpretive approach can be illuminating. It suggests that the current positions of both the government and the commercial sector, if taken to their logical conclusion, would likely be self-defeating. On the one hand, the interpretive perspective counsels against imposing a sharp separation between basic and applied research, arguing instead that the health of the overall R&D system depends on close, intense interactions between the two disciplines. On the other hand, the interpretive viewpoint makes clear that the most important contribution the research university can make to industry, above and beyond the quantity and quality of its graduates, is to help expose private companies to a broad range of new ideas. A company that demands an exclusive, proprietary research relationship may not only be damaging the university, it may also be reducing the value that it will ultimately derive from that relationship.

Many of the best examples of interpretive management in product development can be found in the fashion apparel industry, where customers' tastes are always in flux. Although fashion design does involve well-defined projects – garments must, after all, be created with strict seasonal deadlines – these projects do not harm the essence of the development effort. The core of fashion is the process by which the idea of what is fashionable develops. Fashion is not a problem that is "solved" in the course of a discrete project. Rather, the sense of what is fashionable emerges from a series of conversations among fashion designers, clothing buyers, key customers, garment manufacturers, and fashion writers. The conversations have neither beginning nor end. The question of what is fashionable has no final answer, on the contrary, the whole idea is that the answer keeps changing. New creations – that is, new garments – emerge continually, drawn out of an unfolding, open-ended process. Without this process, there could be no individual projects.

Levi's conversations

One of the fastest-growing fashion companies of recent years is Levi Strauss & Company. Ironically, for the first century of its existence, Levi's never thought of itself as a fashion company at all. Its product – one-style-suits-all denim work pants – was a commodity. In fact, Levi's jeans can be considered a prototypical commodity of mass consumption in the United States, the Model T of the garment industry. Although clothing production has always been difficult to mechanize, the cutting and sewing of jeans was as close to assembly line production as could be found in the outer garment industry.

But the jeans business changed dramatically in the late 1970s, when fashion suddenly started to play a central role. Pricey designer jeans in a multitude of styles proliferated. Denim clothing became a staple not just of work life but of night life. Seeing an opportunity to sell its products at much higher margins, Levi's moved to take advantage of this trend, with great success. In the ensuing years, the company evolved into a true fashion leader, branching out from its traditional jeans line to its highly successful Dockers line of casual clothes and to its new Slates line of dress pants. Adept at anticipating and managing the evolution of style, Levi's posted ten consecutive years of record sales between 1986 and 1996, as its revenues grew from $2.7 billion to $7.1 billion. In recent months, in response to weakening demand for apparel, Levi's has moved aggressively further to sharpen its focus on the fashion end of its business.

In transforming itself from a commodity manufacturer to a fashion company, Levi's has invested heavily in product development. Several times a year, the company prepares new collections for its major product lines. It thinks of these collections in terms of a V-shaped merchandising model. At the back of the store are the perennial items – the backbone of the collection, which generates the bulk of the revenue. These items change little from year to year. At the front of the store are new items just introduced, aimed at the fashion-conscious consumer and geared to a particular season. In the middle are items introduced in earlier collections that have sold well but have not yet earned a place in the company's permanent collection. Products move from the front of the store to the back over their life cycle, and they may be dropped at any time.

In many ways, Levi's method of preparing its collections is consistent with the analytical mode of product development. The effort is organized in a series of distinct phases. There are definite start and end dates and there are "gates" through which the collection must pass as it moves toward the market. Once a design has been introduced and has spent some time on store shelves, its fate can be predicted fairly accurately, and decisions about it can be structured analytically based on hard data.

For the fashion items at the front of the store, however, the analytical approach won't work. There is simply too much uncertainty about fashion trends, customer reactions, and even manufacturing capabilities. Levi's manages the generation of these new-product ideas very differently from the way it manages the collection as a whole. It stresses interpreting customer needs and production capabilities, not simply analyzing them.

For its jeans line, Levi's looks in two different directions for product innovations. One is toward the consumer. The other is toward the finishing process, which in large part determines the look and feel of the garment. In working with both the consumer and the finishing process, the design leader plays a critical managerial role for which there is no term in the analytical lexicon. One way to think about that role is as guiding the flow of a conversation.

For Levi's, the notion of a conversation with the consumer is more than just a metaphor. The company divides the market into age segments and assigns a designer to each segment. The designer is encouraged to become immersed in the segment's culture, to live the life of its members. She goes shopping at the stores where they shop, eats in their restaurants, dances in their clubs, listens to their radio stations, reads their magazines – all in an effort to pick out new trends. The conversation is extended into the company itself through meetings which the designers discuss what they have seen and what they think it means, comparing developments in the lifestyles of different generations.

Levi's is an effective listener, but it is by no means just a listener. Rather, it strives to be an active participant in the conversation. Take the case of baggy jeans – a fashion trend that emerged from the youth culture of the inner city where it became a hallmark of rap singers and their fans. Levi's concluded early on that the trend would spread to the general culture as rap music itself grew in popularity, and the company invested heavily in designs rooted in the trend. But the market began to level off much earlier than the company had expected. At that point, Levi's launched an intensive advertising campaign around the rap theme. The campaign succeeded in generating a second, larger wave of demand for the new fashion, particularly among suburban teenagers. Did Levi's create the baggy jeans fashion? Not exactly. Company managers were not sure why the advertising campaign worked, and they by no means viewed its success as preordained. What is certain, though, is that Levi's advertising was itself as much a part of youth culture as the rap music with which the baggy jeans were originally associated. To the analytical manager, Levi's success would seem to be the product of a mysterious chemistry, an unmanageable chain of serendipitous events. But the fact is that Levi's, by pursuing an open-ended, unstructured form of interpretive management, instigated and guided that chain of events to create a winning product.

The other source of innovation for Levi's jeans is the finishing process. Because current jeans fashions are heavily influenced by a manufacturer's ability to replicate the look and feel of used garments, finishing is central to product development. The basic technology of finishing is straightforward: a garment is laundered to soften its fabric and texture, to alter its fit, and to change its colour – all in ways that aren't easily produced by chemicals and dyes. In addition, finished garments are typically abraded by washing them with stones or pumice or by brushing or sandblasting them in order to produce the lines and creases of used clothes. As much as 80% of the life of a garment is expended in the finishing process.

Because finishing is an inexact science, getting jeans with the desired features into retail stores in a timely manner requires close and continual collaboration among the designers and manufacturers of the garment, the textile mills that supply the denim, the laundries that perform the finishing, and the machine shops that produce the equipment used by the laundries. Experimentation with new techniques is constant, both to create new effects and to reproduce effects already achieved in other ways. The introduction of new techniques has led to a cascade of changes in cooperating industries. Denim fabric has been redesigned to withstand extensive abrasion. Industrial washing machines have been redesigned to stand up to the pounding delivered by the stones and pumice, and they have been equipped with computer controls to adjust to different kinds of stones. The combination of changes in fabrics, techniques and equipment can itself produce new and unexpected effects, leading to further discovery, further experimentation, and further change.

Where so much turns on happenstance, a strictly analytical approach to management would be counterproductive. The analyst's stress on closure would tend to freeze the process, cutting off the continuing stream of discoveries that leads to new leaps in fashion. Not surprisingly, Levi's has come to take as conversational an approach to working with finishers as it takes to learning about customers. A particularly key role in this process has been played by one of the company's outside laundries, American Garment Finishers of El Paso, Texas, and its president, Claude Blankiet. Blankiet combines a formal technical education – he was trained as a chemical engineer – with a strong intuitive sense for fashion and design. He is widely credited with exceptional judgment about the marketability of new effects achieved in the finishing process. Moreover, he is a living example of the interpretive manager.

Over the years, Blankiet has developed an extensive network of contacts in the jeans industry across Asia, Europe, and the United States that helps him stay on top of technical developments. He travels extensively, visiting other laundries as well as washing-machine manufacturers and fabric and garment makers in order to exchange tricks of the trade. By gathering the experiences of others, he expands his own repertoire of techniques for producing or reproducing desired effects; he also pushes the entire finishing industry forward.

Levi's has begun to rely on Blankiet to strengthen communication among its own laundries and laboratories, which has been hampered by a tradition of rivalry and competition. Although these facilities have regularly encountered similar technical problems, they have shared little information. To ensure that popular garments can be produced reliably in large quantities, Levi's wants to improve the ability of laundries to reproduce effects created at other laundries. From the analytical perspective, Blankiet's task is to work out a technical solution to the problem of achieving each desired new finish and then standardize the knowledge and procedures across the network of laundries. But Blankiet's own understanding of his role is more consistent with the interpretive view. Because finishing technology is still highly empirical, without a firm theoretical base, new effects are often achieved inadvertently. Blankiet sees himself as an interpreter who instigates and translates wide-ranging conversations among the laundries. While he helps Levi's achieve better communication among its laundries, he personally seeks not to eliminate the variations in finishing but to exploit those variations as a continuing source of new ideas and insights.

Recently, Levi's jeans appear to have lost a step – slow to exploit the wide-leg jeans style, the latest big fashion trend – and younger consumers have been leaving the brand for other fashion-focused merchandisers. Why did Levi's miss the emerging trend? One reason may be that its fast-growing fashion jeans division has become more structured and formal and has lost some of its earlier flexibility and receptivity to new fashion ideas. The company is now moving to recreate what has been lost. It is setting up another smaller fashion unit and is taking steps to renew the flow of fashion ideas that links the company to the street, to its finishers, and to the rest of the world. In effect, Levi's is seeking to reintroduce the interpretive dimension of management that is so critical to the success of fashion-driven businesses.

Beyond fashion

Fashion apparel is hardly a typical industry, of course, but many of its characteristics are now being replicated in other, very different industries. In many consumer product and service sectors, for example, managers are struggling with unpredictable shifts in customer needs and unforeseen changes in technology that require a steady stream of new and different products. Even Andy Grove, CEO of the archetypal analytical company, Intel, whose product-development activities are dominated by huge design projects with thousands of people racing against tight deadlines to get the latest generation of chips to market, has acknowledged "a deep-seated conviction that our business has some of the characteristics of the fashion industry. You always have to come up with something exciting and new to stay on top." No matter what industry a company competes in, the greater its susceptibility to shifting tastes and technologies, the greater the risk of relying wholly on an analytical style of management.

The need for an interpretive approach tends to be particularly strong in markets or industries that are still in their formative stages. A good recent example is the cellular telephone industry. At the outset, the market for cellular phones was undefined. Even the role the technology would play could not be predicted. Was a cellular phone a toy, or was it a genuine alternative to traditional wire-line systems? Was it basically a car radio, or was it a portable, handheld device? Would demand for the service be limited to a few narrow segments, or would it be universal? The nature of a cellular system, the different components of the infrastructure, the technologies used, the functions provided, the character of competition, the economics of the business – all were unclear.

The companies that have come to dominate the cellular industry all initially managed their cellular divisions using a highly interpretive approach. AT&T housed its cellular operations in Bell Labs, encouraging a climate of open-ended experimentation and discovery. Motorola organized its initial efforts around a core of engineers who operated as a flexible, ad hoc team, drawing in other members of the organization as needed and conversing directly with customers about their needs and desired product features. Matsushita's cellular unit lacked clear functional boundaries, thus encouraging communication between its product-development and manufacturing units. Nokia's cellular business began as a highly entrepreneurial operation with informal design procedures. Salespeople communicated directly with the product development team, often making last-minute changes to product specifications in response to customers' requests.

Once the market began to stabilize in the middle and late 1980s, each of these companies began to reorganize its cellular division, imposing much more formal structures with much more analytical managerial approaches. The transition was most dramatic at AT&T and Matsushita. AT&T moved its cellular operations out of Bell Labs, establishing a stand-alone business unit, Network Wireless Systems, led by experienced managers drawn from other operating divisions. It also introduced a formal five-step product-development process based on a model used throughout the company. Matsushita brought in a manager from its television division to oversee the cellular business and established a clearly defined hand-off point between development and manufacturing, instituting an analytical review to ensure that the product was ready to go into mass production. Motorola and Nokia also embraced a more analytical approach, but they did not abandon the interpretive perspective entirely. Motorola limited customers' access to the development team by appointing a set of project managers to act as points of contact, but these project managers continued to play an interpretive role in communicating between developers and customers. Nokia instituted a formal product-development process with well-defined phases marked by analytical reviews, but it still encouraged cross-functional conversations throughout the process.

When these companies began their shift from the interpretive to the analytical approach, they shared a belief that the cellular business was stabilizing, with increasingly well-defined customer needs and product features. In hindsight, we can see that their assumption was wrong. The cellular business has entered a new period of radical uncertainty. A number of technological, regulatory and competitive developments – the introduction of personal communications services, the growing communications power of personal digital assistants and pagers, the expanding range of cordless phones, the development of satellite systems – have converged in a way that couldn't have been predicted, again casting into doubt the ultimate role that traditional cellular services will play. It may turn out that the four leading competitors, particularly AT&T and Matsushita, acted too quickly in shifting away from their original interpretive approach to management.

The instinct displayed by the cellular competitors – to move to an analytical approach as a market matures – is a common one. After all, as a business grows larger and more complex, its efficiency depends on the establishment of well-defined operating processes and formal management structures. Strong analytical, problem-solving skills become more and more important to effective management. Nevertheless, as radical uncertainty becomes a more pervasive feature of the business environment – as it has in the cellular business – the limitations of a *strictly* analytical model will become progressively more debilitating. The most successful managers will understand both approaches, seeing them as complementary, not antagonistic, and they will be capable of striking a sensible balance between the two.

A different way of seeing

New managers today are capable of taking such a balanced view. Because the pull of the analytical approach is so powerful and its routines so ingrained in management practice, most managers simply can't comprehend the possibility of a different approach. Even at fashion-oriented Levi's, one senior manager told us he looked forward to the day when interpretive conversations among the company's denim finishers would no longer be necessary. He hoped to introduce more scientific knowledge into the finishing process, cross-training designers in relevant technical disciplines so that they would be able to develop and standardize new finishes quickly. He wanted his designers to work "scientifically the way they do it in biotechnology."

Interestingly, however, product development in the biotech industry is not always "scientific" in the way the Levi's manager used the term. Indeed, it sometimes closely resembles the Levi's model of product development. Chiron Corporation, a leading biotech company headquartered directly across the San Francisco Bay from Levi's, provides a good example. Although Chiron uses analytical structures in many areas of its business, its chief executive has embraced an explicitly interpretive role, positioning himself and his company at the center of an extensive network of university and corporate researchers. His strategy has been to draw scientists from all parts of the biotechnology community into a continuing exchange of information with his company's people. To carve out its position as the central node in the research community, Chiron has often had to share its own information about evolving technologies and commercial applications, with the expectation that its interlocutors would divulge information of their own. Outside researchers now routinely seek out the company's researchers to discuss new findings and get advice on new technical problems – a pattern of communication that the company views as one of its major strategic assets.

Chiron's approach mirrors the way Claude Blankiet draws new members into his network of laundries. When Blankiet spots technical problems during his visits to outside laundries, he offers unsolicited solutions in the hope that the laundry will reciprocate by sharing technical secrets of its own. His exchanges, like those of Chiron's researchers, could be viewed from the analytical perspective as transactions wherein information of more or less equal value is traded. But from the interpretive view, they can be understood as the opening gambit in an ongoing conversation.

The idea that the same activity can be at once analytical and interpretive might seem illogical at first. But just as modern physics instructs us to think about light as both particles and waves, so too can a business organization be looked at from either the analytical or the interpretive perspective. One view may be more immediately useful in certain circumstances – as uncertainty increases, for example, the emphasis on interpretation should grow – but the simultaneous use of both lenses will provide managers with deeper insights into their challenges, opening up new possibilities for action.

Consider, for example, the concept of core competency. When a company sets out to determine what it does best, it typically takes an approach, cycling between what it *can* do given its existing resources and what it *might* do given the opportunities presented in the marketplace. This back-and-forth process, essentially interpretive in nature, is almost always fruitful, revealing possibilities as well as new constraints. Too often, however, companies rush to end the process: "These are our core capabilities, and these are the products we will produce, and these are the processes we will use to produce them." The analyst's need for closure terminates the interpreter's search for knowledge. The risk is that, in an unpredictable environment, this kind of closure can be disastrous. The company can end up doing a very good job producing products no one wants to buy.

Interpretive managers, by contrast, constantly question the boundaries of their company's core competency and sometimes even deliberately stray across those boundaries. For example, several manufacturing companies we studied – Matsushita in cellular telephones, Levi's in fashion apparel, Oticon in medical devices – maintain small retail divisions. These divisions are probably not profitable, and they certainly lie outside their companies' areas of core competency. But they provide direct exposure to the consumer, enabling the companies to test new product ideas and to gather the kind of unfiltered information that cannot be supplied by independent retailers. The existence of these outlets cannot be justified through the analytical approach the companies use to evaluate their regular wholesale and retail channels. They can be understood only in an interpretive framework.

Toward a new vocabulary

Interpretive management implies a whole new way of thinking about the work of business executives. Interpretive managers, like Chiron's chief executive, identify and bring together individuals within and outside the company who might have something interesting to say to one another. They arrange, in other words, who should talk to whom. They also take an active role in influencing what people talk about – highlighting, for example, areas or experiences people have in common. Acting much like the host of a party, they introduce new people into groups where conversation seems to be flagging, intervene to suggest a new topic when the people don't seem to be able to discover what they determine have in common, break up groups that are headed iterative for an unpleasant argument, and guide the conversations in a general direction without seeming (or wanting) to dictate the outcome. (See Box 3.2.)

As anyone who has hosted a party knows, these are difficult skills to master. Indeed, for most managers, the interpretive approach remains an entirely foreign concept. It is not taught as an explicit discipline in business schools, it is not part of most executive training programs, and there are few role models available. Until now, we haven't even had a vocabulary for talking about the interpretive approach. As a result, managers often come to important tasks with blinders on, not recognizing even the possibility of an alternative to the analytical approach. Challenges that might more usefully have been treated as open-ended processes, where multiple possibilities could coexist and play off one another, are forced back into the analytical mold where the emphasis is on clarification, on getting things straight, on eliminating the redundant, the ambiguous, and the unknown. The danger is that the rush to clarify often leads to the reification of insight, to the premature freezing of ideas – to the elimination, in fact, of the very conditions that are needed for creativity to flourish. By purging our organizations of what is ambiguous, we risk losing our sense of what is possible.

This is not a risk that concerns most managers today. In fact, managers fear the paralysis of indecision, the danger of *not* deciding on a course of action, more than the elimination of options. They are acutely aware that organizations need closure, otherwise nothing will be accomplished. They try to structure projects that can yield optimal solutions in the face of potentially overwhelming uncertainty. And they have a very well-developed analytical apparatus for doing this. But what they lack – and what the interpretive approach offers – is a way to keep things moving forward without closure, a framework that sees in ambiguity the seeds not of paralysis but of opportunity.

Box 3.2 The work of interpretation

The work of the interpretive manager is very different from that of the analytical manager. Success requires not only a new outlook but also a new set of skills. We would make the following suggestions to managers looking to incorporate an interpretive approach into their day-to-day jobs.

Look for new ways to promote conversations about the future
Because conversation is so central to interpretation, you need to create forums and stimuli for productive, far-ranging conversations. IBM's research division, for example, recently directed its basic scientists to get out of the laboratory and start spending time with customers. "We don't want Capuchin monks in a monastery on a hill," explained former IBM research chief Jim McGroddy. "Rather, we want Franciscans in the street." The visits enable the scientists to solve customers' problems, but that's not their only benefit. The scientists themselves are changed by the experience; they gain a new perspective on their work that can lead to research breakthroughs back in the lab. Recalled McGroddy, "Recently, I ran into a couple of our mathematicians in the parking lot who were on their way to see a customer. Neither of them had visited a customer before, but we set it up for them and made it easy. They came back very excited by what they'd seen, and that affects the research agenda of our division." In a similar vein, Andersen Consulting has created several virtual business environments around the world – simulations of futuristic supermarkets, retail outlets, even entire companies where consultants can meet and talk with their clients about what new technology might help them achieve in the future. The point of these sites is not to predict what will happen but rather to stimulate thinking and discussion about what might happen. Many people, especially engineers, are

uncomfortable with the notion of open-ended, creative conversations. Therefore, you will often need to find ways to kick-start conversations. One conversational gambit that can be highly successful is the adoption of a so-called stretch goal. Whether that goal is actually achieved or not is often immaterial; the point is to force the enterprise out of its customary ways of working, to keep it moving and searching. One of the most famous stretch goals was the 6-Sigma quality target established by Motorola during the 1980s. As longtime Motorola chairman Bob Calvin explained in a recent interview, "It doesn't really matter what the goal is exactly, as long as it is reasonable. The point is to stimulate, to catalyze." Motorola did not, in fact, reach its target, but the 6-Sigma program stimulated many new and highly beneficial collaborations within the company (and later also with its suppliers), a large fraction of which were unanticipated at the outset.

Pick your interlocutors carefully
It's not enough just to talk; you need to talk with the right people. A number of equipment supply companies, for example, spend a lot of time with their lead clients – those customers that have leadership positions in their industry or that use the equipment in the most demanding or most innovative ways. A good lead client is a good interlocutor, capable of moving the conversation forward and widening the circle by bringing in others from its market segment. In the medical devices industry, companies developing new products seek to place the technology first with key users – practitioners with strong reputations in the professional community who will use the innovation in clinical trials and write papers disseminating the results. A similar principle applies to the selection of suppliers. Instead of rebidding its parts purchases every year or so to find the lowest-cost producers, Chrysler now carefully selects one or two key suppliers for each component early on. The goal is not necessarily to select the lowest-cost supplier but rather to find partners who are able and willing to help advance the design of the component throughout the full production life of the vehicle.

Develop alloy people within your organization
In companies facing rapidly changing markets, the role of interpreters – people who can facilitate communication across organizational boundaries – is especially important. In the analytical view, communication is thought of as the exchange of packets of unambiguous information – like Morse code. It requires no interpretation to be understood. More commonly, however, the cultural and linguistic gap between different organizational units is wide, and the message must be interpreted. People who are able to bridge the gaps need to be identified and then encouraged, formally or informally, to act as interpreters. In the company we've studied, the managers and engineers who perform this key function are nicknamed *alloy people*, just as an alloy is an amalgam of two or more metals, an alloy person represents the union of two or more points of view.

4 Business, the Environment and Local Government

Roger Levett

Every company is 'local' to somewhere and what it can or cannot do about the environment will depend on local circumstances. These include the influence of local authorities, training and enterprise councils (TECs) and other public agencies.

This chapter falls into two parts. The first describes what these public agencies active in local economic development *can* do and *are* doing to make the local economy more sustainable. The message of this part is positive: 'greening the local economy' is not impossible or self-contradictory: there *are* methods and approaches which have been shown to bring real benefits for both environment and economy and which other local authorities can copy.

The second part of the chapter tempers the optimism of the first with a discussion of the *limits* to local authority action and in turn the limits to the extent that businesses can sensibly be expected to take the sustainability agenda on and the implications and lessons for policymaking at national as well as local level.

The overall message of the chapter is one that is increasingly familiar throughout the sustainability movement: of creative action at local level making great strides but sooner or later hitting limits that only central government can remove.

This chapter will break new ground in sustainability literature by *not* starting with the customary quotation, obeisance and exegesis of the Brundtland definition of sustainable development. Instead it will simply take as its starting point the notion that human activities are threatening the environment's ability to keep on providing the resources and 'environmental services' – including climate maintenance, water purification and waste decomposition – which we need for survival and basic welfare.

Breathing apart, virtually all the human activities that affect the environment are 'economic': they include extracting raw materials, processing them into products using and consuming those products, and getting rid of the resulting wastes. The *way* in which these threaten future environmental provision is by overloading the natural systems which provide resources and carry out services or, as ecologists put it, exceeding the 'carrying capacity' of the environment. It is this quality of breaking through the resilience and ability of natural systems to 'bounce back' – as it were, snapping the rubber band instead of stretching it – which distinguishes environmental *sustainability* questions from the wider category of environmental *protection* issues.

Carrying capacities arise at all spatial levels, from the ability of a stream to provide for the biochemical oxygen demand of an effluent put into it or a woodland's ability to keep providing a yield of timber year on year, to the combined ability of all the world's forests, farmland and sea plants to mop up extra carbon dioxide added to the atmosphere by power stations, transport, industry, heating, lighting and other uses of fossil fuels.

The idea is gaining acceptance that each geographic region, river catchment and human settlement needs to be thought of as an ecosystem with its own characteristic set of carrying capacity limits. Some continental cities such as Gothenburg and Freiburg are starting to put this idea into practice: trying to measure resource flows and environmental change, to deduce carrying capacity limits from these and to make compliance with these limits the objectives of environmental policies and programmes. This 'ecosystems' approach is advocated in Brugmann (1992) Storksdieck and Otto-Zimmermann (1994) and CEC (1994).

It is proving very difficult and expensive to do this even for local environmental carrying capacities. It is harder still at regional and global level because the complexities and uncertainties increase. Indeed, there is still no *proof* that global warming is really happening, let alone where the environment's carrying capacity for CO_2 and other 'greenhouse' gases lies. We are therefore a long way from the ideal of being able to say, for each area, what the maximum sustainable levels of different environmental pressures are and therefore what levels of each kind of environmental impact businesses can be permitted. For the moment, the only prudent course is to follow some general rules of thumb aimed at reducing the kinds of impact which seem likely to have serious consequences. These could be summarized as:

- Reduce energy and resource consumption and waste production across the board.
- Switch from non-renewable resources to renewable ones being cropped within their replenishment capacity.
- Convert 'one-shot' resource use into circular flows through techniques such as refilling, reuse, recycling and recovery.

This chapter's focus is action by local authorities and other local public agencies in the UK to move economic activity in these directions. This is of course only a subset of environmental actions by business, sustainable development actions by local authorities and local action for economic development. Indeed it is the area where all three of these fields overlap.

Local authority action

Helping businesses improve environmental performance

Local authority economic development activity generally starts from orthodox assumptions about the blanket desirability of business activity, economic growth, conventional employment and so on. Economic development officers and the committees they report to tend to be suspicious of environmentalists and goals which they believe can oppose economic development. (The first of a number of delicious paradoxes which this chapter will uncover is that economic development officers and environmental officers often see themselves in exactly the same way, as outsiders preaching and promoting values which the authority only intermittently and unreliably supports.)

The palest green arguments have therefore been the most acceptable. The simplest, best and most frequently used of these is that if the local authority helps businesses reduce resource use, pollution and wastes, everyone wins both environmentally and commercially. Local people get a cleaner environment. Pressure is taken off transport and waste disposal infrastructure, thus also off local government as provider and regulator. The businesses themselves save money, some of which at least will be spent or invested locally. They also increase their competitiveness and reduce their vulnerability to environmental regulation and hikes in resource and waste disposal costs, both now and in the future. They are therefore more likely to continue to provide jobs and prosperity for the area.

On this argument, helping local businesses improve their environmental performance is just like helping them obtain suitable premises, train their staff, market their products or manage their finances effectively – something which a prudent local authority will do to make sure those businesses remain successful and can continue to make their contribution to the area.

Coventry City Council's programme of environmental advice to industry is a good example. Specialist advisers (funded first under the Urban Programme, then by the European Social Fund) advise small and medium sized companies on issues such as energy conservation, pollution, waste reduction and recycling. Direct savings include:

- A small engineering works was spending £18,000 disposing of contaminated water. The advice given enabled them to eliminate the contamination and the consequent cost.
- A small glazing installer saved £3500 a year as a result of advice given on recycling glass waste.
- A vehicle components coatings company had been ordering resins in 45-gallon drums. There were expensive to dispose of. As a result of advice they switched to bulk containers which were reusable, so saving costs and materials.

Direct visits to companies have proved very valuable. Businesses have been able to identify concrete issues on their premises more easily than at seminars and nothing turns companies on to environmental management better than direct cost savings!

Other Coventry initiatives have included helping the local technical college develop an accredited training course in environmental advice and working in partnership with other local authorities to help the Rover Group and several of its suppliers to pilot the BS7750 environmental management standard cooperatively. Coventry is unusually advanced and committed among UK local authorities. Approaches used more commonly tend to focus on provision of information and encouragement rather than casework.

Development of green business opportunities

If improving resource efficiency is good for *all* businesses, the technologies, products and services which will help them do so will be commercial opportunities for *some* businesses. Many economic development strategies now include a reference to encouraging the environmental sector among the standard motherhood statements about creating a high output, high value-added economy and a highly trained and motivated workforce, building on traditional strengths while responding energetically to new opportunities etc. without which no respectable strategy is complete. But few strategies include actions in support of this aim.

One possible local authority response would be to discriminate in favour of firms at the environmentally better end of any industry. Possible proxies for good environmental performance include possession of a formal environmental policy (only meaningful when combined with some form of management system to ensure that it is implemented and that its success or otherwise is independently assessed and publicly reported), employment of specialist environmental managers, commitments to 'clean technology' approaches and low emissions. Many local authorities are beginning to apply requirements of this sort in their purchasing and tendering, as part of their own environmental management systems. Indeed the government-sponsored local authority adaptation of the EU Eco-Management and Audit Scheme requires that 'management shall ensure that contractors working on the local authority's behalf apply environmental standards equivalent to the local authority's own' (HMSO, 1993). The same criterion could be used as a 'filter' for economic development assistance.

A different approach is to concentrate on developing particular areas of economic activity with environmental benefits. Lothian and Edinburgh Environmental Partnership (LEEP) is a leading current example. It is a non-profit company, core funded largely by Edinburgh City Council and also supported by the regional council, the university and Friends of the Earth Scotland, all of which are represented on its board. It was set up in 1990 specifically to develop business opportunities in three areas chosen for their importance for sustainability: energy efficiency, recycling/waste reduction and sustainable transport. Its aim is to act as a catalyst: to provide advice, development and planning effort or in some cases funding to enable businesses to get started.

Some of LEEP's most successful interventions have been among the smallest.

A few hours of staff advice and a £200 grant for a study visit to a similar business in Milton Keynes enabled an unemployed Edinburgh woman to set up a nappy laundry service which provides parents with an environmentally friendlier alternative to disposables, contracting spare capacity in an energy-efficient hospital laundry to do the washing. Similar small-scale support helped launch Edinburgh's first pedal cycle courier company.

At the other extreme of effort lies the 'billsavers' project currently under development with EU LIFE funding. The basic idea is to finance low-income households to replace obsolete domestic appliances with more energy-efficient new ones and pay back the costs out of the energy savings. If it succeeds it will be the first domestic application of an energy services company approach in the UK.

The project has the active support of energy utilities, appliance manufacturers, technical consultants, the City Council and tenants' organizations. But without LEEP none of these would have felt the project was a high enough priority to put in the research, coordination, negotiation and promotional effort necessary to bring them all together or to do the groundwork to establish technical and financial feasibility and develop appropriate and effective methods of working. This catalytic role was LEEP's distinctive contribution.

LEEP 'adds value' by making possible businesses which would otherwise not get started. It must therefore aim to operate in a 'twilight zone' between those business opportunities which are already sufficiently commercially attractive and well understood to get started *without* any special help and those which are unlikely ever to develop into viable businesses and so do not *warrant* special help.

Inevitably this means LEEP will sometimes devote considerable effort to developing projects which do not work. LEEP established, for example, that the intuitively elegant and attractive idea of combining *collection* of paper for recycling with *delivery* of new recycled stationery to small businesses does not work. The reason? Most companies buy their stationery in occasional big bulk orders with occasional panic afterthoughts requiring instant response. But they want their recyclables taken away on a frequent but regular and reliable routine. The three different schedules just don't match.

It can be argued that a stream of failures provides reassurance that LEEP is really doing its job of pushing back the frontiers of what is possible. However, this is thin consolation for staff having to admit defeat after weeks or months of committed effort on projects of the sort just dismissed in a paragraph each.

Businesses based on delivering local environmental policies

Another approach is for a local authority to help develop businesses to deliver its own environmental agenda. Sheffield went into partnership with a Finnish district heating company to develop a refuse-based district heating scheme; a consortium of London boroughs has done likewise to build the SELCHP (South East London Combined Heat and Power) plant.

In 1983 Glasgow City Council helped establish Heatwise as a separate business to undertake draught-proofing and insulation work to help tackle the city's enormous problems of cold, damp housing, illness and fuel debt caused by a combination of poor thermal performance, low incomes and the cold damp climate.

The hope was that the extra flexibility of an organization outside the council would give both efficient service delivery and the opportunity to use the council's own contributions to 'lever' funding from a variety of government schemes. The project was modelled on Keeping Newcastle Warm, the first of the community insulation projects which exploited the potential to link the Department of Energy's grants to establish insulation projects, the DoE's Homes Insulation Scheme and DHSS Single Payments to pay for insulation and draught-proofing materials, and the Manpower Services Commission's Community Programme which paid the wages of long-term unemployed people for up to a year of work and training on the projects, with tight but workable allowances for supervision and equipment.

By 1993 Heatwise had become the Wise Group, a business empire of six companies employing over 600 people at any one time, providing landscaping, physical property improvements, urban forestry and recycling, as well as energy efficiency, with offshoots in Motherwell outside Glasgow and Newham in East London.

The success was achieved through consistently following the original formula of delivering the local environmental services required by the council reliably, competitively and to high-quality standards, in a format carefully designed to meet the policy aims and criteria of a range of other public funders. Each component of the funding package is negotiated on the basis of the 'leverage' it will achieve through all the others. The various funding bodies are like a ring of Boy Scouts, each sitting on the lap of the one behind: they all sit comfortably for as long as they all sit still.

A weakness of this arrangement is that whenever one Boy Scout gets up and walks away, the whole ring falls down unless the gap is quickly filled. Over the last ten years the turnover of government funding schemes has resembled a game of musical chairs – or, from the point of view of the recipients, hide and seek. Or blind man's buff. None of the original government schemes mentioned still exists. Indeed, of the four government organizations mentioned, only the DoE has not been abolished or transformed.

The Wise Group has only survived, let alone prospered, by devoting large amounts of very high-quality management attention to remaking the funding coalition every time the rules changed. For example when the government replaced the Community Programme with Employment Training, one of the (many) ways the new scheme was meaner was that it paid trainees 'benefit plus' – a small flat rate cash addition to whatever benefits they had previously been claiming – instead of the 'rate for the job'. This was unacceptable to the trade unions, and Glasgow City Council, a staunch Labour authority, said it could not use Wise Group trainees if they were on ET 'benefit plus' rates. After months of negotiation a deal was done: the Wise Group would use European Social Fund (ESF) money to top up the ET payments from 'benefit plus' to 'rate for the job' levels. The unions were happy because the trainees would be getting the rate for the job, the city council was happy because the unions were happy, the ESF administrators were happy because the ET funding made their money go further and the MSC (being renamed Training Agency) was relieved to have secured a substantial and reliable block of take-up for an unpopular and problematic new scheme.

Lessons

Several lessons can be drawn from projects of the sort mentioned:

- *Strong local government helps.* Coventry, Edinburgh, Glasgow and Sheffield are all large authorities with (historically at least) considerable staff and financial resources, and consistent and settled political leadership. Coventry and Sheffield are unitary authorities; Edinburgh and Glasgow so large and powerful as to function in many ways more like partners than subordinates to their respective regions.

- *Business does not always know what is best for business.* A second delicious paradox is that in greening economic development, as indeed in economic development more generally, public agencies and public employees can often help businesses perform better.

- *Progress takes time.* All the main examples took time to hit their stride. They also all built on a long history of earlier experiments and projects. Coventry established its Pollution Prevention Panel – a forum for business and city council representatives to discuss and work cooperatively towards solutions to business environmental problems – as long ago as 1970. This made collaboration with the council on environmental issues part of the normal fabric of business life in the city for a quarter of a century. The habits, methods, contacts and expectations which this long experience built up have been crucial for making possible the more recent initiatives discussed earlier.

  Several people who helped develop the Recycling Cities programme as members of FoE's Projects Unit are now working on Global Action Plan, a programme of support for environmental action by individuals and households. Others are involved in Projects in Partnership, an attempt to break down the behavioural and cultural barriers to better energy efficiency behaviour through cooperation with relevant industry interests.

  The Recycling Cities programme also led to the creation of the National Recycling Forum, a coalition of business, local government and voluntary interests which has sponsored research and information exchange in waste minimization as well as reuse and many of whose policy recommendations have been taken up in the government's draft waste strategy for England and Wales.

- *The private sector has no monopoly of entrepreneurship, innovation or creativity.* In all the main examples quoted, the inspiration and the leading figures came from the voluntary or public sector and were motivated mainly by public good rather than commercial considerations.

Limits to local action to green economic development

The success stories in the last section might prompt the question: if environment is good for businesses and local authorities can promote green business, why isn't the economy getting more sustainable and why are the genuine success stories so few that the same examples crop up over and over again? This second part discusses some of the reasons. It moves from current limitations on local government action to limits on the scope for businesses themselves to promote sustainability and back to a new understanding of the role for central and local government action.

Resource pressures on local government

The first barrier to greening the local economy is very simple: the resource pressures on local government. Economic development and proactive environmental policy are both 'discretionary' functions, where local authorities have *powers* but not *duties*. Cutting them does not lay the council open to legal liabilities like (for example) failing to keep roads or buildings safe or collect the rubbish or produce immediate obvious suffering to local people like (for example) closing old people's homes and sacking teachers. Financial stringency may initially encourage efficiency, but beyond a certain point it simply forces authorities to sacrifice coherent forward-looking strategy to short-term crisis management.

Consider a recent example from an English city authority with a large commercial property portfolio. Most of the property is let to smaller local businesses and in an environmental management exercise the council's role as landlord was identified as an important potential environmental effect. Officers were highly creative in identifying ways that lettings policy and lease conditions could be used to influence the environmental performance of these tenants, for example by requiring minor repairs and refurbishments to be done to high energy-efficiency standards, avoiding use of tropical hardwoods or lead paints, providing cycle as well as car parking and so on.

Many of these suggestions would have cost tenants money, at least in the short term. All would have constrained their behaviour and required them to give management time and attention to matters not normally raised by property leases. This would make renting from the council less attractive than renting comparable properties from private sector landlords without environmental complications. The council would have to reduce its rents to compensate. But the valuers department's main aim was to manage the portfolio so as to maximize rental income to the city. Officers were ready and willing to promote better environmental performance through lettings – but only if, at political level, members accepted the cost. This was not politically realistic at a time when the authority was having to make painful and unpopular service cuts.

Management pressures on local government

In addition to financial restrictions, local government has been subjected to an extraordinary succession of management upheavals in the 1980s and 1990s. At corporate level these have included compulsory competitive tendering (first blue collar, now white collar), the attempted replacement of domestic rates with the poll tax, the ensuing shambles and return to council tax, business rates changes, the Citizens' Charter and the development of performance indicators and (unfortunately neither last nor least) local government review. In addition there have been continual and often arbitrary and unpredictable, changes in the rules and requirements *within* many service areas including housing, education and social services.

Local government review (LGR) has been particularly effective at retarding the best work on environment and economy. Abolition is the greatest threat any authority can face and calls for the best efforts at resistance. The protractedness and complication of the process has ensured that the people seconded to work on it were tied up for long periods. The extended period of uncertainty has made strategic planning difficult for many authorities for years. Finally, by setting the different tiers of local government against each other it has made particularly difficult the sorts of collaboration and partnership which are at the leading edge of both environmental and economic development work.

The effect of these management initiatives is thus a bit like flu: the patient loses the ability to do anything more dynamic than doze in bed while all available energy is devoted to containing and repelling the threat. Our next delicious paradox is therefore that the more exciting and dynamic *management* change becomes, the more static, unambitious and unimaginative an organization's *policies* and *activities* are likely to be. It is no accident that much of the boldest and most creative work has been done by big, stable authorities: those best able to defend themselves against disruptions.

Additionality versus substitution

Another problem is that of 'additionality' versus 'substitution'. This is not peculiar to green economic development: all public intervention in a market economy runs the risk of simply *moving* activity rather than *adding* to it. Enterprise Zones, City Challenge projects and suchlike have been criticized for increasing business activity in their targeted areas by tempting businesses to move in from the surrounding areas.

In the late 1980s smart companies considering major developments would express interest in one potential site in (say) Merseyside, one in the South Wales coalfields, one in Strathclyde and one in Derry (or Kerry) and make sure that the regional economic development agencies in each knew of the others. Top executives could then spend a happy week or two being treated to lavish tours of each region, during which they would invite each set of hosts to better the package of support and inducements offered by the previous ones. Sometimes a second or even third round of visits would be needed to complete the auction.

Much inward investment promotion may thus be a futile 'zero sum game' in which one area only gains benefits by depriving others of them and the only winners are commercial interests cunning enough to play one public agency off against another. The problem is particularly obvious for some kinds of environmental business development. For example, collecting newspapers for recycling is one of the most obvious, tangible and satisfying environmental activities available to ordinary people. Through the 1970s and 1980s, whenever market fluctuations created a little extra demand for newspapers, voluntary groups and local authorities rushed to establish new collections. Each time, the new collections soon oversaturated the market. Merchants responded, as elementary market theory would predict, by driving prices down.

Unfortunately the collectors did not, as elementary market theory says they should, pull out when the price fell below covering their costs. Instead they appealed for subsidies to enable them to continue the great crusade of saving paper. Some councils obliged, mindful of the great public enthusiasm for recycling and the unpopularity of allowing recycling schemes to fail. The result was to allow the merchants to push prices still lower. This drove *un*subsidized paper collections, including some long established ones, out of business.

The lesson for greening local economic development is to concentrate on areas of definite additionality or where more sustainable alternatives substitute for non-environmental. Within the field of recycling, wise authorities (and businesses) have concentrated on recycling of (for example) higher grade office paper or aluminium cans, where industry demand is far greater than supply. Other areas of green business development which are relatively immune to additionality problems include the building of cycle ways and improving energy efficiency in local buildings. In many authorities these are not seen as economic development activities.

The businesses and managers who most need environmental advice and information are precisely those who are least likely to go out of their way to get it. Voluntary measures only reach those who volunteer. Before volunteering for green business activities, business people have at least to believe there is an issue and it is this first step which most smaller British companies have yet to take.

The reason is not at all mysterious. It is the same reason why the Energy Efficiency Office is still, 13 years after its launch, plaintively pointing out that most businesses could cheaply and easily save 20 per cent of their energy bills and why most companies are still not doing it. Any company has to concentrate limited money and management attention on the small number of possible activities which are most important for the future of the business and most businesses will have more urgent priorities than the environment.

Managers of a successful, prospering business will give more attention to developing new products and markets and managing expansion than to making small savings on energy or wastes, particularly where expansion is expected to reduce their proportionate importance to the company. Managers of an unsuccessful, faltering business will generally have far more pressing worries and demands on their time than small-scale resource and environmental impacts and will be uninterested in investments which will only pay back over a future the company may not have.

Limits to commercial viability of sustainability action

Behind these behavioural barriers to business interest in sustainability lies a more intractable problem. Granted that there are enormous opportunities for 'no regrets' actions which both save money and improve the environment. But there are limits beyond which further environmental improvements result in commercial costs.

Sainsbury's, the supermarket chain, provides a good example of both opportunities and limits. Over many years it has worked towards outstanding standards of energy efficiency in the stores, through applying the best individual technologies in refrigeration, lighting and so on, then progressively integrating the different energy uses and using sophisticated monitoring and control technologies. They also stock environmentally preferable alternatives to a number of products, host recycling banks in their car parks and encourage shoppers to reuse their carrier bags by giving a penny refund on each bag reused. But at the same time Sainsbury's have energetically promoted and developed out-of-town superstores which have increased the car dependence and energy intensity of shopping and the relative disadvantage of shoppers without cars.

Even the Body Shop, one of the most environmentally committed companies in the UK, has moved to a site on the outskirts of its home town to which most staff commute by car. In Sweden Volvo's top management recognize that some time in the next few decades environmental and social pressures will greatly reduce the market for the sorts of cars they make. They are devoting considerable resources to developing buses, trams and suchlike so they will be ready when this happens. But meanwhile they continue to make and promote heavy resource-wasteful cars.

It would be naive to accuse any of the companies just discussed of hypocrisy or even inconsistency. Their pro-environmental actions are directed to exactly the same end as their anti-environmental ones: commercial security and success. It is commercially rational for Sainsbury's to devote great attention to energy efficiency because it can achieve significant savings in an important area of corporate costs. The unusually long paybacks Sainsbury's accept reflect their strong cash flow and confidence in the future. Stocking green products is rational because enough customers are prepared to pay the extra and having bottle banks on site gains more goodwill than it costs in parking space.

However Sainsbury's continue to sell cheaper un-green alternatives because most customers still want them and like the other supermarket chains they calculate that the cost and trouble of providing facilities for return of bottles for refilling would be greater than the customer goodwill they would gain. The environmental superiority of refilling will be quite irrelevant to this decision until it is reflected to a significant degree in customer preferences and demands, whereupon Sainsbury's will doubtless oblige – closely followed by Safeway, Tesco, Asda and the others at the point where their respective market shares are threatened.

The need to manage markets

It would be unrealistic to expect any of these companies to behave differently. They are only doing what any company must do if it wishes to stay in business: make the most commercially advantageous decisions possible given current and anticipated market conditions. The great strength of the market system – its impersonal, mechanical, value-free way of allocating resources – is also its great weakness: its inability to recognise or reflect any values or aims which are not embodied in price relationships. '*Free* market' is a peculiarly misleading description for an institution which so rigidly prescribes the factors which can permissibly affect decisions and their relative weightings and punishes those who allow wider considerations to affect their judgements with business failure.

This throws a surprising new light on the government's repeated insistence on the leading role of voluntary action by companies in working towards sustainable development. This is normally seen as a compliment and a liberation to business.

In fact it is an unfair burden: companies can only live up to the expectations being placed on them by damaging their own commercial positions.

The inevitable failure of voluntary business action to deliver serious moves towards sustainability might, in the current political climate, be taken as proof of the impracticality of sustainability. But this is two-edged. A government with different preconceptions – or public opinion after a serious environmental crisis – might conclude that the fault is with the free market for being unsustainable, rather than with sustainability for being incompatible with market forces.

A further delicious paradox is therefore that people wishing to safeguard the credibility and popularity of the market system in the longer term might be wise to press governments to intervene to create market conditions in which businesses can go a lot further towards sustainable behaviour than at present, instead of merely repeating complimentary but impracticable exhortations to the business community.

Central government action is essential

All the frustrations and limitations discussed point to one simple message: there is no substitute for active management of the economy by government to make more sustainable behaviour commercially viable. Many of the local actions described should be seen as pathfinders for central government action rather than alibis for central government inaction. For example the LEEP 'billsavers' project mentioned earlier shines forth as a good deed of demand management in a wicked world of energy sales – but far more environmental impact could be achieved less laboriously through government building a 'least cost planning approach into energy utility regulation' and far more social equity improvement could be achieved through reforming energy tariff structures to charge lower unit prices to small energy users rather than higher ones as at present (see Levett, 1994).

Likewise, ecological tax reform – shifting of taxation off labour and value-added and onto use of natural resources and wastage (which can be thought of as 'value-subtracted') – could, if properly designed and combined with other measures, achieve a great deal more to motivate companies to reduce resource consumption than just advice and exhortation.

Another delicious paradox is that the government's unwillingness to make big, simple, consistent interventions such as ecological tax reform is leading it to reinvent the sort of thicket of arbitrary, cross-cutting localized measures – a bit of fuel levy here, some VAT exemptions there, some landfill tax, recycling credits changing hands at different rates between different types of waste authority, sometimes extended to voluntary groups, sometimes not, a succession of bidding rounds for renewable energy subsidies, each on different terms – which it has consistently been trying to eliminate from the economy in the name of the 'level playing field'.

The future: Redefining economic success

The necessity of central government action does not imply a lack of need for local action. In fact, the opposite is true: central government action to green the economy would greatly increase the benefits of, and the scope for, many of the kinds of local action described.

Indeed a general move towards sustainability would open up a much more profound role for local action on economic development. This chapter started with very light green arguments about environmental improvement and business. The hue has been steadily deepening, but the discussion has so far stayed largely within standard assumptions about the blanket desirability of economic activity.

These assumptions are increasingly being challenged in local consultative processes, being initiated by local authorities under the Local Agenda 21 banner, to decide on the meaning of sustainable development for an area and on action to be taken towards it. *Local Agenda 21: Principles and Process* (LGMB, 1994) includes the following ringing declarations:

> Human wellbeing has social, cultural, moral and spiritual dimensions as well as material ones. Development worthy of the name must seek to support all of these, not some at the expense of others . . . Development and economic growth are quite different things. It is possible to have either without the other . . . We need broader indicators than economic growth to measure development by.

By late 1995 this is already coming to seem part of the standard litany of local government environmentalism. In some local authorities, economic development strategies are being generated through, or heavily influenced by, Local Agenda 21 processes, and are building in concerns for equity and non-economic quality of life as well as for environmental sustainability.

There are clearly limits to how far such approaches are realistic and deliverable in an economy geared to very different aims. But it is only at local level that a new value-based view of the economy and of desirable directions for economic development can be articulated.

Conclusion

Local authorities and other local agencies are already playing a significant role in greening the local economy – and demonstrating that the public sector has a positive and constructive role to play in the economy.

There are limits to how far businesses can go – and therefore to how far public sector action can push them. Government action is essential to move the barriers. Both the government's enthusiasms for voluntary action by businesses and the renewal of the planning system are welcome, but could turn out to be poisoned chalices without corresponding action by the government itself.

References

Brugmann, J. (1992) *Managing Human Ecosystems: Principles for Ecological Municipal Management*, ICLEI, Toronto.

Commission of the European Communities (1994) *European Sustainable Cities: first report of the EU Expert Group on the Urban Environment Sustainable Cities Project*, CEC, Brussels.

HMSO (1993) *A guide to the Eco-Management and Audit scheme for UK Local Government*, HMSO, London.

International Centre for Local Environmental Initiatives (1994) *Guide to Environmental Management for Local Authorities in Central and Eastern Europe: Volume 9: Environmental Issues in Land Use Planning and Economic Development Planning*, I CLEI, Freiburg.

Levett, R. (1994) 'Sustainable pricing structures' in *Town and Country Planning*, October 1994.

Local Government Management Board (1993a) *Greening Economic Development*, LGMB, Luton.

Local Government Management Board (1993b) *A Framework for Local Sustainability*, LGMB, Luton.

Local Government Management Board (1994) *Local Agenda 21 Principles and Process, A Step by Step Guide*, LGMB, Luton.

Storksdieck, M. and Otto-Zimmermann, K. (1994) *Local Environmental Budgeting*, ICLEI, Freiburg.

Section B   Managing People

Few people can doubt that the management of people is central to the success of today's organization. Here Pfeffer, Collins and Porras, Quinn et al. and Ekvall illustrate some of the reasons why. Pfeffer documents the increasing importance of the way staff are managed. Collins and Porras explain why it is more important for leaders to build organizations with good, considerate management than articulate their vision for a grand new product charismatically. Quinn et al. focus on that most modern problem – managing intellectuals, or as Handy neatly expressed it, trying to herd cats. Ekvall describes the characteristics of the creative work climate associated with innovative and adaptive departments.

Pfeffer elaborates on the changing sources of advantage, arguing that product advantages, protected markets, access to finance and economies of scale no longer offer the key advantages but rather that staff, the way they are managed and the culture they work in is what makes the difference between the successful and unsuccessful firm. In this article he discusses the merits of employment security with highly selective hiring of new personnel, the importance of development and training and the advantages and disadvantages of outsourcing. Elsewhere he has elaborated on the merits of self-managed teams and decentralization of decisions, comparatively high compensation linked to performance, extensive training, reduced status distinctions and extensive sharing of financial and performance information in this more open form of management (Pfeffer, 1999).

Collins and Porras aim to destroy two prevailing myths about leaders – that they have charisma and build their companies on great ideas. They draw on research on successful companies like 3M, Sony, Walt Disney and Hewlett-Packard and compare these to companies that have not fared so well. The reserved and un-charismatic leaders, like William McKnight, with over 50 years at the helm of 3M and Masaru Ibuku of Sony, whose initial products failed, appear to have built very successful companies. The authors present a compelling case that what makes the difference is attention to building an organization that is self-sufficient enough to survive the owner's death and continue the innovative tradition he or she initiated.

Quinn and colleagues turn their attention to the business of managing profes-sionals, an area that is burgeoning as human capital becomes ever more central to organizational functioning. Their advice seems almost old-fashioned with its emphasis on recruiting the best, the need for intensive early development and weeding out staff who are not making the grade. However, they recognize the need for, but problems with, getting professionals to share knowledge; after all knowledge is often their product and powerbase. They recommend strong incentives to encourage the process. They also recognize that fancy technology to enable knowledge sharing rarely gets far without a culture to support its use. Finally, they address a structure they see as well suited to managing professionals, a spider's web network, where specialists gather together for short periods to focus on particular projects.

Ekvall describes two studies of creative organizational climate, outlining the open characteristics associated with more innovative organizations and departments. He goes on to try and identify the organizational characteristics associated with adaptive or incremental creativity and with innovative or radical creativity. He concludes that each thrives under slightly differing conditions presenting something of a dilemma for management.

Reference

J. Pfeffer (1999) 'Seven practices of successful organisations', *Health Forum Journal*, 42, Jan/Feb.

5 Competitive Advantage through People

Jeffrey Pfeffer

Suppose that, in 1972, someone had asked you to pick the five companies that would provide the greatest return to stockholders over the next 20 years. And suppose that you had had access to books on competitive success that were not even written. How would you approach your assignment? In order to earn tremendous economic returns, the companies you pick should have some sustainable competitive advantage, something that (1) distinguishes them from their competitors, (2) provides positive economic benefits and (3) is not readily duplicated.

Conventional wisdom then (and even now) would have you begin by selecting the right industries. After all, "not all industries offer equal opportunity for sustained profitability, and the inherent profitability of its industry is one essential ingredient in determining the profitability of a firm."[1] According to Michael Porter's now famous framework, the five fundamental competitive forces that determine the ability of firms in an industry to earn above-normal returns are "the entry of new competitors, the threat of substitutes, the bargaining power of buyers, the bargaining power of suppliers, and the rivalry among existing competitors."[2] You should find industries with barriers to entry, low supplier and buyer bargaining power, few ready substitutes, and a limited threat of new entrants to compete away economic returns. Within such industries, other conventional analyses would urge you to select firms with the largest market share, which can realize the cost benefits of economies of scale. In short, you would probably look to industries in which patent protection of important product or service technology could be achieved and select the dominant firms in those industries.

You would have been very successful in selecting the five top-performing firms from 1972 to 1992 if you took this conventional wisdom and turned it on its head. The top five stocks, and their percentage returns, were (in reverse order): Plenum Publishing (with a return of 15,689%), Circuit City (a video and appliance retailer: 16,410%), Tyson Foods (a poultry producer: 18,118%), Wal-Mart (a discount chain: 19,807%) and Southwest Airlines (21,775%).[3] Yet during this period, these industries (retailing, airlines, publishing, and food processing) were characterized by massive competition and horrendous losses, widespread bankruptcy, virtually no barriers to entry (for airlines after 1978), little unique or proprietary technology, and many substitute products or services. And in 1972, none of these firms was (and some still are not) the market-share leader, enjoying economies of scale or moving down the learning curve.

The point here is not to throw out conventional strategic analysis based on industrial economics but simply to note that the source of competitive advantage has always shifted over time. What these five successful firms tend to have in common is that for their sustained advantage, they rely not on technology, patents, or strategic position, but on how they manage their work force. Our first task is to explore how and why some sources of competitive success that were important in the past are less so now and why the workforce, and how it is organized and managed, is an increasingly important source of competitive advantage.

The very factors that made Southwest Airlines, Wal-Mart, Plenum, and other organizations such as Nordstrom, Lincoln Electric, and the New United Motor plant of the Toyota-GM joint venture so successful are things that are difficult to imitate. That is what provides such competitive leverage, the ability to almost literally make gold out of lead – exceptional economic returns in highly competitive, almost mundane industries. The paradox is that even if we succeed in changing what we do, the basis of sustained competitive success will alter again. At the moment, however, we are a long way from having to worry about that problem.

The changing basis of competitive success

People and how we manage them are becoming more important because many other sources of competitive success are less powerful than they once were. Recognizing that the basis for competitive advantage has changed is essential to develop a different frame of reference for considering issues of management and strategy. Traditional sources of success – product and process technology, protected or regulated markets, access to financial resources, and economies of scale – can still provide competitive leverage, but to a lesser degree now than in the past, leaving organizational culture and capabilities, derived from how people are managed, as comparatively more vital.

Product and process technology

One important source of competitive advantage was product technology, protected by patents or other proprietary know-how. In 1959, Xerox developed and prepared to introduce its first plain-paper copier. Some 13 years later, in 1972, it enjoyed a market share of more than 90% with machines that, although improved, still relied, fundamentally, on the same technological foundation. How many companies, industries, or products today could retain more than 90% of the market on the basis of 13-year-old technology? A quote from the annual report of Sun Microsystems, a computer workstation manufacturer, makes the point: "Sun's avowed intention [is] doubling the performance of its high-end workstations about every 18 months, on average."[4]

Since product life cycles are shortening and new-product introductions are coming much more rapidly, relying on a static product technology for success is increasingly problematic.

Research has shown that new product introductions are vital to most manufacturing firms' growth and prosperity. A Booz, Allen and Hamilton study of over 700 Fortune 1000 companies estimated that new products would provide over 30% of these firms' profits during a five-year period from 1981–1986. The same study suggested that the number of new products introduced by these firms was expected to double compared to the previous five-year period.[5]

The increasing pace of product change means that a technical edge, even once achieved, will erode quickly and must be renewed. The need for continuous innovation and rapid response to market and technological changes virtually requires a work force that delivers superior performance.

Not only is the length of product life cycles diminishing, there is an erosion in the protection provided by patents because of competitors' ability to imitate product innovations. One of the most comprehensive studies of this question examined 48 product innovations of firms in the chemical, drug, electronics, and machinery industries.[6] The study found that, on average, the imitation cost to innovation cost ratio was approximately .65, and the ratio of imitation time to innovation time was about .70.[7] Although patents provided some protection, particularly in pharmaceuticals, the protection was less than one might think. "Contrary to popular opinion, patent protection does not make entry impossible, or even unlikely. Within 4 years of their introduction, 60% of the patented successful innovations . . . were imitated."[8]

Firms sought competitive advantage not only in their product technology, but also in the process technology used to produce the product or service. General Motors was perhaps the archetype of this approach, investing heavily in technology to automate its factories in the 1980s. The company spent some $40 billion for modernization and new facilities, in the process substituting fixed costs for variable costs.[9] In fact, GM spent enough money on capital equipment to have purchased both Honda and Nissan.[10] Unfortunately, it did not get much for that investment.

There are several problems with seeking competitive advantage through investments in process technology. First, little of that technology is proprietary – the people who sell you robots or point-of-sale terminals or software to analyze production or service delivery will sell the robots, terminals and software to your competitors. Your ability to obtain the benefits of, let alone get any advantage from, this technology – which is often widely available and readily understood – depends on your ability to implement it more rapidly and effectively. This almost inevitably involves the skill and motivation of the workforce.

Second, investment in specialized technology is not a substitute for skill in managing the workforce; it actually makes the workforce even more crucial for success. This is because more skill may be required to operate the more sophisticated and advanced equipment, and with a higher level of investment per employee, interruptions in the process are increasingly expensive. This means that the ability to effectively operate, maintain and repair equipment – tasks all done by first-line employees – becomes even more critical.

Paul Adler noted that: "In banks, a fully on-line system integrating numerous branches meant that people at the extremities . . . would have to be absolutely reliable, since any data they entered . . . would be fed instantaneously into all the bank's accounts and corresponding funds transferred instantaneously."[11] He also

noted that in the case of numerically controlled machine tools, in spite of manufacturers' promises, the skill requirements of machinists have remained constant or
increased. They often required expanded training and higher levels of responsibility,
even with the more technologically sophisticated machines.

When the Shenandoah Life Insurance Company spent some $2 million to
computerize its processing and claims operations in the early 1980s, it found that
it got almost nothing for its expenditure – it still required 27 working days and 32
clerks in three departments to handle a policy conversion.[12] Only after the company
changed how it organized and managed its workforce – relying on semi-autonomous
teams of five to seven people, upgrading training and skills and paying more for the
more responsible and more skilled workers – did case-handling time drop and service
complaints virtually disappear. "By 1986, Shenandoah was processing 50% more
applications and queries with 10% fewer employees than it did in 1980."[13]

Finally, investments in process technology provide only limited competitive
advantage because, as the senior manufacturing executive in the papermaking
division of a large forest products company said: "Machines don't make things,
people do." Commenting on the tremendous investment in advanced computer
technology to automate factory processes, one writer perceptively noted: "It is rather
ironic that the application of artificial intelligence to manufacturing is becoming
a popular topic. If intelligence is so helpful in its artificial form, then why have the
benefits of the real intelligence been overlooked so far."[14]

Protected and regulated markets

Another way in which firms achieved competitive success was by avoiding
competition through protected or regulated domestic markets. Some years ago while
visiting Italy, I noticed that there were many Fiats and almost no Japanese cars
– indeed, only about 2000 Japanese cars per year were sold in Italy during the
mid-1980s. This sales level did not reflect the relative prices and product qualities
or consumer tastes, but resulted from a limit on the imports of Japanese cars. Fearful
of the power and success of Fiat after World War II, Japan struck a bargain in which
the Japanese automobile market would be protected from Fiat while the Italian
market would be protected from Japanese automakers.

Regulation can limit competition by setting prices and by restricting entry.[15]
In the United States, for many years entry into transportation industries such
as airlines and trucking was strictly controlled. MCI's success as a provider of
long-distance telephone service came only after the company won a protracted
struggle even to be permitted to operate. The wave of deregulation sweeping the
United States and the rest of the world, however, has eliminated many protected
markets. Moreover, there is some evidence that once deregulated and opened to
competition, markets are difficult to close or reregulate. Thus, these trends seem
to be irreversible.

Access to financial resources

Another traditional source of competitive advantage was access to financial resources. With less efficient capital markets, a firm's ability to finance itself through substantial financial resources afforded protection from competitors less able to acquire the resources necessary to mount a serious challenge. This source of competitive advantage has eroded in the face of increasingly efficient financial markets in which capital moves worldwide on an unprecedented scale. The venture capital industry is now international, so that if US investors, for instance, are unwilling to bear the risk of financing leading-edge technologies in pharmaceuticals, semiconductors, and equipment, foreign investors will take up the slack. Capital is now less important as a source of competitive advantage because the money to finance a good idea, or strong management, is increasingly available to all attractive projects.

Economies of scale

Yet another source of competitive advantage that is now less significant than it used to be is economies of scale. The famous Boston Consulting Group experience curve postulated that a firm that entered a market early and achieved large production volumes would face significantly lower costs as it achieved the benefits of learning as well as more traditional scale economies. Although there is some evidence for the economic benefits of large market share,[16] there is much evidence that this source of competitive advantage is diminishing in importance. The trend toward more fragmented markets, with the need to cater to the specialized tastes of particular subsegments of the population, has been described in detail by Piore and Sabel in their book about flexible specialization.[17] In general, the same computer-aided design and manufacturing technologies that make imitation easier also make it possible to economically design and manufacture a more differentiated product line.

Several examples help make the point. Consider first so-called natural monopolies, such as telecommunications and electric power generation. Even here, evolving technology makes it possible for smaller competitors to exploit market segments effectively. In downtown Chicago, an independent company laid its own fiber optic cable and provides telephone service to a set of commercial clients in that densely populated area. Electric utilities compete with industrial clients that now dispose of their wastes in co-generation facilities, which produce power from the heat. The ability of the Japanese to make car models profitably, even when they sell fewer than 100,000 units per year, has given firms with that capability a tremendous competitive advantage. And finally, the textile industry, particularly suppliers of men's clothing, traditionally competed on the basis of price and did so by making large lots of standard products. With major retailers now wanting to stock leaner inventories and be more responsive to shifting customer tastes and what actually sells, the basis of success has shifted to the ability to deliver the product quickly. "Rather than allowing order response times of one month or more, the lean retailer currently requires 13 days for order fulfillment. In two years, the response time will decrease to 6 days."[18]

Without debating whether scale economies and market share ever provided the advantages that some claimed, it is clear that whatever those advantages, they are smaller now than they once were and will probably be even smaller in the future.

The importance of the workforce and how it is managed

As other sources of competitive success have become less important, what remains as a crucial, differentiating factor is the organization, its employees and how they work. Consider, for instance, Southwest Airlines, whose stock had the best return from 1972 to 1992. It certainly did not achieve that success from economies of scale. In 1992, Southwest had revenues of $1.31 billion and a "mere 2.6% of the US passenger market."[19] People Express, by contrast, achieved $1 billion in revenues after only three years of operation, not the almost 20 it took Southwest. Southwest exists not because of regulated or protected markets but in spite of them. "During the first three years of its history, no Southwest planes were flown."[20] Southwest waged a battle for its very existence with competitors that sought to keep it from flying at all and, failing that, made sure it did not fly out of the newly constructed Dallas-Fort Worth international airport. Instead, it was restricted to operating out of the close-in Love Field, and thus was born its first advertising slogan, "Make Love, Not War." Southwest became the "love" airline out of necessity, not choice.

In 1978, competitors sought to bar flights from Love Field to anywhere outside Texas. The compromise Southwest wrangled permitted it to fly from Love to the four states contiguous to Texas.[21] Its competitive strategy of short-haul, point-to-point flights to close-in airports (it now flies into Chicago's Midway and Houston's Hobby airports) was more a product of its need to adapt to what it was being permitted to do than a conscious, planned move – although, in retrospect, the strategy has succeeded brilliantly. Neither has Southwest succeeded because it has had more access to lower-cost capital – indeed, it is one of the least leveraged airlines in the United States. Southwest's planes, Boeing 737s, are obviously available to all its competitors. It isn't a member of any of the big computerized reservation systems; it uses no unique process technology and sells essentially a commodity product – low-cost, low-frills airline service at prices its competitors have difficulty matching.

Much of its cost advantage comes from its very productive, very motivated and, by the way, unionized work force. Compared to the US airline industry, according to 1991 statistics, Southwest has fewer employees per aircraft (79 versus 131), flies more passengers per employee (2318 versus 848), and has more available seat miles per employee (1,891,082 versus 1,339,995).[22] It turns around some 80% of its flights in 15 minutes or less, while other airlines on average need 45 minutes, giving it an enormous productivity advantage in terms of equipment utilization.[23] It also provides an exceptional level of passenger service. Southwest has won the airlines' so-called triple crown (best on-time performance, fewest lost bags, and fewest passenger complaints – in the same month) nine times. No competitor has achieved that even once.[24]

What is important to recognize now is why success, such as that achieved at Southwest, can be sustained and can not readily be imitated by competitors. There are two fundamental reasons. First, the success that comes from managing people effectively is often not as visible or transparent as to its source. We can see a computerized information system, a particular semiconductor, a numerically controlled machine tool. The culture and practices that enable Southwest to achieve its success are less obvious. Even when they are described, as they have been in numerous newspaper articles and even a segment on '60 minutes', they are difficult to really understand. Culture, how people are managed and the effects of this on their behavior and skills are sometimes seen as the "soft" side of business, occasionally dismissed. Even when they are not dismissed, it is often hard to comprehend the dynamics of a particular company and how it operates because the way people are managed often fits together in a system. It is easy to copy one thing but much more difficult to copy numerous things. This is because the change needs to be more comprehensive and also because the ability to understand the system of management practices is hindered by its very extensiveness.

Thus, for example, Nordstrom, the department store chain, has enjoyed substantial success both in customer service and in sales and profitability growth over the years. Nordstrom compensates its employees in part with commissions. Not surprisingly, many of its competitors, after finally acknowledging Nordstrom's success and the fact that it was attributable to the behaviors of its employees, instituted commission systems. By itself, changing the compensation system did not fully capture what Nordstrom had done, neither did it provide many benefits to the competition. Indeed, in some cases, changing the compensation system produced employee grievances and attempts to unionize when the new system was viewed as unfair or arbitrary.

Achieving competitive success through people involves fundamentally altering how we think about the workforce and the employment relationship. It means achieving success by working with people, not by replacing them or limiting the scope of their activities. It entails seeing the workforce as a source of strategic advantage, not just as a cost to be minimized or avoided. Firms that take this different perspective are often able to successfully outmanoeuvre and outperform their rivals. In the remainder of this chapter, I address two issues – training and the use of contingent workforce – to show how viewing people as a source of success changes the formulation of both public policy and managerial strategy.

Training and skill development

If competitive success is achieved through people, then the skills of those people are critical. Consequently, one of the most obvious implications of the changing basis of competitive success is the growing importance of having a workforce with adequate skills. Historical studies show that between 1929 and 1982, education prior to work accounted for 26% of the growth in the productive capacity of the United States, with learning on the job contributing to an additional 55%. It seems clear that: "Learning in school and learning on the job are by far the most important factors behind American economic growth and productivity in this century, and will determine the nation's economic prospects in the next."[25] The evidence, however, is that skill problems in the US workforce are widespread and growing.

There are several reasons why many organizations provide less training than is optimal. First, unlike many other countries, the United States presently has no specific public policy designed to encourage training. Although such expenditures are obviously tax-deductible, in many countries there is a requirement that 1% or so of payroll (wages) be spent on training. If less than the prescribed amount is spent, the difference goes to the government as tax. Also, unlike many other countries, there is little coordination from the government, industry associations, or other collective organizations to formulate training policy and standards and to facilitate the training enterprise. For instance, in New Zealand, legislation has established co-ordinating bodies for training in various industries, and these bodies tend to be active in setting standards, developing curricula, implementing certification, and so forth.

Second, the costs of training funded by the company are clear and immediate, but the benefits are often long term and may, in fact, accrue to other organizations. If I train someone and the person leaves to work for another employer, then the other organization obtains the benefits of my organization's expenditures. Economic theory, consequently, suggests that general training, of use in numerous jobs, be funded by the trainee, who, after all, stands to reap the benefits. Firm-specific training, for skills that are of use primarily to a particular organization, should be funded by that organization. Of course, what constitutes general or firm-specific training is likely to be very much open to question and firms will therefore have a tendency to under-invest in skill development.

Third, training's benefits are inherently long term. Under the pressure of short-term budget or profit pressure, training, particularly in the United States, is often the first thing to be cut. Every dollar saved on skill building this year flows immediately to pre-tax profit and the loss of competitive position that may be caused is less clearly visible and, in any event, will probably occur only sometime in the future.

This, however, does mean that organizations that choose to do so can use training, and the skills developed thereby, as a competitive weapon. As one example, consider the New United Motor automobile assembly plant in Fremont, California, a joint venture of Toyota and General Motors. Under the agreement establishing the joint venture, a certain proportion of the production was to go to Toyota and a portion to GM. When the Nova was being produced for GM at the plant, and sales weren't sufficient to keep the plant busy, rather than laying off workers, the company gave them other tasks such as painting and repair, and trained them extensively in statistical process control (SPC), how to work in groups, how to analyze jobs and the work process and so forth. The plant manager at the time remarked that in the 1990s, having a skilled and committed workforce would be the key to success in the automobile industry and wanted to ensure that this facility would be competitive with the best in the world. Indeed, many of the Japanese transplant automobile assembly facilities surprised people with the extensive training they provided workers. Often, selected workers were sent to Japan prior to the start-up and workers were routinely given as much as four times the amount of initial training that was customary in the US automobile industry. This training obviously costs money, but the Japanese believed that it would produce a workforce with the skills to provide a competitive advantage in an industry facing excess manufacturing capacity.

Using training to gain a competitive edge is diffusing to US automakers as well. When General Motors opened a new truck plant in Fort Wayne, Indiana, that relied not only on new technology but also on team-based production, both workers and management went through intensive training in group problem solving and interpersonal dynamics.[26] The 3000 employees at the factory received 1.9 million hours of training, or about 633 hours per worker, to learn the new technology and develop skills in working in teams.

In a world in which your competitors treat training as a luxury, don't know how to organize and deliver it, and don't link it tightly to the strategic objectives of the business, your organization's ability to maintain appropriate training can produce real competitive advantage. Moreover, public policies that facilitate, encourage, or enable training enhance the competitiveness of those who are subject to those policies.

The 'externalization' of employment

If competitive success is achieved through people – if the workforce is, indeed, an increasingly important source of competitive advantage – then it is important to build a workforce that has the ability to achieve competitive success and that cannot be readily duplicated by others. Somewhat ironically, the recent trend toward using temporary help, part-time employees, and contract workers, particularly when such people are used in core activities, flies in the face of the changing basis of competitive success. This raises the questions of why these practices seem to be growing, what effects they have on the ability to achieve advantage through people, and what the implications are for organizations that might follow a different strategy.

At the most fundamental level, it is obvious that, at the limit, if all employees are temps or contract workers, or even if they are part-timers, this cannot serve as a basis of distinction. As is the case with technological equipment, the temporary agencies will furnish staff to all customers. Outside contractors will work for anyone, and part-timers, many of whom are in that status involuntarily, have insufficient attachment or commitment to a particular organization to provide it with some comparative advantage. Consider the case of professional services, such as law, accounting, or management consulting. Why use McKinsey, the consulting firm, or Jones, Day, the large law firm, or KPMG Peat Marwick, the accounting firm, and pay a premium price to do so, if these companies simply hired contract or temporary workers? The distinctive competence of a professional services firm is the skill of its staff and if those people can be obtained just as readily elsewhere, and if they have no attachment to a particular firm, then the competitive position of the organization is diminished. This is why many well-managed professional services firms emphasize recruitment, selection, and building strong cultures to retain the skilled employees who constitute the basis of their success. To the extent that people are a source of competitive success for firms other than those in professional services, the same logic applies.

Nevertheless, taking employees out of the organization or diminishing their attachments to it is a growing trend.[27] For instance, between 1970 and 1984, the temp industry outgrew the GNP by almost 2 to 1 and grew 21% faster than even the computing equipment industry over that same time period.

The reasons behind this growth are many. It is often much quicker to staff using these sources of labor. Hiring a so-called permanent employee requires possibly posting the job, collecting applications, screening, and making a final selection. Getting a temporary requires a phone call, and the person can often be there within an hour. Speed in filling the position is a mixed blessing, however. On the one hand, you get someone quickly. On the other hand, the absence of the formal process may mean you have people who would not meet the regular requirements.

A second reason for using contract or temporary workers is that the unit may not have authorization to hire. Many organizations manage head count much more stringently than they manage monetary budgets. This permits them to trumpet figures like sales per employee, or, in the case of government, for political leaders to announce that they have reduced the size of government. However, if all one has done is replace regular employees with outsiders or temporaries, the presumed savings may be illusory or worse.

Third, the use of contingent employees is a buffer to absorb fluctuations in demand while avoiding the morale problems that layoffs engender. The traumatic 1985 layoffs at Apple, an organization with a strong culture, caused many managers to want to avoid a repeat of the situation. One way was to use very lean staffing levels and contingent workers to do the additional work. A study of 442 private firms observed that both the seasonality and cyclicality of demand affected the use of temporaries. However, neither factor affected the extent of contracting out.[28] The use of contingent employment to buffer a set of critical, core employees is one that is compatible with achieving competitive advantage through the workforce.

Finally, one of the most important reasons why organizations use contingent employees is that they cost less. The issue of cost is complex, as there are many costs (and possibly offsetting benefits) that need to be accounted for. In many organizations, as at Apple, a facilities charge is levied for permanent employees, since they need work space, but not for contingent workers. Of course, this cost saving is illusory if one has temporary workers who actually occupy space continuously.

Temporary and contract employees may also cost less because they are paid less and do not receive the benefits – particularly health insurance, retirement, and vacation – of regular employees. Katherine Abraham reported that: "The average wages for less-skilled workers . . . employed in the business service sector are from 15 to 30% lower than average wages for workers holding similar jobs in manufacturing[29] and a study of contract workers in petrochemical facilities found that such workers earned less even after numerous characteristics were statistically controlled.[30] Wages, however, are often the same or even higher for contingent workers in high-skilled occupations. The evidence is that benefits are not offered on a pro rata basis to part-time employees[31] and are less likely to be offered to low-skilled workers in business services compared to the same jobs in manufacturing.[32]

Many of the benefits of using contingent employees are immediate and measurable. The disadvantages or costs are more likely to accrue over time and occur in ways that make them less readily captured by traditional accounting systems. Consequently, there is a tendency for organizations, particularly those under immediate financial pressure, to overuse these arrangements and thereby lose the opportunity to achieve some market advantage through their workforce.

The biggest disadvantage of contingent employment arrangements is the difficulty in obtaining loyalty, dedication, or willingness to expend extra effort on behalf of the organization. One Hewlett-Packard executive commented, 'They don't tend to be dedicated to the corporate ideal. . . . They're here to make money, not to fulfill the corporate vision.'[33]

The costs of reduced productivity, diminished motivation, and less commitment to the organization can be "large and sometimes subtle . . .".[34]

The use of contingent workers also affects the likelihood of the organization's obtaining strategic advantage through training and the development of a skilled workforce. Contingent work arrangements preclude the organization's capturing the benefits of any firm-specific knowledge or capabilities that the employees may develop. More important, the work arrangements themselves discourage training and development – hiring temporaries or outside contractors is, after all, sometimes done to enable the organization to change its skill set or avoid taking the time and incurring the cost to develop its own people.

A contingent, poorly trained workforce can be a dangerous one in the wrong setting. In the chemical industry, maintenance and repair tasks are often contracted out, with contract employees performing about one-third of that work during regular operations and half of the work in upgrading or repairing equipment.[35] These less educated, experienced, and trained workers are associated with the growing number of serious accidents in petrochemicals. From January to June 1991: "of the 11 workplace accidents known to involve explosions, fires, and spills in the United States petrochemical industry . . . nine were reported to involve contract employees."[36] In nursing, the use of temporary agencies to solve staffing shortages had two adverse effects. With a short-term palliative, the organizations seldom addressed their fundamental problems. Quality control was a major problem. Temp nurses were used in positions for which they were not qualified; they worked excessive hours for several different clients; and the poor performers were simply reassigned to a different hospital until the performance deficiencies were again noticed.[37]

The appropriate use of a contingent workforce involves first understanding the real sources of success in one's business and then ensuring that key activities are performed by people with enough connection to the organization that they are likely to do a good job and to receive the necessary training and skill development, either through on-the-job learning or through more formal programs. Wal-Mart sees an important component of its success coming from customer service and from the ability to tap into localized knowledge of customer wants and needs. Seeking advantage in part through its workforce, the company staffs itself to have the opportunity to obtain a more dedicated and skilled set of employees.

The allure of the immediate cost and benefit savings may be seductive but the costs of contingent employees can be high. The critical decision involves deter-mining whether people will be a source of distinct competitive advantage and, if so, in what activities they are the most critical. Contingent employees should be used with great caution in such activities.

Considering the issues of training and contracting out provides two concrete illustrations of how thinking about the extent to which sustainable competitive advantage originates from the workforce helps us make sound decisions about policies and practices related to managing the workforce. It is by making the right choices about managing people that firms such as Nordstrom, New United Motor, Wal-Mart, Lincoln Electric, and Southwest Airlines achieved their well-known success.

References

1 Michael E. Porter, *Competitive Advantage* (New York: Free Press, 1985), 1.
2 Ibid., 4.
3 'Investment winners and losers', *Money*, October 1992, 133.
4 George Stalk, Jr. and Thomas M. Hout, *Competing Against Time* (New York: Free Press, 1990), 141.
5 Billie Jo Zirger and Modesto A. Maidique, 'A model of new product development: an empirical test', *Management Science* 36, 1990, 867.
6 Edwin Mansfield, Mark Schwartz, and Samuel Wagner, 'Imitation costs and patents: an empirical study', *The Economic Journal* 91, 1981, 907–918.
7 Ibid., 909.
8 Ibid., 913.
9 Maryann Keller, *Rude Awakening: The Rise, Fall, and Struggle for Recovery of General Motors* (New York: William Morrow, 1989), 213.
10 Richard Pascale, *Managing on the Edge* (New York: Simon & Schuster, 1990), 73.
11 Paul Adler, 'New technologies, new skills', *California Management Review* 29, 1986, 10.
12 'Management discovers the human side of automation', *Business Week*, 29 September, 1986, 70.
13 Ibid.
14 M. Hossein Safizadeh, 'The case of workgroups in manufacturing operations', *California Management Review* 33, 1991, 61.
15 George J. Stigler, 'The theory of economic regulation', *Bell Journal of Economics and Management Science*, 1971, 3–21.
16 Robert Buzzell and Bradley T. Gale, *The PIMS Principles: Linking Strategy to Performance* (New York: Free Press, 1987).
17 Michael J. Piore and Charles E. Sabel, *The Second Industrial Divide* (New York: Basic Books, 1984).
18 John T. Dunlop and David Weil, Human Resource Innovations in the Apparel Industry: An Industrial Relations System Perspective. Unpublished ms. (Cambridge, MA: Harvard University, 1992).
19 Bridget O'Brian, 'Southwest Airlines is a rare air carrier: it still makes money', *The Wall Street Journal*, 26 October 1992, A1.
20 James Campbell Quick, 'Crafting and organizational culture: Herb's hand at Southwest Airlines', *Organizational Dynamics* 21, Autumn 1992, 47.
21 O'Brian, 'Southwest Airlines', A7.
22 Quick, 'Crafting an organizational culture', 50.

23 O'Brian, 'Southwest Airlines', A1.

24 Ibid., A7.

25 Anthony P. Carnevale and Harold Goldstein, 'Schooling and training for work in America: an overview', in Louis A. Ferman, Michele Hoyman, Joel Cutcher-Gershenfeld, and Ernest J. Savoie (eds) *New Developments in Worker Training: A Legacy for the 1990s* (Madison, WI: Industrial Relations Research Association, 1990), 40.

26 'Where the jobs are is where the skills aren't', *Business Week*, 19 September 1988, 106.

27 Jeffrey Pfeffer and James N. Baron, 'Taking the workers back out: recent trends in the structuring of employment', in Barry M. Staw and L.L. Cummings (eds) *Research in Organizational Behavior*, vol. 10 (Greenwich, CT: JAI Press, 1988), 257–303.

28 Katherine G. Abraham, 'Restructuring the employment relationship: the growth of market-mediated work arrangements', in Katherine G. Abraham and Robert B. McKersie (eds) *New Developments in the Labor Market* (Cambridge, MA: MIT Press, 1990), 106.

29 Ibid., 101–102.

30 James B. Rebitzer, Short-Term Employment Relations and Labor Market Outcomes: Contract Workers in the U.S. Petrochemical Industry. Unpublished ms. (Cambridge, MA: MIT, Sloan School of Management, 1991).

31 S. D. Nollen and V. H. Martin, *Alternative Work Schedules, Part 2: Permanent Part-Time Employment* (New York: Amacom, 1978).

32 Abraham, 'Restructuring the employment relationship', 102.

33 L. Reibstein, 'More companies use free-lancers to avoid cost, trauma of layoffs', *The Wall Street Journal*, 18 April 1986, 21.

34 Michael J. McCarthy, 'Managers face dilemma with temps', *The Wall Street Journal*, 5 April 1988, 31.

35 Keith Schneider, 'Study finds link between chemical plant accidents and contract workers', *New York Times*, 30 July 1991, A10.

36 Rebitzer, 'Short-term employment relations and labor market outcomes', 3.

37 Walt Bogdanich, 'Danger in white: the shadowy world of temp nurses', *The Wall Street Journal*, 1 November 1991, B1, B6.

6 Building a Visionary Company

James C. Collins and Jerry I. Porras

> Above all, there was the ability to build and build and build – never stopping, never looking back, never finishing – the institution. . . . In the last analysis, Walt Disney's greatest creation was Walt Disney [the company].
>
> Richard Schickel, *The Disney Version*[1]

The builders of visionary companies tend to be clock builders, not time tellers. They concentrate primarily on building an organization – building a ticking clock – rather than on hitting a market just right with a visionary product idea. They take an architectural approach and concentrate on building the organizational traits of visionary companies. The primary output of their efforts is not the tangible implementation of a great idea, the expression of a charismatic personality, the gratification of their ego or the accumulation of personal wealth. Their greatest creation is *the company itself* and what it stands for.[2]

Our research punched holes in two widely held and deeply cherished myths that have dominated popular thinking and business school education for years: the myth of the great idea and the myth of the great and charismatic leader. We found that creating and building a visionary company absolutely does not require *either* a great idea *or* a great and charismatic leader. In fact, we found evidence that great ideas brought forth by charismatic leaders might be *negatively correlated* with building a visionary company. These surprising findings forced us to look at corporate success from an entirely new angle. They also have implications that are profoundly liberating for corporate managers and entrepreneurs alike.

The myth of the 'great idea'

On 23 August 1937 two recently graduated engineers in their early twenties with no substantial business experience met to discuss the founding of a new company. However, they had no clear idea of what the company would make. They only knew that they wanted to start a company with each other in the broadly defined field of electronic engineering. They brainstormed a wide range of initial product and market possibilities, but they had no compelling 'great idea' that served as the founding inspiration for the fledgling company.

Bill Hewlett and Dave Packard decided to first start a company and *then* figure out what they would make. They just started moving forward, trying anything that might get them out of the garage and pay the light bills. According to Bill Hewlett:

> When I talk to business schools occasionally, the professor of management is devastated when I say that we didn't have any plans when we started – we were just opportunistic. We did anything that would bring in a nickel. We had a bowling foul-line indicator, a clock drive for a telescope, a thing to make a urinal flush automatically, and a shock machine to make people lose weight. Here we were, with about $500 in capital, trying whatever someone thought we might be able to do.[3]

The bowling foul-line indicator didn't become a market revolution. The automatic urinal flushers and fat-reduction shock machines didn't go anywhere, either. In fact, the company stumbled along for nearly a year before it got its first big sale – eight audio oscilloscopes to Walt Disney for work on the movie *Fantasia*. Even then, Hewlett-Packard continued its unfocused ways, sputtering and tinkering with a variety of products, until it got a boost from war contracts in the early 1940s.

Texas Instruments (TI), in contrast, traces its roots to a highly successful initial concept. TI began life in 1930 as Geophysical Service, Inc., 'the first independent company to make reflection seismograph surveys of potential oil fields, and its Texas labs developed and produced instruments for such work.'[4] TI's founders formed their company to exploit a *specific* technological and market opportunity.[5] TI started with a 'great idea'. HP did not.

Neither did Sony. When Masaru Ibuka founded his company in August 1945, he had no specific product idea. In fact, Ibuka and his seven initial employees had a brainstorming session – *after* starting the company – to decide what products to make. According to Akio Morita, who joined the company shortly after its founding: 'The small group sat in conference and for weeks they tried to figure out what kind of business this new company could enter in order to make money to operate.'[6] They considered a wide range of possibilities, from sweetened bean-paste soup to miniature golf equipment and slide rules.[7] Not only that, Sony's first product attempt (a simple rice cooker) failed to work properly and its first significant product (a tape recorder) failed in the marketplace. The company kept itself alive in the early days by stitching wires on cloth to make crude, but sellable, heating pads.[8] In comparison, Kenwood's founder, unlike Ibuka at Sony, appeared to have a specific category of product in mind. He christened his company with the name 'Kasuga Wireless Electric Firm' in 1946 and 'since its foundation', according to the *Japan Electronics Almanac*, 'Kenwood has always been a specialist pioneer in audio technology.'[9]

Like fellow legendaries Ibuka and Hewlett, Sam Walton also started without a great idea. He went into business with nothing other than the desire to work for himself and a little bit of knowledge (and a lot of passion) about retailing. Walton started in 1945 with a single Ben Franklin franchise five-and-dime store in the small town of Newport, Arkansas. 'I had no vision of the scope of what I would start,' Walton commented, 'but I always had confidence that as long as we did our work well and were good to our customers, there would be no limit to us.'[10] He wrote in *Made in America*:

Somehow over the years folks have gotten the impression that Wal-Mart was something that I dreamed up out of the blue as a middle-aged man, and that it was just this great idea that turned into an overnight success. But [our first Wal-Mart store] was totally an outgrowth of everything we'd been doing since [1945] – another case of me being unable to leave well enough alone, another experiment. And like most overnight successes, it was about twenty years in the making.[11]

According to Walton biographer Vance Trimble: 'Other retailers were out there [in 1962] trying to do just what he was doing. Only he did it better than nearly anyone.'[12]

HP, Sony, and Wal-Mart put a large dent in the widely held mythology of corporate origins – a mythology that paints a picture of a far-seeing entrepreneur founding his or her company to capitalize on a visionary product idea or visionary market insight. This mythology holds that those who launch highly successful companies usually begin first and foremost with a brilliant idea (technology, product, market potential) and then ride the growth curve of an attractive product life cycle.

Indeed, few of the visionary companies in our study can trace their roots to a great idea or a fabulous initial product. Nordstrom started as a small, single-outlet shoestore in downtown Seattle (when John Nordstrom, just returned from the Alaska Gold Rush, didn't know what else to do with himself).[13] Merck started merely as an importer of chemicals from Germany.[14] Procter & Gamble started as a simple soap and candle maker – one of 18 such companies in Cincinnati in 1837.[15] Motorola began as a struggling battery eliminator repair business for Sears radios.[16]

Furthermore, some of our visionary companies began life like Sony – with outright failures. 3M started as a failed corundum mine, leaving 3M investors holding stock that fell to the barroom exchange value of 'two shares for one shot of cheap whiskey'.[17] Not knowing what else to do, the company began making sandpaper. 3M had such a poor start in life that its second president did not draw a salary for the first 11 years of his tenure. In contrast, Norton Corporation, 3M's comparison in the study, began life with innovative products in a rapidly growing market, paid steady annual dividends in all but one of its first 15 years of operations, and multiplied its capital fifteenfold during the same time.[18]

Bill Boeing's first airplane failed ('a handmade, clumsy seaplane copied from a Martin seaplane' which flunked its Navy trials) and his company faced such difficulty during its first few years of operations that it entered the furniture business to keep itself aloft![19] Douglas Aircraft, in contrast, had superb initial success with its first airplane. Designed to be the first plane in history to make a coast-to-coast non-stop trip and to lift more load than its own weight, Douglas turned the design into a torpedo bomber which he sold in quantity to the Navy.[20] Unlike Boeing, Douglas never needed to enter the furniture business to keep the company alive.[21]

Waiting for 'the great idea' might be a bad idea

In all, *only three* of the visionary companies began life with the benefit of a specific, innovative and highly successful initial product or service – a 'great idea': Johnson

& Johnson, General Electric, and Ford. And even in the GE and Ford cases, we found some slight dents in the great idea theory. At GE, Edison's great idea turned out to be inferior to Westinghouse's great idea. Edison pursued direct current (DC) system, whereas Westinghouse promoted the vastly superior alternating current (AC) system, which eventually prevailed in the US market.[22] In Ford's case, contrary to popular mythology, Henry Ford didn't come up with the idea of the Model T and *then* decide to start a company around that idea. Just the opposite. Ford was able to take full advantage of the Model T concept because he already had a *company* in place as a launching pad. He founded the Ford Motor Company in 1903 to capitalize on his automotive engineering talent – his third company in as many years – and introduced five models (Models A, B, C, F, and K) before he launched the famous Model T in October 1908.[23] In fact, Ford was one of 502 firms founded in the United States between 1900 and 1908 to make automobiles – hardly a novel concept at the time. In contrast to the visionary companies, we traced the founding roots of 11 comparison companies much closer to the great idea model: Ames, Burroughs, Colgate, Kenwood, McDonnell Douglas, Norton, Pfizer, R. J. Reynolds, Texas Instruments, Westinghouse and Zenith.

We found that the visionary companies were less likely to have early entrepreneurial success than the comparison companies. *We found a negative correlation between early entrepreneurial success and becoming a highly visionary company.* The long race goes to the tortoise, not the hare.

If you are a prospective entrepreneur with the desire to start and build a visionary company but have not yet taken the plunge because you don't have a 'great idea', we encourage you to lift from your shoulders the burden of the great idea myth. Indeed, the evidence suggests that it might be better to *not* obsess on finding a great idea before launching a company. Why? Because the great idea approach shifts your attention away from seeing the company as your ultimate creation.

The company itself is the ultimate creation

In courses on strategic management and entrepreneurship, business schools teach the importance of starting first and foremost with a good idea and well-developed product/market strategy and *then* jumping through the 'window of opportunity' before it closes. But the people who built the visionary companies often didn't behave or think that way. In case after case, their actions flew in the face of the theories being taught at the business schools. We had to *shift from seeing the company as a vehicle for the products to seeing the products as a vehicle for the company.*

Compare GE and Westinghouse in their early days. George Westinghouse was a brilliant product visionary and prolific inventor who founded 59 other companies besides Westinghouse.[24] Additionally, he had the insight that the world should favour the superior AC electrical system over Edison's DC system, which it eventually did.[25] But compare George Westinghouse to Charles Coffin, GE's first president. Coffin invented not a single product. But he sponsored an innovation of great significance: the establishment of the General Electric Research Lab, billed as

'America's first industrial research laboratory'.[26] George Westinghouse told the time; Charles Coffin built a clock. Westinghouse's greatest creation was the AC power system; Coffin's greatest creation was the General Electric Company.

Luck favours the persistent. The builders of visionary companies were highly persistent, living to the motto: Never, never, *never* give up. But what to persist *with*? Their answer: The company. *Be prepared to kill, revise or evolve an idea* (GE moved away from its original DC system and embraced the AC system), *but never give up on the company*. If you equate the success of your company with success of a specific idea – as many businesspeople do – then you're more likely to give up on the company if that idea fails; and if that idea happens to succeed, you're more likely to have an emotional love affair with that idea and stick with it too long, when the company should be moving vigorously on to other things. But if you see the ultimate creation as the company, not the execution of a specific idea or capitalizing on a timely market opportunity, then you can persist beyond any specific idea – good or bad – and move toward becoming an enduring great institution.

Dave Packard echoed the clock-building orientation in a 1964 speech: 'The problem is, how do you develop an environment in which individuals can be creative? I believe that you have to put a good deal of thought to your organizational structure in order to provide this environment.'[27] In 1973, an interviewer asked Packard what specific product decisions he considered the most important in the company's growth. Packard's response didn't include one single product decision. He answered entirely in terms of organizational decisions: developing an engineering team, a pay-as-you-go policy to impose fiscal discipline, a profit-sharing programme, personnel and management policies, the 'HP Way' philosophy of management and so on. In a fitting twist, the interviewer titled the article, 'Hewlett-Packard chairman built company by design, calculator by chance'.[28]

Similarly, Masaru Ibuka's greatest 'product' was not the Walkman or the Trinitron; it was Sony the company and what it stands for. Walt Disney's greatest creation was not *Fantasia* or *Snow White* or even Disneyland; it was the Walt Disney Company. William Procter and James Gamble's most significant contribution was not hog fat soap, lamp oils or candles, for these would eventually become obsolete; their primary contribution was something that can never become obsolete: a highly adaptable organization with a 'spiritual inheritance'[29] of deeply ingrained core values transferred to generation after generation of P&G people.

We ask you to consider this crucial shift in thinking – the shift to seeing the company itself as the ultimate creation. If you're involved in building and managing a company, this shift has significant implications for how you spend your time. It means spending less of your time thinking about specific product lines and market strategies and spending more of your time thinking about organization design.

We don't mean to imply that the visionary companies never had superb products or good ideas. They certainly did. And most of them view their products and services as making useful and important contributions to customer' lives. Indeed, these companies don't exist just to 'be a company': they exist to do something useful. But we suggest *that the continual stream of great products and services from highly visionary companies stems from them being outstanding organizations, not the other way around.*

The myth of the great and charismatic leader

When we ask executives and business students to speculate about the distinguishing variables – the root causes – in the success of the visionary companies, many mention 'great leadership'. They point to George Merck, Sam Walton, William Procter, James Gamble, William E. Boeing, R. W. Johnson, Paul Galvin, Bill Hewlett, Dave Packard, Charles Coffin, Walt Disney, J. Willard Marriott, Thomas J. Watson and John Nordstrom. They argue that these chief executives displayed high levels of persistence, overcame significant obstacles, attracted dedicated people to the organization, influenced groups of people toward the achievement of goals and played key roles in guiding their companies through crucial episodes in their history.

But – and this is the crucial point – so did their counterparts at the comparison companies! Charles Pfizer, the Gilman brothers (Ames), William Colgate, Donald Douglas, William Bristol, John Myers, Commander Eugene F. McDonald (Zenith), Pat Haggarty (TI), George Westinghouse, Harry Cohn, Howard Johnson, Frank Melville. A systematic analysis revealed that the comparison companies were just as likely to have solid 'leadership' during the formative years as the visionary companies.

In short, we found no evidence to support the hypothesis that great leadership is the distinguishing variable during the critical, formative stages of the visionary companies.

Charisma not required

A high-profile, charismatic style is absolutely not required to successfully shape a visionary company. Indeed, we found that some of the most significant chief executives in the history of the visionary companies did not have the personality traits of the archetypal high-profile, charismatic visionary leader.

Consider William McKnight. If you're like most people, you know little or nothing about William McKnight. As of 1993, he had not made it onto *Fortune* magazine's 'National Business Hall of Fame'.[30] Few articles have ever been written about him. His name doesn't appear in the *Hoover's Handbook* sketch of the company's history.[31] When we started our research, we're embarrassed to say, we didn't even recognize his name. Yet the company McKnight guided *for 52 years* (as general manager from 1914 to 1929, chief executive from 1929 to 1949 and chairman from 1949 to 1966) earned fame and admiration with businesspeople around the world; it carries the revered name Minnesota Mining and Manufacturing Company (or 3M for short). 3M is famous; McKnight is not. We suspect he would have wanted it exactly that way.

McKnight began work in 1907 as a simple assistant bookkeeper and rose to cost accountant and sales manager before becoming general manager. We could find no evidence that he had a highly charismatic leadership style. His biographer described him as 'a good listener', 'humble', 'modest', 'slightly stooped', 'unobtrusive and soft-spoken', 'quiet, thoughtful, and serious'.[32]

Masaru Ibuka of Sony had a reputation as being reserved, thoughtful and introspective.[33] Bill Hewlett reminded us of a friendly, no-nonsense, matter-of-fact, down-to-earth farmer from Iowa. Messrs Procter and Gamble were stiff, prim, proper and reserved – even deadpan.[34]

We've worked with quite a few managers who have felt frustrated by all the books and articles on charismatic business leadership and who ask the sensible question: 'What if high-profile charismatic leadership is just not my style?' Our response: Trying to develop such a style might be wasted energy. For one thing, psychological evidence indicates that personality traits get set relatively early in life through a combination of genetics and experience and there is little evidence to suggest that by the time you're in a managerial role you can do much to change your basic personality style.[35] For another – and even more important – our research indicates that you don't need such a style anyway.

We do not deny that the visionary companies have had superb individuals atop the organization at critical stages of their history. They often did. Furthermore, we think it unlikely that a company can remain highly visionary with a continuous string of mediocre people at the top. In fact we found that the visionary companies did a better job than the comparison companies at developing and promoting highly competent managerial talent from inside the company and they thereby attained greater *continuity* of excellence at the top through multiple generations. But, as with great products, perhaps *the continuity of superb individuals atop visionary companies stems from the companies being outstanding organizations, not the other way around.*

An architectural approach: Clock builders at work

As in the case of Charles Coffin versus George Westinghouse, in our study we noticed differences between the two groups of early shapers. The key difference, we believe, is one of orientation – the evidence suggests to us that the key people at formative stages of the visionary companies had a stronger organizational orientation than in the comparison companies, regardless of their personal leadership style. As the study progressed, in fact, we became increasingly uncomfortable with the term 'leader' and began to embrace the term 'architect' or 'clock builder'. The following comparisons further illustrate what we mean by an architectural, or clock-building, approach.

Citicorp versus Chase

James Stillman, Citicorp's president from 1891 to 1909 and chairman to 1918, concentrated on organizational development in pursuit of his goal to build a great national bank.[36] He transformed the bank from a narrow parochial firm into 'a fully modern corporation'.[37] He oversaw the bank as it opened new offices, instituted a decentralized multidivisional structure, constructed a powerful board of directors composed of leading CEOs and established management training and recruiting programmes (instituted three decades earlier than at Chase).[38] *Citibank 1812–1970* describes how Stillman sought to architect an institution that would thrive far beyond his own lifetime.

Wal-Mart versus Ames

The key difference between Sam Walton and the leaders at Ames is not that he was a more charismatic leader, but that he was much more of a clock builder – an architect. This was true even in Walton's own eyes, as he wrote in *Made in America*:

> What nobody realized, including a few of my own managers at the time, was that we were really trying from the beginning to become the very best operators – the most professional managers – that we could. There's no question that I have the personality of a promoter. But underneath that personality, I have always had the soul of an operator, somebody who wants to make things work well, then better, then the best they possibly can. I was never in anything for the short haul; I always wanted to build as fine a retailing organization as I could.[39]

For example, Walton valued change, experimentation and constant improvement. But he didn't just preach these values, he instituted concrete *organizational* mechanisms to stimulate change and improvement. Using a concept called 'A Store Within a Store', Walton gave department managers the authority and freedom to run each department as if it were their own business.[40] He created cash awards and public recognition for associates who contribute cost saving and/or service enhancements ideas that could be reproduced at other stores. He created 'VPI (Volume Producing Item) Contests' to encourage associates to attempt creative experiments.[41] He instituted merchandise meetings, to discuss experiments that should be selected for use throughout the entire chain and Saturday morning meetings, which often featured an individual employee who tried something novel that worked really well. Profit sharing and employee stock ownership produced a direct incentive for employees to come up with new ideas, so that the whole company might benefit. Tips and ideas generated by associates got published in the Wal-Mart internal magazine.[42] Wal-Mart even invested in a satellite communications system 'to spread all the little details around the company as soon as possible'.[43] In 1985, stock analyst A. G. Edwards described the ticking Wal-Mart clock:

> Personnel operate in an environment where change is encouraged. For example, if a store associate makes suggestions regarding [merchandising or cost savings ideas], these ideas are quickly disseminated. Multiply each suggestion by over 750 stores and by over 80,000 employees (who can potentially make suggestions) and this leads to substantial sales gains, cost reductions and improved productivity.[44]

Whereas Walton concentrated on creating an organization that would evolve and change on its own, Ames leaders dictated all changes from above and detailed in a book the precise steps a store manager should take, leaving no room for initiative.[45] Whereas Walton groomed a capable successor to take over the company after his death (David Glass), the Gilmans had no such person in place, thus leaving the company to outsiders who did not share their philosophy.[46] Whereas Walton passed along his clock-building orientation to his successor, post-founder CEOs at Ames recklessly pursued disastrous acquisitions in a blind, obsessive pursuit of raw growth for growth's sake, gulping down 388 Zayre stores in one bite. In describing Wal-Mart's key ingredient for future success, David Glass said 'Wal-Mart associates will find a way' and 'Our people are relentless'.[47] Ames CEO of the same era said: 'The real answer and the only issue is market share.'[48] Sam Walton died with his creation intact and the belief that it could prosper long beyond him, stronger than ever. Shortly before he died in 1992 he set audacious goals for the company out to the year 2000, displaying a deep confidence in what the company could achieve independent of his presence.[49]

Walt Disney versus Columbia Pictures

Quick, stop and think: Disney. Can you create a clear image or set of images that you associate with Disney? Now do the same thing for Columbia Pictures. If you're like most people, you can conjure up images of what Disney means, but you probably had trouble with Columbia Pictures.

In the case of Walt Disney, it is clear that Walt brought immense personal imagination and talent to building Disney. He personally originated many of Disney's best creations, including *Snow White* (the world's first-ever full-length animated film), the character of Mickey Mouse, the Mickey Mouse Club, Disneyland and EPCOT Centre. By any measure, he was a superb time teller. But, even so, in comparison to Harry Cohn – Disney's counterpart at Columbia Pictures – Walt was much more of a clock builder.

Cohn 'cultivated his image as a tyrant, keeping a riding whip near his desk and occasionally cracking it for emphasis, and Columbia had the greatest creative turnover of any major studio due largely to Cohn's methods'.[50] We could find no evidence of any concern for employees by Cohn. Neither could we find any evidence that he took steps to develop the long-term capabilities or distinct self-identity of Columbia Pictures as an institution.

The evidence suggests that Cohn cared first and foremost about becoming a movie mogul and wielding immense personal power in Hollywood (he became the first person in Hollywood to assume the titles of president *and* producer) and cared little or not at all about the qualities and identity of the Columbia Pictures Company that might endure beyond his lifetime.[51] Cohn's personal purpose propelled Columbia Pictures forward for years, but such personal and egocentric ideology could not possibly guide and inspire a company after the founder's death. Upon Cohn's death, the company fell into listless disarray, had to be rescued in 1973 and was eventually sold to Coca-Cola.

Throughout his life, Walt Disney paid greater attention to developing his company and its capabilities than did Cohn at Columbia. In the late 1920s, he paid his creative staff more than he paid himself.[52] In the early 1930s, he established art classes for all animators, installed a small zoo on location to provide live creatures to help improve their ability to draw animals, invented new animation team processes (such as storyboards) and continually invested in the most advanced animation technologies.[53] In the late 1930s, he installed the first generous bonus system in the cartoon industry to attract and reward good talent.[54] In the 1950s, he instituted employee 'You Create Happiness' training programmes and, in the 1960s, he established Disney University to orient, train and indoctrinate Disney employees.[55] Harry Cohn took none of these steps.

Granted the Disney film studio languished for nearly 15 years after his death as Disneyites ran around asking themselves, 'What would Walt do?'[56] But the fact remains that Walt, unlike Cohn, created an institution much bigger than himself, an institution that could still deliver the 'Disney Magic' to kids at Disneyland decades after his death.

The message for CEOs, managers and entrepreneurs

One of the most important steps you can take in building a visionary company is not an action, but a shift in perspective. We're doing nothing less than asking you to make a shift in thinking as fundamental as those that preceded the Newtonian revolution, the Darwinian revolution and the founding of the United States.

If you're involved in building and managing a company, we're asking you to think less in terms of being a brilliant product visionary or seeking the personality characteristics of charismatic leadership, and to think more in terms of being an *organizational* visionary and building the characteristics of a visionary company.

Indeed, we're asking you to consider a shift in thinking analogous to the shift required to found the United States in the 1700s. Prior to the dramatic revolutions in political thought of the 17th and 18th centuries, the prosperity of a European kingdom or country depended in large part on the quality of the king (or, in the case of England, perhaps the queen). If you had a good king, then you had a good kingdom. If the king was a great and wise leader, then the kingdom might prosper as a result.

Most of what's required to build a visionary company *can be learned*. You don't have to sit around waiting until you're lucky enough to have a great idea. You don't have to accept the false view that until your company has a charismatic visionary leader it cannot become a visionary company. There is no mysterious quality or elusive magic. Indeed, once you learn the essentials, you – and all those around you – can just get down to the hard work of making your company a visionary company.

References

1 Richard Schickel, *The Disney Version* (New York: Simon & Schuster, 1968), pp. 44, 363.
2 The original inspiration for this analogy came from a lecture series on intellectual history and the Newtonian Revolution entitled 'The origin of the modern mind', taught by Alan

Charles Kors, Professor of History, University of Pennsylvania, and captured on audiotape as part of the Superstar Teacher Series from the Teaching Company, Washington, DC.

3 Hewlett-Packard Company Archives, 'An interview with Bill Hewlett', 1987.

4 'Research packed with PhDs', *Business Week*, 22 December 1956, p. 58.

5 John McDonald, 'The men who made TI', *Fortune* (November 1961), p. 118.

6 Akio Morita, *Made in Japan* (New York: Dutton, 1986), pp. 44–57.

7 Nick Lyons, *The Sony Vision* (New York: Crown, 1976), pp. 4–5.

8 Morita, op. cit., pp. 44–57.

9 *Japan Electronics Almanac*, 1988, p. 282.

10 Vance Trimble, *Sam Walton* (New York: Dutton, 1990), p. 121.

11 Sam Walton with John Huey, *Sam Walton: Made in America* (New York: Doubleday, 1992), p. 35.

12 Trimble, op. cit., pp. 102–104.

13 John W. Nordstrom, *The Immigrant in 1887* (Seattle, WA: Dogwood Press, 1950), pp. 44–50; 'Nordstrom History', company publication, 26 November 1990.

14 *Values and Visions: A Merck Century* (Rahway, NJ: Merck, 1993), pp. 13–15.

15 'Procter & Gamble Chronology', company publication; Oscar Schisgall, *Eyes on Tomorrow: The Evolution of Procter & Gamble* (New York: Doubleday, 1981), pp. 1–14; Alfred Lief, *It Floats: The Story of Procter & Gamble* (New York: Rinehart, 1958), pp. 14–32.

16 Harry Mark Petrakis, *The Founder's Touch* (New York: McGraw-Hill, 1965), pp. 62–63.

17 *Our Story So Far* (St. Paul, MN: 3M Company, 1977), p.51.

18 Charles W. Cheape, *Norton Company: A New England Enterprise* (Cambridge, MA: Harvard University Press, 1985), p. 12.

19 Robert J. Serling, *Legend and Legacy: The Story of Boeing and Its People* (New York: St Martin's Press, 1992), pp. 2–6.

20 'Take-off for the business jet', *Business Week*, 28 September 1963.

21 Rene J. Francillon, *McDonnell Douglas Aircraft Since 1920* (Annapolis, MD: Naval Institute Press, 1988), pp. 1–12.

22 Grover and Lagai, *Development of American Industries*, 4th edition, 1959, p. 491.

23 Robert Lacey, *Ford: The Men and the Machine* (New York: Ballantine Books, 1986), pp. 47–110.

24 *Centennial Review*, Internal Westinghouse Document, 1986.

25 Ibid.

26 Leonard S. Reich, *The Making of American Industrial Research: Science and Business at GE and Bell, 1876–1926* (Cambridge: Cambridge University Press, 1985), pp. 69–71. (*Author's note*: We cannot verify that GE's lab was definitely America's first, but we do know that it preceded Bell Labs, one of the other early labs, by a full 25 years.)

27 Dave Packard, 'Industry's new challenge: the management of creativity', Western Electronic Manufacturers' Association, San Diego, 23 September 1964, courtesy Hewlett-Packard Company Archives.

28 'Hewlett-Packard chairman built company by design, calculator by chance', *The AMBA Executive* (September 1977), pp. 6–7.

29 Schisgall, op. cit., p. xii.

30 'National business hall of fame roster of past laureates', *Fortune*, 5 April 1993, p. 116.

31 *Hoover's Handbook of Corporations, 1991*, p. 381.

32 Mildred Houghton Comfort, *William L. McKnight, Industrialist* (Minneapolis: T.S. Denison, 1962), pp. 35, 45, 182, 194, 201.

33 Morita, op. cit., p. 147.

34 Schisgall, op. cit., pp. 1–15.

35 Camille B. Wortman and Elizabeth F. Loftus, *Psychology* (New York: McGraw-Hill, 1992), pp. 385–418.

36 Harold van B. Cleveland and Thomas F. Huertas, *Citibank 1812–1970* (Cambridge, MA: Harvard University Press, 1985), p. 32.

37 Ibid., p. 301.

38 Ibid., pp. 41, 301; and John Donald Wilson, *The Chase* (Boston, MA: Harvard Business School Press, 1986), p. 25.

39 Walton with Huey, op. cit., pp. 78–79.

40 'America's most successful merchant', *Fortune*, 23 September 1991.

41 Much of the detail in this section comes from Walton with Huey, op. cit., pp. 225–232.

42 Trimble, op. cit., p. 274.

43 Walton with Huey, op. cit., p.225.

44 Trimble, op. cit., p. 121.

45 'Industry overview', *Discount Merchandiser* (June 1977).

46 'Gremlins are eating up the profits at Ames', *Business Week*, 19 October 1987.

47 'David Glass won't crack under fire', *Fortune*, 8 February 1993, p. 80.

48 'Pistner discusses Ames strategy', *Discount Merchandiser* (July 1990).

49 Goals for the year 2000, from a letter we received from a Wal-Mart director in 1991.

50 *International Directory of Company Histories* (Chicago, IL: St James Press, 1988), vol. 2, p. 135.

51 Clive Hirschhorn, *The Columbia Story* (New York, NY; Crown, 1989).

52 *The Disney Studio Story* (Hollywood, CA: Walt Disney, 1987), p. 18.

53 Ibid.; and Schickel, op. cit., p. 180.

54 *The Disney Studio Story* (Hollywood, CA: Walt Disney, 1987), p. 42.

55 *Personnel* (December 1989), p. 53.

56 John Taylor, *Storming the Magic Kingdom* (New York: Ballantine Books, 1987), p. 14.

7 Managing Professional Intellect: Making the Most of the Best

James B. Quinn, Philip Anderson and Sydney Finkelstein

In the post-industrial era, the success of a corporation lies more in its intellectual and systems capabilities than in its physical assets. The capacity to manage human intellect – and to convert it into useful products and services – is fast becoming the critical executive skill of the age. As a result, there has been a flurry of interest in intellectual capital, creativity, innovation and the learning organization, but surprisingly little attention has been given to managing professional intellect. This oversight is especially surprising because professional intellect creates most of the value in the new economy. Its benefits are immediately visible in the large service industries, such as software, healthcare, financial services, communications, and consulting. But in manufacturing industries as well, professionals generate the preponderance of value – through activities like research and development, process design, product design, logistics, marketing, or systems management. Despite the growing importance of professional intellect few managers have systematic answers to even these basic questions: What is professional intellect? How can we develop it? How can we leverage it?

What is professional intellect?

The true professional commands a body of knowledge – a discipline that must be updated constantly. The professional intellect of an organization operates on four levels, presented here in order of increasing importance:

Cognitive knowledge (or know-what) is the basic mastery of a discipline that professionals achieve through extensive training and certification. This knowledge is essential, but usually far from sufficient, for commercial success.

Advanced skills (know-how) translate "book learning" into effective execution. The ability to apply the rules of a discipline to complex real-world problems is the most widespread value-creating professional skill level.

Systems understanding (know-why) is deep knowledge of the web of cause and effect relationships underlying a discipline. It permits professionals to move beyond the execution of tasks to solve larger and more complex problems and to create extraordinary value. Professionals with know-why can anticipate subtle interactions and unintended consequences. The ultimate expression of systems understanding is highly trained intuition – for example, the insight of a seasoned research director who knows instinctively which projects to fund and exactly when to do so.

Self-motivated creativity (care-why) consists of will, motivation, and adaptability for success. Highly motivated and creative groups often outperform groups with greater physical or financial resources. Without self-motivated creativity, intellectual leaders can lose their knowledge advantage through complacency. They may fail to adapt aggressively to changing external conditions and particularly to innovations that obsolesce their earlier skills – just as the techniques of molecular design are superseding chemical screening in pharmaceuticals today. That is why the highest level of intellect is now so vital. Organizations that nurture care-why in their people can simultaneously thrive in the face of today's rapid changes and renew their cognitive knowledge, advanced skills, and systems understanding in order to compete in the next wave of advances.

Intellect clearly resides in the brains of professionals. The first three levels can also exist in the organization's systems, databases, or operating technologies, whereas the fourth is often found in its culture. The value of intellect increases markedly as one moves up the intellectual scale from cognitive knowledge to self-motivated creativity. Yet most enterprises focus virtually all their training attention on developing basic (rather than advanced) skills and little or none on systems or creative skills.

Most of a typical professional's activity is directed at perfection, not creativity. Customers primarily want professional knowledge delivered reliably and with the most advanced skill available. Although there is an occasional call for creativity, most of the work done by accounting units, hospitals, software companies, or financial service providers requires the repeated use of highly developed skills on relatively similar, though complex, problems. People rarely want surgeons, accountants, pilots, maintenance personnel, or nuclear plant operators to be very creative. Managers clearly must prepare their professionals for the few emergencies or other special circumstances that require creativity, but they should focus the bulk of their attention on delivering consistent, high-quality intellectual output.

Because professionals have specialized knowledge and have been trained as an elite, they often tend to regard their judgement in other realms as sacrosanct as well. Professionals generally hesitate to subordinate themselves to others or to support organizational goals not completely congruous with their special viewpoint. That is why most professional firms operate as partnerships and not as hierarchies, and why it is difficult for them to adopt a unified strategy.

Members of every profession tend to look to their peers to determine codes of behavior and acceptable standards of performance. They often refuse to accept evaluations by those outside their discipline. Many doctors, for example, resist the attempts of HMOs and insurance companies to tell them how to practice medicine.

Such a posture is the source of many professional organizations' problems. Professionals tend to surround themselves with people who have similar backgrounds and values. Unless deliberately fractured, these discipline-based cocoons quickly become inward-looking bureaucracies that are resistant to change and detached from customers. Consider the many software or basic research organizations that become isolated inside larger organizations, creating conflicts with other professional groups such as marketing or manufacturing departments.

Developing professional intellect

At the heart of the most effective professional organizations we have observed are a handful of best practices for managing intellect that resemble successful coaching more than anything else.

Recruit the best

The leverage of intellect is so great that a few topflight professionals can create a successful organization or make a lesser one flourish. Marvin Bower essentially created McKinsey & Company; Robert Noyce and Gordon E. Moore spawned Intel; William H. Gates and Paul Allen built Microsoft; Herbert W. Boyer and Robert A. Swanson made Genentech; and Albert Einstein put Princeton's Institute for Advanced Study on the map. But even such organizations must find and attract extraordinary talent.

It is no accident that the leading management consultants devote enormous resources to recruiting and that they heavily screen the top graduates of the leading business schools. Microsoft interviews hundreds of highly recommended people for each key software designer it hires, and its gruelling selection process tests not only cognitive knowledge but also the capacity to think about new problems under high pressure. The Four Seasons Hotel often interviews 50 candidates to make one hire. Venture capital firms, recognizing talent and commitment as the most critical elements for their success, spend as much time selecting and pursuing top people as they do making quantitative analyses of projects.

Because the most qualified professionals want to work with the best in their field, leading organizations can attract better talent than their lesser competitors. The best commercial programmers, for example, seek out and stay with Microsoft largely because they believe Microsoft will determine where the industry will move in the future and because they can share the excitement and rewards of being at that frontier. But second-tier organizations are not destined always to lag behind. Managers who understand the importance of the right kind of talent can pull a jujitsu reversal on industry leaders by acquiring such talent. When CEO Marshall N. Carter led State Street Bank's entry into the rapidly emerging custodials business, he hired world-class data-processing managers to seed his new organization. Today State Street handles $1.7 trillion in custodial accounts, and virtually all its senior managers have data processing rather than traditional banking backgrounds.

Force intensive early development

Professional know-how is developed most rapidly through repeated exposure to the complexity of real problems. Thus for most professionals, the learning curve depends heavily on interactions with customers. Accordingly, the best companies systematically put new professionals in contact with customers, where they work under the watchful eye of an experienced coach. Microsoft, for example, assigns new software developers to small teams of three to seven people. Under the guidance of mentors, the developers participate in the design of complex new software systems at the frontier of users' needs.

The legendary 80-hour weeks and all-nighters that give investment bankers and software developers their bragging rights serve a more serious developmental purpose: they enable the best talent to move up a learning curve that is steeper than anyone else's. On-the-job training, mentoring, and peer pressure can force professionals to the top of their knowledge ziggurat. Although burnout can be a problem if people are pushed too far, many studies show that intensity and repetition are critical to developing advanced skills in fields as diverse as the law and piloting aircraft.

People who go through these intensive experiences become noticeably more capable and valuable – compared with their counterparts in less intensively managed organizations – within six months to a year. If they are properly coached, they also develop a greater in-depth feel for systems interactions (know-why) and identify more with the company and its goals (care-why). The most successful organizations ensure such growth through constantly heightened (preferably customer-driven) complexity, thoroughly planned mentoring, substantial rewards for performance, and strong incentives to understand, systematize, and advance the discipline. The great intellectual organizations all seem to develop deeply ingrained cultures that emphasize these values. Most others do not.

Constantly increase professional challenges

Intellect grows most when professionals buy into a serious challenge. Leaders of the best organizations tend to be demanding, visionary and intolerant of half-hearted efforts. They often set almost impossible 'stretch goals' – as did Hewlett-Packard's William R. Hewlett (improve performance by 50%), Intel's Gordon Moore (double the number of components per chip each year), and Motorola's Robert W. Galvin (achieve 6-sigma quality). Some professionals may drop out in response to such demands. Others will substitute their own even higher standards. The best organizations constantly push their professionals beyond the comfort of their book knowledge, simulation models, and controlled laboratories. They relentlessly drive associates to deal with the more complex intellectual realms of live customers, real operating systems, and highly differentiated external environments and cultural differences. Mediocre organizations do not.

Evaluate and weed

Professionals like to be evaluated, to compete, to know they have excelled against their peers. But they want to be evaluated objectively and by people at the top of their field. Hence, heavy internal competition and frequent performance appraisal and feedback are common in outstanding organizations. As a result, there is a progressive winnowing of talent. For example, at Andersen Consulting, only 10% of the carefully selected professional recruits move on to partnerships – a process that takes 9 to 12 years. Microsoft tries to force out the lowest-performing 5% of its highly screened talent each year. Great organizations are unabashed meritocracies; great organizations that fail are often those that forget the importance of objective praise and selective weeding.

Leveraging professional intellect

Conventional wisdom has long held that there are few opportunities for leverage in professional activities. A pilot can handle only one aircraft at a time; a chef can cook only so many different dishes at once; a researcher can conduct only so many unique experiments; a doctor can diagnose only one patient's illness at a time. In such situations, adding professionals at the very least multiplies costs at the same rate as benefits. In the past, growth most often brought diseconomies of scale as the bureaucracies coordinating, monitoring, or supporting the professionals expanded faster than the professional base. Universities, hospitals, research firms, accounting groups, and consultancies all seemed to pay the price.

For years, there were only two ways in which many organizations could create leverage: by pushing their people through more intensive training work schedules than their competitors or by increasing the number of 'associates' supporting each professional. The latter practice even became the accepted meaning of the term *leverage* in the fields of law, accounting, and consulting.

But new technologies and management approaches are changing the traditional economics of managing professional intellect. Organizations as diverse as Merrill Lynch, Andersen Worldwide, and NovaCare have found effective ways to link new software tools, incentive systems, and organizational designs in order to leverage professional intellect to much higher levels. Although each organization has developed solutions tailored to the specific needs of its business, there are a handful of common underlying principles.

Boost professionals' problem-solving abilities by capturing knowledge in systems and software

The core intellectual competence of many financial organizations – such as Merrill Lynch and State Street Bank – lies in the human experts and the systems software that collect and analyze the data that are relevant to investment decisions. A few financial specialists working at headquarters leverage their own high-level analytical skills through close interactions with other specialists and "rocket scientist" modelers, and through access to massive amounts of data about transactions. Proprietary software models and databases leverage the intellect of those professionals, allowing them to analyze markets, securities, and economic trends in ways that otherwise would be beyond their reach. Software systems then distribute the resulting investment recommendations to brokers at retail outlets who create further value by customizing the center's advice in order to meet the needs of individual clients. If one thinks about this organization as a center connected to customers at multiple points of contact, or nodes, leverage equals the value of the knowledge multiplied by the number of nodes using it. Value creation is enhanced if experimentation at the center increases know-why and incentive structures stimulate care-why.

Merrill Lynch's retail brokerage business follows the basic structure outlined. Roughly 18,000 Merrill Lynch brokers operate out of more than 500 geographically dispersed offices to create custom investment solutions for clients. The typical retail broker is not a highly skilled financial professional with years of advanced training. Yet the firm's brokers serve millions of clients worldwide with sophisticated investment advice and detailed, up-to-date information on thousands of complex financial instruments. Information systems make this extraordinary leverage possible.

Electronic systems capture Merrill Lynch's aggregate experience curve, quickly enabling less trained people to achieve performance levels ordinarily associated with much more experienced personnel. The firm's computer network ensures that the retail brokers' cognitive knowledge is current and accurate. Merrill Lynch's information technologies allow the centre to capture and distribute to the brokerage offices information about transactions, trading rules, yields, securities features, availability, tax considerations and new offerings. Proprietary software, available on-line, serves as an instant training vehicle. It ensures that all brokers adhere to current regulations, make no arithmetic or clerical errors, and can provide customers with the latest market information. Capturing and distributing the firm's knowledge base through software allows Merrill Lynch to leverage the professional intellect at its core.

Information technology allows a large modern brokerage to be both efficient and flexible. At the center, it can achieve the full information power and economies of scale available only to a major enterprise. Yet local brokers can manage their own small units and accounts as independently as if they alone provided the service on a local basis. Their reward system is that of local entrepreneurs. The center functions primarily as an information source, a communications coordinator, or a reference desk for unusual inquiries. Field personnel connect with the center to obtain information to improve their performance, rather than to ask for instructions or specific guidance. At the same time, the center can electronically monitor local operations for quality and consistency. Most operating rules are programmed into the system and changed automatically by software. Electronic systems replace human command-and-control procedures. They also can eliminate most of the routine in jobs, free up employees for more personalized or skilled work, and allow tasks to be more decentralized, challenging, and rewarding.

Overcome professionals' reluctance to share information

Information sharing is critical because intellectual assets, unlike physical assets, increase in value with use. Properly stimulated, knowledge and intellect grow exponentially when shared. All learning and experience curves have this characteristic. A basic tenet of communication theory states that a network's potential benefits grow exponentially as the nodes it can successfully interconnect expand numerically. It is not difficult to see how this growth occurs. If two people exchange knowledge with each other, both gain information and experience linear growth. But if both then share their new knowledge with others – each of whom feeds back questions, amplifications, and modifications – the benefits become exponential. Companies that learn from outsiders – especially from customers, suppliers, and specialists such as advanced design or software firms – can reap even greater benefits. The strategic consequences of exploiting this exponential growth are profound. Once a company gains a knowledge-based competitive edge, it becomes ever easier for it to maintain its lead and ever harder for its competitors to catch up.

Overcoming professionals' natural reluctance to share their most precious asset, knowledge, presents some common and difficult challenges. Competition among professionals often inhibits sharing, and assigning credit for intellectual contributions is difficult. When professionals are asked to collaborate as equals in problem solving, slow response is common as specialists try to refine their particular solutions to perfection. Because professionals' knowledge is their power base, strong inducements to share are necessary.

Even then, the tendency of each profession to regard itself as an elite with special cultural values may get in the way of cross-disciplinary sharing. Many professionals have little respect for those outside their field, even when all parties are supposedly seeking the same goal. Often, in manufacturing companies, researchers disdain product designers, who disdain engineers. In healthcare, basic researchers disdain physicians (because "they don't understand causation"). Physicians disdain both researchers (who "don't understand practical variations among real patients") and nurses (who "don't understand the discipline"). Nurses disdain both doctors and researchers (who lack true "compassion"). And all three groups disdain administrators (who are "non-productive bureaucrats").

To facilitate sharing, Andersen Worldwide has developed an electronic system linking its 82,000 people operating in 360 offices in 76 countries. Known as ANet, the Tl and frame-relay network connects more than 85% of Andersen's professionals through data, voice and video interlinks. ANet allows Andersen specialists – by posting problems on electronic bulletin boards and following up with visual and data contacts – to self-organize instantly around a customer's problem anywhere in the world. ANet thus taps into otherwise dormant capabilities and expands the energies and solution sets available to customers. Problem-solving capacity is further enhanced through centrally collected and carefully indexed subject, customer-reference, and resource files accessible directly through Anet or from CD-ROMs distributed to all offices.

Initially, Andersen spent large sums on hardware, travel, and professional training to encourage people not only to follow up on network exchanges but also to meet personally to discuss important problems – with disappointing results. Major changes in incentives and culture were needed to make the system work. Most important, participation in ANet began to be considered in all promotion and compensation reviews. To stimulate a cultural shift toward wider use of ANet, senior partners deliberately posed questions on employees' E-mail files each morning "to be answered by 10." Until those cultural changes were in place, ANet was less than successful despite its technological elegance.

Organize around intellect

In the past, most companies aimed to enhance returns from investments in physical assets: property, plant, and equipment. Command-and-control structures made sense when management's primary task was to leverage such physical assets. For example, the productivity of a manufacturing facility is determined largely by senior managers' decisions about capital equipment, adherence to standardized practices, the breadth of the product line, and capacity utilization. With intellectual assets, on the other hand, individual professionals typically provide customized solutions to an endless stream of new problems.

Inverting organizations

Many successful enterprises we have studied have abandoned hierarchical structures, organizing themselves in patterns specifically tailored to the particular way their professional intellect creates value. Such reorganization often involves breaking away from traditional thinking about the role of the center as a directing force.

Consider NovaCare, the largest provider of rehabilitation care and one of the fastest-growing healthcare companies in the United States. Its critical professional intellect resides in its more than 5000 occupational, speech, and physical therapists. As professionals, they work alone to customize their expertise for individual patients at 2090 locations in 40 states. To be of greatest value, they must be highly trained and constantly updated on the best practices in their fields.

By organizing around the work of its therapists, NovaCare achieves considerable leverage. To focus their time on serving patients' needs, the organization frees the therapists from administrative and business responsibilities by, for example, arranging and managing their contracts with care facilities, scheduling and reporting on treatments they give, handling their accounting and credit activities, providing them with training updates, and increasing their earnings through the company's marketing capabilities.

NovaCare's software system, NovaNet, captures and enhances much of the organization's systems knowledge, such as the rules with which therapists must comply and the information they need about customers, schedules, and billing; it highlights for executives those trends or problem areas most pertinent to future operations. NovaNet collects information from all therapists about, for example, their costs and services, techniques that have worked well and changing care patterns in different regions. This information is vital for recruiting, training, motivating, and updating therapists.

To facilitate the collection and analysis of knowledge, NovaCare records its therapeutic care activities in ten-minute blocks. This detailed information creates a database that can be used by a diverse group of stakeholders: caregivers, hospitals, clinics, payers, government agencies, executives, and outside financial and regulatory bodies. NovaCare utilizes extensive peer and customer reviews in evaluating its therapists' work and (based on the time units captured in NovaNet) rewards them on the amount and quality of the care they deliver.

NovaCare's professionals are highly self-sufficient; they have tremendous autonomy on questions involving patient care. Therapists can give orders to all intermediate line organizations. The company's regional and functional specialists in accounting, marketing, purchasing and logistics exist primarily to support the therapists. Even CEO John H. Foster refers to the therapists as "my bosses." The leverage of NovaCare's organizational structure is "distributive" – that is, the support organization efficiently distributes logistics, analysis, and administrative support to the professionals. But it does not give them orders.

NovaCare has thus inverted the traditional organization. The former line hierarchy becomes a support structure, intervening only in extreme emergencies – as might the CEO of a hospital or the chief pilot of an airline. The function of former line managers changes: instead of giving orders, they are now removing barriers, expediting resources, conducting studies, and acting as consultants. They support and help articulate the new culture. In effect, line managers evolve into staff people. (See Figure 7.1.)

Inverted organizations like NovaCare make sense when individual experts embody most of the organization's knowledge, when they do not have to interact with one another to solve problems, and when they customize their knowledge at the

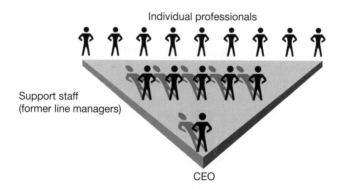

The center provides support services that leverage the professionals in the field. Inverted organizations are appropriate when individual professionals have enough expertise to be self-sufficient and can act independently to meet specific customer needs. Many healthcare providers, technical troubleshooting units, and universities are inverted organizations.

Figure 7.1 In inverted organizations, field experts becomes bosses

point of contact with customers. The software behind inverted systems must serve two somewhat conflicting goals: rules enforcement and professional empowerment. First, because professionals often resist regimentation, the software forces NovaCare's therapists to provide information in a consistent format, to comply with corporate rules and external regulations and to originate the information necessary to monitor quality, costs and trends for the organization's overall operation. Second, the software captures and distributes to professionals all the knowledge the company has built up over time so they can do their jobs better or more efficiently. That knowledge includes information about customers, professional databases, analytical models, successful solutions to problems, and access to specialized sources of knowledge.

Inverted organizations pose some unique managerial challenges. The apparent loss of formal authority can be traumatic for former line managers. And field people who are granted formal power may tend to act more and more like specialists with strictly "professional" outlooks and to resist any set of organizational rules or business norms. Given those tendencies and without a disciplining software, field people often don't stay current with details about their organization's own complex internal systems. And their empowerment without adequate information and controls embedded in the company's technology systems can be dangerous. A classic example is the rapid decline of People Express, which consciously inverted its organization and enjoyed highly empowered and motivated point people but lacked the systems or the computer infrastructures to enable them to adapt as the organization grew.

If such organizations fail, it is usually because despite much rhetoric about inversion – their senior managers did not support the concept with thoroughly overhauled performance-measurement and reward systems. Inverted systems rarely work until field people largely determine their "support people's" wages, promotions and organizational progress. Former line people are reluctant to take this last crucial step. In our studies of more than 100 major structural changes in 60 large service organizations, less than 20% of the organizations had changed their performance-measurement systems significantly and only about 5% had changed their reward systems (*Information Technology in the Service Society*, National Academy Press, 1993). Without such changes, the complications were predictable: people continued to perform according to the traditional measures.

Creating intellectual webs

In NovaCare's business, the professional therapists who create value are largely self-sufficient individual contributors. The inverted organization, coupled with the right software and incentives, allows NovaCare to enhance its therapists' productivity while giving them the operating autonomy they need. In other businesses, professional intellect is called on to create value by solving problems that exceed the capabilities of any solo practitioner. When problems become much more complex or less well defined, no one person or organization may know exactly what their full dimensions are, where key issues will ultimately reside, or who may have potential new solutions.

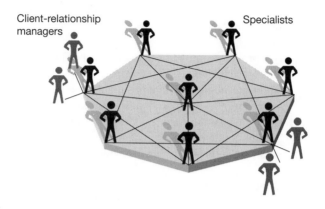

Spider's webs form to accomplish a particular project and disband when the project is completed. They are appropriate when knowledge is dispersed among many specialists, who must provide a coordinated solution to a complex customer problem. Many consulting firms, investment banks, research consortia, and medical diagnostic teams make use of spider's webs.

Figure 7.2 In spider's webs, a few experts team up to meet a specific challenge

To tackle such problems – and to leverage their own intellectual assets to the maximum – a number of companies are using a form of self-organizing network that we call a *spider's web*. We use this term to avoid confusion with other, more traditional network-like forms more akin to holding companies or matrix organizations. Typically, a spider's web brings people together quickly to solve a particular problem and then disbands just as quickly once the job is done. The power of such interconnections is so great that even with a modest number of collaborating independent professionals (eight to ten), a spider's web can leverage knowledge capabilities by hundreds of times. (See Figure 7.2.)

Consider Merrill Lynch's mergers and acquisitions group. At the firm's center, specialists work primarily with others in their own disciplines – for example, acquisitions, high-yield financings, or equity markets. But when a large financing opportunity emerges, the project becomes an intellectual focal point and a team of specialists from different locations forms to pursue each individual deal. Such projects are so complex that, as one executive says: "No one can be a know-everything banker. You can't have only specialists doing their own thing, and the client is not interested in dealing with multiple specialists." The key problem is focusing Merrill Lynch's rich but dispersed talents on a single customer's problem for a short time. Client-relationship managers, who best understand the customer's integrated needs, usually coordinate these teams, but they don't have direct, hierarchical control over team members.

Despite the current popularity of virtual organizations and of networks, few companies understand when and how to use networked forms to leverage professional intellect. As the Merrill Lynch example shows, networks can flexibly combine high specialization in many different disciplines with multiple geographic contact points and a sharp focus on a single problem or customer set. But without the firm's specifically tailored promotion and compensation evaluation processes, the system probably would not work.

At Merrill Lynch, individuals work with many different colleagues on a variety of projects over the course of a year. All of them submit a confidential evaluation on everyone with whom they have worked closely. People are willing to share knowledge and cooperate because their compensation is attached to this mosaic of peer relationships, and compensation is a major motivating factor in this business. There are enough close personal team contacts to allow a truly multifaceted picture of an individual's performance. According to one vice president of the mergers and acquisitions group: "In addition to profits generated, people are evaluated on how well they throw themselves into various projects, work with different groups to meet priorities, and meet clients' needs. The culture penalize those who fail to be team players or to meet clients' needs. Under these rules, spider's webs have worked well in our relationship world. In our transactional world, however, we generally win by having the best specialists for that transaction."

Because each spider's web is unique in its purpose, patterns, and organizational power relationships, there is no single "best way" to manage all of them. For many projects, there may not be a single authority center. Often if the goal, problem, or solution is sufficiently clear, decisions may occur through informal processes if the parties agree. When the various centers of excellence need to operate in a highly coordinated fashion, they may delegate temporary authority to a project leader – as when widely dispersed researchers present a contract proposal. In other cases, the organization may designate one person as the lead in order to force decisions or to make final commitments – as when an insurance or investment banking consortium faces a deadline.

How groups communicate and what they voluntarily communicate are as important as the advanced knowledge each center of excellence may have. For virtually all purposes, however, encouraging shared interests, common values, and mutually satisfying solutions is essential for leveraging knowledge in these structures. Research suggests that to accomplish this goal, network managers should force members to overlap on different teams in order to increase continuity of contact, joint learning, and informal information sharing; purposely keep hierarchical relations ill defined; constantly update and reinforce project goals; avoid overly elaborate rules for allocating profits to individual nodes; develop continuous mechanisms for updating information about the external environment (for example, tax code changes, customer needs, or scientific results); involve both clients and peers in performance evaluations; and provide node members with both individual and team rewards for participation. Such consciously structured management interactions can mitigate the most common failures and frustrations.

The other key leverage factor in most spider's webs is technology. Electronics allow many more highly diverse, geographically dispersed, intellectually specialized talents to be brought to bear on a single project than ever before. Because public telecommunications networks allow interconnection almost anywhere, the key to effective network systems generally lies in software that provides a common language and database for communications, captures critical factual data about external environments, helps players find knowledge sources (usually through electronic menus, web browsers like Netscape, or bulletin boards), and allows interactive sharing and problem solving. Each node will of course have its own specialized analytical software. But networking, groupware, and interactive software, along with a culture of and incentives for sharing, are the keys to success in these systems.

Much can be done to leverage professional intellect through extraordinary recruitment, training, and motivational measures. But, increasingly, managing human intellect alone is not enough. More radical organizational structures, supported by specifically designed software systems, are essential to capture, focus, and leverage capabilities to the fullest. Such systems have become the glue that both joins together highly dispersed service-delivery centers and leverages the critical knowledge bases, intellectual skills, and accumulated experience in professional organizations. They also bond professionals to the organization by providing them with databases, analytical models, and communication power that they cannot find elsewhere. These tools enable professionals to extend their performance beyond their personal limits, allowing them to achieve more inside the organization than they could on their own.

No organizational form is a panacea. In fact, many different forms often coexist successfully in the same company. Properly used, each helps a company attract, harness, leverage, and deploy intellect for a quite different purpose. Consequently, each requires a carefully developed set of cultural norms supported by software and by performance-measurement and reward systems tailored to the organization's specific purposes.

8 Organizational Conditions and Levels of Creativity

Göran Ekvall

Two levels of creativity can be identified whether we look at the concept from the product, the person or the process point of view. The one is radical and revolutionary, the other adaptive and confirmatory. Some results are presented that indicate differing influences on higher and lower level creativity. It is argued that the issue of innovation in organizations harbours a couple of basic dilemmas which requires an understanding of the psychology of creativity.

New research questions

The understanding of creative products, persons and processes, that has emerged through research during the 20th century, provides a valid basis for formulating hypotheses about organizational structures, systems and processes that stimulate or block creative acts. Conditions that restrict free and open communications, such as rigid bureaucratic rules and instructions, 'holy' hierarchies and detail controlling supervision, keep creativity down, because new mental structures, new constellations, come into being when knowledge, experiences, ideas from widely differing and distinct domains meet. Such meetings can more easily appear when there are few restrictions to the members' possibilities to move mentally inside and outside the organization and be able to confront variety. As creative thinking questions established ways of doing things, conservative values, strategies and policies, that support the conventional, are blocking creativity. Those that ask for change stimulate it. As incubation phases and subconscious mental activities are elements of the creative problem-solving process, time for retreat, reflection and relaxation promotes the processes, and subsequent time pressure, heavy workload and stress reactions hamper them. As risk taking and anxiety are ingredients of creative acts, culture elements that make risk taking and failure less threatening and dangerous promote creative behaviour, whereas in situations where creative initiatives are met with suspicion, defensiveness and aggression, the fear of failure becomes strong and holds creativity back.

These propositions have support in research reports and in management textbooks on creativity and innovation in organisations (Amabile, 1988; Hage and Aiken, 1970; Hall, 1977; Peters and Waterman, 1982; Woodman, 1995). We have some solid knowledge about the organizational conditions that enhance and those that block creativity in general terms. There are also indications and hypotheses about differential influences related to the two levels or, if we prefer, the two kinds of creativity (Ekvall, 1996).

Do some organizational characteristics promote lower, more adaptive, creative acts but impede more radical creativity? And do some conditions that stimulate the radical block the adaptive kind of creative acts? Two studies that shed light on these questions will now be presented.

A study at a chemical company

This was a study of four divisions of a middle-sized Swedish industrial company, producing chemicals for other industries, i.e. paper, pulp, detergents and others. Each division had its own product development, marketing and sales. Three of them also had their own production facilities, whereas the fourth used one of the others as subcontractor. The study had a broad scope concerning the domains studied (history, strategies, philosophies, policies, structures, leadership, processes, climates, job satisfaction, profits and innovations) and the research methods applied (document analysis, interviews, questionnaires, direct observations, group discussions).

The analyses are geared to the issue of differences in innovative achievements between the divisions and the organizational conditions influencing the innovative outcomes (Ekvall, 1988, 1991, 1996; Ekvall, Arvonen and Nyström, 1987; Nyström, 1991).

The four divisions (we can call them A, B, C and D) showed fundamental differences in history, age, culture, strategies, leadership and innovative achievements.

Division A, the oldest, was a traditional process plant, with its roots in the late 19th century. It produced some basic chemicals and had a given market share for those mature products. No development activities about products existed. The organization was of the traditional, hierarchical style and the leadership was patriarchal.

Division B produced a chemical that was of later date than those of the A division. The prospects for the chemical were bright, the sales volume had grown substantially. These successes were the result of purposeful market-oriented development work. Project groups were established with customers in order to adapt the chemical to new applications and better to meet the needs of the customer. There prevailed a rational systematic, achievement-oriented culture, an administrative functioning style, stressing systems, procedures, goals. The leadership reinforced these values and principles.

The C division had about the same size and was of the same age as the B division. But in contrast to B, which was a one-product business, it contained several product lines and it had both mature and younger products and furthermore a lot of new product development projects were in progress. The leadership was democratic and relations oriented and emphasized integration and synergies between old and new parts of the business. Values of creativity and flexibility were salient elements of the culture.

The D division was the youngest. At the time of the study it was a large product project for a new chemical system that had recently appeared on the market. The concept had its roots in the C division. The leadership and the culture were of the typical entrepreneurial style. The product concept later became a great commercial success.

Comparison between the B and C divisions are feasible; they were of the same size and age, roughly. Both were complete plants with their own development, production, marketing and sales functions. They however differed considerably in the case of creativity and innovation: the B division being a one-product business, striving to adapt its concept to new applications and new customers and the C division being a multiproduct business with a mix of mature and young products and many new product development projects going on. The innovative activities at the B division were of a typical adaptive sort, whereas the C division presented a clear example of radical innovation strivings. These justify a proposition that adaptive, lower level creative acts were prevailing at the B division and radical, higher level, creative acts at the C division.

A questionnaire was handed out to all white-collar and supervisory personnel in the divisions. The items consist of statements about practice and behaviour patterns in the organization, which the respondent has to agree or disagree with. Examples:

Tasks are clearly defined.
Rules and principles are stressed.
There is a clear tendency for risk taking here.

In six of the 15 indexes there were statistically significant differences between B and C, shown in Table 8.1.

The indexes where no differences were observed belonged to three different domains: information and personnel policy; climate of challenge and achievement orientation; trust, openness and harmony in relations. Both B and C scored quite high in those domains.

Table 8.1 shows that B division scored higher than C on only two indexes, order/structure/plan and goal clarity. The differences on order/structure/plan is substantial, the largest of the differences.

Table 8.1 Mean scores on organizational indexes: white-collar and supervisory employees

	Divisions		
Index	*B*	*C*	*Diff.*
Order/structure/plan	1.77	1.12	.65***
Goal clarity	1.73	1.56	.17+
Risk taking	1.37	1.92	−.55**
Freedom	1.95	2.33	−.38*
Playfulness/humour	1.66	1.96	−.30*
Debates	.96	1.35	−.39*
Livelifulness/dynamism	1.68	2.05	−.37*

Scale 0–3: +p < .10 * p < .05 ** p < .01 *** p < .001

Table 8.2 Mean scores on items of the order/structure/plan index

	Divisions		
Index	*B*	*C*	*Diff.*
Operations are strictly planned and organized	1.58	.82	.76***
One is exacting about plans being followed	1.85	1.13	.72***
Everyone knows what is expected of him/her	2.04	1.37	.67***

Scale 0–3

In Table 8.2 the three items that carried the main part of the difference in this index are presented.

The results indicate that the strict, rational, structured culture and praxis prevailing in the B division appeared to promote adaptive creativity and the second-order innovations that characterized the product strategies and achievements. The C division, with its looser structure, more freedom, higher risk inclination and debating, dynamic and playful atmosphere tended to stimulate creative acts of the higher, first-order kind, that paved the way to new projects and products.

A study at a mechanical company

This study was carried out in Sweden (Ljungkvist, 1993). The author used the Creative Climate Questionnaire (CCQ) (Ekvall, 1991 and 1996), to compare different parts of a multinational company that produces systems and machinery for packing foodstuffs and is very successful on the world market.

The company's product development function is divided into two departments; one working with design of new products, the other with improvements of old established products.

The CCQ is a 50-item questionnaire covering ten dimensions: challenge, freedom, idea-support, trust, dynamism, playfulness, debates, conflicts, risk taking, idea time. All dimensions except conflicts are positively related to an organization's degree of creativity and innovativeness (Ekvall, 1996). The items are phrased in the same way as those in the questionnaire described in the previous example. The CCQ items are all about climate – the behaviours, attitudes and feelings – characterizing the life in the organization.

The study included two random samples of ten design engineers each, from the department for development of new products and from the department of product improvements. Table 8.3 shows the mean scores in the climate indexes for the two samples.

The results are evident. The designers in the new product department perceived a more creativity promoting and stimulating climate than the design engineers in the product improvement department did. The management of the R&D function declared that they 'accepted' a lower level of creativity in the product improvement department than in the new product department, from which they thus expected higher levels of creativity.

Table 8.3 Mean scores in CCQ indexes for two departments

Index	New products	Departments Improvements	Diff.
Challenge	2.26	1.98	.28 n.s.
Freedom	2.12	1.72	.40*
Idea support	2.12	1.70	.42*
Trust	2.02	1.82	.20 n.s.
Dynamism	2.06	1.64	.42*
Playfulness	2.08	1.90	.18 n.s.
Debates	1.08	1.64 ·	.44*
Conflicts[1]	.76	1.18	−.42*
Risk taking	1.82	1.39	.43*
Idea time	1.80	1.43	.37*

Scale 0–3. * p < .05

[1] The conflict dimension, in the CCQ operationalized by items concerning ego and power tensions in the organization, has in all studies so far showed negative correlations with all the other dimensions, debates (tensions between ideas) included. Person collisions (conflicts) have come out as obstacles to creativity and innovation in the studies, as opposed to idea collisions (debates that have shown positive relations).

Table 8.4 CCQ mean scores for the two divisions compared to mean scores for other organizations

	High-tech project	New product department	Mechanical company	Product improvement department	Five 'stagnated' organizations
Challenge	2.36	2.26	1.80	1.98	1.63
Freedom	2.00	2.12	1.70	1.72	1.53
Idea support	1.83	2.12	1.50	1.70	1.08
Trust	2.23	2.02	1.60	1.82	1.28
Dynamism	2.20	2.06	1.60	1.64	1.40
Playfulness	2.30	2.08	1.70	1.90	1.40
Debates	1.85	2.08	1.60	1.64	1.05
Conflicts	.30	.76	1.00	1.18	1.40
Risk taking	1.57	1.82	1.20	1.39	.53
Idea time	1.40	1.80	1.10	1.43	.97

Scale 0–3

Both departments were living up to expectations, as the company is very successful with its product goals and strategies. This makes comparisons with other companies, whose creative achievements are known, apt.

In Table 8.4 the two departments' mean scores on the climate indexes are compared to mean scores of three other organizations (Ekvall, 1996):

1 A large product development project in high-tech, lasting for three years and with 30 engineers working full time in the project. The climate was measured each third month with the CCQ. (The scores in Table 8.4 are means of these measurements.) The product, a new type of operator station for defence systems, was rated as comprising several original spearhead technical solutions. Creative acts of the 'higher' level were no doubt occurring in this project.

2   The product development department of a large mechanical company operating in an old business line characterized by incremental product changes. The companies in this trade watch each other keenly and product changes of the same kind tend to appear at the same time in their programmes. The adaptive kind of creativity might be the hallmark of this product development department (Ekvall, 1990).

3   Five 'stagnated' organizations. Small companies or independent divisions of larger companies, all being in difficult economical circumstances, at the time of the study, due to lack of new products and/or updating their old products. It is reasonable to assume that these organizations were uncreative and had been so for a couple of years.

The climate pattern of the new products department is similar to that of the high-tech project. The pattern of the product improvement department is near the mechanical company's and is significantly different from the stagnated organizations', in the positive direction, which places its climate between the climates of highly creative and uncreative organizations. The climate picture as defined by the CCQ indexes seems to reflect the two levels of organizational creativity; the product improvement department can be assumed to exhibit a climate typical of organizations where adaptive creativity is practised and the new products department can, in the same way, be assumed to show a climate representative of organizations where radical creative acts occur frequently.

Discussion

The data indicate that creative acts in companies are related to organizational variables. The relationships are, as usual in organizational settings, complex from the causality point of view. Climate aspects stimulate or hamper creativity, but creative outcomes then influence climate.

The CCQ data may be interpreted as indicating that the differences in organizational variables between the two levels of creativity is a matter of degree; the constructs are positive for both kinds of creativity, but more is required for radical creativity to occur than for adaptive, the exception being conflicts, where the case is reversed.

We can speculate about effects of 'too much' of some climate dimensions. For example: What will happen if risk taking and freedom are being stressed harder than previously by management in an organization working with incremental innovations and thus practising adaptive creativity? It is probable that highly creative people, those with an 'innovative style' in Kirton's terminology, will be stimulated and respond by presenting more radical ideas and problem solutions than before. The 'adaptors', on the other hand, will be uneasy and lose energy and motivation to solve problems. It is not probable that people who, due to personality dispositions, are adaptive problem solvers will turn into radical thinkers. The organizational effect will accordingly be that the adaptive creativity fades away and more innovative creative acts tend to appear, provided that the organization harbours some innovative thinkers, who respond to the new management signals and that recruiting more such employees is possible. If the strategy aims purely at exchanging adaptive innovations for radical innovations, the effects are adequate. If, however, the idea with the stronger push for risk taking and freedom is to reach a balance of adaptive and radical creativity and a mix of improvement and new product achievements, the decreasing motivation and morale among the adaptive problem solvers may become a problem. This dilemma of having 'innovators' and 'adaptors' understand and accept each other's ways of approaching and solving problems and working together is discussed by Kirton (1987). The case with the two different departments, one for product improvements and another for development of new products might be regarded as an attempt to manage the dilemma.

A still more intricate issue is that of organizational dimensions where high scores may block the radical creativity and innovation but promote the adaptive.

The study at the chemical company provides an indication that strict and clear structures, policies and rules are hindrances to higher level, innovative creativity and that more loose, vague and variable structures are prerequisites for such radical creative acts to be prevalent in the organization. The C division (with its radical innovation strategy and outcomes) showed low scores on items about order, structure, planning. The adaptively inclined B division, however, had high scores, which supports the assumption that its systematic, structured organizational functioning favoured the appearance of adaptive creative acts.

The reason that strict and plain organizational principles and practice hamper the radical, higher level creativity and promote the adaptive, lower level creativity is found in the nature of creative processes and of creative personalities. As creative processes consist in 'making new and valuable connections' and as the more apart the connected elements are at the outset, the more creative the outcome will be, it is reasonable to assume that organizational conditions that support meetings of ideas, knowledge, experiences and standpoints, which are highly different, prepare the way for radical creative processes to come up. A loose structure and elastic practice facilitates such encounters. That kind of structure allows the members of the organization to search for information and viewpoints freely and not be restricted to using only formal channels and contacts. Furthermore the lower stress laid on time schedules, strict planning and fixed role assignments entails time and freedom for initiatives, experimentation, reflection and 'incubation', which raises the chances for 'shifts in perception' to occur.

The radical problem solver is very content with a vague and loose structure. His/her ways of intellectual, motivational and emotional functioning fit such situations. Strict, rigid, formal organizational settings are experienced as uneasy and fettering and are resisted. Kirton (1987) has described the 'innovator' as a person who challenges rules, dislikes routine work and takes control in unstructured situations. The latter tendency implies that highly creative persons are stimulated by vague, unstructured situations because those present possibilities for them to make scope for their own new 'mental configurations'. Researchers of the creative personality have maintained that highly creative persons are characterized by 'tolerance of ambiguity' (Rogers, 1962; Stein, 1962). It might be that they are not only tolerant of the vagueness, they are even motivated by it.

The Adaptor personality as described by Kirton (1987) is the psychological pendant to the bureaucratic structure with its stress on precision, methods, stability and conformity. They are the kind of people who 'seek solutions to problems in tried and understood ways', who 'reduce problems by improvement and greater efficiency, with maximum of continuity and stability'. The Norwegian scholar Paul Moxnes has described this kind of personality as socio-structure dependent and found that they tend to become anxious in loose, vague, fluid situations (Moxnes, 1978). The Adaptor needs a clearly defined context in order to feel well and be able to utilize his/her capabilities at work. And when solving problems it becomes necessary to operate within that context and not put the safe frame at risk.

Goal clarity probably has similar effects on the creativity in the organization as structure and order, even if the results of the study at the chemical company were not strongly indicative.

The elaboration of the mission, goals and strategies of the company and disseminating this to the members of the organization is a management principle and procedure aimed at consistency and guidance, and at the same time supposed to engender meaning and commitment. The principle has been named MBO (management by objectives) in management philosophy. The energy, initiatives and problem-solving efforts of the employees are expected to be geared to the company's stated goals and support the goal attainment. Management by objectives has developed in opposition to bureaucratic management by strict rules and prescriptions to give more scope for discretion and initiatives to the members of the organization.

Clear mission statements, goals and strategies entail a structure different from the bureaucratic, but still a structure. The business lines, the expected achievements in different aspects and the main routes are laid out by top management. Inside this framework departments and teams are expected to use initiatives and discretion to have their work contribute to the goal attainment. This kind of structure supports creativity because of the amount of freedom it allows. Departments, teams and individuals have to organize their work and set their targets at their own discretion, inside the frames given, in order to promote the overall goal. It is however the adaptive kind of creativity that grows best in the MBO culture. It is a situation where the Adaptor feels at home and becomes productive as a problem solver. Steady improvements alongside the set avenues are expected. Some basic, governing values in the MBO culture are very much the same as in the bureaucratic culture; consistency, predictability, risk avoidance. The main difference is the higher trust in people's capacities to take on responsibility characterizing MBO. The values that MBO have in common with the bureaucratic systems tends to make the scope for radical creativity on problems of work organization and methods more narrow than the general frame of goals and strategies would permit.

Elaborated goals and strategies that are clearly announced in the company are intended to work as fixed guiding stars and guideways for initiatives and plans. Highly creative individuals with their 'innovator style' of approaching problems are frustrated when things are settled and indisputable. Their drives are to question the established, to reformulate problems and goals, not to stay mentally inside frames that are given, traditional and accepted. The MBO principles do not permit much scope for such ambitions, especially not where the principles have been introduced in organizations with deep-rooted bureaucratic values.

The difficulties of generating innovations in large organizations have had growing attention during the 1980s and 1990s. The rigidity and inertia of large, bureaucratic systems are considered as the basic problem. The common conclusion is creative ideas are not taken care of in such systems. Some of the modern management trends such as MBO and decentralization can be assumed to promote creative acts, mainly of the adaptive kind, but other tendencies that are pushing pace, efficiency and productivity, like 'time management', 'lean production', 'just in time', 'reengineering' and 'cutting down product development time', might be pressing down even the lower (adaptive) kind of creativity and probably blocking the more radical (Mellström, 1995). Layoffs due to the rationalizations or to shrinking markets have deteriorating effects on the rate of creative behaviors (Amabile and Conti, 1995).

The TQM (total quality management) movement has introduced strict control systems and procedures not only in production but in almost all operations and functions. It has been argued that TQM implies a renaissance of Taylorism (Boje and Windsor, 1993). If this is so, and quality has become a cardinal all-embracing light approached by scientific management methods, there has come a second unconditional goal, besides efficiency, whose application has a similar complicated relation to creativity and innovation.

The fundamental problem with radical innovation in organizations can be described as consisting of a number of interrelated dilemmas:

- The fact that creativity on the one hand, and time pressure, speed and stress on the other are counteracting forces.
- The fact that organizational principles, systems and procedures aimed at structure and stability do shrink the scope for high-level creativity but allow adaptive creativity.
- The necessity of ample resources to bring forth radical innovations in modern high-tech industries implies large organizations with many people, frequent cooperation and joint ventures, where two or more companies are co-actors, which requires structures and procedures for co-ordination and control, i.e. the sort of organizational mechanisms that reduce the chances for radical creative acts to appear.
- The fact that companies in highly competitive markets must create the means for long-term development by having high efficiency in their operations, which brings in strategies, systems and structures which are problematic from the creativity point of view.
- The experiences of the difficulty of having Adaptors and Innovators cooperate because they challenge each other's beliefs and basic values.

The dilemmas have been observed and expressed not only by organization theorists but also by management people, who try to find ways to overcome them. There are still, however, plenty of managers who deny the problem and argue that radical innovations can be brought forth by strict planning and follow-up systems.

There is even much material with that kind of message included in textbooks and courses on project management. The trend seems nevertheless to be towards a broadening awareness of the problem, which probably is a consequence of the constantly increasing requirements for innovations in the world of business.

These growing insights can be traced in strategic statements and policy documents. They are also revealed in metaphorical phrases flitting around in the organization as normative cultural elements, such as 'love and care for the kids as much as the grown-ups', 'don't shoot the skunks', 'stand the mavericks and wild cats'. Examples of organizational strategies to manage the dilemmas are of many kinds: special departments for evaluation of ideas and finding funding and promoters inside the company for the promising ideas – Kodak's 'office of innovation' for example (Rosenfeld and Servo, 1984); giving R&D people time for 'free projects' as with 3M; establishing company funds, for high-risk projects, where departments and subsidiaries can apply for grants – the Perstorp system of a variety of funds being an example (Nordberg, 1983); starting separate subsidiaries for development of new products, where the structures, rules, administrative principles, policies and economic targets of the mother company are not applied – this being probably the most common strategy; running idea and innovation campaigns during a limited time and directed towards specified problems, like the Volfram campaign at Volvo (Ekvall, 1990).

There have been success stories as well as failures reported for all these kinds of strategy. The variance in outcomes is probably due to differences in the top managers' understandings of the basic character of the problem and the differences in ways to put the strategies into practice according to the diverging understandings.

The thesis of this chapter is that the problem of innovation in organizations is rooted in the nature of creative processes and creative persons and that the two different kinds of creativity that have been identified are differentially facilitated by organizational conditions. This creates organizational dilemmas. These dilemmas cannot be wiped out because creative processes and the creative personality are given. The dilemmas must, however, be managed as companies must have capacity for radical changes in different aspects in order to survive in the long run and they must at the same time earn the money day by day by effective operations to make the resources for the development work. The keys to success in the inevitable balancing act are to be found in understanding and paying regard to the nature of creative processes and creative persons in the construction and application of the organizational strategies aimed at managing the dilemmas.

References

Amabile, T. M. (1988) 'A model of creativity and innovation in organizations', *Research in Organizational Behaviour*, vol. 10, pp. 123–67.

Amabile, M. and Conti, R. (1995) 'What down-sizing does to creativity', *Issues and Observations*, vol. 15, no. 3, Greensboro: Center for Creative Leadership.

Arieti, S. (1976) *Creativity: The Magic Synthesis*, New York: Basic Books.

Barron, F. (1969) *Creative Person and Creative Process*, New York: Holt, Reinehart and Winston.

Besemer, S. P. and O'Quin, K. (1987) 'Creative product analysis. Testing a model by developing a judging instrument', in S. G. Isaksen, (ed.) *Frontiers of Creativity Research*, Buffalo: Bearly Ltd.

Boje, D. M. and Windsor, R. D. (1993) 'The resurrection of Taylorism: total quality management's hidden agenda', *Journal of Organizational Change Management*, vol. 6, no. 4.

De Bono, E. (1971) *The Mechanism of Mind*, Middlesex: Penguin Books.

Ekvall, G. (1988) *Förnyelse och Friktion*, Stockholm: Natur and Kultur.

Ekvall, G. (1990) *Idéer, Organisationsklimat och Ledningsfilosofi*, Stockholm: Norstedts.

Ekvall, G (1991) 'The organizational culture of idea-management: a creative climate for the management of ideas', in J. Henry and D. Walker (eds) *Managing Innovation*, London: Sage Publications.

Ekvall, G. (1996) 'Organizational climate for creativity and innovation', *European Journal of Work and Organizational Psychology*, vol. 5, no. 1, pp. 105–23.

Ekvall, G., Arvonen, J. and Nyström, H. (1987) *Organisation och innovation*, Lund: Studentlitteratur.

Ghiselin, B. (1952) *The Creative Process*, New York: New American Library.

Ghiselin, B. (1963) 'Ultimate criteria for two levels of creativity', in C. W. Taylor and F. Barron (eds) *Scientific Creativity*, New York: Wiley and Sons.

Guilford, J. P. (1967) *The Nature of Human Intelligence*, New York: McGraw-Hill.

Hage, J. and Aiken, M. (1970) *Social Change in Complex Organizations*, New York: Random Hansey, Inc.

Hall, R.H. (1977) *Organizations: Structure and Process* (2nd edn), Englewood: Prentice-Hall, Inc.

Kaufmann, G. (1980) *Problemløsning og Kreativitet*, Oslo: Cappelens Forlag.

Kirton, M. J. (1987) 'Adaptors and innovators. Cognitive style and personality', in S. G. Isaksen (ed.) *Frontiers of Creativity Research*, Buffalo: Bearly Ltd.

Koestler, A. (1964) *The Act of Creation*, New York: Dell.

Kris, E. (1952) *Psychoanalytical Explorations in Art*, New York: International Universities Press.

Ljungkvist, P. (1993) *Bolagiseringens Effekter på Innovationsklimat och Kommunikationsmönster*, Magisteruppsats: Högskolan i Halmstad.

Maslow, A. H. (1962) 'Emotional blocks to creativity', in S. J. Parnes and H. F. Harding (eds) *A Source Book for Creative Thinking*, New York: Scribner's Sons.

Mellström, U. (1995) *Engineering Lives. Technology, Time and Space in a Male World*, University of Linköping.

Moxnes, P. (1978) *Angst og Organisasjon*, Oslo: Gyldendal Norsk Forlag.

Nordberg, S. (1983) *Perstorps Kretaive Bas – en unik väg mot förnyelse*, Konferens-paper, Liber Förlag.

Nyström, J. (1990) 'Organizational innovation' in M. A. West and J. L. Farr (eds) *Innovation and Creativity at Work: Psychological and Organizational Strategies*, Chichester: Wiley.

Nyström, J. (1991) *Technological and Market Innovation – Strategies for Product and Company Development*, Chichester: Wiley and Sons.

Peters, T. and Waterman, R., Jr. (1982) *In Search of Excellence*, New York: Harper and Row.

Poincaré, H. (1970) 'Mathematical creation' in P. Vernon (ed.) *Creativity*, London: Penguin Books.

Rogers, C.R. (1962) 'Towards a theory of creativity', in S. J. Parnes and H. F. Harding (eds) *A Source Book for Creative Thinking*, New York: Scribner's Sons.

Rosenfeld, R. and Servo, J. (1984) 'Business and creativity. Making ideas connect', *The Futurist*, August.

Simonton, D. K. (1984) *Genius, Creativity and Leadership*, Cambridge: Harvard University Press.

Smith, G. J. W. (1981) 'Creation and reconstruction', *Psychoanalysis and Contemporary Thought*, vol. 4, pp. 275–86.

Smith, G. and Carlsson, I. (1990) 'The creative process. A functional model based on empirical studies from early childhood to middle age', *Psychological Issues*, vol. 57.

Stein, M.I. (1962) 'Creativity as an intra- and inter-personal process', in S. J. Parnes, and H. F. Harding (eds) *A Source Book for Creative Thinking*, New York: Scribner's Sons.

Wallas, G. (1926) *The Art of Thought*, London: Watts.

Wertheimer, M. (1945) *Productive Thinking*, New York: Harper.

Woodman, R. W. (1995) 'Managing creativity' in C. M. Ford and D. A. Gioia (eds) *Creative Action in Organizations*, London: Sage Publications.

Part 2

Innovation

Section C Policy and Management

This section presents chapters which discuss innovation policy and innovation management. They discuss different routes to innovation, the dangers of innovating, lean enterprise, attention to staff needs and the way new ideas are put across. Rothwell illustrates some key theories of innovation, noting how these have changed over time. Kay sounds one of his characteristic warnings, here on the dangers of being first to market and the better odds often associated with technological following. Womack and Jones present their case for a form of lean enterprise that allows for skill development, combining cross-disciplinary team working with job rotation to retain career development. Dyson, the successful inventor, like Semler, seems to believe that a very open climate and commitment to service are important and central to his innovative medium size business. 3M is a large organization that, unlike many organizations of comparable size, seems to have succeeded in maintaining a high rate of innovation. Shaw suggests use of narrative is one of the reasons why.

Rothwell outlines some of the ways in which people have tried to make sense of innovation and how a belief in the primacy of technological push gave way to an understanding of the role of market demand and subsequently to an understanding of the role of feedback, parallel development and more systemic models of innovation. He goes on to outline some of the strategies used by successful innovative organizations.

Kay provides a short chapter on the dangers of being the first mover – first out with the new product and how often fast followers, who copy the new idea, turn out to win the race in the long run, whether the field is computing (Microsoft over Apple), pharmaceuticals (Zantac or Tagamet) or domestic electric products (Sony over EMI). Kay contends it is the organization that has the best marketing, distribution, technical expertise and the like that often gains the lion's share of the market.

Womack and Jones point out the failings of the German, US and Japanese management systems. The German stress on technical expertise has led to the neglect of cross-disciplinary working, the US individualistic 'every company for itself' ethos has inhibited cooperation across the value chain and the Japanese stress on obligation and maintaining relationships has led to a facility for incremental improvement within a particular area but one that can burn itself out. The authors argue that their idea of lean enterprise allows companies to have their cake and eat it. Accepting cross-disciplinary team working is the order of the day, they advocate procedures to ensure this does not inhibit career development such as learning on the job and job rotation that includes substantial periods aimed at skill development. They cite the Unipart university as an example of a firm that has taken this approach to heart.

Dyson, of bagless vacuum cleaner fame, expounds his management philosophy, which could be summarized as care and diligence. First, he and his young staff care about the product, they aim to design a beautiful and efficient machine that they are constantly improving. Staff are expected to be thorough rather than fast. Dyson also makes a point of attracting good staff by paying them well, giving them good food, a convenient bus service and nice surroundings. He treats his customers with equal care, replacing any faulty machines the next day or repairing them. He has encouraged a climate of openness through the use of open plan offices, monthly meetings with him and a more private forum and suggestions boxes for the introverted to say what is wrong. He has removed all trappings of bureaucracy – discouraging all memos, avoiding job demarcation and banning suits.

Swathes of industry run on bullet points. Shaw et al. point out the failings of this approach to planning with admirable clarity. Instead they advocate a form of strategic storytelling as a means of conveying key relationships and insights more effectively than bullets and in a way that gains more attention and buy in. They describe the use of this practice at 3M, a company famed for its stories as much as its innovation, a fact which Shaw et al. do not believe is merely coincidence.

9 Towards the Fifth-generation Innovation Process

Roy Rothwell

Manufacturing companies are today faced with intensifying competition and a turbulent economic environment. To some extent, technology is seen as a means by which firms can strive to adapt to the requirements of this difficult and uncertain environment. On the other hand, rapid rates of technological change and associated shorter product cycles are themselves part of the difficulty, as is the increased blurring of long-established industrial boundaries – Kodama's (1985) process of 'technological fusion'. The growing complexity and pace of industrial technological change are forcing firms to forge new vertical and horizontal alliances and to seek greater flexibility and efficiency in responding to market changes. This adaptation process is leading some companies towards greater and more strategically directed integration and networking with external agencies and to the adoption of a sophisticated electronic toolkit in their design and development activities to enhance developmental flexibility, speed and efficiency. In the language of this chapter, these leading edge innovators are beginning to take on elements of the fifth-generation (5G) innovation process.

The first-generation innovation process

(1950s–mid-1960s)

During the first 20 years or so following World War II, the advanced market economies enjoyed unparalleled rates of economic growth largely through rapid industrial expansion. There was the emergence of new industries based largely on new technological opportunities, e.g. semiconductors, pharmaceuticals, electronic computing and synthetic and composite materials; at the same time there was the technology-led regeneration of existing sectors, e.g. textiles and steel and the rapid application of technology to enhance the productivity and quality of agricultural production. These developments lead to rapid growth of the consumer white goods, consumer electronics and automobile industries (Freeman et al., 1992).

Science and technology were seen to have the potential for solving society's greatest ills. These attitudes were reflected at governmental level and public technology support policies focused largely on the supply side, i.e. on stimulating scientific advance in universities and government laboratories and the supply of skilled manpower, with some financial support for major R&D programmes in companies (normally in the United States, in relation to defence and space requirements). In manufacturing companies the main corporate emphasis was on R&D to create new product ranges and on manufacturing build-up to satisfy the burgeoning demand for them.

Under these conditions it is perhaps not surprising that the process of the commercialisation of technological change, i.e. the industrial innovation process, was generally perceived as a linear progression from scientific discovery, through technological development in firms, to the marketplace. This first generation, or technology push, concept of innovation (Figure 9.1) assumed that 'more R&D in' resulted in 'more successful new products out'. With one or two notable exceptions, little attention was paid to the transformation process itself (Carter and Williams, 1957) or to the role of the marketplace in the process (Cook and Morrison, 1961).

Figure 9.1 Technology push (first generation)

The second-generation innovation process

(Mid-1960s–early 1970s)

Towards the second half of the 1960s, while manufacturing output continued to grow and general levels of prosperity remained high, in many countries manufacturing employment was more or less static or grew at a much reduced rate, while manufacturing productivity increased considerably (Rothwell and Soete, 1983). During this period of relative prosperity there was corporate emphasis on growth, both organic and acquired, and a growing level of corporate diversification. Levels of industrial concentration increased, with more importance being placed on static-scale economies. While new products were still being introduced, these were based mainly on existing technologies and in many areas supply and demand were more or less in balance.

During this period of intensifying competition, investment emphasis began to switch from new product and related expansionary technological change towards rationalisation technological change (Clark, 1979, Mensch et al., 1980). This was accompanied by greater strategic emphasis on marketing, as large and highly efficient companies fought for market share. Perceptions of the innovation process began to change, with a marked shift towards emphasising demand side factors, i.e. the marketplace. This resulted in the emergence of the second-generation or 'market-pull' (sometimes referred to as the 'need-pull') model of innovation shown in Figure 9.2. According to this simple sequential model, the market was the source of ideas for directing R&D, which had a merely reactive role in the process.

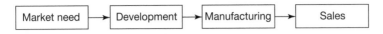

Figure 9.2 Market pull (second generation)

One of the primary dangers inherent in this model was that it could lead companies to neglect long-term R&D programmes and become locked in to a regime of technological incrementalism as they adapted existing product groups to meet changing user requirements along maturing performance trajectories (Hayes and Abernathy, 1980). In doing so they ran the risk of losing the capacity to adapt to any radical market or technological changes that occurred.

The third-generation innovation process

(Early 1970s–mid-1980s)

The early to late 1970s, with two major oil price rises, was a period marked by high rates of inflation and demand saturation (stagflation), in which supply capacity generally outstripped demand and by growing structural unemployment. Companies were forced to adopt strategies of consolidation and rationalization, with growing emphasis on scale and experience benefits. There was associated concern with accountancy and financing issues, leading to a strategic focus on cost control and cost reduction.

During a decade of severe resource constraint, it became increasingly necessary to understand the basis of successful innovation in order to reduce the incidence of wasteful failures and, indeed, it was approximately during this period that the results of a number of detailed empirical studies of the innovation process were published (Cooper, 1980; Hayvaert, 1973; Langrish et al., 1972; Myers and Marquis, 1969; Rothwell, 1976; Rothwell et al., 1974; Rubenstein et al., 1976; Schock, 1974; Szakasitz, 1974; Utterback, 1975). Successful innovation process could be modelled on the basis of a portfolio of wide-ranging and systematic studies covering many sectors and countries. Essentially, these empirical results indicated that the technology push and need pull models of innovation were extreme and atypical examples of a more general process of interaction between, on the one hand, technological capabilities and, on the other market needs (Mowery and Rosenberg, 1978). This third generation interactive, or 'coupling', model of innovation is illustrated in Figure 9.3.

The overall pattern of the innovation process can be thought of as a complex net of communication paths, both intra-organizational and extra-organizational, linking together the various in-house functions and linking the firm to the broader scientific and technological community and to the marketplace (Rothwell and Zegveld, 1985 p.50).

The third-generation innovation model was seen by most western companies, certainly up the mid-1980s or so, as presenting best practice. It was still essentially a sequential process, but in this case with feedback loops.

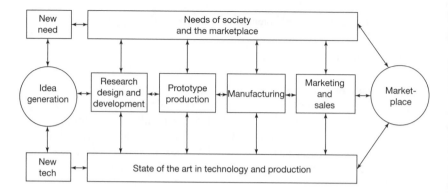

Figure 9.3 The coupling model of innovation (third generation)

There were in some cases strong intersectoral differences concerning the rank order of importance of the different factors (suggested by research) (Rothwell et al., 1974). These factors are divisible, according to Rothwell (1992b), into two groups, namely, project execution and corporate level.

Project execution factors
*   Good internal and external communication; accessing external know-how.
*   Treating innovation as a corporate-wide task; effective interfunctional co-ordination; good balance of functions.
*   Implementing careful planning and project control processes: high quality up-front analysis.
*   Efficiency in development work and high-quality production.
*   Strong marketing orientation: emphasis on satisfying user needs; development emphasis on creating user value.
*   Providing a good technical and spares service to customers: effective use of education.
*   Effective product champions and technological gatekeepers.
*   High-quality, open-minded management; commitment to the development of human capital.
*   Attaining cross-project synergies and interproject learning.

Corporate level factors
*   Top management commitment and visible support for innovation.
*   Long-term corporate strategy with associated technology strategy.
*   Long-term commitment to major projects (patient money).
*   Corporate flexibility and responsiveness to change.
*   Top management acceptance of risk.
*   Innovation-accepting, entrepreneurship-accommodating culture.

Success was rarely associated with performing one or two tasks brilliantly, but with doing most tasks competently and in a balanced and well co-ordinated manner.

At the very heart of the successful innovation process were 'key individuals' of high quality and ability; people with entrepreneurial flair and a strong personal commitment to innovation.

Fourth-generation innovation process

(Early 1980s–early 1990s)

The early 1980s heralded a period of economic recovery with companies initially concentrating on core businesses and core technologies (Peters and Waterman, 1982). This was accompanied by a growing awareness of the strategic importance of evolving generic technologies, with increased strategic emphasis on technological accumulation (technology strategy). The emergence of new generations of IT-based manufacturing equipment led to a new focus on manufacturing strategy (Bessant, 1991). The notion of global strategy emerged (Hood and Vahlne, 1988) and there was a rapid growth in the number of strategic alliances between companies (Contractor and Lorgange, 1988; Dodgson, 1993; Hagedoorn, 1990), often with government encouragement and support (Arnold and Guy, 1986; Haklisch et al., 1986; Rothwell and Dodgson, 1992). Not only large firms, but also innovative small firms were engaging in intensive external networking activity (Docter and Stokman, 1987; Rothwell, 1991). Shortening product life cycles meant that speed of development became an increasingly important factor in competition leading firms to adopt so-called time-based strategies (Dumaine, 1989). A crucial feature of this period was the recognition in the West that the remarkable competitive performance of Japanese companies in world markets was based on considerably more than the combination of technological imitation, JIT relationships with primary suppliers and efficient, quality-oriented production procedures. The Japanese, it was realized, were powerful innovators in their own right and there were features of the Japanese

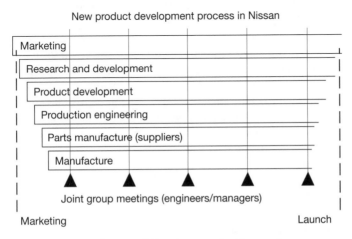

Figure 9.4 Example of the integrated (fourth-generation) innovation process

new product development system that enabled them to innovate more rapidly and efficiently than their western counterparts.

Two of the salient features of innovation in leading Japanese companies (the basis of the fourth-generation innovation model) are *integration* and *parallel development*. Innovating Japanese companies integrate suppliers into the new product development process at an early stage while at the same time integrating the activities of the different in-house departments involved, which work on the project simultaneously (in parallel) rather than sequentially (in series). This so-called 'rugby' approach to new product development (Imai et al., 1985) is one of the factors contributing to high Japanese production efficiency through the process of 'design for manufacturability'. Even when completely simultaneous development is not possible or, as in the case of science-based sectors such as pharmaceuticals, not necessary, a degree of functional overlap with intensive information exchange is essential. A usefully illustrative example of the fourth-generation, or integrated, innovation process as practised in Nissan is given in Figure 9.4 (Graves, 1987).

Towards the fifth-generation innovation process

Today leading companies remain committed to some technological accumulation (technology strategy); strategic networking continues; speed to market (time-based strategy) remains of importance; firms are striving towards increasingly better integrated product and manufacturing strategies (design for manufacturability); greater flexibility and adaptability are being sought (organizational, manufacturing, product); and product strategies are more strongly emphasizing quality and performance features. In addition, growing concern over the degradation of the physical environment, which is resulting in intensifying regulatory activity, is once again placing regulatory issues firmly on the corporate strategy agenda (Rothwell, 1992a). At the same time that companies are attempting to implement this complex set of strategies, the world economy has faltered following the period of rapid growth around the mid-1980s, and levels of unemployment and business failure rates have grown apace, with many companies struggling hard to remain in profit.

Of the various dominant elements of corporate strategy already mentioned, perhaps the one that has attracted most attention during the late 1980s and the early 1990s is that of speed of development. Being a 'fast innovator' is seen increasingly as an important factor determining a company's competitiveness, especially in areas where rates of technological change are high and product cycles are short. Thus, during a period of increasing resource constraints, many companies are faced with the need to accelerate product development rates in an intensely competitive environment.

Being the first to market with a new product or new model that offers customers economic benefit carries with it certain obvious advantages such as greater market share, experience curve benefits, monopoly profits and increased customer satisfaction (Reiner, 1989). Being late to market, however, can carry significant penalties in terms of reduced market share and profitability, especially where product life is

short (Rudolph, 1989). Even in cases where being first is not of paramount importance, the ability to be 'fast' or 'timely' can be advantageous. *Certainly the ability
to control product development speed can be seen as an important core competence.*
Attempting significantly to increase development speed with no multiplication
of resources, might carry 'hidden' costs such as increased errors and an aversion
to attempting more radical innovation (Crawford, 1992). Several authors have
suggested that there is a time/cost trade-off such that as development times shorten,
development costs do in fact increase.

In considering the time/cost trade-off it is clear that a number of factors need to
be considered, among the most important of which are:

the direct benefits of being first (or fast) to market
the direct costs of accelerating product development
the indirect costs of accelerating product development
the influence of timeliness on customer satisfaction
the penalties accompanying lateness
the short-term versus the long-term perspective.

If a company is faced with trade-offs between being late, being sub-optimal in
production efficiency and spending more on R&D then, *ceteris paribus*, in terms of
reduction in profit over the product's life, the latter option generally is the least costly
while the first option is the most costly (Sommerlatte, 1990).

There exists evidence to suggest that a number of leading innovators today are
adopting a variety of practices that are now shifting them towards a third and even
more favourable cost/time curve, i.e. towards even faster development speed and
greater efficiency. These practices include internal organizational features, strong
inter-firm vertical linkages, external horizontal linkages and, more radically, the
use of a sophisticated electronic toolkit. The organization, practice, technology and
institutional scope of product development in leading innovators, taken together,
represent a shift towards the fifth-generation innovation process, a process of systems
integration and networking (SIN).

*The process is essentially a development of the parallel, integrated process in
which the technology of technological change is itself changing.*

Twenty-four factors have been identified as being involved in increasing
development speed and efficiency. Some of them impact mainly on speed, some on
efficiency, while others offer improvement along both dimensions. Many of these
factors are far from new and are well established in the literature on successful
industrial innovation (Rothwell, 1992b). They are:

1 *An explicit time-based strategy.* Given the scope of activities that needs to be
  addressed in order to accelerate product development appreciably, it is unlikely
  that significant gains could be achieved unless the issue was tackled on a broad
  front. This means that being a fast innovator must be at the forefront of corporate
  strategy.
2 *Top management commitment and support.* Visible top management commitment and support is a significant factor in determining successful innovation.

It is also important in achieving faster product development speed (McDonough and Barczac, 1991). Certainly the lack of senior management support is a major reason for product development delays and without this support speed is unlikely to become a feature of corporate culture (Gupta and Wileman, 1990). Moreover, top management should be involved in the development process from the very beginning since, where late involvement occurs, this often results in design changes that are highly costly (Sommerlatte, 1990).

3 *Adequate preparation: mobilizing commitment and resources.* This comprises what Ansoff (1992) terms building platforms for change. It involves careful project evaluation, analysis and planning and, centrally, gaining commitment, understanding and support from the corporate entity and from staff who will be involved in the project. Gaining consensus helps to prevent projects facing a 'resistance ladder' to change. In addition platform building involves adequate training and the acquisition of new skills where necessary.

4 *Efficiency at indirect development activities.* Activities such as project control, project administration and co-ordination can account for up to 50% of total project development time (Sommerlatte, 1990). Clearly, actions that render these activities more efficient have potential for significantly reducing development times and costs.

5 *Adopting a horizontal management style with increased decision making at lower levels.* The greater empowerment of managers at lower levels reduces the number of approvals required and the reduction in hierarchy reduces approval delays (Dumaine, 1989). These should contribute to enhancing the efficiency of indirect development activities, not least through reducing communication complexity and facilitating decision making.

6 *Committed and empowered product champions and project leaders.* Empowered product champions and project leaders (and *shusas* in Japan) (Graves, 1991) can play an important role in achieving both successful and faster new product development (Gupta and Wileman, 1990; Rothwell and Teubal, 1977). In projects with technical leaders, their possession of general business skills in addition to their technical capabilities is important to achieving greater development speed (McDonough and Spital, 1984). Development speed is also associated with a participative style of project leadership (McDonough and Barczac, 1991).

7 *High-quality initial product specification (fewer unexpected changes).* Not surprisingly, when the initial definition of product requirements is flawed, it results in unplanned changes during product development and can be a major factor in delay (Gupta and Wileman, 1990). It will also add significantly to development costs. High-quality up-front analysis including, centrally, a deep understanding of user requirements, is therefore essential in firms committed to speedier and more efficient product development.

8 *Use of integrated (cross-functional) teams during development and prototyping (concurrent engineering).* This is what Imai et al. (1985) refer to as the 'rugby' approach to product development. It is the core of innovation as a parallel process. Where parallel activities take place outside the framework of the fully integrated team, then continuous interfunctional interaction (information

integration) is essential throughout the periods of functional overlap (Clark and Fujimoto, 1991). The concurrent approach to product development is also known as simultaneous engineering. Especially at the design/manufacturing interface, the use of CAD systems can increase development speed and efficiency while at the same time ensuring optimum 'manufacturability'. Concurrent engineering ensures that most significant design changes occur during early development phases when the cost of modification is relatively low.

9   *Commitment to across-the-board quality control.* A company clearly can speed up product development if it is willing to cut corners in the process. In doing so, however, it is likely to incur high downstream costs and delays when it is faced with remedial design activity. Sometimes the results of skimped early-stage design activity show up only following commercial launch when direct modification costs are extremely high, as are indirect costs due to damaged reputation. According to Hewlett-Packard (1988), total quality control in product development is an essential feature in raising overall product development efficiency, including reduced cycle times.

10 *Incremental development strategy.* There is evidence to suggest that one reason Japanese manufacturers achieve relatively rapid product cycles is that they aim for smaller technological steps between successive models (Clark and Fujimoto, 1989). This 'small-step' strategy is aided by the fact that each model in the series is subjected to continuous improvement over its life cycle. Using this approach ensures that new technology is, in general, incorporated into products sooner to the greater satisfaction of customers. Over-emphasis on 'cheap and fast' incremental changes does, however, carry the danger that more radical changes with high long-term profit potential can be rejected or ignored (Crawford, 1992).

11 *Adopting a 'carry-over strategy'.* This refers to the utilization of significant elements of earlier models in the most recent designs. Examples are the use in the new Airbus A330 and A340 aircraft of existing wide-body fuselage cross-sections and the A310 tail fin, and the use in the top-of-the-range Toyota Lexus of a modified version of the floor pan of the well-established and successful Camry. This strategy can not only increase development speed and reduce development costs, but it can also reduce manufacturing start-up costs and afford more rapid manufacturing start-up.

12 *Product design combining the old with the new.* This relates to factor 1 but refers to the use of major elements of existing designs as the basis for creating new product types, rather than new models of existing types. A good example of this was the use by Black & Decker of existing drill components to help create their highly successful hot air (heat gun) paint stripper. The heat gun contained about two-thirds of its components in common with the drill, making it a marginal cost device to develop, manufacture, distribute and service. A complete redesign some two years later held very few components in common with the original design, but by then Black & Decker were market leaders with a highly profitable curve.

13 *Designed-in flexibility.* This refers to the creation of designs that contain inherent flexibility or technological slack such that they can be subsequently stretched

into a design family of significant variants. With those so-called 'robust designs' (they are robust with respect to changing customer requirements and market segmentation), the cost of the original design might be high, but the subsequent costs of creating new family members often over a period of many years, are relatively modest. A good example of a robust design is the Boeing 747. Robust designs enable companies to combine scale and experience economies in production (high commonality of parts) with economies of scope (wide product variety), while at the same time offering the customer enhanced choice of models and enhanced learning benefits in both use and servicing (Rothwell and Gardiner, 1988). The point is that the design family approach is essentially *strategic* in that the speed and efficiency gains accrue over the longer term.

14 *Economy in technology.* The economy in technology concept relates, in a sense, to the robust design principle. There are two aspects to this strategy: the first is the aim to apply a particular basic technological capability/understanding across the widest possible range of products (provided this does not jeopardize the overall competitiveness – inclusive cost competitiveness – of the products) (Ruffles, 1986); the second is to design core subassemblies that can be used across an extended range of products.

15 *Close linkages with primary suppliers.* Close and early linkages with suppliers can reduce development costs and increase development speed. This has long been a feature of product development in Japan, where suppliers can be a integral part of the development process and today it appears increasingly to be occurring in Europe and the United States with the emergence of true supplier/ manufacturer partnerships (Lamming, 1992; Maier, 1988; Rothwell, 1989). Supplier/manufacturer partnerships can also provide considerable advantages downstream from product development:

> Rather than simply demanding that their key suppliers cut costs overnight, as GM is now doing, Chrysler enlisted supplier support to make design and engineering changes that would add value and boost productivity. As a result, Chrysler's parts suppliers have turned in 3,900 suggestions that have saved the company an estimated $156 million in production costs.
>
> (McWhirter, 1992)

16 *Up-to-date component database.* Creating a comprehensive, up-to-date database on new component and materials characteristics and availability and the status of preferred suppliers, can facilitate design start-up and reduce the overall design cycle. It can also help ensure that new products contain the best available component/materials technology to the greater satisfaction of users.

17 *Involving leading-edge users in design and development activities.* Users who are technologically strong and innovation demanding can assist in increasing development speed and reducing development costs especially if, as in the case of partnering suppliers, they become actively involved in product development. Perhaps the most obvious example of this is when the user is also the inventor of the new product and had created a rough prototype for own use before transferring the design to the manufacturer. In this case, development times are shortened and development costs are effectively subsidized through

the user's initial and subsequent design and technological contributions (von Hippel, 1988; Shaw, 1986). Leading-edge users can also make a significant contribution to later developments along the product's design trajectory (Rothwell, 1986).

18 *Assessing external know-how.* Accessing external know-how has long been acknowledged as a significant factor in successful innovation. Gold (1987) argues that the use of external R&D can also speed up new product development, as can buying or licensing in existing technology. This latter contention is lent some support by Stalk and Hout (1990) who, commenting on the ability of Sun Microsystems to achieve very fast development cycles, state: 'Sun will use any off-the-shelf technology if the performance of its workstations can be enhanced. Each new Sun system is said to offer twice the performance of its predecessor for nearly the same price.' Mansfield (1988) found, across a range of industries, that both the time and the cost of product development for products that were based mainly on existing external technology were less than for those relying mainly on in-house development, and that the effects were particularly strong in Japan. McDonough and Barczac (1991), on the other hand, failed to find any relationship between project speed and the use of external technology. Accessing external know-how and licensing in external technology should reduce the cost of technological development in cases where the firm is seeking to incorporate technology outside its areas of core competence. In cases of technology fusion, external alliances should, on the face of it, help to reduce both the time and the cost of developing radical new products.

19 *Use of computers for efficient intra-firm communication and data sharing.* Not surprisingly, efficient information flows contribute to efficient product development. Increasingly, computer-based systems are being used to enhance intra-firm information efficiency:

> In an attempt to simplify information flow, Yoshiro Maruta (president, KAO Corporation, 1989) notes that in his company information is fed directly to those concerned through a computerised information network. Thus, long complex hierarchical communication paths are simplified.
> (Millson et al., 1992, p.58)

> During the second half of the 1980s, Black & Decker succeeded in increasing the number of new product productions while simultaneously reducing product lead times, a process in which computerised linkages played a key role. By reorganising the design staffs and developing a computer-aided design system that links the company worldwide, B&D has been able to halve its design cycle.
> (Stalk and Hout, 1990)

20 *Use of linked CAD systems along the production chain (supplier, manufacturer, users).* Not only are electronic (CAD) linkages important across the design/ manufacturing interface *within* firms, but they are also a powerful tool for closer integration *between* firms at the supplier/manufacturer and the manufacturer/ customer interfaces. For example, electronic manufacturer/ supplier design

linkages are becoming an increasingly common feature in the design of application-specific semiconductors (ASICs).

21 *Use of fast prototyping techniques.* One of the advantages of the use of information technology in product design is that the 3D-CAD images thus generated can, using a variety of techniques, be rapidly transferred into physical prototypes (Juster, 1992; Kruth, 1991). These can be of considerable value, not only for in-house test purposes, but also in gaining early-stage customer feedback. Fast prototyping can significantly reduce development time and cost.

22 *Use of simulation modelling in place of prototypes.* Replacing physical prototyping by simulation modelling can significantly enhance overall development efficiency. This approach is being utilized increasingly in industries as diverse as automobiles, pharmaceuticals, aeroengines, mould manufacturing and electronics. Hewlett-Packard's Loveland Instrument Division, for example, uses electronic product development (electronic design, simulation analysis, prototype testing), involving specially developed printed circuit board CAD tools, which has reduced PCB design cycle times from an average of 27 days in 1981 to nine days in 1987; and in pharmaceuticals the notion of 'designer drugs' owes much to the use of computer simulation techniques.

Simulation does not obviate the need for physical prototyping completely. Indeed, to omit this practice entirely would in most cases be too risky. Simulation does, however, reduce the number of required physical prototype builds considerably, as well as the time and resources required to reach the final physical prototyping stage of the development cycle.

23 *Creating technology demonstrators as an input to simulation.* In fields for which the various critical parameters and operating relationships are well understood, simulation modelling can be relatively straightforward (e.g. in circuit design). In other areas, however, basic data have to be generated as inputs to simulation models and this can have implications for the balance of expenditure between basic and more downstream technological activity. Rolls-Royce Aeroengines, who have increasingly used simulation techniques to enhance the efficiency of their product development activities, have been compelled to shift from the traditional 'make-it-and-break-it' approach to engine development (building and testing a series of physical prototypes, a costly and time-consuming process) to a more scientific approach, in which the percentage of R&D devoted to basic technological understanding has been increased (over a ten-year period from about 8% to about 25%) (Ruffles, 1986). The 'technology demonstrators' created through this shift to greater basic engineering activity were a crucial input to Rolls-Royce's new engine simulation models.

24 *Use of expert systems as a design aid.* The use of computer-based product design and simulation techniques enables innovators to embark on electronics-based heuristics. Several companies have taken this process further and have developed design-related expert systems. A Hewlett-Packard expert system, used in HP's electronic test equipment plant, analyses each new printed circuit design and improves manufacturability. This has, over a three-year period, reduced failure rates across 36 products by 84% and manufacturing time by 85%. In Japan, Canon have developed Optex, an expert system for TV camera

lens design which, in 1988, saved the company $700,000. As an example of its effectiveness, Optex reduced one design task from six person-months (four people working for one and a half months) to half a person month (one person working for two weeks) (Feigenbaum et al., 1988).

This list provides some indication of the nature and scope of the actions leading innovator companies are taking to enhance the speed, efficiency and flexibility of their product development activities. These include centrally integrated and parallel development processes, strong and early vertical linkages, devolved corporate structures and the use of electronics-based design and information systems. At the same time, as mentioned earlier, innovation has increasingly involved horizontal linkages such as collaborative pre-competitive research, joint R&D ventures and R&D-based strategic alliances, i.e. innovation is becoming more of a *networking process*. The factors listed will not apply equally to radical new product developments and developments along established design trajectories; neither will they apply equally across industry sectors or even to all firms within a sector. Taken together, however, these factors do define the main enabling features of the emerging innovation process, which is one of systems integration and networking (SIN). The characteristics, in terms both of underlying strategic elements and the primary enabling factors are:

1   *Underlying strategy elements*
   – Time-based strategy (faster, more efficient product development)
   – development focus on quality and other non-price factors
   – emphasis on corporate flexibility and responsiveness
   – customer focus at the forefront of strategy
   – strategic integration with primary suppliers
   – strategies for horizontal technological collaboration
   – electronic data-processing strategies
   – policy of total quality control.

2   *Primary enabling features*
   Greater overall organization and systems integration:
   – parallel and integrated (cross-functional) development process
   – early supplier involvement in product development
   – involvement of leading-edge users in product development
   – establishing horizontal technological collaboration where appropriate.

   Flatter, more flexible organizational structures for rapid and effective decision-making:
   – greater empowerment of managers at lower levels
   – empowered product champions/project leaders/*shusas*.

   Fully developed internal databases:
   – effective data-sharing systems
   – product development metrics, computer-based heuristics, expert systems
   – electronically assisted product development using 3D-CAD systems and simulation modelling

- linked CAD/CAE systems to enhance product development flexibility and product manufacturability.

Effective external data link:
- co-development with suppliers using linked CAD systems
- use of CAD at the customer interface
- effective data links with R&D collaborators.

The fifth generation process is essentially one of *lean innovation*.

Discussion

This chapter has discussed the evolution, during the post-World War II period, of changing perceptions – and to a large extent changing practice – of what constitutes the dominant model of best practice in the innovation process, from the simple series technology push model of the 1950s to the parallel and integrated model of the 1980s. The reality is more complex, in that even today all types of innovation process continue to exist in various forms. To some extent this diversity is a result of sectoral differences, i.e. innovation in certain consumer products has a strong market pull flavour, innovation in assembly industries is becoming more integrated and parallel in nature, while innovation in science-based industries such as pharmaceuticals leans more towards the 'science discovers, technology pushes' mode. However, even in areas like pharmaceuticals, few would argue for a pure technology push mode, and perhaps the coupling model with its feedback loops and market linkages, and with the addition of limited functional overlap, applies best. Certainly the many success/failure studies of innovation performance during the 1970s suggested that the coupling (3G) model more often led to success than did its linear predecessors. The use of electronic product design tools can be incorporated into any of the innovation models.

In the case of innovations involving the development of a major new technology, it would be unwise to opt initially for a fully parallel process. Such radical innovations are characterized by high technological uncertainty and a parallel process might not allow sufficient time for technological learning and the proper assessment of alternative technological pathways before major resources are committed.

Unforeseen technical problems could require costly changes across the entire innovation system. Thus, with radically new innovations, a 3G process with limited functional overlap is probably best although, as the project develops and technological uncertainty is reduced, the degree of overlap could be increased. Electronic development tools and data-sharing systems can, of course, be used in such radical developments since information-processing efficiency is important for all types of innovation, from the incremental to the radical. The point is, it is important that fundamental technological uncertainties are largely resolved before the innovation system engages in parallel development, i.e. with radical innovations adequate technology demonstrators are an essential prerequisite to 5G.

A third important point is that the balance between technology push and need pull as a *motivation* for innovation might vary considerably over the industry cycle.

In the new wave biotechnology industry, for example, which began very much in the technology push mode with basic discoveries in monoclonal antibodies and recombinant DNA at universities, increasingly greater influence has been imposed by the marketplace (need pull). The point is, it is often only as a basic technology develops and its application possibilities become evident that new uses and users emerge, at which stage the marketplace plays a greater role in directing the pace and direction of technological change. Further, as the field matures, the nature of technological change frequently shifts from the radical to the incremental. At all stages in the field's development, however, the process of matching technological capabilities to market needs remains central to success.

A fourth point is that in cases where there is convergence towards an industry-dominant design, the nature of innovatory activity can shift from an emphasis on product change to one of manufacturing process change (Abernathy and Utterback, 1978). In such cases firms can become introspective in their innovation selection criteria (manufacturing cost focus), rejecting, on the one hand, technological possibilities for radical product change and, on the other, failing to respond to significant market shifts. This progressive dominance of a single corporate function, in this case manufacturing, runs counter to the 'balance of functions' which is the hallmark of successful innovators and technically progressive firms. Essentially this internally directed technological change process is one in which the necessary internal and external linkages and interactions are lacking.

Returning to the 5G innovation process, its main characteristics are:

- Greater overall organizational and systems integration (including external networking).
- Flatter and more flexible organizational structures, including devolved decision making.
- Fully developed internal databases.
- Electronically assisted product development.
- Effective external electronic linkages.
  In short, the key aspects of the process are:
- Integration.
- Flexibility.
- Networking.
- Parallel (real-time) information processing.

Underlying all these features is the requirement for across-the-board quality control reflecting the importance of 'getting it right first time'. Many of the features of 5G are already in place in innovators that have mastered the 4G process: parallel and integrated operations, flatter structures, early and effective supplier linkages, involvement with leading customers and horizontal alliances. The most radical feature of 5G is the use of a powerful electronic toolkit to enhance the efficiency of these operations. While electronic measuring and computational devices and analytical equipment have for many years been important aspects of industrial innovation, *5G represents a more comprehensive process of the electronification of innovation across the whole innovation system.* Electronic development tools (and a more parallel development process) are becoming increasingly a feature of product development not only in manufacturing (hardware), but also in software (Quintas, 1993).

Many companies are already utilizing information and communication technology (ICT) to facilitate their innovatory and related activities. For example, companies with split R&D facilities have, during the 1980s, increasingly utilized electronic mail and video-conferencing as part of their day-to-day operations (Howells, 1992). In order to capture the full potential benefits of ICT, however, firms will need to develop the appropriate strategies and commit the necessary resources for equipment purchase and, perhaps more importantly, for adequate training programmes and this especially will be the case for multinationals operating global strategies. (In the case of multinationals operating across a variety of languages, perhaps a major advantage of linked compatible CAD systems is that they can communicate using a common technical/visual language.)

Some companies are already well along the pathway towards adopting and mastering the 5G electronic toolkit and towards developing the appropriate strategies:

- Hewlett-Packard makes considerable and growing use of electronic product development techniques and CAD/CAE, including inter-plant linkages (e.g. computer data storage products are designed in Bristol, UK and the design data are sent directly on-line to the manufacturing plant at Boeblingen, Germany).
- Ford of Europe has installed a 'worldwide engineering release system' which links between plants and shares design and manufacturing information. The company has integrated its telecoms strategy with its business strategy and has given considerable attention to the implementation of interactive remove CAD/CAM applications (Mansell and Morgan, 1991).
- Boeing designed its new 777 aircraft on a 500-workstation, two mainframe computer network using a sophisticated 3D-CAD program. This simplified aircraft design cut development costs and greatly facilitated ongoing design changes and customer design inputs (Abrahams, 1990).

Industrial innovation can be depicted as a process of know-how accumulation, or learning process, involving elements of internal and external learning (Figure 9.5). Electronic product development tools can themselves become a powerful factor in company learning. Mastering the 5G process will itself involve considerable learning, including organizational learning and this will be far from costless in terms of time and of equipment and training expenditures. The potential long-term benefits, however, are very considerable. Essentially the main benefits of 5G derive from the efficient and real-time handling of information across the whole system of innovation, including internal functions, suppliers, customers and collaborators, i.e. 5G is a process of parallel information processing, one in which electronic information processing and the more traditional informal face-to-face human contact operate in a complementary manner. The formalized information contained within electronics-based systems complements the tacit knowledge embodied in the individuals involved in innovation, while computer-based heuristics (expert systems) might succeed in capturing some of this tacit knowledge.

Internal learning

• R, D and D – learning by developing
• Learning by testing
• Learning by making – production learning
• Learning by failing
• Learning by using in vertically integrated companies
• Cross-project learning

External or joint internal/external learning

• Learning from/with suppliers
• Learning from/with lead users
• Learning through horizontal partnerships
• Learning from/with the S&T infrastructure
• Learning from the literature
• Learning from competitors' actions
• Learning through reverse engineering
• Learning from acquisitions or new personnel
• Learning through customer-based prototype trials
• Learning through servicing/fault finding

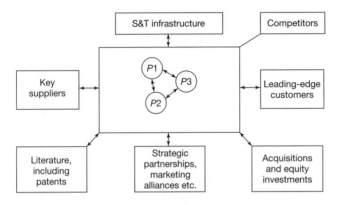

Figure 9.5 Innovation as a process of know-how accumulation

In general electronic systems will act to enhance the efficiency with which tacit know-how is deployed.

A significant factor in Japanese competitive success is the quality of informal information exchange during product development, including interchanges at the supplier interface, leading to fast, efficient and flexible development (and manufacturing) processes. This factor, it might be expected, would lead to greatest advantage in the case of complex assembly-type products and with systems integrators (e.g. automobiles, machinery, electrical equipment, aerospace) rather than in the science-based and process-based sectors (e.g. pharmaceuticals, chemicals). In the former sectors, innovation is more system based (many actors, great diversity of components and subassemblies) while in the latter it is internalized to a greater extent, with less input variety (Pavitt and Patel, 1992). It is significant in this respect that Mansfield (1988) found Japanese time and cost advantages over US competitors to be more significant in machinery (including computers), instruments and electrical equipment than in chemicals (including pharmaceuticals).

It is tempting to speculate that in assembly-type industries the 5G process, properly deployed, might, given the process's inherent information processing efficiency, help to redress the product development (and manufacturing) speed and efficiency advantages enjoyed by Japanese manufacturers.

References

Abernathy, W. I. and Utterback, J. M. (1978) 'Patterns of industrial innovation', *Technology Review*, vol. 80, no.7, June–July.

Abrahams, P. (1990), 'The fledgling learns to fly', *Financial Times*, 18 October, p. 18.

Ansoff, H. I. (1992), 'Managing discontinuous strategic change', in H. I. Ansoff, A. Biseman and P. M. Storm (eds), *Understanding and Managing Strategic Change*, North Holland Publishing Company, Amsterdam.

Arnold, E. and Guy, K. (1986) *Parallel Convergency: National Strategies in Information Technology*, Frances Pinter, London.

Bessant, J. (1991) *Managing Advanced Manufacturing Technology*, NCC Blackwell, Oxford.

Carter, C. and Williams, B. (1957) *Industry and Technical Progress*, Oxford University Press, London.

Clark, J. (1979) 'A model of embodied technical change and employment', mimeo. Science Policy Research Unit, Sussex University, Falmer Press, Sussex.

Clark, K. B and Fujimoto, T. (1989) 'Lead time in automobile product development: exploring the Japanese advantage', *Journal of Engineering and Technology Management*, vol. 6, pp. 25–58.

Clark, K. B. and Fujimoto, T. (1991) *Product Development Performance*, Harvard Business School Press, Boston, MA.

Contractor, F. J. and Lorgange, P. (1988) *Cooperative Strategies in International Business*, Lexington Books, Lexington, MA.

Cook, L. G. and Morrison, W. A. (1961) *The Origins of Innovation*, Report No. 61-GP-214. June. General Electric Company, Research Information Section, New York, NY.

Cooper, T. G. (1980) 'Project new prod: factors in new product success', *European Journal Marketing*, vol. 14, no. 5/6.

Crawford, C.M. (1992) 'The hidden costs of accelerated product development', *Journal of Product Innovation Management*, vol. 9, pp. 188–99.

Docter, J. and Stokman, C. (1987) 'Innovation strategies of small industrial firms', in R. Rothwell and J. Bessant (eds) *Innovation: Adaptation and Growth*, Elsevier, Amsterdam.

Dodgson, M. (1993) *Technological Collaboration in Industry*, Routledge, London.

Dumaine, B. (1989) 'How managers can succeed through speed', *Fortune*, 13 February.

Feigenbaum, E., McCorduck, P. and Nii, H. P. (1988) *The Rise of the Expert Company*, Macmillan, London.

Freeman, C., Clark, J. and Scete, L. (1992) *Unemployment and Technical Innovation*, Frances Pinter, London.

Gold, B. (1987) 'Approaches to accelerating new product development', *Journal of Product Innovation Management*, vol. 4, pp. 81–88.

Graves, A. (1987) 'Comparative trends in automotive research and development', DRC Discussion Paper No. 54, Science Policy Research Unit, Sussex University, Brighton, Sussex.

Graves, A. (1991) *International Competitiveness and Technology Development in the World Automobile Industry*, D. Phil. thesis, Science Policy Research Unit, Sussex University, Brighton.

Graves, S. B. (1989) 'Why costs increase when projects accelerate', *Research Technology Management*, March–April, pp. 16–18.

Gupta, A. S. K. and Wileman, D. L. (1990) 'Accelerating the development of technology-based new firms', *California Management Review*, vol. 32, no. 2, Winter, pp. 24–44.

Hagedoorn, J. (1990), 'Organizational needs of inter-firm co-operation and technology transfer', *Technovation*, vol. 10, no. 1, pp. 17–30.

Hasklisch, C. S., Fusfeld, H. I. and Levinson, A. D. (1986) *Trends in Collective Industrial Research*, Centre for Science and Technology Policy, Graduate School of Business Administration, New York University, New York, NY.

Hayes, R. and Abernathy, W. J. (1980) 'Managing our way to economic decline', *Harvard Business Review*, July–August.

Hayvaert, C.H. (1973) *Innovation Research and Product Policy: Clinical Research in 12 Belgian Industrial Enterprises*, Catholic University of Louvain, Belgium.

Herbert, R. and Hoar, R. W. (1982) *Government and Innovation: Experimenting with Change*, Final Report ETIP, National Bureau of Standards, Washington DC, NBS-GCR-ETIP-82-10.

Hewlett-Packard (1988) *Hewlett Packard and Engineering Productivity*, Design Center, Hewlett Packard, Palo Alto, CA.

Hewlett-Packard Company (1989) *The Promise and Measure of CAD*, Co. Graphics Symposium, Milano, Italy.

von Hippel, E. (1988) *The Sources of Innovation*, Oxford University Press, Oxford.

Hood, N. and Vahlne, J. E. (1988) *Strategies in Global Competition*, Croom Helm, London.

Howells, J. (1992) Going global: the use of ICT networks in R&D', Working Paper No. 6, Programme for Information and Communication Technologies, University of Newcastle, Newcastle-upon-Tyne, April.

Imai, K., Nonaka, I. and Fakeuchi, H. (1985) 'Managing the new product development', in K. Clark and F. Hayes (eds) *The Uneasy Alliance*, Harvard Business School Press, Boston, MA.

Juster, N. P. (1992) 'A summary of rapid prototyping processes', *Computer-Aided Rapid Prototyping*, Department of Mechanical Engineering, Leeds University, Leeds.

Kodama, P. (1985), 'Japanese innovation in mechatronics technology', *Science and Public Policy*, vol. 13, nò. 1, February, pp. 44–51.

Kruth, J. P. (1991), 'Material increase manufacturing by rapid prototyping techniques', *Annals of the CIRP (Collège International pour l' Étude Scientifique des Techniques de Production Mechanique)*, vol. 40, no. 2, pp. 603–614.

Lamming, R. (1992) *Supplier Strategies in the Automotive Components Industry: Development towards Lean Production*, D. Phil. thesis. Science Policy Research Unit, University of Sussex, Brighton.

Langrish, J., Gibbons. M., Evans. W. G. and Jevons, F. R. (1972) *Wealth from Knowledge*, Macmillan, London.

Maier, H. (1988) 'Partnerships between small and large firms: current trends and prospects', Conference on Partnerships between Small and Large Firms, EC, Brussels, 13–14 June.

Mansell, R. and Morgan, K. (1991) *Communicating across Boundaries: The Winding Road to Broadband Networking*, vol. 7, Perspectives on Advanced Communications for Europe, EC, Brussels.

Mansfield, E. (1988) 'The speed and cost of industrial innovation in Japan and the United States: external vs. internal technology', *Management Science*, vol. 34, no. 19, pp. 1157–1168.

McDonough, E. F. and Barczac, G. (1991) 'Speeding up new product development: the effects of leadership style and source of technology', *Journal of Product Innovation Management*, vol. 8, pp. 203–211.

McDonough, E. F and Spital, F. C (1984) 'Quick-response new product development', *Harvard Business Review*, vol. 62, pp. 52–53.

McWhirter, W. (1992) 'Chrysler's second amazing comeback', *Time*, November, p. 50.

Mensch, G., Kaash, K. Kleinknecht. A. and Schnapps, R. (1980) *Innovation Trends and Switching between Full- and Under-Employment Equilibrium*, 1950–1978, International Institute of Management, Discussion Paper Series, Berlin, January.

Millson, M. R., Raj, S. P. and Wileman, D. (1992) 'A survey of major approaches for accelerating new product development', *Journal of Product Innovation Management*, vol. 9, pp. 53–69.

Mowery, D. C. and Rosenberg, N. (1978) 'The influence of market demand upon innovation: a critical review of some recent empirical studies', *Research Policy*, vol. 8.

Myers, S. and Marquis, D. G. (1969) *Successful Industrial Innovation*, National Science Foundation, Washington DC.

Nelson, R. (1993) private communication, National Bureau of Economic Research Inc. April, Stanford, CA.

Pavitt, K. and Patel, P. (1992) 'Contemporary patterns of technological change', mimeo, Science Policy Research Unit, Sussex University, Brighton.

Peters, T. J. and Waterman, R. W. (1982) *In Search of Excellence*, Harper and Row, New York, NY.

Quintas, P. (1993) 'A product-process model of innovation in software development', CICT Centre mimeo, Science Policy Research Unit, Sussex University, Brighton.

Reiner, G. (1989) 'Winning the race for new product development', *Management Review*, vol. 78, no. 8, pp. 52–53.

Roessner, D. (1979) 'The local government market as a stimulus to industrial innovation', *Research Policy*, vol. 8, pp. 340–362.

Rothwell, R. (1976) *Innovation in Textile Machinery: Some Significant Factors in Success and Failure*, Science Policy Research Unit, Occasional Paper Series No. 2, June.

Rothwell, R. (1984) 'Technology-based small firms and regional innovation potential: the role of public procurement', *Journal of Public Policy*, vol. 4, no. 4, pp. 307–332.

Rothwell, R. (1986) 'Innovation and re-innovation: a role for the user', *Journal of Marketing Management*, vol. 2, no. 2, pp. 109–123.

Rothwell, R. (1989) 'SMEs, inter-firm relationships and technological change', *Entrepreneurship and Regional Development*, vol. 1, pp. 275–291.

Rothwell, R. (1991) 'External networking and innovation in small and medium-sized manufacturing firms in Europe', *Technovation*, vol. 11, no. 2, pp. 93–112.

Rothwell, R. (1992a) 'Industrial innovation and environmental regulation: some lessons from the past', *Technovation*, vol. 12, no. 7, pp. 447–458.

Rothwell, R. (1992b) 'Successful industrial innovation: critical factors for the 1990s', *R&D Management*, vol. 22, no. 3, pp. 221–238.

Rothwell, R. and Dodgson, M. (1992) 'European technology policy evolution: convergence towards SMEs and regional technology transfer', *Technovation*, vol. 12, no. 4, pp. 223–238.

Rothwell, R. and Gardiner, P. (1988) 'The strategic management of re-innovation', *R&D Management*, vol. 18, no. 2, April, pp. 147–160.

Rothwell, R. and Soete, L. (1983) 'Technology and economic change', *Physics in Technology*, vol. 14, no. 6, November, pp. 270–277.

Rothwell, R. and Teubal, M. (1977) 'SAPPHO revisited: a re-appraisal of the SAPPHO Data', in K. A. Stroetman (ed.) *Innovation, Economic Change and Technology Policies*, Birkhauser, Basel and Stuttgart.

Rothwell, R. and Zegveld, W. (1985) *Reindustrialization and Technology*, Longman, Harlow.

Rothwell, R., Freeman, C., Horsley, A., Jervis, V. T. P., Robertson, A. B. and Townsend, J. (1974) 'SAPPHO updated: Project SAPPHO Phase II', *Research Policy*, vol. 3, no. 3, pp. 258–291.

Rubenstein, A. H., Chakrabarti, A. K., O'Keefe, R. D., Sonder, W. E. and Young, H. C. (1976) 'Factors influencing success at the project level', *Research Management*, vol. XIX, no. 3, pp. 15–20.

Rudolph, S. E. (1989) *What Smart Companies are Doing in New Product Development*, Centre for Product Development, Arthur D. Little, Cambridge, MA.

Ruffles, P. C. (1986) 'Reducing the cost of aero engine design', *Aerospace*, vol. 13 no. 9, pp. 10–19.

Schock, G. (1974) *Innovation Processes in Dutch Industry*, TNO, Policy Studies and Information Group, Appeldoorn.

Shaw, B. (1986) *The Role of the Interaction between the Manufacturer and the User in the Medical Instrument Manufacturing Process*, D.Phil. thesis, Science Policy Research Unit, Sussex University, Brighton.

Sommerlatte, T. (1990) 'Raising technology development productivity', *Enterprise, Innovation and 1992*, TII, Luxembourg.

Stalk, G. and Hout, T. M. (1990) 'Competing against time', *Research Technology Management*, March–April, pp. 19–24.

Szakasitz, G. D (1974) 'The adoption of the SAPPHO method in the Hungarian electronics industry', *Research Policy*, vol. 3.

Utterback, J. M. (1975) *The Process of Innovation in Five Industries in Europe and Japan*, Centre for Policy Alternatives, MIT Press, Cambridge, MA.

10 Why the Last Shall be First and the First Shall Fade Away

John Kay

History teaches that innovative companies are rarely the most successful. Imitators use distribution and marketing to catch up.

Have you heard of Berkey or Ampex? Gablinger or Chux? Perhaps you should have, because each occupies an important place in the history of product innovation. Berkey produced the first handheld electronic calculators, Ampex the first video recorders. Gablinger developed low-alcohol lager and Chux sold the first disposable nappies.

Or perhaps you should not, because none of these companies made a commercial success of their innovations. Today the calculators we use are probably made by Casio, our video recorder comes from Matsushita; our low-alcohol beer is Miller Lite, our nappies are made by Procter & Gamble. In each of these markets the innovator was swept away.

As the future of EMI hangs in the balance, it is a good moment to recall that this company has one of the most remarkable records of innovation of any in the world. EMI was a pioneer in television and computing and its CAT scanner transformed radiography. It has not made any of these products for many years. Our televisions come from Sony, our computers from International Business Machines or Dell and GE is market leader in scanners.

Xerox looks like an exception to this sorry catalogue. The company was first into the photocopier market and, even if its dominance was ultimately challenged by Canon, it remains a large and successful company today. But Xerox was also a pioneer in fax machines and personal computers. Each of these eventually proved to be a success – but not for Xerox Corporation.

As we all know, it was Apple that developed the personal computer market. But Apple's leadership quickly disappeared when IBM came on the scene. Apple then jumped ahead by introducing the graphical user interface. Its windows and mice brought personal computing within the reach of everyone. But it is Microsoft that does this now.

The business world is not kind to pioneers. Contrast EMI's experience with that of Britain's most successful company of the past two decades – Glaxo Wellcome. Each had, in the 1970s, a product that would ultimately take the US healthcare market by storm. Both the CAT scanner and anti-ulcerants were to win Nobel Prizes for the British scientists who invented them.

But there the similarities end. EMI was proud to employ Geoffrey Houndsfield, who invented the scanner. It established a US distribution network and manufacturing facility to exploit his innovation – and was quickly crushed by the superior political, marketing and technical skills of GE.

James Black, who developed anti-ulcerants, did not work for Glaxo, but for SmithKline. Glaxo's Zantac was an imitative product, second to market. US distribution was initially contracted out to Hoffman La Roche, the only foreign-owned drug company previously to have enjoyed success in US distribution. The superior marketing skills of Glaxo and its partners enabled Zantac to overtake SmithKline's Tagamet and become the world's best-selling drug. Glaxo's achievement was based not on the speed or quality of its innovation but on its commercial skills in exploiting it.

What is true of technical innovation is also true of innovation in business process. Direct Line is inevitably losing market share to Johnny-come-lately established insurers. American Express may have pioneered plastic money, but it was to be Citibank, Bank of America and even Sears Roebuck that were to capture the market with Mastercard, Visa and Discover.

Next and Ratners identified unexploited market niches – fashionable clothing for older women and jewellery cheaper than you imagined buying – only to find that established retailers could do the same job at least as well.

And what we see as a first mover advantage is often only that because we now think of the successful innovator as the first mover. Many spreadsheet programs were developed in the 1980s and Lotus succeeded not because it was the first or best but because it was the product available at the moment the market was ready to take off. Even if you know how a market will develop, timing is a matter of luck – or of quite exceptional skill.

There are two closely related lessons. One is that being first is not often very important. The other is that innovation is rarely a source of competitive advantage on its own. Individuals and small companies can make a great deal of money out of good new ideas. The success of large established corporations – Matsushita, Philip Morris, IBM or General Electric – is generally based on other things: their distribution capability, their depth of technical expertise, their marketing skills. And time and again these characteristics enable them to develop the innovative concept far more effectively than the innovators themselves.

This is not to say that there is no role in business for the great innovator. After all, General Electric was built on the extraordinary fecundity of Thomas Edison's mind, the Ford motor company on the abilities of its eponymous founder. The imagination of Walt Disney created a company that is still without parallel or rival. Perhaps Akio Morita of Sony occupies a similar place in the annuals of modern business.

However, while many chief executives may see themselves as Edisons, or Fords, Disneys or Moritas, few actually are. Genius is indeed a source of competitive advantage, but necessarily a rare one. So when you are told that the key to future business success is to see the future more quickly or more clearly than other people, ask which cases in business history illustrate the point. And try to remember Berkey and Ampex, Gablinger and Chux.

11   From Lean Production to Lean Enterprise

James P. Womack and Daniel T. Jones

It's useful to look anew at the three pre-eminent industrial traditions: the German, the American and the Japanese. Each has derived different strengths by trying to satisfy the needs of either the function, the individual or the company. The conventional wisdom has been that the three traditions, whose shortcomings are the product of these unavoidable trade-offs, are mutually exclusive. We disagree. In the course of our extensive research on German, US and Japanese companies, it has occurred to us that there is a fourth approach. We believe that our model of the lean enterprise will satisfy the needs of the individuals, functions *and* companies. The end result will offer greater value to the customer than the existing traditions can.

The German tradition

The backbone of German industry has been its intense focus on deep technical knowledge organized into rigidly defined functions. Individuals progress in their careers by climbing the functional ladder. And companies strive to defend their positions in a value chain by hoarding proprietary knowledge within their technical functions.

The consequence of this focus has been great technical depth and an ability to compete globally by offering customized products with superior performance. The weakness of the German tradition, strikingly apparent in the 1990s, is its hostility to cross-functional cooperation. Mercedes-Benz, for example, requires three times the number of hours Toyota requires to engineer and manufacture a comparable luxury car, largely because the engineering functions won't talk to each other. Mercedes makes durable, high-performance cars, but with too many labour-intensive loops in the development process and too little attention to manufacturability. The same holds true for almost all German industries, which have discovered that the world will no longer buy enough customized goods at the high prices required to support the system's inherent inefficiency.

The American tradition

The individual has always been at the centre of US society. At the beginning of this [20th] century, the lack of strong functional and craft traditions and the willingness of suppliers to collaborate with assemblers were major advantages in introducing continuous flow and mass production.

But extreme individualism created its own needs. In the post-war era, managers sought portable professional credentials (e.g. an MBA) and generic expertise independent of a particular business (e.g. finance). And rather than stressing cooperation, each company in a value chain, itself acting as a individual, sought to create its own defendable turf.

The consequence was that US industry gradually became as functional as German industry, but self-preservation, rather than a desire for technical knowledge, drove functionalism in the United States. At the same time, the 'every company for itself' tendency most evident in hard times greatly reduced the ability of US companies to think together about the entire value stream. Even though the willingness of Americans to innovate by breaking away from employers and traditional intercompany relationships imparts a real advantage today in nascent industries like information processing and biotechnology, this extreme individualism has caused the United States to lose its lead in efficient production.

The Japanese tradition

The Japanese have stressed the needs of the company, which is hardly surprising given the centuries-old feudal tradition of obligation between companies and employees and between big companies and their smaller suppliers and distributors. Government policy, with its focus on production rather than individual consumption, has reinforced this emphasis. The enormous benefit of the Japanese tradition has been the ability of big companies to focus on the needs of the entire value stream unimpeded by functional fiefdoms, career paths within functions and the constant struggles between members of the value stream to gain an advantage over each other.

But such an exclusive focus on the company produces corresponding weaknesses, which have become apparent over time. For example, the technical functions are weak in most Japanese companies despite the overwhelming dominance of engineers in management. Because most engineers have spent practically all their careers on cross-functional teams developing products or improving production processes, they have got better and better at applying what they already know. But the creation of new knowledge back in the technical functions has languished. As a result, many Japanese companies (from Toyota in cars to Matsushita in consumer electronics) that prospered by commercializing and incrementally improving well-understood product and process technologies have now largely cleared the shelf of available ideas for generating fundamentally new, innovative products and processes.

Sony is a case in point. The company recently acknowledged that, for the first time in its history, no dramatic product breakthroughs were imminent and that it would try to defend its competitive position by adopting lean techniques to cut costs in its increasingly mature product lines. We applaud, of course, whenever a company adopts lean techniques. However, these should complement rather than substitute for innovation. Sony must address the weakness of its core technical functions in addition to becoming lean.

Another weakness inherent in the Japanese system is that preserving feudal relationships has become more important than responding to shifts in the market. During the last five years, Japanese companies with massive export surpluses should have redeployed production so that their output in a given region corresponded more closely to sales in the region. Instead, constraints on reassigning employees to new enterprises and abandoning traditional second- and third-tier suppliers caused many big companies to invest in additional domestic capacity for making the same families of products. This is why so many companies, including the model company Toyota, found themselves in deep trouble when the yen strengthened.

New models for careers, functions and the company

The critical challenge for managers today is to synchronize the needs of the individual, the function, the company and the value stream in a way that will yield the full benefits of the lean enterprise while actually increasing individual opportunities, functional strength and the well-being of member companies. Achieving this balance will require new management techniques, organizational forms and principles of shared endeavour.

Alternating career paths

If we have learned anything in recent years about the value stream, it is that individuals must be totally dedicated to a specific process for the value stream to flow smoothly and efficiently. The old division of labour, which shuttled the product from department to department, must give way to a recombination of labour so that fewer workers, organized in focused teams, can expedite the value flow without bottlenecks or queues. Similarly, functional specialists involved in product development must completely focus on their task in a team context.

But there is a problem. The individual facing permanent assignment to a cross-functional team is being asked to abandon his or her functional career path. At the same time, key functions face the loss of power and importance. When both individuals and functions feel threatened by streamlined processes, these processes won't be streamlined for very long.

The solution is a career path that alternates between concentration on a specific value stream (a family of products) and dedicated, intense knowledge building within functions. These functions must include a new process management function (in place of industrial engineering and quality assurance) that instils a process perspective in everyone from the top to the bottom of the company.

In following this new career path, the individual's know-how will still be growing. But the value stream itself will get his or her undivided attention for extended periods. Making this model work will be the primary task of the human resource function, which is responsible for ensuring that each individual has a coherent career – a key to attracting and retaining employees.

The concept of an alternating career path has nothing to do with matrix organizations, in which everyone has two bosses. In this new model, the process leader rates an individual's performance while an individual is dedicated to a process, but the function head rates performance while the individual is back in the function. The career planner in human resources, the function head, and the process leader decide jointly where the individual should go next.

Honda has embraced this approach in Japan and North America, particularly for engineers. When engineers join Honda, they go through a rotation, common in Japanese companies, that begins with several months on a production line, followed by short stints in marketing and sales. Honda's practice then diverges from the Japanese norm of assigning engineers to and keeping them in process teams. At Honda, the young engineer's first extended assignment is on a product development team, where he or she performs routine engineering calculations. This assignment continues for the life of the development activity, or up to three years.

After this job, the young engineer is assigned to his or her technical speciality within the engineering department to begin a skills-upgrading process. As part of this phase, the individual is assigned to an advanced engineering effort involving a search for new techniques or capabilities that the company wants to master. The engineer is then typically reassigned to a development team for a new product to perform more complex engineering tasks that call on his or her newly acquired knowledge. After this development effort, the engineer goes back to the 'home' engineering function to begin another learn-apply-learn cycle.

Functions become schools

The problem with functions in most companies today is that they perform the wrong tasks. Purchasing should not purchase. Engineering should not engineer. Production should not produce. In the lean enterprise, functions have two major roles. The first is to serve as a school. They should systematically summarize current knowledge, search for new knowledge and teach all this to their members, who then spend time on value-creating process teams. (See Boxes 11.1 and 11.2.)

Box 11.1 Unipart: turning functions into schools

Britain's Unipart Group has gone further than most companies in turning its functions into schools as part of the company's effort to become lean. Unipart was created in 1987, when Rover sold a collection of disparate, highly autonomous functions to employees. Unipart then turned these functions into independent divisions, which included auto-parts manufacturing; warehousing, distribution, marketing and sales of Unipart's and others' auto components; information systems; and video production.

John Neill, Unipart's CEO, pushed each Unipart business to become lean on its own. But auto-parts manufacturing was clearly the most successful. Its plants that make fuel tanks and exhaust systems for cars, which learned lean techniques from Honda's and Toyota's British plants, won the UK Factory of the Year Award in 1989 and 1993.

When Neill decided that the auto-parts manufacturing business should teach the other businesses its secrets, he quickly realized that given their history of operating autonomously, this was much easier said than done. He also realized that if things did not change, Unipart would fail to leverage the knowledge of a practice leader, and, because the businesses were interdependent to a certain extent, the laggards would prevent the whole company from becoming as lean as possible.

To tackle these problems, Neill created 'Unipart University'. He made each business responsible for finding the best practice in its field, customizing it for Unipart and then teaching it to the other businesses and their partners. In other words, each Unipart business, complete with its own 'faculty' is a centre of expertise. 'Through this forum we share the best available learning with our colleagues,' Neill says.

The Information Technology Faculty, which resides in the information-systems company, for example, is responsible for upgrading IT skills throughout Unipart. And the Industries Faculty, which resides in the manufacturing company, is playing the lead role in teaching its suppliers as well as the warehouse operation the process management techniques it gleaned from Honda and Toyota. In the case of the warehouse operation, this entails teaching it how to work with its major suppliers so that together they can fill orders on time, which will enable the warehouse operation to cut its inventories.

The 'deans' of the faculties, most of whom are the heads of the businesses, sit on the Deans Group, which steers the university, ensures that problems are discussed company wide and initiates research on ways to solve them. The Deans Group recently charged two faculties with a critical task: researching how to select and develop leaders of self-managed, shop floor teams. As part of that effort, the group from the industries and warehousing faculties visited Japan and the United States as well as Honda's and Toyota's British operations.

'Our vision,' Neill says, 'is to build the world's best lean enterprise. That means continuously integrating training, or should I say learning, into the decision-making systems of the company.'

Box 11.2 Lucas: undermined from without and within

By implementing lean techniques, Lucas plc, a British supplier of mechanical and electrical components to the automotive and aerospace industries, made great strides in improving product quality and on-time deliveries. But after about seven years, progress ground to a halt in some operations because key customers had not similarly adopted lean thinking. And other operations began to backslide as Lucas plant managers and functional departments resisted changes that they saw as threats to their power.

Lucas was one of the first British companies to adopt lean techniques when it recruited University of Birmingham Professor John Parnaby in 1983 to head a new process improvement function. Parnaby quickly introduced the concepts of the Toyota Production System throughout Lucas, with extremely promising initial results. For example, a Lucas aerospace component plant halved its lead times and work-in-progress inventories and a truck component plant doubled its inventory turns and boosted the portion of orders delivered on time from 25% to 98%. Thanks to such improvements, Lucas began to overcome its reputation among customers as the 'Prince of Darkness'.

But problems soon emerged. An electrical component factory that had embraced lean techniques, for example, found itself backsliding because big customers like Rover and Ford had not yet made their operations lean. As a result, these customers continued to place orders in an unpredictable fashion. To cope, the factory had to maintain relatively high inventories, a cardinal sin in lean production. True to form, workers began to rely on the inventories as a safety net and the lean factory began to gain weight.

Within Lucas, the new process improvement function was soon locked in a struggle with the traditional, vertical functions – marketing, product development, engineering and production – over the former's efforts to improve efficiency. One plant installed a production line to manufacture a mechanical system in a continuous flow. But ignoring Parnaby's protests, the engineering function bought and installed some expensive, inflexible machines which, as is typical of such equipment, were difficult to switch from making one type of component to making another. As a result, the plant had to revert to batch production and inventories and inefficiencies quickly increased.

Internal conflict at Lucas was also evident at a plant for making truck components when the product design function refused the advice of the process management function. The latter developed a component that promised to be superior to competitors' offerings, but it turned out that the component couldn't be manufactured to the tolerances required. If a cross-functional design team including process management and production engineering had overseen the project, this folly could have been avoided.

Discouraged by all the battles within and without, Parnaby scaled back his efforts to institute lean thinking at Lucas. Hard hit by slumps in its key markets in the 1990s, Lucas has seen its profits wither, has suffered from management turmoil and has dramatically shrunk its product offerings and slashed its payrolls. The company has also been a rumoured takeover target. The person who must contend with these problems is George Simpson, who was to assume the helm of Lucas. As the chairman of Rover, the British automaker, Simpson has used lean production to improve Rover's competitiveness dramatically. He will undoubtedly try to force Lucas to carry on the lean revolution it began over a decade ago.

The second role of functions is to develop guidelines – the best practices – for, say, purchasing or marketing and to draw up a roster of those companies eligible to be long-term partners in the value stream (suppliers, in the case of the purchasing department). With their counterparts in companies up and down the value stream, functions should also develop rules for governing how they will work together to solve problems that span the companies and for establishing behavioural codes so that one company does not exploit another.

So who actually performs the tasks that these functions traditionally handled? Cross-functional product development and production teams should select suppliers, develop products and oversee routine production activities. The traditional purchasing department, for example, should define the principles of enduring relationships with suppliers, draw up the roster of eligible suppliers and strive to improve continuously the performance of every supplier. The product development team should perform the purchasing department's traditional job of deciding to obtain a specific amount of a specific item at a target price from a specific supplier for the life of the product.

The experience of Nissan's British subsidiary provides a striking example of what can happen when a purchasing department rethinks its mission. Nissan had serious problems during the 1989 production launch of the Primera, its first car designed for the European market, when several suppliers disrupted production by failing to deliver workable parts in time. The normal course of action in Britain would have been to replace the miscreants. Instead, Nissan's British purchasing department teamed up with the Nissan R&D centre to place supplier development teams of Nissan engineers inside each supplier for extended periods to improve their key processes. Nissan's theory was that setting high standards and giving the suppliers advice on how to meet them would produce superior results. Two years later, when Nissan began production of the Micra, a new small car, this approach had transformed these suppliers from the Nissan subsidiary's worst into its best.

What is the role of other functions? Marketing defines principles of enduring relationships with customers and/or distributors and identifies suitable partners. The traditional marketing and sales tasks of specifying the product, taking orders and scheduling delivery become the work of the product development and production teams. Engineering defines the best engineering practices, which it teaches to engineers. It also searches for new capabilities, such as new materials to reduce weight in its products. By undertaking such jobs, the engineering function extends the expertise of the discipline by finding ways to overcome the shortcomings of today's products and processes. It can then apply its new knowledge to the next generation of products or to entirely new products. The product development team performs all routine engineering; it solves problems that have been solved before for similar products.

Finally, a new process management function (which still does not exist in the vast majority of companies) does three things: it defines the rules for managing cross-functional teams and the continuous flow of production, including quality assurance; it teaches team leaders in product development and production how to apply these rules; and it constantly searches for better approaches. The old departmental structures within production – moulding, painting, assembly, quality assurance – disappear into the continuous flow production teams in charge of making families of products.

While functions become 'support' for value-creating process teams, every function paradoxically has a deeper and more coherent knowledge base than was possible when it divided its attention between thinking and doing. Moreover, this knowledge base is more relevant to the company's long-term needs because function members returning from value-creating assignments in the processes bring new questions for the function to answer. Constantly applying knowledge in this way fights the tendency of all intellectual activities to veer off into abstractions when left in isolation.

12   A New Philosophy of Business

James Dyson

As often as I am asked about my design philosophy, I am cross-examined as to how I run my business. People see the numerical and financial success of the product and want to know how it was done. It is never enough to say that it is down to the qualitative difference of the vacuum cleaner and, to be fair, there may well be more to it than that. But a business philosophy is a difficult thing to distil out of the daily workings of a company, because you never really know how you do it, you just do it. It's like asking a horse how it walks. I thought, perhaps, if I tried to explain everything we do that other companies probably do not do, then people might be able to work out the philosophy for themselves.

Everyone who starts work at Dyson makes a vacuum cleaner on their first day

This is true from the lowliest member of staff to a non-executive director like former trade minister Richard Needham who joined us in 1995 to advise on export. Quite apart from being fun, making you feel good and reinforcing my conviction that anyone can do anything, it means that everyone in the company understands how the cleaner is put together, how it works and why, because of its design, it is better.

Everyone then takes it home and uses it, so that they can see its benefits in its natural environment, and get a grasp of the company's *raison d'être*. They have to pay £20 if they want to keep it forever, though. That's another thing worth knowing: you don't get anything for nothing! The idea is that everyone understands the whole product, even though they may only be working on a small part of it. It is, in fact, a core element of the next point.

A holistic approach to design

When we moved into a new factory in Malmesbury in 1995, we commissioned a rising star, Chris Wilkinson, to make some alterations internally and externally that transformed the building, including a jaunty tubular and sheet tension structure to provide shade to the offices.

Deirdre designed the lilac, lavender and purple interior colour scheme and we designed and built the high-tech office tables. We also bought Vitara chairs, designed by Antonio Citerio, at great expense (£400 each) for every employee. A chair, after all, is the most important piece of furniture in the office. At Dyson we care about people's bottoms.

The offices are open plan so that everyone can communicate easily and feels part of the same team. The graphics and engineering people are in the geographical centre of the office and that reflects the centrality of design and engineering to the whole operation. But there are no department boundaries or borders or walls, fences, ditches, moats, ha-has or minefields: freedom of movement and of expression is total.

I hope in this way to make everyone design conscious and to feel encouraged to make creative contributions.

Engineering and design are not viewed as separate

Designers are as involved in testing as engineers are in conceptual ideas. Elsewhere in industry, designers just design the look of the product and maybe sketch the odd part. Then engineers design the mechanics of the product. Test engineers do the testing. And model makers make the models. And machinists machine things. At Dyson, uniquely, we see *no* barriers between these disciplines – everyone in the department does everything. This way, everybody understands the implications of what they are doing and enjoys total creative freedom. And it goes further.

Everyone is empowered to be creative and knowledgeable

Or at least to feel that creative contributions are encouraged. In practice, of course, most ideas come from within whichever department they are supposed to come from, but not always. The idea of putting our helpline number on the handle of the machine (we are the only company to do this) came from Jackie on the service desk. And, when we were having trouble getting the motor seal to seal properly every time, someone else from the service department, a chap called Pete, discovered that if you did up the screws in cylinder head manner (in a prescribed order) they would be 100% effective.

No memos – ever

First of all, memos are just a way of passing the buck, avoiding the buck, avoiding the issue and abdicating responsibility. Second, memos only generate memos, then memos responding to the memo responding to the memo and then . . . I could go on but it would be as boring as the memo. Third, and most importantly, however much they multiply nobody every reads them.

Dialogue is the founding principle for progress. Talk to people, they listen. Monologue leads only to monomania. Memos are also tacky, soulless and get lost. I would rather people did less, if it means doing what they do properly, and a memo, though quicker than a conversation, is far more likely to lead to a misunderstanding.

By the way, computer messages are the pits and E-mail is even lower. The graphics are so appalling I just can't get interested enough to read them. I am considering banning those as well.

No one wears suits and ties

Every company needs an image. The smaller and less established you are, the more important that image becomes. And it is not a nebulous, intangible thing – like a reputation for ruthlessness, charm or efficiency – but a real, concrete and visible thing that people can take away with them, like a souvenir implanted in the brain, that keeps your company and your way of thinking, locked in their mind – even before they have seen what you are trying to sell – crystallized in its simple, comprehensible motif.

Now it may be that the not wearing of suits has taken on an importance for me that is greater than it really is. It should not, after all, become a stricture, because that is to make the practice as much a uniform as the miserable outfit it is trying to avoid. The fundamental principle is this: I do not want my employees thinking like businessmen. I do not want them sitting round a table with me or with anyone else and coming out with the same old crap as you would expect from a businessman. As soon as they start thinking like businessmen they will think that the company is all about making money and it is not. I have no time for businessmen; they are the suited pen-pushers who have always endeavoured to stifle creativity. And while what I choose to wear is entirely up to me and not open to question, I have chosen also to discourage my employees from wearing suits, because it seems to me the best way to instil in them my own heartfelt conviction in the theory of difference for the sake of difference.

A man in jeans and a T-shirt has nothing to hide behind – and will not feel compelled to hide behind conformity in anything else. He will be less likely, therefore, to come out with conformist remarks. We want people really to think about the business and come out with radical remarks – it is merely an offshoot that you provide people with, something to recall about you, that instantly tells them what sort of company you are. For me, personally, it has become almost symbolic of my difference, of my not putting on airs and graces. The old cliché that springs unsuppressably to mind is all about getting what you see.

I first got obsessed with this idea in the mid-1980s. (It was, in fact, a friend of mine in France, Diane Bauer, who also looks after some of our affairs over there, who first put the idea into my head. I happened to mention on the way to a meeting that I hated wearing suits. She looked astonished and said: 'Then stop wearing them.' And so I did.) It was after a meeting with a company called Millikan, the largest private company in America when I had to give a lecture to a panel of 24 people. Now, in business circles on the East Coast, you were simply not taken seriously unless you wore a traditional IBM suite with a sober tie, but I walked into the boardroom without one, took off my jacket and tossed it on the floor and told them that ties make you go deaf in your old age.

'It restricts the motion of your larynx,' I explained, 'and is known to hasten the onset of deafness.' And at that, 24 of the most powerful men in America immediately took of their jackets and ties and relaxed. They are a funny lot. If they go into the office on a Saturday they will always, without fail, wear jeans, trainers and ghastly lumberjack shirts – it is just another kind of uniform, as soulless and restrictive to creative thought as a suit.

I read once about a company, I think it may even have been IBM, that issued all its staff with T-shirts bearing the company logo. Torn between showing loyalty to the company, appreciation for the chairman's generosity, and not wanting to appear too casual, they all put the T-shirts on over suits. The same mentality is reflected in their quaint old tradition of mufti day, when everyone goes to work without a suit, one day a year and gives their daughter a dollar for charity. Not a tactic that would squeeze much of a donation out of us.

It may be that I attach too much significance to this, for you never know what really makes people behave the way they do. But from the evidence of institutions that depend on uniforms – primarily school, armies and prisons – it seems that they have been developed merely to encourage conformity and discipline. If I were organizing a military campaign such things might be useful.

I am not a fanatic about it and there is always the odd misfit. New employees tend to wear suits and ties out of habit, but they go after six to eight weeks. The suits and ties that is, not the employees – I don't take it *that* seriously.

A suit is like a biker's leathers or a fireman's protective kit: it is merely protection. People wear one because if you look the part, if you look efficient, sober and reliable, people will assume that you are and you can get away with being inadequate. Show up for marketing meeting in your underpants, though, and you have to be pretty damned impressive to pull it off.

I'd rather the qualities of my employees shone through in what they did, rather than what they wore. That is why I employ brilliant young graduates with no experience at all. I want free thinkers who can take the company forward and have revolutionary ideas.

My own justification for not wearing a suit is the same. I want people to make their judgements about me for deeper reasons than what I wrap myself in to keep out the cold. And then, of course, it becomes embroiled in this culture of difference. People come to see us and go away thinking of people who look relaxed, behave efficiently and think differently and they think to themselves, as they undo the inside button of their shiny green double-breasted suit and pluck up their matching trousers at the knee to stop them creasing, as they take their seat on the train home from Chippenham: 'Now there is a refreshing company.'

To be totally honest, I did wear a suit to work once. It was the day Prince Charles came to look round the factory and it was not, before you leap to conclusions, done out of toadying royalism. Deirdre insisted that I wear the armour so that HRH wouldn't feel out of place.

A café not a canteen

We operate in two shifts at the factory, so lunches and breaks are taken from 10.00am through to 7.00pm and since there is nothing in walking distance, we clearly needed our own restaurant. It was also important to create a kind of social focus or at least the sort of atmosphere where employees would find it easy to get to know each other.

I couldn't bear the thought of a 'canteen' or anything at all resembling mass catering – I wanted something a bit more Conranny, with the nearest thing to fresh Italian food that we could do in the south of England. I am not the sort of swollen-gutted, excruciating business luncher that sets off in the limo for four hours of beef and claret every day at noon and comes back to do little more than gurgle and fart all afternoon. I eat on-site like everyone else and I needed someone who could rustle up pastas and salad.

It also happened that there was an antiques shop in Malmesbury that was also a delicatessen. Judith Hughes, my PA, latched onto it like a shot as a source for lunches – reinforcing my own long-held belief that antique dealers are usually gourmets. Taste in food and taste in objets d'art clearly walk hand in hand across the palate of life. And it was the existence of this deli-antiquary that inspired the formula for our café – a place that would be run by antique dealers who liked food. A lace dealer called Jane appeared to run it for me, and recruited more dealers to help: good, wholesome, vegetable-biased, unfried food was just around the corner.

The staff were not, as you might expect, by any means chuffed. They wanted pasties and chips, bacon and eggs, pies and chips, sausages and chips. Not fusilli, pesto sauces, aubergines au gratin, rocket salad, cherry tomatoes, fennel, steamed fish, snails, kiwi fruit, carrot and orange soup or fruit salads. But after only a few days Jane was doing 450 lunches a day for a delighted staff, who were going back unbloated, free of the tyranny of cholesterol, their skins luminous with health, their organically fuelled bodies trim as a *Baywatch* lifeguard. And Jane was hunting for more antique dealers.

If you are ever in Malmesbury, by the way, I recommend the kedgeree.

Encourage employees to be different, on principle

This is part of my anti-brilliance campaign. Very few people can be brilliant. Those who are rarely do anything worthwhile. And they are over-valued. You are just as likely to solve a problem by being unconventional and determined as by being brilliant. And if you can't be unconventional, be obtuse. Be deliberately obtuse, because there are five billion people out there thinking in train tracks and thinking what they have been taught to think.

If you go in and are illogical, then half the time people will laugh at you and half the time you will strike up something interesting because you have stopped everyone else from thinking logically, which has failed to provide a solution. Be a bit whacko and you shake people up a bit. And we all need shaking up.

Methodologically it even makes a bit of sense, in that, to bastardize a dictum of Mr Sherlock Holmes, when you have eliminated the logical, whatever remains, however illogical, must be the answer. So why not start there? I probably only think this because I can never be bothered to think anything through logically, but we'll let it go. At any rate, to be different is something we try to instil in all our staff, because, for the reasons just given, we don't want people behaving like businessmen, but behaving like normal human beings and treating the customer as a friend.

Don't relinquish responsibility once the sale is made

For as long as their Dyson is under guarantee our customer has the unique and, though I say so myself, rather charming entitlement to phone the hotline on the handle and, if necessary, a brand new machine will be delivered by first thing the next morning, totally free. And, once the guarantee is over, the customer is ever afterwards entitled to ring the hotline and the machine will be picked up immediately, repaired by us and returned by courier.

We do not use some outside engineer who arrives when he feels like it, asks for a cup of tea, scratches his bottom for a while and then says, 'What you need is a new vacuum cleaner. This one's finished.'

It may sound like an expensive service for us to run, but real service, like real innovation, is what people want more than anything and people are so delighted when they discover that we will immediately send them a new machine that their call of complaint becomes a call of gratitude. They phone up steaming because something has gone wrong with their very expensive vacuum cleaner (although it rarely does) and end up deliriously happy because they are about to get a new one.

Employ graduates straight from university

The basic reason for this is that they are unsullied. They have not been strapped into a suit and taught to think by a company with nothing on its mind but short-term profit and early retirement. We are trying to do things differently from everyone else, so it's easier to teach fresh graduates this new way and enable them to challenge established beliefs, than to retrain someone with 'experience'. Sometimes some of our staff do lack knowledge, but there is now a cadre of experienced and talented managers and this combination provides and extraordinarily energetic and intelligent stratum of managers which is what gives Dyson its strength.

I began employing graduates because I was so appreciative of the opportunities given to me when I was younger by Jeremy Fry. He, after all, had taken me on when I was still an undergraduate. And as soon as I had graduated he gave me carte blanche on the Sea Truck project and entrusted me with running the business from the start. I enjoyed and benefited from the responsibility of learning things by doing, rather than being taught by superiors. That was what made me feel I was a pioneer.

So when I first set up Prototypes Ltd to develop the vacuum cleaner I started employing engineering graduates from the Royal College of Art – and we now have about 20 RCA graduates in Malmesbury. It never occurred to me that they wouldn't be able to do everything brilliantly. And they did.

When I began building Dyson Appliances I employed fresh graduates for graphics, marketing, production, tooling and export. And their enthusiasm, intelligence, inventiveness and resourcefulness has been the most emotional and rewarding part of the adventure. They're getting old now though – the average age of our employees has just hit 25.

Our competitors sometimes say, as a way of belittling the company's achievement, that all we are good at is marketing. Well, all our marketing has been done by Rebecca Trentham, from a standing start as a languages graduate from Oxford and all our products have been designed and engineered by new graduates.

The atmosphere and spirit generated by these young people learning the business for themselves is something we would never have got by employing old hacks to teach them.

Not to forget, of course, that the young unemployed are cheaper to employ than most, which was a great help in the early, cash-strapped days. But their pay rises quickly – if not as quickly as they would like.

Meet the staff as equals – they are

Although during the course of daily life I speak to most of the staff at one time or another, I speak to them, as a group, about once a month. And, because we have expanded so fast, I now have to do that in three goes: talking with the morning shift at 1.45pm, the evening shift at 2.05pm and the office at 5.00pm.

I talk, by and large, for about ten minutes about anything from marketing issues – such as what our competitors are doing and what we are doing about it – to management changes, how our overseas subsidiaries are doing, advertising campaigns and property purchases. When, for example, we became involved with Sir Ranulph Fiennes' solo expedition to the Antarctic, I introduced him to everyone and he gave a small talk, which probably made a nice change from listening to me wittering on.

We also address the kinds of social issue that I am sure most good companies do, such as the canteen, shift changeovers and pensions. And then the staff fire at me whatever questions they like, although we also run clinics for that, which are a better forum for the less extrovert individuals and a suggestions box for the positively retiring, whose letters are always answered personally.

I do spend a lot of time walking around the factory, but it is a mistake to live under the illusion that one is therefore communicating – for it is usually the same people who approach and ask you questions and offer their opinions. The advantage of the soap box occasion is that you are setting aside time especially to communicate aspects of the business that all the staff should know about and other things that directly affect their welfare. It is eyeball-to-eyeball contact and there is always a very palpable atmosphere: sometimes very positive and upbeat and sometimes difficult when news is not so good.

The meetings offer a good time to reaffirm our philosophy – and I think it is fair to call it a philosophy rather than just a 'company policy', for it is not a way of 'doing' that we impose on anybody, but a way of 'being' that I find is generally most productive. For example it is often in these meetings that I remind people that the assembly lines need not be in a hurry. Speed is not important and neither are numbers. The only thing that is important is doing everything carefully, thoroughly and vigilantly. New assembly workers, used to the methods of other manufacturers in the market, have sometimes become accustomed to a mentality that works at full speed all day to achieve mere numbers, at the expense of care and quality.

Feedback from the floor, when it concerns production, usually centres around the quality of components fed to the line by subcontractors. It is a crucial melting pot of ideas that enables us to share with the assembly staff our management experience and efforts with the subcontractors, at the same time as they describe the end results of our efforts. So useful is this proving, that we have arranged, in future, for subcontractors to attend the meetings. Hope they can take it.

The final assembly is done entirely by hand

There is very little mechanization in our assembly lines, which is rather unusual. It allows us total flexibility to lengthen or shorten the line when we need to, to add or remove people or to add new lines at a moment's notice, change the assembly method, change the design of the product. It does mean that we rely more than others on the skill of our assembly staff but it allows us that 'can do' attitude that is anathema to British manufacturing otherwise. And we do take pride that the work is done by hand and say so when we can, rather than pretend that everything is built by robots and is therefore somehow better.

Everything in the factory is, in fact, done by hand, because we do not keep the tooling here or manufacture any of the components, thus keeping nasty, heavy, dirty machinery out of the place and making it feel more like a craft workshop – albeit a very modern one – than a factory.

We do spend a lot of time supervising our many subcontractors but our skills are in designing and making vacuum cleaners, not in the processes of making components. In our cleaner, quieter, more pleasant factory we are all able to concentrate our minds on engineering, testing and quality control, which is what makes our customers happy and our business the success that it is.

We pay our staff well

In addition to very good rates of pay (which have resulted in most of Malmesbury and the surrounding area beating a path to our door) we pay a flat premium, on a weekly basis, that is subject to full attendance, as a reward for reliable and loyal staff. Everyone has life insurance and a company pension, 22 days' holiday a year, paid sick leave and leaves early on Friday. The café is heavily subsidized (a lunch of top continental cuisine, healthy as a walk in the country still gives you change out of two quid) and we run a free bus service from Chippenham.

Japanese influences

To the outside world some of our ideas may appear to be rather Japanese in their conception. But that is only because they are not very British. We have none of the corny Japanese ideas, like the exercises or mantras, forgoing of holidays and chronic presenteeism (though we do run football, netball and squash activities), but I have noticed one or two things in our approach which, while we were not aware that they were particularly Japanese, have certain similarities.

I have mentioned iterative development as part of innovation and that extends to the workplace. Like the Japanese, we are never satisfied with the product and are always trying to improve it. We take any complaint very seriously, even if it arises out of the customer's own error (such as failure to read the instructions) and solve the problem. Customer feedback is our way of foretelling and directing our future and we spare no expense in acting on that feedback.

We are aware – as the Japanese are – that the strength of our business does not lie with the quality of the directors and senior managers, but with the quality, effort, intelligence and, above all, enthusiasm of everyone else.

We are fascinated, to the point of obsession, with the product. We do not, perhaps, attain quite the delirious object fetishism of the Japanese, but are determined that whatever we produce should be perfect, as well as exciting and beautiful. It is this that allows us to maintain ownership of our product and without it we do not have a business.

Dealing with suppliers

There are four straightforward requirements that we have of our suppliers: that they should provide (a) what we order, (b) at the time stipulated, (c) in the correct quantity and (d) to the quality stipulated.

I wish.

The thing is that if they let us down in any of those areas, not only their future business with us but, more importantly, our business with our customers will suffer. The trouble is that suppliers seldom see beyond our role as the cash provider for whatever they ship – 'Right, Dyson, we've sent off a truck load of bits of plastic to your gaff, where's the money?'

They are not all like this, of course. But it only takes one to stop the whole production line and that, in turn, demoralizes the staff.

We have some very good suppliers, with whom we have shared the success of our business and I try to make the best of them the watermark by which I select and judge the others. A good example of what I look for is the attitude of Adrian Hill of Belpar Rubber. Back in November 1992 he flew over to Italy, when the tooling was finished, to help me assemble the first off-tooling samples – he had made all the rubber parts and was so keen to make sure that they all worked properly, cared so much about his own business fulfilling all that was asked of it, that he insisted on being there himself when they were first put to use. Belpar is a very successful small family business and has been a major supplier to Dyson ever since.

As we grew, we realized that we had to work constantly with our increasing army of suppliers to improve both quality and technology. To this end I am grateful to a man called David Brown, of Motorola in Swindon, who in September 1995 introduced me to a quality scheme of theirs called 6-Sigma. Under this excellent programme, which involves us redesigning parts as required and suppliers altering their production methods to accommodate it, and going through a rigorous checking process themselves, we have worked with them to reduce rejects to six parts per million.

We depend on our suppliers and they know that. Many of them put their faith in us in the early days, trusting us to succeed, believing that our initially small orders would become reasonable. They have adapted well to our spiralling demand for extra products and changes in design, and it has been good to share our success with them.

We have a similar relationship with our retailers, most of whom were initially asked to put their faith in a small company, with the promise of greater things to come. Although shops and mail order catalogues are our immediate purchasers, we are very much attuned to the existence of the consumer as our ultimate customer and depend on the skill and enthusiasm of retail staff. We encourage them to buy and use the vacuum cleaners themselves and to attach our point-of-sale labels to the machines so that the people who walk into the shops get a picture of the whole story. We in turn are aware that we must support them with promotion and advertising.

And that, from the comfort of our bottoms and the state of our digestion to the quality of our parts and products, is how we do things at Dyson. And I think it is it good way. It has worked for me at least. A note of caution though: it wouldn't count for diddly if our vacuum cleaner had a bag.

13 Strategic Stories: How 3M is Rewriting Business Planning

Gordon Shaw, Robert Brown and Philip Bromiley

At 3M, we tell stories. Everyone knows that, in our earliest days, a share of 3M stock was worth a shot of whiskey in a local St Paul bar. We tell stories about how we failed with our first abrasive products and stories about how we invented masking tape and wet-or-dry sandpaper. More recently, we've been telling the story about one of our scientists who, while singing in a choir, wished he had bookmarks that wouldn't fall out of the hymnal and later created Post-it Notes.

We train our sales representatives to paint stories through word pictures so that customers will see how using a 3M product can help them succeed. At employee award ceremonies, we tell stories about the programmes and people being recognized to explain what happened and why it's significant.

Maybe our story-intensive culture is just an accident, but we don't think so. We sense that it's central to our identity – part of the way we see ourselves and explain ourselves to one another. Stories are a habit of mind at 3M and it's through them – through the way they make us see ourselves and our business operations in complex, multidimensional forms – that we're able to discover opportunities for strategic change. Stories give us ways to form ideas about winning.

So it's remarkable that we typically discard storytelling when we do our strategic planning. After all, that's the formal process by which we lay out how we're going to win.

At one level it's odd, but at another level it isn't at all, since virtually all business people plan using lists, outlines and bullets. In any event, over the course of several years overseeing strategic planning at 3M, Gordon Shaw, the lead author of this chapter, became uncomfortably aware that 3M's business plans failed to reflect deep thought or to inspire commitment. They were usually just lists of 'good things to do' that made 3M functionally stronger but failed to explain the logic or rationale of winning in the marketplace.

He began to suspect that the familiar, bullet-list format of the plans was a big part of the problem. After critiquing hundreds of plans, he started to look for a more coherent, compelling way to present them. With strategic narratives, he found that form. (See Box 13.1.) Individuals in 3M now use strategic narratives in their planning processes, not only to clarify the thinking behind their plans but also to capture the imagination and the excitement of the people in their organizations.

Box 13.1 The science of stories

Stories are central to human intelligence and memory. Cognitive scientist William Calvin describes how we gradually acquire the ability to formulate plans through the stories we hear in childhood. From stories, a child learns to 'imagine a course of action, imagine its effects on others, and decide whether or not to do it' (*Scientific American*, October 1994). In a very fundamental way, then, storytelling and planning are related.

Stories also play an important role in learning. Language researchers studying how high school students learn found that the story-based style of *Time* and *Newsweek* was the best way to learn and remember. When the researchers translated American history textbooks into this format, they found that students recalled up to three times more than they did after reading traditional textbooks.

Cognitive psychologists have established that lists, in contrast, are remarkably hard to remember because of what is referred to as the *recency* and *primacy* effects: people mainly remember the first and the last items on a list but not the rest of it, and – more dangerous yet – their memory is guided by their interests. They remember what they like or find interesting; they do not recall the whole.

A good story (and a good strategic plan) defines relationships, a sequence of events, cause and effect and a priority among items – and those elements are likely to be remembered as a complex whole. That likelihood, supported by a substantial amount of cognitive science, argues strongly for strategic planning through storytelling.

What's wrong with bullets?

In every company we know, planning follows the standard format of the bullet outline. It fits the way we're used to writing and presenting information. It's economical. It reduces complex business situations to a few, apparently clean points. It allows for conversation around the issues and gives presenters the freedom to move, modify, clarify and revise on the fly. In a sense, the bullet list may be an artifact of the way business takes place in the course of strategic planning: it mirrors the character of meetings and the high-pressure pace of the manager or planner who must reduce the complex to short and clear.

So what's the problem?

If the language we use in writing strategic planning reports were only a matter or presentation, of the way we package ideas and offer them to others, it would not matter much how we wrote them. But writing is thinking. Bullets allow us to skip the thinking step, genially tricking ourselves into supposing that we have planned when, in fact, we've only listed some good things to do.

Bullet lists encourage us to be intellectually lazy in three specific, and related, ways.

Bullet lists are typically too generic; that is, they offer a series of things to do that could apply to any business

They fail to focus an organization on the specifics of how it will win in its particular market. Witness this selection from a planning document submitted by a 3M business unit. The planners proposed three 'major strategies':

*   reduce high delivered costs
*   reduce international parent head count by three
*   explore sales cost reductions
*   determine vision for traditional products and appropriately staff
*   continue to reduce factory costs
*   refine unit cost management system
*   reduce process and product costs
*   accelerate development and introduction of new products
*   increase responsiveness.

What's proposed is so general that it could fit any business at any point in its maturity and, by the way, the bullet points are not vague because we've disguised proprietary information. This is a typical level of detail for business plans. Basically, these planners propose to keep doing good things faster, cheaper and with more attention to the market.

The problem here is not incompetence; good managers drafted this plan. They know their business unit and, if asked, could probably provide the detail to turn an empty phrase like 'determine vision for traditional products' into a story about market analysis, positioning and strategic action. But we can't tell that from their plan.

Neither can their executive reviewers. And, more critically, neither can the people who need to get behind the plan and make it happen.

But any of these abstract proposals could be part of a powerful strategic plan. If 'increase responsiveness' means 'improve on-time delivery', for example, it might set a company apart from its competition – if the norm in this business is to be late and unpredictable. But we certainly can't tell that from this plan.

Bullets leave critical relationships unspecified

Lists can communicate only three logical relationships: sequence (first to last in time); priority (least to most important or vice versa); or simple membership in a set (these items relate to one another in some way, but the nature of that relationship remains unstated). And a list can show only one of those relationships at a time. When we present a list, either orally or in writing, we leave other critical relationships unspecified. Our audience can fill in the blanks from their own view of things or we can do it, adjusting what we say to the responses we receive from them.

Sometimes, this approach can be politically savvy, making the list palatable to a variety of people who may have different points of view. Lists leave us room to move and, in moving, to protect our sense of mastery, certainty and control. However, in the end, lists present only an illusion of clarity – and it can be an expensive illusion. If the plan doesn't specify critical relationships among issues, it can't demonstrate that we really know what we're doing or where we're going. We can't see the whole picture.

Bullets leave critical assumptions about how the business works unstated

Consider these major objectives from a standard five-year strategic plan:

- Increase market share by 25%.
- Increase profits by 30%.
- Increase new product introductions to ten a year.

Implicit in this plan is a complex, but unexplained, vision of the organization, the market and the customer. However, we cannot extrapolate that vision from the bullet list. The plan does not tell us how these objectives tie together and, in fact, many radically different strategies could be represented by these three simple points.

Does improved marketing (for example) increase market share, which results in increased profits (perhaps from economies of scale), thus providing funds for increased new product development?

Or maybe new product development will result in both increased profits and market share at once:

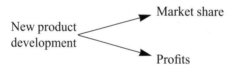

Alternatively, perhaps windfall profits will let us just buy market share by stepping up advertising and new product development:

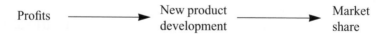

These different models make radically different assumptions about how the world works. Indeed, these three simple items – profit, market share and new product development – can relate in many other plausible ways as well. Without being clear about which set of assumptions they favour, planners cannot seriously think through their plans. Without knowing which assumptions the planners are making, senior managers cannot seriously evaluate or modify the plans. And without understanding the business assumptions, subordinates face just another list of objectives without any confidence that those goals can be reached and without an essential sense of excitement.

The narrative logic of strategic stories

Planning by narrative is a lot like traditional storytelling. Like a good storyteller, the strategic planner needs to set the stage – define the current situation in an insightful, coherent manner. That involves analyzing the industry's economics, its key success factors and the forces that drive change. It also involves defining basic tensions and relationships: Which capabilities and objectives do we have and which do the other players have? What do we believe the other players intend to do? How do our key success factors compare with those of our competitors? Some of these factors are straightforward but others involve complex analysis.

Next, the strategic planner must introduce the dramatic conflict. What challenges does the company face in this situation? What critical issues stand as obstacles to success? In some cases, the main challenge will be exploiting new technological opportunities. In other cases, it will be coping with high costs in a commodity market.

Finally, the story must reach resolution in a satisfying, convincing manner. The plan must tell us how the company can overcome obstacles and win. The conclusion requires a logical, concise argument that is specific to the situation and leads to the desired outcomes.

Requiring that a plan have a narrative logic forces to the surface the writer's buried assumptions about cause and effect. The act or writing a full, logical statement encourages clear thinking and brings out the subtlety and complexity of ideas.

Indeed, sometimes we sit down to write believing we have a clear idea, but our difficulty in getting it down on paper exposes the flaws in our thinking.

Presenting a plan in narrative creates a richer picture of strategy not only for the plan's authors but also for its intended audience. Readers are made privy to the author's thought processes, so they know far more than they would if they read a bullet list. When assumptions are made explicit, they can be discussed and held up against senior managers' own mental models. Executives are in a better position to evaluate the plan critically, ask more penetrating and insightful questions and offer more useful advice. As one 3M manager said, 'If you read just bullet points, you may not get it, but if you read a narrative plan, you will. If there's a flaw in the logic, it glares right out at you. With bullets, you don't know if the insight is really there or if the planner has merely given you a shopping list.' (See Box 13.2.)

A word of caution. For this approach to work, the story can't be just a list of bullets connected by 'and then and then, and then . . .' Rather, it must be a recasting and rethinking of the parts of the plan and their relationships with one another. It must tell a story of a struggle between opponents in which the good guy triumphs by doing a series of smart things in the right order.

Box 13.2 Building a story that works

Robert Brullo, a 23-year 3M veteran, needed to figure out what to do about his division's relationship with Hoechst, the German chemical company. Since the early 1980s, his fluoropolymer group had enjoyed a cordial, arm's length relationship with Hoechst, which had been first a supplier, then a manufacturer, for 3M. That arrangement had worked well for a long time, but it was no longer enough.

Hoechst had recently developed a new resin, called THV, that remained flexible at very low temperatures. It was a product with huge potential. Hoechst, however, did not have the skills necessary to develop or market applications. 3M did. Simply acquiring THV did not make sense for 3M; the cost was too high and Hoechst already had a manufacturing facility, which 3M would not want to duplicate. A joint venture between the two organizations might ultimately have made the most sense, but Brullo knew that 3M does not enter into such agreements easily or often.

Brullo thought about how to resolve the business issue facing his division. Whatever he decided, getting senior management behind him would be a challenge. He realized that a bullet-style plan could not elicit, or reflect, the serious thinking he needed to do. He decided to write a narrative-style plan instead.

'I said to myself, I'm going to write this like a book – make it like a story – so that anybody can pick up the plan, read it, and understand our situation.'

Brullo talked with subordinates and read related business plans. He wrote the plan on his own, however. His description of writing that first draft captures the painful, exhilarating process of thinking through a difficult problem:

'I'd sit there knowing it wasn't coming, and then all of a sudden I'd have a flash of brilliance. I spent two days at home just getting my thoughts down on paper. I had sheets and sheets full of ideas. Finally, I started writing out the actual story.'

Brullo spent two weeks working on his plan. Once he'd written a 30-page draft, his subordinates critiqued it and he rewrote it more than once, preparing to present the plan to the company's senior management.

On the day of his presentation, he began by turning off the overhead projector, saying, 'I'm going to have fun today.' Top managers started whispering that they could see a disaster coming. The business unit involved highly complex science and it competed in a highly complex industry, so following a detailed plan would have been challenging for the audience had they been listening to a less talented storyteller. However, Brullo walked them easily through descriptions of the players, the critical issues and the proposed resolution. He knew the material cold; his carefully crafted stories had become part of him.

By the end of the presentation, top management was on board. Brullo's presentation became the foundation for a joint venture between 3M and Hoechst. An observer at the presentation reported later:

> When Bob got up and presented, I could see the strategies to win. I could see these strategies changing the basis of competition. I could see the critical issues being identified and I could see the key success factors for that part of the business. People could see the connections as he went from one section of his presentation to the next. They could see how the business was evolving, and they could see, ultimately, how the business was going to win.

Brullo says: 'To me, the point is to communicate an insight, not simply a bunch of numbers or a bunch of bullet points. It keeps coming down to the same thing – you have to be able to show that the insight is there.'

Dyneon, the new joint venture, was formed in August 1996. Managers developing the new organization over the coming months met with far less mistrust and misunderstanding than most international joint ventures involve. The narrative allowed them to identify potential problems. For example, the strategic story highlighted the importance of addressing specific needs of users in the automotive and semiconductor industries. From its inception, Dyneon jumped on those issues, establishing teams that included people from both companies.

Today Brullo leads Dyneon as its first president. The 600-employee, $350 million business is almost two years into the joint venture agreement. 3M is the majority owner. Thus far Dyneon's financial and operational performance has surpassed expectations. Brullo has used the narrative format in subsequent strategic plans as the basis for two other joint venture proposals. One of those joint ventures was completed soon after.

Bullets versus strategic stories: An example

A good story has a point that becomes clear through the telling. Likewise a good plan lays out a vision – not just a generic platitude, but a fully enunciated statement of how the business creates value. Rather than reflecting an inward focus (for example, 'to be the leading supplier of widgets'), the vision says how we will make a significant contribution to the customer.

Consider, as an example, our Global Fleet Graphics Division. Once upon a time, the substantive piece of the 1992 business plan for the division might have looked something like this:

- Increase our market share from 40% to 50%.
- Regain product-development leadership position.
- Increase sales closings by 50%.

Today we would craft the plan in the form of a narrative. Although what follows is highly condensed and it is partly disguised (all the numbers have been changed, for example, it illustrates the value of telling a strategic story).

Setting the stage

Global Fleet Graphics makes premium, durable graphic-marking systems for buildings, signs, vehicles and heavy equipment. The corporate logos and graphics we see on fleets of package delivery trucks, tractor trailers and airplanes are typical examples.

Fleet Graphics now faces more demanding customers and more aggressive competitors than it has in previous years. Customers want design flexibility and larger graphics without higher cost. Some customers want easy-to-remove products, while others want durable ones. Bus operators want graphics that cover the windows yet still allow passengers to see out. Total sales of graphic materials have increased, but sales of traditional, painted graphics have declined due to their high cost. 3M has 40% of the market and for some years has been the technological leader.

Fleet Graphics faces three major competitors: AmeriGraphics, GraphDesign, and FleetGlobal. AmeriGraphics has begun to expand its product line by using our older technologies as the patents expire. Its global share has grown from 10% in 1982 to 16% today. GraphDesign uses direct distribution and new manufacturing capabilities to compete on price but has experienced quality problems. Its market share has dropped from 18% to 15% in the last ten years. The quality of FleetGlobal's products is comparable to ours, but they sell at a lower price. Its share has grown from 24% in 1982 to 28% today.

In short, we are losing our patent advantages at the same time that we face three strong competitors that are using low-cost strategies.

Dramatic conflict

Without radical changes, Fleet Graphics will not be profitable in the near future. We can expect rapid price erosion once all competitors bring very similar products to market. Given 3M's higher overhead, we cannot compete in a price-competitive business without a technological advantage.

Our vision: Incremental product or process improvements will not solve this problem. We plan to transform the industry through several technological advances. At the heart of this transformation will be a move from analogue to digital printing and storage technology. In addition, the quality and economics of the final product will be improved using new film and adhesive technologies. The strategy we propose draws on diverse areas of 3M.

First, we propose a quantum change in Global Fleet Graphics' production system that will allow us to deliver products much more quickly and at a competitive price. Rather than focus on cost reduction through incremental process changes, we have tried to rethink the entire way we produce fleet graphics. We have contacted numerous R&D areas at both the corporate and divisional levels to locate appropriate and adaptable technologies. The search has resulted in a radical plan for a new, more flexible, lower cost graphics production system.

Many graphics will be produced and stored digitally. We will convert manual, analogue, silk-screen printing into digital form by scanning the art and cleaning it up on a computer screen. We will then be able to send it digitally anywhere in the world. Global Fleet Graphics will create a central repository of images that can be electronically transmitted to production facilities worldwide. IT estimates that the system will cost 33 million and be operational in 24 months.

The repository dramatically decreases product delivery time from as much as four weeks to as little as three hours. It also drastically reduces inventory.

Second, we propose development of a new generation of patented technologies and products to differentiate our offerings from competitors'. Three such products are already in the works. We are in the late stages of developing adhesives and films that can cover windows but allow people to see out. Only the final product definition and design work still need to be done; design should be completed in five months. Manufacturing has begun to work on production facilities to ensure adequate capacity worldwide.

In addition, we are now close to answering our customers' need for graphics that can be applied to many non-traditional surfaces (such as corrugated truck sidings and flexing surfaces (such as European trucks with canvas sides). Films for these applications already exist in our labs.

And our new adhesives will make graphics easier to install. The Adhesives Division has a product that remains tacky for a time so that graphics can be positioned and repositioned. When the placement is correct, a second adhesive system is activated to bond the graphics in place. The repositioning capacity decreases installation time by 30%, resulting in substantial cost savings.

Third, we need to upgrade our sales and marketing staffs' skills to match their capabilities with the technology-driven strategy. We will put substantial effort into field testing and marketing. Technical, marketing and sales personnel will fieldtest the new products both domestically and overseas. Simultaneously, we will develop and test modifications to the product as well as produce sales and other supporting documentation.

Before we launch the new products, sales, marketing and technical service personnel will train all sales reps in how to use and sell the new technology. Training will include both technical and communication skills related to calling on top-level executives: reps will receive intensive training in how to talk those customers' language and they will also be able to handle technical questions on their own. Training will begin one year from now and we expect it to take six months.

Resolution: How we win

To summarize, Global Fleet Graphics has drawn on diverse technological skills at 3M to create a proposal for transforming its business. What has been a hard-copy, analogue, design materials business will become a more fully global, digital, electronic-imaging and repository business. Combining new films with new adhesives will create substantial value and reduce overall cost in both the manufacturing and application of graphics. By these means, Global Fleet Graphics will maintain and enhance its profitability and industry leadership.

We believe that this new graphics system will radically transform the industry in a manner consistent with 3M's overall corporate strategy-regaining technological advantage on both the product and process fronts. The competition may duplicate some parts of this strategy (for example, the electronic storage of graphic images) but that will take time. We should have an advantage for several years even in those areas. Other areas have patent protection and our advantages can be sustained for a decade or more.

Even such a condensed narrative demonstrates the relative complexity that a strategic story reveals. When readers finish the complete narrative, they will know how 3M intends to increase its market share from 40% to 50%. They will know which product and process developments should, when combined, launch a new generation of fleet graphics. And they will be able to imagine that, given those new products and processes, as well as new training opportunities, sales representatives might well improve their performance by 50%. Just as important, readers will understand that hundreds and hundreds of players must contribute in order for the plan to succeed.

In a recent 3M survey, employees asked management to 'allow us to get excited about where we are going' and to provide evidence of management's confidence and excitement about 3M's future. We believe that casting our plans for the future as compelling stories can help us do just that. The ultimate success of our plans depends on how effectively we inspire the people who make those plans happen.

This final role of narrative plans – generating excitement and commitment in both superiors and subordinates – may be the most important. A well-written narrative strategy that shows a difficult situation and an innovative solution leading to improved market share can be galvanizing – and it is certainly more engaging than a bulleted mandate to 'increase market share by 5%'. When people can locate themselves in the story, their sense of commitment and involvement is enhanced. By conveying a powerful impression of the process of winning, narrative plans can motivate and mobilize an entire organization.

Section D Partnership and Networks

The high cost of development and the tendency to disaggregate means that partnerships with other organizations are now a prominent part of business life. Tidd, Bessant and Pavitt examine the various forms of interorganizational partnerships used to help advance innovation. DeFillippi and Arthur explain how collaboration works in an industry that has long run very successfully through a network of partnerships, a form of project-based enterprise that seems to be on the increase. Dyer and Ouchi and Lewis and Lytton elaborate on the merits of long-term relationships with suppliers.

Tidd, Bessant and Pavitt examine the role of collaboration in the development of new technologies, products and processes. They outline the different forms these take from loose consortia and networks to more formal joint ventures, licensing and subcontracting and examine what each has to offer different industries. They describe how these partnerships are used to gain access to new technologies and new markets, stressing the importance of an organization's position in one or more innovation networks. They go on to examine trends in collaborative activity and certain characteristics that appear to be important in the management of cross-organizational ventures. They point out that in addition to short-term cost savings collaboration offers the longer term advantage of learning new competencies.

DeFillippi and Arthur describe the project-based enterprise round which most film making, and for that matter a good deal of the construction, legal and software industries are organized. Typically, staff come together strictly for the duration of the project and then disband. For a management science attached to the company as the key unit of analysis and holder of organizational knowledge, this form of enterprise seems paradoxical and, as DeFillippi and Arthur make clear, this poses a challenge for certain classic management assumptions. In practice however project-based enterprise seems to work very well. The slack inherent in film production allows ample time for junior staff to watch, interact with and learn from their more skilled superiors, in effect acting as informal apprentices in the presence of masters. Rehiring seems to work partly, as has been argued earlier in this book, on reputation but is also dependent on the particular network you belong to. Often the same or similar teams, with diverse skills, come together to work on successive projects. The industry works through the social capital of numerous overlapping networks.

Dyer and Ouchi attempt to explain how it is that the Japanese have produced higher quality at lower cost by developing partnerships with particular suppliers. On average they use fewer suppliers than their western counterparts and maintain relationships with suppliers over a long period, even helping weaker suppliers develop. The gains are partly a matter of reduced transaction costs and inventory but also a matter of increased trust and commitment. Dyer and Ouchi explain how the Japanese build trust through stock exchange and employee transfers to the point where both manufacturer and supplier are willing to make customized investments. Many organizations have found the idea works well in the West too.

Lewis and Lytton show that partnerships with suppliers is just as appropriate for small firms as large. They build trust with suppliers partly through open book accounting. Ken Lewis CEO of Dutton summarizes the advantages of a long-term Japanese style relationship with suppliers as on-time delivery, reduced paperwork and costs for manufacturers and the possibility of forward planning and prompt payment for suppliers.

14   Learning through Alliances

Joe Tidd, John Bessant and Keith Pavitt

Firms collaborate for a number of reasons:

- to reduce the cost of technological development or market entry
- to reduce the risk of development or market entry
- to achieve scale economies in production
- to reduce the time taken to develop and commercialize new products.

In any specific case, a firm is likely to have multiple motives for an alliance. However, for the sake of analysis it is useful to group the rationale for collaboration into technological, market and organizational motives (Figure 14.1). Technological reasons include the cost, time and complexity of development. In the current highly competitive business environment, the R&D function, like all other aspects of business, is forced to achieve greater financial efficiency and to examine critically whether in-house development is the most efficient approach.

Figure 14.1 A model of collaboration

In addition, there is an increasing recognition that one company's peripheral technologies are usually another's core activities and that it often makes sense to source such technologies externally, rather than to incur the risks, costs and most importantly of all, timescale associated with in-house development. The rate of technological change, together with the increasingly complex nature of many technologies, means that few organizations can now afford to maintain in-house expertise in every potentially relevant technical area.

Many products incorporate an increasing range of technologies as they evolve, for example, automobiles now include much computing hardware and software to monitor and control the engine, transmission, brakes and in some cases suspension. For example, when developing the Jaguar XK8, Ford collaborated with Nippondenso in Japan to develop the engine management system and ZF in Germany to develop the transmission system and controls. In addition, there is a greater appreciation of the important role that external technology sources can play in providing a window on emerging or rapidly advancing areas of science. This is particularly true when developments arise from outside a company's traditional areas of business or from overseas.

Two factors need to be taken into account when making the decision whether to 'make or buy' a technology; the transaction costs, and strategic implications.[1] Transaction cost analysis focuses on organizational efficiency, specifically where market transactions involve significant uncertainty. Projects involving technological innovation will feature uncertainties associated with completion, performance and pre-emption by rivals. Projects involving market entry will feature uncertainties due to lack of geographical or product market knowledge. In such cases firms are often prepared to trade potentially high financial returns for a reduction in uncertainty.

Generally, the fewer potential sources of technology, the lower the bargaining power of the purchaser and the higher the transaction costs. Transaction costs are increased where a potential purchaser of technology has little knowledge of the technology. In this respect the acquisition of technology differs from subcontracting more routine tasks such as production or maintenance work, as it is difficult to specify contractually what must be delivered.[2]

As a result, the acquisition of technology tends to require a closer relationship between buyers and sellers than traditional market transactions, resulting in a range of possible acquisition strategies and mechanisms. The optimal technology acquisition strategy in any specific case will depend on the maturity of the technology, the firm's technological position relative to competitors and the strategic significance of the technology.[3] Some form of collaboration is normally necessary where the technology is novel, complex or scarce. Conversely, where the technology is mature, simple or widely available, market transactions such as subcontracting or licensing are more appropriate. However, the cumulative effect of outsourcing various technologies on the basis of comparative transaction costs may limit future technological options and reduce competitiveness in the long term.[4]

In practice, therefore, transaction costs are not the most significant factors affecting the decision to acquire external technology. Factors such as competitive advantage, market expansion and extending product portfolios are more important.[5] Adopting a more strategic perspective focuses attention on long-term organizational effectiveness, rather than short-term efficiency. The early normative strategy literature emphasized the need for technology development to support corporate and business strategies and therefore technology acquisition decisions began with an evaluation of company strengths and weaknesses. The more recent resource-based approach emphasizes the process of resource accumulation or learning.[6] Competency development requires a firm to have an explicit policy or intent to use collaboration as an opportunity to learn rather than minimize costs. This suggests that the acquisition of external technology should be used to complement internal R&D, rather than being a substitute for it. In fact, a strategy of technology acquisition is associated with diversification into increasingly complex technologies.[7]

For successful technology acquisition the choice of partner may be as important as the search for the best technology. For both partners, the transaction costs will be lower when dealing with a firm with which they are familiar: they are likely to have some degree of mutual trust, shared technical and business information, and existing personal social links. (See Box 14.1.)

Box 14.1 Philips and Sony

The alliance between Philips and Sony to develop, produce and commercialize the compact disc (CD) is a good example of the multiple objectives of strategic alliances.

Philips had developed the prototype for the CD by 1978, after six years of development, but recognized that it would be difficult for the company to turn the concept into a world standard. Philips had previously experienced the commercial failure of its video laser disc system. Therefore, in 1979, Philips approached Sony to form a strategic alliance. Sony was chosen because it had the requisite development and manufacturing capability and provided access to the Japanese market. Also, like Philips, Sony had recently suffered commercial defeat with its Betamax video format.

Philips had developed the basic prototypes of the recording technologies, but the two firms jointly developed the commercial chips necessary for the modulation, control and correction of the digital signal. Sony also developed three integrated circuits which eliminated 500 components, making the CD player smaller, cheaper to produce and more reliable.

Philips and Sony quickly moved to establish their technology as the international standard, both by official and de facto means. Their format was adopted by the influential Electronic Association of Japan, which effectively blocked competing standards from Japanese manufacturers. Moreover, both firms used their in-house recording and pressing facilities to produce CD recordings, CBS/Sony in Japan and Philips/PolyGram in Germany, and thus ensure a supply of music titles. In 1982 the CD was launched in the Japanese market and in Europe and the USA in 1983. Sales of CD players and recording exceeded all forecasts: 3 million players in 1985, 9 million in 1986, a cumulative total of 59 million CD recordings by 1985 and 136 million by 1986.

In short, the alliance between Philips and Sony had many motives, including access to complementary technologies, economies of scale in production, establishment of international standards and access to international markets. It was successful because in each case the motives of the respective partners were complementary, rather than competitive.

There is also a growing realization that exposure to external sources of technology can bring about other important organizational benefits, such as providing an element of 'peer review' for the internal R&D function, reducing the 'not invented here' syndrome and challenging in-house researchers with new ideas and different perspectives. In addition, many managers realize the tactical value of certain types of externally developed technology. Some of these are increasingly viewed as a means of gaining the goodwill of customers or governments, of providing a united front for the promotion of uniform industry-wide standards and to influence future legislation.

The UMIST survey of more than 100 UK-based alliances confirms the most common reasons for collaboration for product development are in response to changing customer or market needs.[8] Although many firms formed alliances in an effort to reduce the time, cost or risk of R&D, they did not necessarily realize these benefits from the relationship. Around half believed that collaboration made development more complicated and costly. The study also identified a number of potential risks associated with collaboration:

* leakage of information
* loss of control or ownership
* divergent aims and objectives, resulting in conflict.

The problem of leakage is greatest when collaborating with potential competitors, as it is difficult to isolate the joint venture from the rest of the business and therefore it is inevitable that partners will gain access to additional skills or knowledge. Consequently, a firm may lose control of the venture, resulting in conflict between partners.

Forms of collaboration[9]

Alliances can be characterized in a number of different ways. Horizontal relationships include cross-licensing, consortia and collaboration with potential competitors of sources of complementary technological or market know-how. Vertical relationships include subcontracting, and alliances with suppliers or customers. The primary motive of horizontal alliances tends to be access to complementary technological or market know-how, whereas the primary motives for vertical alliances is cost reduction. An alternative way of viewing alliances is in terms of their strategic significance or duration (Table 14.1). In these terms, contracting and licensing are tactical, whereas strategic alliances, formal joint ventures and innovation networks are strategic and more appropriate structures for learning. We discuss each of these in turn.

Subcontracting

The subcontracting of non-core activities has become popular in recent times. Typically, arguments for subcontracting are framed in terms of strategic focus, or

Table 14.1 Forms of collaboration

Type of collaboration	Typical duration	Advantages (rationale)	Disadvantages (transaction costs)
Subcontract	Short term	Cost and risk reduction, Reduced lead-time	Search costs, product performance and quality
Cross-licensing	Fixed term	Technology acquisition	Contract cost and constraints
Consortia	Medium term	Expertise, standards, share funding	Knowledge leakage Subsequent differentiation
Strategic alliance	Flexible	Low commitment Market access	Potential lock-in Knowledge leakage
Joint venture	Long term	Complementary know-how Dedicated management	Strategic drift Cultural mismatch
Network	Long term	Dynamic, learning potential	Static inefficiencies

'sticking to the knitting', but in practice most subcontracting or outsourcing arrangements are based on the potential to save costs; suppliers are likely to have lower overheads and variable costs and may benefit from economies of scale if serving other firms.

Resource dependence and agency theory are more commonly used to explain vertical relationships and are concerned with the need to control key technologies in the value chain. The seminal work of von Hippel[10] and subsequent work by others have encouraged firms to identify and form relationships with 'lead' users and more recently perceptions of the practices of Japanese manufacturers have led many firms to form closer relationships with suppliers.[11] Indeed closer links between firms, their suppliers and customers may help to reduce the cost of components, through specialization and sharing information on costs.[25]

Traditionally such relationships have been short-term, contractual arm's length agreements focusing on the issue of the cost, with little supplier input into design or engineering. In contrast the 'Japanese' model is based on long-term relationships and suppliers make a significant contribution to the development of new products. In certain sectors, particularly machine tools and scientific equipment, there is a long tradition of collaboration between manufacturers and lead users in the development of new products.

Technology licensing

Licensing offers a firm the opportunity to exploit the intellectual property of another firm, normally in return for payment of a fee and royalty based on sales. Typically, a technology licence will specify the applications and markets in which the technology may be used and often will require the buyer to give the seller access to any subsequent improvements in the technology.

In practice, the relative costs and benefits of licensing-in will depend on the nature of the technologies and markets and strategy and capability of the firm. A survey of more than 200 firms in the chemical, engineering and pharmaceutical industries found that the most important reasons for licensing were related to the speed of access, rather than cost. Factors such as quickly acquiring knowledge required for product development, keeping pace with competitors and increasing sales were found to be most important and factors such as the cost of development least important.[12] The study found that the most significant problems associated with licensing-in were entry costs such as the choice of suitable technology and licenser and the loss of control of decision making.

Research consortia

Research consortia consist of a number of organizations working together on a relatively well-specified project. They may take many different forms, the most centralized being pooled investment in a common research facility or new venture, and the least centralized being co-ordinated research co-located in the various member firms. Typically, European firms have favoured the former, whereas American firms have tended to adopt the latter type. Japanese firms appear to favour a hybrid form in which shared facilities are used in parallel to co-ordinated in-house research. These differences in structure are due to technical, competitive and legal reasons.

The original research consortia were the industry-based research associations formed in the UK during World War I. They were funded by a combination of government funds and contributions from member firms. Many of the associations have survived and are now commercial contract research organizations. The concept of research associations transferred to Japan in the 1950s and a number of research consortia were formed to support the development of the automobile component industry. However, the goals and structure of the Japanese consortia are very different from those in the UK.

In Japan, the Technology Research Association system provides a structure to bring together firms from a wide range of different industries. Unlike their British counterparts, the Japanese associations tend to be temporary organizations and are disbanded when the project is completed, whereas the British associations have tended to become permanent organizations. Members of the Japanese associations tend to be large firms with extensive in-house R&D capabilities, whereas members of British associations tend to be much smaller companies with little in-house R&D. Finally, the Japanese associations tend to be in high-technology areas, whereas the British associations originally concentrated on support for mature industries.

The United States was relatively late to adopt research consortia because of a strong belief in the efficiency of a free market economy resulting in severe anti-trust (anti-monopoly) legislation, which made it difficult to organize consortia.[13]

There are significant differences between Japanese and US research consortia.[14] Almost all members of the Japanese consortia conduct research in member firms, compared to less than half of the US consortia members. The US consortia favour separate joint facilities and research in universities. Therefore the Japanese and US consortia face different organizational problems. The biggest problem the Japanese must tackle is how to co-ordinate research in member firms, whereas the biggest problem for the Americans is how to manage technology transfer from the centre to the member firms. In addition, the Japanese consortia are more focused on applied product development and pilot production, whereas the US consortia tend to concentrate on idea generation and technical feasibility studies.

Strategic alliances

Strategic alliances, whether formal or informal, typically take the form of an agreement between two or more firms to co-develop a new technology or product. Whereas research consortia tend to focus on more basic research issues, strategic alliances involve near-market development projects. However, unlike more formal joint ventures, a strategic alliance typically has a specific end goal and timetable and does not normally take the form of a separate company.

Joint ventures

There are two basic types of formal joint venture: a new company formed by two or more separate organizations, which typically allocate ownership based on shares of stock controlled; or a more simple contractual basis for collaboration. The critical distinction between the two types of joint venture is that an equity arrangement requires the formation of a separate entity. In such cases management is delegated to the joint venture, which is not the case for other forms of collaboration. (See Box 14.2.)

Box 14.2 Airbus industries

Airbus Industrie was formed in France in 1969 as a joint venture between the German firm MBB and French firm Aerospatiale, to be joined by CASA of Spain in 1970 and British Aerospace in 1979. At that time the international market for civil aircraft was dominated by the US firm Boeing, which in 1984 accounted for 40% of the airframe market in the non-communist world. The growing cost and commercial risk of airframe development had resulted in consolidation of the industry and a number of joint ventures.

   The partners identified an unfilled market niche for a high-capacity/short–medium-range passenger aircraft, as more than 70% of the traffic was then on routes of under 4600 km. Thus the Airbus A300 was conceived in 1969. The A300 was essentially the result of the French and German partners, the former insisting on final assembly in France, the latter gaining access to French technology. The first A300 flew in 1974, followed by a series of successful derivatives such as the A310 and the A320. The British partner played a leading role in the subsequent projects, bringing both capital and technological expertise to the venture.

> Airbus demonstrates the complexity of joint ventures. The primary motive was to share the high cost and commercial risk of development. On the one hand, the French and German participation was underwritten by their respective governments. This fact has not escaped the attention of Boeing and the US government, which provides subsidies indirectly via defence contracts. On the other, all partners had to some extent captive markets in the form of national airlines, although almost three-quarters of all Airbus sales were ultimately outside the member countries. Finally, there were also technology motives for the joint venture. For example, BAe specializes in development of the wings and Aerospatiale the avionics. Both MBB and CASA have used Airbus to develop their own technological competencies.

Innovation networks[26]

Where there are high transaction costs involved in purchasing technology, a network approach may be a more appropriate framework for analysis than a market model. Any firm will have a group of partners with which it does regular business – universities, suppliers, distributors, customers and competitors, for instance. Over time mutual knowledge and social bonds develop through repeated dealings, increasing trust and reducing transaction costs. Therefore a firm is more likely to buy or sell technology from members of its network.[15]

Organizational networks have two characteristics which affect the innovation process: activity cycles and instability.[16] The existence of activity cycles and transaction chains creates constraints within a network. The repetition of transactions is the basis of efficiency, but systemic interdependencies create constraints to change. For example, the Swiss watch industry was based on long-established networks of small firms with expertise in precision mechanical movements, but as a result was slow to respond to the threat of electronic watches from Japan. However, as the role of a network is different for all its members, there will always be reasons to change the network and possibilities to do so. This inherent instability and imperfection means that networks develop over time. A network can never be optimal in any generic sense, as there is no single reference point, but is inherently adaptable. Analogies with neural networks would suggest that these two characteristics are the basis for learning. Different types of network will present different opportunities for learning (Table 14.2).

Table 14.2 Competitive dynamics in network industries

	Type of network	
	Unconnected, closed	*Connected, open*
System attributes	Incompatible technologies	Compatible across vendors and products
	Custom components and interfaces	Standard components
Firm strategies	Control standards by protecting proprietary knowledge	Shape standards by sharing knowledge with rivals and complementary markets
Source of advantage	Economies of scale, customer lock-in	Economies of scope, multiple segments

Source: Adapted from Garud, R. and Kumaraswamy, A. (1993) 'Changing competitive dynamics in network industries', *Strategic Management Journal*, 14, 351–369

For example, Japan has a long tradition of formal business groups, originally the family-based zaibatsu and, more recently, the more loosely connected keiretsu. The best known groups are the three ex-zaibatsu – Mitsui, Mitsubishi and Sumitomo – and the three newer groups based around commercial banks – Fuji, Sanwa and Dai Ichi Kangyo (DKB). There are two types of keiretsu, although the two overlap. The vertical type organizes suppliers and distribution outlets hierarchically beneath a large, industry-specific manufacturer, for example Toyota Motor. These manufacturers are in turn members of keiretsu which consist of a large bank, insurance company, trading company and representatives of all major industrial groups. These inter-industry keiretsu provide a significant internal market for intermediate products.

In theory, benefits of membership of a keiretsu include access to low-cost, long-term capital and access to the expertise of firms in related industries. This is particularly important for high-technology firms. In practice, research suggests that membership of keiretsu is associated with below average profitability and growth[17] and independent firms like Honda and Sony are often cited as being more innovative than established members of keiretsu. However, the keiretsu may not be the most appropriate unit of analysis, as many newer, less formal clusters of companies have emerged in modern Japan.

Patterns of collaboration

Industry structure and technological and market characteristics result in different opportunities for joint ventures across sectors, but other factors determine the strategy of specific firms within a given sector.

In general, large firms use joint ventures to acquire technology, while smaller firms place greater emphasis on the acquisition of market knowledge and financial support.

Joint venture activity is high in the chemical, mechanical and electrical machinery sectors, as firms seek to acquire external technological know-how in order to reduce the inherent technological uncertainty in those sectors. In contrast, joint ventures are much less common in consumer goods industries, where market position is the result of product differentiation, distribution and support. If obtaining complementary assets or resources is a primary motive for collaboration, we would expect alliances to be concentrated in those sectors in which mutual ignorance of the partner's technology or markets is likely to be high.[18] Similarly, joint ventures would occur more frequently between partners who are in industries relatively unrelated to one another and that such alliances are likely to be short lived as firms learn from each other. Surveys of alliances in so-called high-technology sectors such as software and automation appear to confirm that access to technology is the most common motive. Market access appears to be a more common motive for collaboration in the computer, microelectronics, consumer electronics and telecommunications sectors.

Given the problems of management and organization, potential for opportunistic behaviour and the limited success of alliances it might be expected that the popularity of alliances might decline as firms gain experience of such problems. However, according to the Co-operative Agreements and Technology Indicators (CATI) database the number of technology alliances increased from fewer than 300 in 1990 to more than 430 in 1993.

Overall, the number of alliances has increased over time and networks of collaboration appear to have become more stable, being based around a number of nodal firms in different sectors. These networks are not necessarily closed, but rather represent the dynamic partnering behaviour of large, leading firms in each of the sectors. The nodal firms are relatively stable, but their partners change over time. Contrary to the claims of globalization, the number of domestic alliances has increased faster than international ones. This trend is particularly strong in the United States. Distinct sectoral patterns exist. In the heavy electrical equipment and aerospace industries, most of the collaborative activity is confined within each of the triad regions: Europe, Japan and North America. In contrast, most of the activity in the chemical and automotive sectors is across the triad regions. This suggests that the primary motive for collaborating with domestic firms is access to technology, but market access is more important in the case of cross-border alliances.

A study of how 23 UK and 15 Japanese firms acquired technology externally identified the conditions under which each particular method is favoured. The relative importance of different external sources to each of the UK-based companies is summarized in Figure 14.2. Each of these sources is discussed in turn and examples provided.

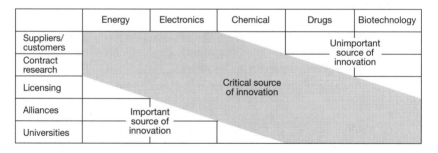

Figure 14.2 Relative importance to UK-based firms of external sources of technology

Source: Adapted from Tidd, J. and Trewhella, M. (1997) 'Organizational and technological antecedents for knowledge acquisition', *R&D Management*, 27(4): 358–75.

Universities

In the UK universities are a widely used external source of technology. These relationships range from support for PhD candidates, extra mural research awards for post-doctoral staff to carry out research in a specific area, to more formal contract research and collaborative schemes such as the LINK scheme jointly funded by the DTI and a number of companies to conduct pre-competitive research in a specified area. Firms use university research for a number of reasons: to access specialist technical support; to extend in-house research; and to provide a window on emerging technologies.

Extensions to existing in-house research typically involve using universities to conduct either fundamental research, aimed at gaining a better understanding of an underlying area of science, or more speculative extensions to existing in-house programmes which cannot be justified internally because of their high risk or because of limited in-house resources. For example, Zeneca has made extensive use of universities to undertake fundamental studies into the molecular biology of plants and the cloning of genes. Although not key technologies, access to state-of-the-art knowledge in these areas is vital to support a number of the organization's core agricultural activities. Similarly, CRL, the research organizations of Thorn, utilized technology originally developed at Edinburgh and Cambridge universities in its spatial light modulators and ultra-low power consumption gas sensors, respectively.

University-funded research can also be used as windows on emerging or rapidly advancing fields of science and technology. Companies view access to such information as being critical in making good decisions about if or when to internalize a new technology.

Research consortia

Consortia, defined as multifirm collaborations, take two main forms, between competitors or between non-competing firms. Firms commonly collaborate with competitors in the development of pre-competitive technologies. This form of collaboration is particularly attractive when supported by government or EU funds, as in the case of the Framework Programme for European Research and Technological Development.

Nevertheless, even in consortia involving non-competing firms, it appears that vested interests can sometimes lead to difficulties. For example, in the collaboration between auto manufacturers and oil companies aimed at reducing toxic emissions from car exhausts, there exist serious differences of opinion between these two groups of firms about whether the main thrust of the research should be directed towards improved engine efficiencies or towards better gasoline formulations.

Licensing

Licensing is one of the most widely used methods for acquiring technology. The main attraction is that it enables firms rapidly to establish positions in new technical areas, particularly in those which complement existing core skills.

In some cases, however, there is a reluctance to license in technology which may adversely affect the differentiation of end products, if customers became aware of the fact. Many firms express concerns regarding the constraints imposed by international licensing agreements, specifically the common requirement to 'grant back' any improvements made to the technology. For example, ICI claims increasing globalization and concentration within the chemical industry as reducing the scope for licensing technology. For these reasons an increasing number of firms are careful to license only components of any process or product in order to allow scope for subsequent improvement and differentiation.

Customers and suppliers

Many firms collaborate with customers to develop technologies or products. The main motives for this are either to gain customer credibility or 'buy-in' or jointly to develop technology that could subsequently be used to satisfy other customers, which will depend on how typical the customers' needs are. For example, most international energy and construction firms have policies of collaboration with customers overseas and source technologies from countries in which they wish to sell products. Such collaborations are an important factor in gaining the goodwill of both potential customers and national governments, which exert a major influence over most of its customers.

Equity and company acquisition

In recent years, acquisition has again become a popular means of acquiring technology. Normally, the rationale is to establish a position quickly in a particular technical area. However, feelings about the effectiveness of this route are mixed; many acquisitions have suffered from the loss or demotivation of key staff or have failed to realize their expected potential for other reasons. Nevertheless, a few companies claim spectacular successes among their acquisitions. The common factors here appear to be prior experience of the markets in which the new technology would be used and a compatible culture between the two organizations. For example, Eli Lilly identified a small US company, Agouron Pharmaceuticals, working on an enzyme believed to be a catalyst in tumour growth. The company considered this technology sufficiently promising to invest $4.5m in acquiring an 8% stake in the company and first claim to any resulting drugs.

Intra-company transfer

In addition to the more obvious sources of external technology already reviewed, managers highlight the changing balance between three potential sources of internally generated technology, specifically the respective role of internal venture groups, corporate research laboratories and divisional R&D facilities. The main issue facing firms today is the share of resources of the central or corporate laboratories, which are normally large, multidisciplinary research establishments, with at least an element of corporate funding and the divisional or business unit R&D facilities, which are funded by, and support, one particular business.

Effect of technology and organization

It is possible to identify two dimensions which affect companies' attitudes towards technology acquisition: the characteristics of the technology and the organization's 'inheritance' (Table 14.3). Together, these eight factors determine the knowledge acquisition strategy of a firm.

Table 14.3 Links between technology acquisition strategy, organizational factors and characteristics of technology

Organizational and technological factors	Acquisitional mechanism (most favoured/alternative)	Rationale for decision
Corporate strategy		
Leadership	In-house R&D/equity acquisition	Differentiation, first mover, proprietary technology
Follower	Licence/customers and suppliers/contract	Low-cost imitation
Fit with competencies		
Strong	In-house R&D	Options to leverage competencies
Weak	Contract/licence/consortia	Access to external technology
Company culture		
External focus	Various	Cost effectiveness of source
Internal focus	In-house/joint venture	Learning experience
Comfort with new technology		
High	In-house corporate/university	High risk and potential high reward
Low	Licence/customers and suppliers/consortia	Lowest risk option
Characteristics of the technology		
Competitive importance		
Base	Licence/contract/customers/ suppliers	Cost effective/secure source
Key	In-house R&D/joint venture	Maximize competitive advantage
Pacing	In-house corporate/university	Future position/learning
Emerging	University/in-house corporate	Watching brief
Complexity		
High	Consortia/universities/suppliers	Specialization of know-how
Low	In-house R&D/contract/suppliers	Division of labour
Codifiability		
High	Licence/contract/university	Cost effectiveness of source
Low	In-house R&D/joint venture	Learning /tacit know-how
Credibility potential		
High	Consortia/customer/government	High-profile source
Low	University/contract/licence	Cost effectiveness of source

Source: Adapted from Tidd, J. and Trewhella, M. (1997) 'Organizational and technological antecedents for knowledge acquisition', *R&D Management*,

The relevant characteristics of the technology include:

- competitive significance of the technology
- complexity of the technology
- codifiability, or how easily the technology is encoded
- credibility potential, or political profile of the technology.

An organization's inheritance encompasses those characteristics which, at least in the short run, are fixed and therefore represent constraints within which the R&D function develops its strategies for acquiring technology. These include:

- corporate strategy, for example, a leadership versus follower position
- capabilities and existing technical know-how
- culture of the firm, including receptivity to external knowledge
- 'comfort' of management with a given technical area.

Competitive significance

The competitive significance of the technology is the single most important factor influencing companies' decisions about how best to acquire a given technology.

Strategies for acquiring pacing technologies, i.e. those with the potential to become tomorrow's key technologies, vary. For example, some organizations, such as AEA Technology, seek to develop and maintain at least some in-house expertise in many pacing technologies, so they will not be 'wrong-footed' if conditions change or unexpected advances occur. Other firms, such as Kodak, also recognize the need to monitor developments in a number of pacing technologies, but see universities or joint ventures as the most efficient means of achieving this. The company sponsors a large amount of research in leading universities throughout the world and has also set up a number of joint venture programmes with firms in complementary industries. Guinness, for example, identified genetic engineering as a pacing technology and seconded a member of staff to work at a leading university for three years. Thus, the company has successfully internalized the technology, understands its potential and is well placed to evaluate new developments in the area or to take advantage of any changes in legislation and public attitudes.

Most companies look to acquire base technologies externally or in the case of non-competitive technologies, by cooperative efforts. Companies recognize that their base technologies are often the core competencies of other firms. In such cases, the policy is to acquire specific pieces of base technology from these firms, who can almost always provide better technology, at less cost, than could have been obtained from in-house sources. Materials testing, routine analysis and computing services are common examples of technical services now acquired externally.

Complexity of the technology

The increasingly interdisciplinary nature of many of today's technologies and products means that, in many technical fields, it is not practical for any firm to maintain all necessary skills in-house. This increased complexity is leading many organizations to conclude that, in order to stay at the forefront of their key technologies, they must somehow leverage their in-house competencies with those available externally. For example, the need to acquire external technologies appears to increase as the number of component technologies increases. In extreme cases of complexity networks of specialist developers may emerge which serve companies which specialize in systems integration and customization for end users.

Codifiability of the technology

The more that knowledge about a particular technology can be codified, i.e. described in terms of formulae, blueprints and rules, the easier it is to transfer and the more speedily and extensively such technologies can be diffused.

Knowledge that cannot easily be codified, often termed 'tacit' is, by contrast, much more difficult to acquire, since it can only be transferred effectively by experience and face-to-face interactions. All else being equal, it appears preferable to develop tacit technologies in-house. In the absence of strong intellectual property rights (IPR) or patent protection, tacit technologies provide a more durable source of competitive advantage than those which can easily be codified.

For example, Kodak maintains all its strategies technologies in-house, even if these are considered mature, because of the large amount of tacit know-how embodied in even these technologies. The existence of difficult-to-codify tacit knowledge is one of the factors that has allowed it to maintain a competitive advantage in one particular core technology, even though the basic features of this technology have been in use for over 100 years. The difficulty of maintaining a competitive advantage when technology is easily codifiable is highlighted by Guinness, which developed a small plastic, gas-filled, device that gives canned beer the same creamy head as a keg beer. This 'widget' initially provided the company with a source of competitive advantage and extra sales, but the innovation was soon copied widely throughout the industry, to the extent that widgets are now almost a requirement for any premium canned beer.

Credibility potential

The credibility given to the company by a technology is a significant factor influencing the way companies decide to acquire a technology. Particular value is placed on gaining credibility or goodwill from governments, customers, market analysts and even from the company's own top management, academic institutions and potential recruits. For example, Celltech's collaboration with a large US chemical firm appears to have enhanced the former's market credibility. Not only did the collaboration demonstrate the organization's ability to manage a multimillion dollar R&D project, but by the numerous patents and academic publications that arose from it were also felt to have improved the company's scientific standing.

Corporate strategy

One of the most important factors affecting the balance between in-house generated and externally acquired technology is the degree to which company strategy dictates that it should pursue a policy of technological differentiation or leadership. For example, Kodak distinguishes between two types of technical core competencies: strategic, i.e. those activities in which the company must be a world leader because they represent such an important source of competitive advantage; and enabling, i.e. skills required for success, but which do not have to be controlled internally. Although all strategic activities are retained in-house, the company is prepared to access enabling technologies externally, if the overall technology is sufficiently complex.

Firm competencies

An organization's internal technical capabilities are another factor influencing the way in which it decides to acquire a given technology. Where these are weak, a firm normally has little choice but to acquire from outside, at least in the short run, whereas strong in-house capabilities often favour the internal development of related technologies, because of the greater degree of control afforded by this route. In such cases, the main driving force behind the acquisition strategy is speed to market. For example, speed to market is a critical success factor for many firms in consumer markets. Such firms select the technology acquisition method that provides the fastest means of commercialization. When the required expertise is available in-house, this route is normally favoured because it allows greater control of the development process and is therefore usually quicker. However, where suitable in-house capabilities are lacking, external sourcing is almost always faster than building the required skills internally. Gillette, for example, found that one of its new products required laser spot-welding competencies that the company lacked and given the limited market window was forced to go outside to acquire this technology.

Company culture

Every company has its own culture, that is 'the way we do things around here'; here we are concerned with the underlying values and beliefs that play an important role in technology acquisition policies. A culture of 'we are the best' is likely to contribute towards a rather myopic view of external technology developments and limit the potential for learning from external partners. Some organizations, however, consistently reinforce the philosophy that important technical developments can occur almost anywhere in the world. Consequently, staff in these companies are encouraged to identify external developments and to internalize potentially important technologies before the competition. However, in practice few firms have formal 'technology scouting' personnel or functions.

For example, Glaxo emphasizes that companies need to guard against becoming captives of their own in-house expertise, since this limits the scope of its activities to what can be achieved through internal resources. Kodak's philosophy is that world-class organizations must access technology wherever it resides and that a culture of 'not invented here' is a prescription for second-class citizenship in the global marketplace. For example, Japan is now the centre of this organization's worldwide efforts in molecular beam epitaxy, a method of growing crystals for making gallium arsenide chips. A key role for overseas laboratories is to monitor technology developments in host countries. Local champions from around the world are closely networked so that technical advances made in one geographic location are rapidly disseminated around the organization as a whole. Such is this company's determination to maintain a 'window' on potential sources of technology that it has set up joint ventures with many large and small companies worldwide, including links with Matsushita, Canon, Nikon, Minolta, Fuji and Apple.

Management comfort

The degree of comfort management has with a given technology manifests itself at the level of the individual R&D manager or management team, rather than at the level of the organization as a whole. Management comfort is multifaceted. One aspect is related to a management team's familiarity with the technology. Another reflects the degree of confidence that the team can succeed in a new technical area, perhaps because of a research group's track record of success in related fields. Attitude to risk is also a factor.

All else being equal, the more comfortable a company's managers feel with a given technology, the more likely that technology is to be developed in-house. For example, the current business of Zeneca Seeds was built on the basis of providing an outlet for the parent organization's in-house biotechnology expertise. This means that the concept of world-leading in-house technology sits very comfortably with the organization's top management, which is reflected by the fact that annual in-house R&D expenditure exceeds the firm's annual capital expenditure by a considerable margin. Similarly, AEA Technology's core technologies of plant life extension, environmental sciences, modelling and land remediation treatment all derive from its nuclear industry background. Top management's comfort with these technologies has led them to encourage staff to build on these skills and to use these as a spring-board for diversification into new scientific areas.

Managing alliances for learning

So far we have discussed collaboration as a means of accessing market or technological know-how or acquiring assets. However, alliances can also be used as an opportunity to learn new market and technological competencies, in other words to internalize a partner's know-how. Seen in this light, the success of an alliance becomes rather more difficult to measure.

Collaboration is an inherently risky activity and less than half achieve their goals. A study of almost 900 joint ventures found that only 45% were mutually agreed to have been successful by all partners.[27] Reasons for failure include strategic divergence, procedural problems and cultural mismatch.

If learning is a major goal, it is necessary for partners to have complementary skills and capabilities, but an even balance of strength is also important. The more equal the partners, the more likely an alliance will be successful. Both partners must be strong financially and in the technological, product or market contribution they make to the venture. A study of 49 international alliances by management consultants

McKinsey found that two-thirds of the alliances between equally matched partners were successful, but where there was a significant imbalance of power almost 60% of alliances failed.[19] Consequently, in the case of a formal joint venture equal ownership is the most successful structure, 50–50 ownership being twice as likely to succeed as other ownership structures. This appears to be because such a structure demands continuous consultation and communication between partners, which helps anticipate and resolve potential conflicts, and problems of strategic divergence. Factors which contribute to the success of an alliance include:[20]

- the alliance is perceived as important by all partners
- a collaboration 'champion' exists
- a substantial degree of trust between partners exists
- clear project planning and defined task milestones are established
- frequent communication between partners, in particular between marketing and technical staff
- the collaborating parties contribute as expected
- benefits are perceived to be equally distributed.

This suggests that firms must learn to design alliances with other firms, rather than pursue ad hoc relationships. By design we do not mean the legal and financial details of the agreement, but rather the need to select a partner which can contribute what is needed and needs what is offered, of which there is sufficient prior knowledge or experience to encourage trust and communication, to allow areas of potential conflict such as overlapping products or markets to be designed out. Partners must specify mutual expectations of respective contributions and benefits. They should agree on a business plan, including contingencies for possible dissolution, but allow sufficient flexibility for the goals and structure of the alliance to evolve. It is important that partners communicate on a routine basis, so that any problems are shared. Without such explicit design, collaboration may make product development more costly, complex and difficult to control.

Thus the success of an alliance depends to a large extent on what can be described as operational and people-related factors, rather than strategic factors such as technological, market or product fit. The most important operational factors are agreement on clearly stated aims and responsibilities and the most important people factors are high levels of commitment, communication and trust.

Mutual trust is clearly a significant factor, as the main risks of collaboration are leakage of information and potential conflict of aims and objectives. Trust may exist at the personal and organization levels. Clearly, high levels of interpersonal trust are necessary to facilitate communication and learning in collaboration, but interorganizational trust is a more subtle issue. Organizational trust may be defined in terms of organizational routines, norms and values which are able to survive changes in individual personnel.[21] In this way organizational learning can take place, including new ways of doing things (operational or lower level learning) and doing new things through diversification (strategic or higher level learning). Organizational trust requires a longer time horizon to ensure that reciprocity can occur, as for any particular collaborative project one partner is likely to benefit disproportionately.

Table 14.4 Determinants of learning through alliances

		Factors which promote learning
A	*Intent to learn*	
1	Competitive posture	Cooperate now, compete later
2	Strategic significance	High, to build competencies, rather than to fix a problem
3	Resource position	Scarcity
4	Relative power balance	Balance creates instability, rather than harmony
B	*Transparency for learning*	
5	Social context	Language and cultural barriers
6	Attitude towards outsiders	Exclusivity, but absence of 'not invented here'
7	Nature of skills	Tacit and systemic, rather than explicit
C	*Receptivity or absorptive capacity*	
8	Confidence in abilities	Realistic, not too high or too low
9	Skills gap	Small, not too substantial
10	Institutionalization of learning	High, transfer of individual learning to organization

Source: Adapted from Hamel, G. (1991) 'Learning in international alliances', *Strategic Management Journal*, 12, 91

In this way organizational trust may mitigate against opportunistic behaviour. However, in practice this may be difficult where partners have different motives for an alliance for differential rates of learning.

It is possible to identify three factors which affect learning through alliances: intent, transparency and receptivity (Table 14.4). Intent refers to a firm's propensity to view collaboration as an opportunity to learn new skills rather than to gain access to a partner's assets. Thus where there is intent, learning takes place by design rather than by default, which is much more significant than mere leakage of information. Transparency refers to the openness or 'knowability' of each partner and therefore the potential for learning. Receptivity, or absorptiveness, refers to a partner's capacity to learn. Clearly, there is much a firm can do to maximize its own intent and receptivity and minimize its transparency. Intent to learn will influence the choice of partner and form of collaboration. Transparency will depend on the penetrability of the social context, attitudes towards outsiders, i.e. clannishness, and the extent to which the skills are discrete and encodable. Explicit knowledge, such as designs and patents are more easily encoded than tacit knowledge.

The conversion of tacit to explicit knowledge is a critical mechanism underlying the link between individual and organizational learning.[22] Through a process of dialogue, discussion, experience sharing and observation individual knowledge is amplified at the group and organizational levels. This creates an expanding community of interaction, or 'knowledge network', which crosses intra-and inter-organizational levels and boundaries. These knowledge networks are a means to accumulate knowledge from outside the organization, share it widely within the organization and store it for future use. Therefore, the interaction of groups with different cultures, whether within or beyond the boundaries of the organization, is a potential source of learning and innovation.

Organizational structure and culture will determine absorptive capacity in inter-organizational learning. Culture is a difficult concept to grasp and measure, but it helps to distinguish between national, organizational, functional and group cultures.[23] Differences in national culture have received a great deal of attention in studies of cross-border alliances and acquisitions and the consensus is that national differences do exist and that these affect both the intents and ability to learn. In general, British and US firms focus more on the legal and financial aspects of alliance, but rarely have either the intent or ability to learn through alliances. In contrast, French, German, and Japanese firms are more likely to exploit opportunities for learning.[24] The issue of national stereotypes aside, there may be structural reasons for these differences in the propensity to learn.

For example, Japanese firms have good historical reasons for exploiting alliances as opportunities for learning. Initially, western firms typically entered Japan through alliances in which they provided technology in return for access to Japanese sales and distribution channels. This exchange of technology for market access appeared to offer value to both sides. However, while the western partner often remained dependent on the Japanese partner for distribution and sales, the Japanese partner typically built up its technological skills and became less reliant on the western partner. As a result, in the 1980s European and US partners began to lose technological leadership in many fields and were forced to trade distribution and sales channels at home for access to the Japanese market. Therefore collaboration has shifted from relatively simple and well-defined licensing agreements or joint ventures, to more complex and informal relationships which are much more difficult to manage.

Most recently firms from the United States and Europe have begun to use alliances for operational learning. Operational learning provides close exposure to what competitors are doing in Japan and how they are doing it. For example, to learn how Japanese partners manage their production facilities, supplier base or product development process. This is not possible from a distance and requires close alliances with potential competitors. However, fewer firms in the West have exploited fully the potential of alliances for strategic learning, that is the acquisition of new technological and market competencies.

In contrast, many US and British firms find it difficult to learn through alliances. This appears to be because firms focus on financial control and short-term financial benefits, rather than the longer term potential for learning. For example, firms will attempt to minimize the number and quality of people they contribute to a Japanese joint venture and the time committed. As a result, little learning takes place and little or no corporate memory is built up.

Summary

Essentially, firms collaborate to reduce the cost, time or risk of access to unfamiliar technologies or markets. Transaction costs analysis focuses on the static, short-term trade-offs between developing an innovation in-house versus external mechanisms, whereas a strategic learning framework focuses on the dynamic, longer term potential for acquiring new technological, market or organizational competencies. The precise form of the collaboration will be determined by the motives and preferences of the partners, but their choice will be constrained by the nature of the technologies and markets, specifically the degree of complexity and tacitness. The success of an alliance depends on a number of factors, but organizational issues dominate, such as the degree of mutual trust and level of communication. The transaction costs approach better explains the relationship between the reason for collaboration and the preferred form and structure of an alliance. The strategic learning approach better explains the relationship between the management and organization of an alliance and the subsequent outcomes.

References

1   McGee, J. E. and Dowling, M. J. (1994) 'Using R&D cooperative arrangements to leverage managerial experience', *Journal of Business Venturing*, 9, 33–48.

2   Hauschildt, J. (1992) 'External acquisition of knowledge for innovations – a research agenda', *R&D Management*, 22(2), 105–110.

3   Welch, J. A. and Nayak, P. R. (1992) 'Strategic sourcing: a progressive approach to the make or buy decision', *Academy of Management Executive*, 6(1), 23–31.

4   Bettis, R. A., Bradley, S. P. and Hamel, G. (1992) 'Outsourcing and industrial decline', *Academy of Management Executive*, 6(1), 7–21.

5   Atuaheme-Gima, K. and Patterson, P. (1993) 'Managerial perceptions of technology licensing as an alternative to internal R&D in new product development: an empirical investigation', *R&D Management*, 23(4), 327–336.

6   Robins, J. and Wiersema, M. I. (1995) 'A resource-based approach to the multi-business firm', *Strategic Management Journal*, 16(4), 277–300.

7   Grandstand, O., Bohlin, E., Oskarsson, S. and Sjoberg, N. (1992) 'External technology acquisition in large multi-technology corporation', *R&D Management*, 22(2), 111–133.

8   D. A. Littler (1998) *Risks and Rewards of Collaboration*, UMIST.

9   Bleeke, J. and Ernst, D. (1993) *Collaborating to Compete*. John Wiley & Sons, New York.

10   Von Hippel, E. (1998) *The Sources of Innovation*. Oxford University Press, Oxford.

11   Nishiguchi, T. (1994) *Strategic Industrial Sourcing: The Japanese advantage*. Oxford University Press, Oxford.

12   Atuaheme-Gima, K. and Patterson, P. (1993) 'Managerial perceptions of technology licensing as an alternative to internal R&D in new product development: an empirical investigation', *R&D Management*, 23(4), 327–336.

13   Gibson, D. V. and Rogers, E. M. (1994) *R&D Collaboration on Trial*. Harvard Business School Press, Boston.

14   Aldrich, H. E. and Sasaki, T. (1995) 'R&D consortia in the US and Japan', *Research Policy*, 24(2), 301–316.

15   Bidault, F. and Fischer, W. A. (1994) 'Technology transactions: networks over markets', *R&D Management*, 24(4), 373–386.

16   Hakansson, H. (1995) 'Product development in networks', in Ford, D. (ed.), *Understanding Business Markets: Interaction, relationships and networks*. The Dryden Press, New York, 487–507.

17   Nakateni, I. (1984) 'The economic role of financial corporate groupings', in Masahiko Aoki (ed.) *The Economic Analysis of the Japanese Firm*. North-Holland, Amsterdam, 227–258.

18   Balakrishnan, S. and Koza, M. P. (1995) 'An information theory of joint ventures', in Gomez-Mejia, L.R. and Lawless, M.W. (eds) *Advances in Global High-Technology*

Management: Strategic alliances in high technology. JAI Press, Greenwich, Conn., Vol. 5 Part B, 59–72.

19   Bleeke, J. and Ernst, D. (1993) *Collaborating to Compete.* John Wiley & Sons, New York.

20   Bruce, M., Leverick, F. and Littler, D. (1995) 'Complexities of collaborative product development', *Technovation*, 15(9), 535–552.

21   Dodgson, M. (1993) 'Learning, trust, and technological collaboration', *Human Relations*, 46(1), 77–95.

22   Nonaka, I. and Takeuchi, H. (1995) *The Knowledge-Creating Company.* Oxford University Press, Oxford.

23   Levinson, N. S. and Asahi, M. (1995) 'Cross-national alliances and interorganizational learning', *Organizational Dynamics*, Autumn, 50–63.

24   Hamel, G. (1991) 'Competition for competence and inter-partner learning within international strategic alliances', *Strategic Management Journal*, 12, 83–103; Jones K. K. and Shill, W. E (1993) 'Japan: allying for advantage', in Bleeke, J. and Ernst, D. (eds) *Collaborating to Compete.* John Wiley & Sons, New York, 115–144; Sasaki, T. (1993) 'What the Japanese have learned from strategic alliances', *Long Range Planning*, 26(6), 41–53.

25   Leonard-Barton, D. and Sinha, D. (1993) 'Developer–user interaction and user satisfaction in internal technology transfer', *Academy of Management Journal*, 36(5), 1125–1139.

26   Nohria, N. and Eccles, R.G. (1991) *Networks and Organizations.* Harvard Business School Press, Boston.

27   Harrigan, K.R. (1986) *Managing for Joint Venture Success.* Lexington Books: Lexington, Mass.

15 Paradox in Project-based Enterprise: The Case of Film Making

Robert J. DeFillippi and Michael B. Arthur

Two interdependent manifestations of the new economy are the rise of project-based careers and the creation of temporary organizations for project-based work. In industries such as film, construction and semiconductors, work is frequently organized around projects, whose employees are subcontractors who move among different employing firms.[1] Project-based enterprises (companies formed to pursue a specific project outcome) and project-based careers (careers habitually moving from one project to another) are most typically found where complex, non-routine tasks require the temporary employment and collaboration of diversely skilled specialists. Similar trends toward project-based organizing can be found in knowledge-intensive professional service firms in fields such as law, management consulting and architecture.[2]

Project-based enterprises challenge several tenets of current strategic management theory. For example, one tenet of strategic management theory is that firms develop and leverage 'core competencies' or key resources over time.[3] How can a project-based enterprise accumulate its core competencies when it rents all its human capital? And how can tacit knowledge and knowledge transfer unfold without a stable cadre of experienced personnel? A second tenet of strategic management theory is that firms create competitive advantage through their possession and use of non-imitable resources.[4] How can project-based enterprises create competitive advantage when its knowledge-based resources are embodied in highly mobile project participants? A third tenet is that competencies are accumulated through firms competing to recruit and develop human capital.[5] How is this human capital assembled and what market and social processes facilitate its identification, evaluation, and selection for project-based activities?

Industry context

Film making is an industry where project-based enterprises have long flourished. Although Hollywood is associated with the dominance of major film studios such as Warner Brothers and MGM, the industry has a long tradition of independent film making dating back to the 1920s. Unlike the major studios of the time, independent film companies did not typically employ their actors under long-term exclusive contracts, did not own expensive studio facilities and did not employ permanent staffs of scriptwriters, special effects technicians, custom designers and other technical support personnel. In the 1950s, the Hollywood studios found the costs of maintaining permanent stables of film-making talent and the employment practices that had grown within those stables prohibitively expensive. The old studio system of film production gave way to the example set by independent filmmakers.[6]

The market uncertainty and demand volatility of the industry require filmmakers to develop competencies in: the identification and recruitment of talented commercial and artistic project participants; and the management of complexities spanning co-ordination of cast, production crews, elaborate sets and sophisticated audio, visual and special effects technologies. These project-specific, knowledge-based competencies can be an important source of competitive advantage and project success.[7] Similar relationships between specialized industry competencies and commercial success have been observed in high-technology firms.[8] However, both sets of observations stop short of identifying how knowledge-based competencies are accumulated and transferred.

Studies in product development suggest that firms having families of sequentially related product development projects often retain core members of successful prior projects to serve on derivative successor projects.[9] These ideas support strategic management approaches concerned with leveraging a firm's knowledge-based human resources.[10] The absence of traditional governance mechanisms for integrating creative and managerial talents directs attention toward the market and social processes occurring among independent film-making participants.

Career context

As the movement toward independent film making unfolded, the industry became characterized by 'core' and 'peripheral' groups. Core groups obtained financing from the seven major Hollywood film studios (as they continued to be called). Peripheral groups used persistent independent producers or 'fly-by-night' single film sponsors. Core groups were more apt to employ similar sets of commercial and artistic personnel on multiple projects, for whom network processes were critical in explaining inter-project employment. In contrast, peripheral groups demonstrated far less continuity of association or employment. Employees in both groups seeking to stay in the industry had to seek regular re-employment and career progression as companies formed to make a single film were successively established and dissolved.[11]

One way for film crews to sustain themselves and their careers is through 'wholly outsourced teams' that provide the continuity independent film companies lack. However, the performance of such teams suggests a curvilinear relationship to film performance, with moderate levels of prior shared project experience correlating with the highest levels of film success. Hence, film projects can suffer from too little or too much prior experience of members having worked together on previous film projects.[12] Despite contrary claims – from, for example, manufacturing – film crews' prior experience working together is not a direct substitute for more traditional governance systems.[13]

In sum, it remains unclear how film-making strategy and its implementation relates to industry participants' prior film experience. In particular, it is still unclear how industry and career processes influence and are influenced by successive project-based enterprise activities.

The research setting

This chapter describes field research into the creation of an independently produced UK–US feature film. The project had large budget financing by a major Hollywood studio (the studios still have a strong presence in financing films, leasing facilities, and securing distribution channels). The project also employed actors and actresses with proven box office appeal and it had built an experienced commercial and artistic support crew, many of whom had worked together on prior film projects.[14] As a condition for access, the names of both the film project (code name *Omega*) and its participants have been disguised to assure the confidentiality of all reported events of the project and its participants. Eight artistic roles were scriptwriter, lead actor, production set designer, art director, wardrobe supervisor, sound mixer, animal consultant and chief make-up artist. These roles are creative/artistic in that they are identified with the creation of the artistic elements (visual, narrative, musical) of the film product. Eight commercial roles were executive producer, producer, associate producer, second assistant director, production co-ordinator, production accountant, production manager and production runner.

Paradox in project-based enterprise

The project-based enterprise confronts several assumptions behind traditional strategic management thought, concerned broadly with the temporary nature of the enterprise and with career investments within it. For more than 20 years, temporary enterprises have sustained a relatively permanent and resilient independent film industry. Moreover, the independent film industry provides an opportunity to observe project-based enterprise in relatively pure form. In other prominent examples, such as after building construction, legal proceedings or software writing, the principal company or companies involved are expected to remain in business and find new work. In independent film making, the producing company is essentially disbanded once the film is released. The notion of temporary enterprises sustaining a permanent industry presents a paradox.

Strategy precedes enterprise formation

The film project *Omega* began to form during the shooting of a modestly financed independent film *Alpha* some eight years earlier. The experience of producing *Alpha*, one of the 'sleeper' hits of the year, generated such a sense of camaraderie among the principal actors, director and several production staff that they collectively agreed to seek out some future film project on which to collaborate. The box office success enabled Peter, *Alpha*'s visionary entrepreneur, to 'write his own rules' and retain creative control for the follow-up *Omega* project. Peter's 'rules' included sharing his evolving vision for *Omega* with an ever widening network of actors, writers and consultants expert in the substantive themes and settings for *Omega*. Included in the draft consultations were the principal actors and production crew from *Alpha*.

Meanwhile, Paul, the producer, had 'been friends for about 15 years' with Peter and had helped with the production of *Alpha*. Paul flexed his reputation as a producer, pitching the 'sought-after' *Omega* project to multiple prospective backers and won a 'very aggressive' deal. It was a deal in which the film was 'very much Peter's vision' while Paul's job was to 'manage the financial side of it' and bring the film to fruition. Thus, the strategic vision of the film, incorporating both artistic and business perspectives, was largely in place before the formal film-making enterprise was formed.

From its inception, the film-making enterprise is distinct from the continuing entity at which much strategic management thinking is targeted.[15] The project-based enterprise inherits its strategic vision, rather than shapes its own. Moreover, the vision is temporary and geared to one specific product rather than multiple related products. The enterprise also inherits its funding and is typically not required to generate further income before its dissolution.

Structure/staffing are temporary

A film company, as a new company, recruits all its personnel from outside. In the *Omega* case, Peter and Paul had clear ideas of the key people they each wanted to work with on the artistic and business sides respectively. Big-budget film projects are such time-pressured, performance-driven undertakings that requisite abilities must be available from the outset. For this reason, there is a bias toward hiring artistic and commercial crews with significant prior film experience in the project tasks assigned to them. This bias toward industry experience is clearly evident in the previous film credits of the 16 interviewed participants in *Omega*. Everyone except the entry-level production runner had no fewer than a half dozen major film credits in their background.

The flip side is that accumulated human resources are also temporary and highly variable. The executive producer reflected on the changing size and composition of the production company during the first two months of production: 'It's just very odd going from employing 20 people just two months ago to our current employment of over 190 people. This week, because the main construction is finished, we'll be losing 40 or 50 construction people. And then a year later, to all intents and purposes, it is over.' Physical assets are also temporary. The *Omega* production company rented office space from a British film studio, leased office equipment for its business staff and outsourced all camera and lighting equipment as part of its contracting with crews. Even the physical setting for much of *Omega*'s shooting was temporary. The realistic looking set of structures that were created in the 90 days prior to film shooting were dismantled almost immediately on the film's completion.[16]

Capital investments are temporary

Human and physical asset arrangements are symptomatic of the short-term, project-specific capital investments through which independent film making is financed. The 'massive' front-end financing required obligates the business side, in the words of the production accountant, 'to advise the investors of the cost position on a weekly basis'. Moreover, if investors 'aren't happy, everyone knows it' and those investors are reportedly 'ready to desert if they feel it is going very, very wrong'. This obligation to investors means that it is not unusual for the production accounting/control function to be one of a film company's most important and heavily staffed functions, controlling all costs while giving the artistic crew 'everything they need to make the film'.

A principal reason for this heavy staffing is that film making is continually subject to unanticipated interruptions. For example, unanticipated weather changes can halt outdoor location shooting, the absence of a key cast member can delay a scene or a fragile ego can fail to respond to new priorities, resulting in significant cost overruns and schedule delays. Because all the company's resources are dedicated to only a single production task, there is little or no opportunity to deploy any of these resources to alternative uses during such delays. Meanwhile, human and physical capital resources are still being charged to the production company's costs, whether these resources are engaged in film production or not. As a result, production planning and production cost forecasts must be continually revised with every unanticipated delay in the film company's schedule.

The overall effect of these temporary capital investments is to constrain the level of autonomy for the project-based enterprise. Accountability to investors regarding capital budgeting is a daily responsibility. Moreover, upon project completion there is no strategic decision between returns to investors (dividends) and retained earnings. All of the revenues are returned to the investors, while the former leaders of the enterprise must look for new work and fresh capital.

Enterprise dissolution precedes outcomes

Staffing follows a predictable sequence in film making, with a small core of people typically involved in pre-production, a growing number during film production and a small creative core in post-production. This ramping up and ramping down of project staffing reflects the highly task-contingent nature of project-based enterprise hiring. Very few film project employees participate in all stages of production. Symbolic of this pattern of progressive dissolution is the departure of actors and actresses before post-production and their and other crew members' engagement in new projects before editing and release of the current project have taken place.

The release of a film to the general public symbolizes both the dissolution of the enterprise and the beginning of strategic outcomes. In recent years, this effect has been moderated by 'sneak previews' which gauge audience reaction before the film is finalized. However, preview activity aside, the main idea in independent film making is to wind down the enterprise before revenue generation, critical reviews and any industry awards are received.

In theory, the old studio system was better placed on this score and – like Honda in automobile design – could keep the team intact to measure and respond to public reaction.[17] Strategic management theory largely endorses a more interactive approach to product or service delivery and customer feedback. In independent film making there is greater pressure to get it right the first time, since a film, once released, cannot generally be revised for a second distribution.[18]

Idleness is necessary

During a typical day of film shooting at *Omega*, different crews of project specialists alternated between frenetic activity and enforced idleness. These alternating patterns of activity and idleness are only imperfectly anticipated by the sequence of film shoots planned for the day. Particular crews can anticipate likely activities, but cannot be certain about the exact time their services will be required. Hence, what appears as idleness on the film set is more akin to vigilant readiness to be mobilized on a moment's notice.

The work rhythms of film making contribute to a learning-by-watching phenomenon. It is often during periods of vigilant waiting that senior project team members provide opportunities to demonstrate specific craft routines to neophyte crew members or to answer questions from their junior crew members regarding previous activities performed by the senior crew members. Lull periods of crew activities also provide an opportunity to observe how tasks outside one's current role are performed by other members of other specialized crews. The opportunities on this particular film included the chance to observe, as one student intern put it, 'the world's top cameraman and one of the world's top make-up artists'.

The necessity of idleness runs counter to traditional themes of productive effectiveness. Even relatively mundane work cannot be scheduled with productive efficiency in mind. Moreover, the value of idleness for reflection and learning can be overlooked by the proponents of lean production systems and other efficiency-focused strategists.[19] When idleness is factored in, the strategic assumption is that the returns to learning will accrue to the employing enterprise. However, in independent film making, those returns to learning will principally benefit a new enterprise formed for a subsequent project.

Inconsequential jobs are sought after

One of the camera crews observed during the *Omega* project had three experienced camera team members (each with a highly specialized role) and two student interns (whose roles were much more vaguely defined). The students' tasks centered around getting coffee, snacks or equipment for the veteran crew. However, closer observation revealed that each senior camera crew member explicitly provided opportunities for the interns closely to observe the performance of their well-practised craft. This 'learning by watching experienced crew members' was relatively widespread among the most junior members of each crew. Another intern working with the script team spent much of her free time observing how others on her team performed their tasks and co-ordinated with other teams on the project.

Performance of the mundane tasks of getting coffee or tea is a time-honored socialization ritual for new crew members and both their performance and attitudes are duly noted. The neophyte's behaviour is incidental to the current project, but is seen as indicative of his or her commitment and compatibility for performing more demanding tasks in future projects. Perhaps the most junior role on any film project is that of a 'runner', who literally runs around the set to deliver information or material (e.g. script revisions, stage props) as needed. In the process, the runner becomes exposed to the complex, chaotic interconnections among specialized film crew activities. The art director reported that 'three to four years as a runner' made his career. 'In the runner's role you make of it what you can, you watch and learn, you're working with great people.'

In sum, low-responsibility, inconsequential jobs assume a delayed importance in film making. Inconsequential jobs are sought after because of the career benefits they offer the job holder. In turn, they also make the prospective learning benefits available to other, later, enterprises. In essence, the least responsible positions in a project enterprise are the ones in which neophytes are socialized into the shared values and uncodified tacit knowledge of their community of practice.[20]

Career mobility drives industry stability

It is the nature of independent film making that neither Paul, one of the most respected producers, nor Peter, even after his success with *Alpha*, was permanently employed by any studio. Instead, the studios had regular access to talented producers and directors from whom to pick for their next investments. The studios' access to Peter and Paul gets mirrored in the two principals' further access to artistic and business talent. Peter and Paul were able to draw on their range of personal contacts to appoint principal lieutenants. Those lieutenants in turn filled out the rest of the crew. In Paul's words: 'Everyone comes with a team because the job is too big for any one person.'

Most *Omega* project participants described their industry as a small, socially interconnected network and it was through inclusion in that network that future project opportunities were identified. These opportunities included, but were not limited to, working with one's immediate crew. One example is Peter's observation that a director's 'ability to choose the right shot' came through hard-earned experience, however, it also required the tacit support of lighting and camera staff (around such things as close-ups, reversals, tracking, and eyeline adjustments) to make the shot work.

Each film project sustains or enhances each project member's network of industry contacts, any one of whom may provide the lead or recommendation for future project opportunities. This contrasts with modern strategic management ideas about returns to intellectual capital and tacit knowledge becoming assets of one particular firm.[21]

Career success, enterprise failure?

In the long run, it is box office and ancillary market gross of the film relative to its production and distribution costs that determines financial success. The producer and director are held most accountable, but others share in their concern to meet budgets and release a successful film. The ideal outcomes are both box office success and widespread acclaim through 'Oscar' nominations and awards for professional and technical roles. The chance to brag about being involved with a hit movie is reported as a powerful draw for getting involved, as well as an opportunity to exonerate people who had difficulty delivering on the set. One key contributor with budgetary problems acknowledged his work had 'cost too much' but that he hoped that people would 'take on board why it went over budget' once his contribution to the final film was witnessed by sponsoring studio executives.

However, the liabilities of film project failure vary by the type of project role a person holds. Production support people who are skilled in maintaining a tight schedule, a smooth pace of production and a relaxed, collaborative atmosphere are valued, whether the films they produce are financially successful or not. Similarly, artistic support personnel who contribute discrete, identifiable artistic components to the project (i.e. theme music, costuming, cinematography) may enhance their reputation by receiving award nominations for their contributions to money-losing films. An interesting subtlety here is bargaining over titles to ensure the possibilities of Oscar nomination. One key collaborator noted: 'There's no Oscar for being an associate producer and there is for screen writing – so that's a better title.'

Strategic management thinking emphasizes a classical, neo-military perspective that subordinates personal goals to those of the firm.[22] However, in the film industry, the reverse appears to be largely the case. In the long run, the success of a particular enterprise is seen as incidental. The industry's continuing success becomes synonymous with the accomplishments of its principal participants and it is those successes, rather than enduring company successes, that get celebrated.

Discussion

Each of the reports just presented exhibits a contrast between strategic management theory's assumption of the permanence – or aspirations to permanence of the firm and the project-based enterprise's temporary status. In the film-making example, no capital investments convert to fixed assets, no revenues are retained, no structure or positions are permanent and no returns to learning accrue for future projects. The common assumption that the health of an industry derives from the health of its most enduring firms does not apply in film making. How, then, can strategic thinking be applied to the project-based enterprise and with what implications for the related outcomes of industrial competitiveness and economic returns?

Independent film making presents a phenomenon that is prevalent but is more disguised in other situations. In situations such as law (cases), software writing (packages), construction (buildings) and in the pursuit of innovation culminating in new products or services, there is a similar underlying project-based structure. Also, recent thinking about careers envisions a series of projects, where people's principal loyalties are directed toward project outcomes rather than toward continuing dependency on the present employer.[23] These observations suggest that independent film making may exhibit in relatively pure form a model of organizing that is broadly and increasingly applicable to other fields of strategic endeavor. What, then, might be learned and what might be generalizable from the film-making example?

Human and social capital are interdependent

Peter and Paul got to know each other, chose to work together (on *Alpha*), got to know each other better still and chose to work together again (on *Omega*) over a prolonged period of engagement in the same industry. Human capital (each knowing their own trade) and social capital (each knowing one another) appear inextricably linked in their still-unfolding relationship. In turn, Peter and Paul each went to his separate network, using social capital to locate further human capital resources to build the film crew. In turn again, principal lieutenants did the same thing with their crews. The system worked through reputation, which may be viewed as an estimate of human capital conveyed over social capital channels.

Project participants at *Omega* described the continuing nature of this interplay between their skills (human capital) and their work relationships (social capital). The participants also expressed hopes about how this interplay would continue to evolve, through their skills becoming better recognized by others, leading to invitations to join future projects and further extend their human and social capital assets. Thus, human and social capital – in contrast to the separate treatment they receive in the strategic management literature – form a self-reinforcing cycle of career competencies that propel a person through successive projects.[24] The cycle can, of course, reverse itself if a person is seen to perform below expectations.[25]

Creative and commercial communities

A particular aspect of human and social capital interdependence concerns the relationships between artistic/creative groups and business groups. The basis for interaction between the groups was to be found in the cooperation between Peter and Paul tracing back to the project's origination. The extension of that interaction came in everyday activities on the film set, as each group worked in almost constant dialogue with the other. Whatever the limitations of this dialogue on creative freedom, it did mean that creative ambitions were held accountable to and calibrated against original budget estimates for the film. Similar conversations (for example, between innovation-oriented and efficiency-oriented project participants) can be found in studies of small firm positioning and high-technology companies.[26] However, it is exceptional for the two sides to be in as close and continuing a dialogue as in the independent film-making example.

The pressure of everyday film making meant that both technical and collaborative attributes were valued. *Omega*'s non-artistic participants described themselves as having been selected for participation in *Omega* and other projects because of both sets of attributes. In this context, social skills are a direct component of human capital, as well as the means through which new social capital is accumulated. Conversely, people who developed a reputation for being difficult to work with then also needed to possess considerable technical talent or box office appeal to compensate for their social deficiencies. In sum, functional separation and hierarchical channels – that is, the structure usually associated with strategy – were of little help in resolving everyday dilemmas. Relationships – including relationships across creative and commercial divisions – drove the enterprise along, as has been observed in studies of knowledge management in Japanese firms and in new venture formation in biotechnology.[27]

Principals, professionals and apprentices

Film project participants occupy one of three occupational niches. Principals may be described as those people behind initial strategy formation and funding of the enterprise. In *Omega*, the principals were the director and producer, which is typical for film projects, and to a lesser extent the star performers who had agreed to return for a new collaboration. Next come the key professionals hired by the principals to apply particular artistic or commercial competence in support of the adopted strategy and whose arrival usually coincides with the founding of the enterprise. Finally, there come apprentices, interns and runners at early stages of their careers who are allowed to join the enterprise to perform mundane but necessary tasks.

In many respects, the film project resembles Handy's 'shamrock' form of organization involving a professional core, outsourced specialist providers and flexible, part-time or temporary groups of workers.[28] However, there are some important distinctions. First, everyone is temporary, along with the enterprise. Second, from an industry standpoint, the 'core' may be seen as the second key professional group through which films regularly get made, even as producers, directors and movie stars come and go. Third, the most dedicated and the most driven to learn of all three groups are often the temporary or 'peripheral' workers. It is also from this group that future principals and professionals will emerge and in turn take responsibility for the health of the industry. In sum, the distinctions among principals, professionals and apprentices reflect dynamic industry and career development processes rather than enduring social stratification.[29]

Career and industry episodes

The project-based enterprise serves separate purposes for its participants' careers and for the evolution of the industry. On the one hand, *Omega*'s participants will employ their film credits to seek new assignments. Each participant's learning is particular to the project role he or she performed and to the unfolding of his or her own career. Personal successes (for example, in set design or special effects) will enhance the prospect of offers to work on new projects coming on stream. On the other hand, the industry will move on to commission new films to follow *Omega*. *Omega*'s press reviews and box office performance will become known and that knowledge will inform future initiatives undertaken by industry principals and their prospective backers. The project-based enterprise represents a meeting ground between discrete career and industry episodes.

Over time, the industry develops a collective memory, informed by films such as *Omega*, of what worked and what didn't, of new special effects and audience tastes.[30] Meanwhile, project participants develop their own memories, informed by the accumulating set of credits earned and experiences involved.[31] What is distinctive here is that there is no place for 'organizational memory' as conventionally presented in strategic management theory.[32] Instead, the film-making enterprise offers an extreme case of the organization's memory disappearing once its project tasks are accomplished. However, by then the enterprise will have played an important transitory role in the episodic learning of both the industry at large and its individual participants.

Who needs the firm?

Remarkable by its absence from these interpretations is any reference to the long-term significance of the firm. Peter and Paul leveraged their separate networks to establish the resources to make the film. The focal firm – the project-based enterprise – provided a temporary meeting ground between the industry and project participants. Professional guilds appeared to provide a partial, although limited, institutional framework. So too did 'Hollywood' through its central role as a source of large-scale project financing, bankable stars and access to distribution channels. However, Hollywood was valued as a regional cluster of competencies, a place to access the overall scale and diversity of resources, rather than as the location of any particular firm.

What appeared to sustain the ability of *Omega*'s principals to realize their artistic and commercial vision was their access to geographically clustered networks of US (Hollywood) and UK (London) film industry resources. No single firm or institution was an indispensable source of project-relevant resources. However, effective access to and membership in the geographically concentrated industry networks of the US and UK film industries were indispensable requirements for organizing the necessary resources and competencies for the *Omega* film project. The firm, whether as the source of funding, the project-based enterprise itself or the vehicle to provide project resources, seemed little more than an administrative convenience.[33]

Conclusion

The evidence from the film industry calls for strategic management theory to incorporate a dynamic, multicommunity perspective into the mainstream of its ideas. The evidence further suggests that the perspective needs to be sensitive to shifting combinations of human and social capital and the further evolution of these through people's career investments. The proposed perspective leads away from firm-centric formulations of strategic activity.

The concept of project-based enterprise leads strategic inquiry toward such questions as: How are project-based enterprises of varying size, complexity and risk initiated through network mobilization? How are the knowledge and experience of project-based enterprises disseminated within multiple communities and transferred to subsequent enterprises? How is economic value created and appropriated among the multiple communities that participate in project-based enterprises? What are the respective roles of geographically concentrated industry regions versus electronically mediated virtual communities in fostering project-based enterprise activities?

These questions direct strategic inquiry toward issues of community and career progression that are inevitably intertwined with the creation and performance of both project-based enterprises and the industries in which they flourish.

References

1 On film, see C. Jones and R. J. DeFillippi, 'Back to the future in film: combining industry- and self-knowledge to meet career challenges of the 21st century', *Academy of Management Executive*, 10/4 (1996): 89–103. On construction, see R. G. Eccles, 'The quasifirm in the construction industry', *Journal of Economic Behavior and Organization*, 2 (1981): 335–357. On semiconductors, see A. Saxenian, *Regional Advantage: Culture and Competition in Silicon Valley and Route 128* (Boston, MA: Harvard University Press, 1994).

2 C. Jones, 'Careers in project networks: the case of the film industry', in M. B. Arthur and D. M. Rousseau, eds., *The Boundaryless Career* (New York, NY: Oxford University Press, 1996), pp. 58–75; W. H. Starbuck, 'Learning by knowledge-intensive firms', *Journal of Management Studies*, 29/6 (1992): 713–740.

3 C. K. Prahalad and G. Hamel, 'The core competence of the corporation', *Harvard Business Review*, 68/3 (1990): 79–91; I. Nonaka and H. Takeuchi, *The Knowledge-Creating Company* (New York, NY: Oxford University Press, 1995).

4 R. Reed and R. J. DeFillippi, 'Causal ambiguity, barriers to imitation and sustainable competitive advantage', *Academy of Management Review*, 15/1 (1990): 88–102.

5 See, for example, O. Nordhaug, *Human Capital in Organizations: Competence, Training and Learning* (Oslo: Scandanavian University Press, 1993).

6 T. Bohn, R. Stromgren, and D. Johnson, *Light and Shadows: A History of Motion Pictures*, 2nd edition (Sherman Oaks, CA: Alfred Publishing Co., 1978).

7 D. Miller and J. Shamsie, 'The resource-based view of the firm in two environments: the Hollywood film studios from 1936 to 1965', *Academy of Management Journal*, 39/3 (1996): 519–543.

8 J. Raelin, *Clash of Cultures* (Boston, MA: Harvard Business School Press, 1991).

9 S. C. Wheelwright and K. B. Clark, *Revolutionizing Product Development* (New York, NY: Free Press, 1992).

10   A. Brookings, *Intellectual Capital* (London: International Thomson Business Press, 1996); A. A. Lado, N. G. Boyd, and P. Wright, 'A competency model of sustained competitive advantage', *Journal of Management*, 18 (1992): 77–91.

11   C. Jones and W. Hesterly, *Network Organization: Alternative Governance Form or Glorified Market?* Working Paper, Carroll School of Management, Boston College, 1996. See also Jones (1996), op. cit., and Jones and DeFillippi, op. cit.

12   C. Jones, W. Hesterly, B. Lichtenstein, S. Borgatti, S. Tallman, *Intangible Assets of Teams: How Human, Social and Team Capital Influence Project Performance in the Film Industry*, Working Paper, Carroll School of Management, Boston College, 1996.

13   L. Argote, 'Group and organizational learning curves: individual, system and environmental components', *British Journal of Social Psychology*, 32 (1993): 31–51.

14   Jones et al., op. cit.

15   Prahalad and Hamel, op. cit.

16   P. Ghemawat, *Commitment: The Dynamic of Strategy* (New York, NY: The Free Press, 1991).

17   K. Clark and T. Fujimoto, *Product Development Performance* (Boston, MA: Harvard Business School Press, 1991).

18   The recent release of the *Star Wars* trilogy is not a contradiction, since the first release was commercially successful and made possible a second release featuring enhanced special effects but no change in plot, dialogue, or characters.

19   J. P. Womak, D. T. Jones, and D. Roos, *The Machine that Changed the World* (New York, NY: Rawson Associates, 1990).

20   J. S. Brown and P. Duguid, 'Organizational learning and communities of practice: towards a unified view of working, learning and organization', *Organization Science*, 2/1 (1991): 40–57.

21   Nonaka and Takeuchi, op. cit. For extended ideas about learning and new firm formation, see A. Saxenian, 'Beyond boundaries: open labor markets and learning in Silicon Valley', in M. B. Arthur and D. M. Rousseau, eds., *The Boundaryless Career* (New York, NY: Oxford University Press, 1996); R. E. Miles and C. C. Snow, 'Twenty-first century careers', in M. B. Arthur and D. M. Rousseau, eds., *The Boundaryless Career* (New York, NY: Oxford University Press, 1996).

22   K. R. Andrews, *The Concept of Corporate Strategy* (Homewood, IL: Irwin, 1971).

23   M. B. Arthur, M. P. H. Claman, and R. J. DeFillippi, 'Intelligent enterprise, intelligent careers', *Academy of Management Executive*, 9/4 (1995): 7–22.

24   On human capital, see Nordhaug (1993), op. cit.; on social capital, see R. S. Burt, *Structural Holes* (Cambridge, MA: Harvard University Press, 1992).

25   One senior project participant expressed concern that his shortcomings in performing up to expectation on Omega might reduce the likelihood of his being invited to participate in future projects by some of his Omega peers and superiors. When the Omega project subsequently went to reshoot some parts of the film in Hollywood, this person was not invited to participate on that phase. The apparent failure in human capital, highlighted through social exchanges on the set of the film, appeared to contribute to a negative reputation effect which in turn might reduce access to future project opportunities.

26   On small firm positioning, see C. Hendry, M. B. Arthur, and A. M. Jones, *Strategy Through People: Adaptation and Learning in the Small–Medium Enterprise* (New York, NY: Routledge, 1995); on high technology, companies see Raelin, op. cit.

27   G. Hedlund, 'A model of knowledge management and the N-form corporation', *Strategic Management Journal* (Special Issue: 'Strategy: search for new paradigms'), 15 (1994): 73–90; D. L. Deeds, D. DeCarolis, and J. Coombs, 'The impact of timing and firm capabilities on the amount of capital raised in an initial public offering: evidence from

the biotechnical industry', in B. Keys and L. N. Dosier, eds., *Academy of Management Annual Meeting Best Paper Proceedings*, 1996.

28 C. Handy, *The Age of Unreason* (Boston, MA: Harvard Business School Press, 1990).

29 The processes we describe appear to have much in common with recent ideas about communities of practice. Brown and Duguid, op. cit.; J. Orr, 'Sharing knowledge, celebrating identity: war stories and community memory in a service culture', in D. Middleton and D. Edwards, eds., *Collective Remembering: Memory in Society* (Beverly Hills, CA: Sage, 1990).

30 J. C. Spender, *Industry Recipes* (Oxford: Basil Blackwell, 1989).

31 A. Bird, 'Careers as repositories of knowledge: considerations for boundaryless careers', in M. B. Arthur and D. M. Rousseau, eds., *The Boundaryless Career* (New York, NY: Oxford University Press, 1996), pp. 150–168.

32 R. R. Nelson and S. G. Winter, *An Evolutionary Theory of Economic Change* (Cambridge, MA: Belknap/Harvard Press, 1982).

33 In the language of recent chaos and complexity theory, the firm becomes a temporary 'attractor' in the self-organizing behaviour of industry participants. See, for example, D. Parker and R. Stacey, *Chaos, Management and Economics* (London, Institute of Economic Affairs, 1994).

16 Japanese-style Partnerships: Giving Companies a Competitive Edge

Jeffrey H. Dyer and William G. Ouchi

Are supplier relationships critical to Japanese firms' success? And why are Japanese suppliers more cooperative and willing to take risks than US suppliers?

Evidence from an increasing number of industries and sources suggests that much of the Japanese success can be attributed to Japanese-style business partnerships. Consider the auto industry, for example. From 1965 to 1989, the combined Japanese market share of worldwide passenger car production jumped from 3.6 percent to 25.5 percent. In striking contrast, the market share of US firms dropped from 48.6 percent to 19.2 percent.[1] Moreover, by the early 1980s, Japanese firms had achieved a 20 percent to 25 percent cost advantage, per car, versus US automakers, while receiving customer satisfaction scores 50 percent higher than those of competing US cars. Can we attribute the astonishing Japanese success to their partnership approach? Consider the following:

- American automakers are more vertically integrated than their Japanese counterparts, with approximately 48 percent of parts manufactured internally as opposed to 25 percent for Japanese automakers.
- Even though US automakers are more vertically integrated, they contract directly with 1500 to 3000 parts suppliers for the parts they don't make. Toyota, by contrast, works with approximately one-tenth that number, buying more – in many instances, entire subsystems – from each supplier.
- A study conducted by Bain & Company found that the total cost of components for a Japanese car was more than 20 percent below that of a comparable US model in 1984. A similar comparison of component costs reported in *Fortune* indicated that, in 1985, US automakers spent an average of $3350 on parts, materials and services for small cars (priced at $6000), while the average Japanese company spent $2750 – a cost saving of more than 22 percent that was achieved mainly 'through more efficient vendor relations'.[2] While the gap has narrowed, Japanese automakers still have a cost advantage over US makers.
- Japanese-owned plants in the United States purchase more than 50 percent of their auto components from Japanese suppliers (these Japanese suppliers sometimes have operations in the United States). As a result, even in their US plants, they enjoy a $700-per-vehicle cost advantage over US automaker plants or about 10 percent of the retail cost of a small car.[3]

- Japanese automakers develop new vehicles at least 30 percent faster than US automakers, which means that products include the latest in technology.[4] Apparently, this advantage is due largely to Japan's subcontracting structure. According to Clark: 'In US companies, the projects in our sample were heavily influenced by the traditional system in which suppliers produced parts under short-term, arm's-length contracts and had little role in design and engineering. In the Japanese system, in contrast, suppliers are an integral part of the development process: they are involved early, assume significant responsibility, and communicate extensively and directly with product and process engineers.'[5] Japanese suppliers frequently give automakers a head start in development by starting work on projects even before they are assured of winning the project.

If US companies are to adopt Japanese inter-company practices successfully, they must understand how and why they work. Consequently, two questions are critical:

1   Why are Japanese-style partnerships more productive than either buying suppliers or customers (vertically integrating) or rotating business across numerous suppliers?
2   Why are Japanese suppliers so cooperative and willing to take risks? (Doesn't that make them overly dependent?)

What is a Japanese-style partnership?

A Japanese-style partnership (JSP) is an exclusive (or semi-exclusive) supplier–purchaser relationship that focuses on maximizing the efficiency of the entire business system (value chain). These supplier partners are typically called *kankei-gaisha* (affiliated companies) in Japan and are considered to be the vertical keiretsu of the parent company. (Companies that are not *kankei-gaisha* are typically referred to as *dokuritsu-gaisha* or independent companies. Independent companies will often work with parent firms in much the same way as the *kankei-gaisha*.) Our findings are primarily from a two-year study of 50 *kankei-gaisha* in the automobile industry compared to 50 US supplier–US automaker relationships.

The goal of Japanese partnerships is to increase quality while minimizing the total value-added costs that both the supplier and the purchase incur. In short, the goal is to create a 'see-through' value chain where both parties' costs and problems are visible. Then both parties can work jointly to solve the problems and expand rather than split the pie. JSPs also take advantage of economies of scale in both production and transaction costs.

In summary, the key characteristics of JSPs in the auto industry are:

- Long-term relationships and commitments with frequent planned communication, which reduces transaction costs and eliminates intercompany inefficiencies.

- Mutual assistance and a focus on total cost and quality, working together to minimize *total* value chain costs (not just unit costs).
- Willingness to make significant customized investments in plant, equipment and personnel as well as share valuable technical information.
- Intensive and regular sharing of technical and cost information to improve performance and set prices, which share equally the rewards of the relationships.
- Trust-building practices like owning stock (e.g. stock swaps), transferring employees, having guest engineers and using flexible legal contracts that create a high degree of goal congruence and mutual trust (see Table 16.1 for a comparison of the traditional US model of vendor relations with the Japanese partnering model).

Table 16.1 Characteristics of vendor relations in the United States and Japan

Traditional US model	*Japanese partnering model*
Department or firm focus, 'optimize firm efficiency'	Business system focus (include supplier/customer economics), 'optimize value chain efficiency'
Emphasis on unit cost/price (minimum quality standards)	Emphasis on full value chain (systems) costs as well as on improving quality
Manufacturer defines needs; specialization of activities; sequential planning	Joint efforts to define needs and problem solve; highly integrated operations and planning
Communication is sporadic, problem driven; little sharing of information or assistance	Communication is frequent and planned; continuous sharing of information and assistance
General investments; uniform approach	Customized investments to meet unique customer or supplier needs (e.g. in information systems, people, manufacturing equipment, etc.)
Precise contracts that split economic benefits beforehand	Flexible contracts that adjust to split economic gains fully as market conditions change
No additional collateral bonds; arm's length relationship	Numerous collateral bonds employed to build trust and align the firms' financial fortunes and safeguard customized investments

Why are JSPs more efficient?

JSPs realize economic benefits not available to firms that either vertically integrate or keep a large supplier base. There are usually three types of benefit: (1) fewer direct suppliers, (2) customized investments and (3) forced competition.

Fewer direct suppliers

It is no secret that reducing the total number of direct suppliers can lower costs while increasing quality. Using fewer suppliers can create value by providing economies of scale and experience curve benefits that lower either transaction costs or production costs.

Reducing transaction costs

Transaction costs, as defined here, are all the costs associated with effecting an exchange (e.g. information gathering and analysis, negotiation, contracting, product movement costs and so on). While most managers understand that greater economies of scale can reduce production costs, many fail to consider the extent to which they also affect transaction costs. A 1985 study of sourcing for wiring harnesses (electrical wiring) comparing the number of suppliers used by Toyota and a US automaker revealed that Toyota gave virtually 100 percent of its volume to two suppliers while the US manufacturer used more than 20 different suppliers.[6]

The total costs of managing multiple suppliers can quickly add up. For example, in 1986, General Motors employed approximately 3000 purchasing people to procure goods and services for 6 million cars (2000 cars per buyer). In contrast, Toyota employed 340 people to procure goods and services for 3.6 million cars (10,590 cars per buyer).[7] Thus, GM's procurement costs were approximately five times higher than Toyota's. (In fact, the difference was greater because the GM buyers were buying only 50 percent of the value of the car – due to higher vertical integration – while Toyota buyers were buying 75 percent.) Why are the purchasing departments within US automakers so large? Apparently, they were created to rotate the business and reduce the company's dependence on any one supplier. When asked why GM has so many suppliers, one executive explained: 'Our purchasing activities are huge and extensive. Most activities have been geared to making sure we don't get stung by an unscrupulous supplier out there.'[8]

Reducing production costs

Within most industries, as cumulative production experience in producing a product or service increases, quality is improved and costs are reduced. More specifically, each time accumulated experience doubles, costs per unit typically fall (in real terms, adjusted for inflation) by 10 percent to 30 percent, with comparable increases in product quality.[9]

By applying the partnership approach, Japanese automakers have consolidated their business with a few highly efficient suppliers and created conditions that permit the suppliers to make the investments necessary to accelerate down the experience curve and to share the full advantage of this volume (and the resulting lower costs per unit) with the carmakers. When a Japanese supplier wins a contract with Nissan or Toyota, it is essentially guaranteed four years of business (or the life of the model). Moreover, if the supplier performs up to expectations, it can usually win the business for the next model as well. Naturally, these practices encourage long-term plans and investments. Suppliers invest in developing ideas and plans for the next model well in advance. Engineers from the two companies have long-term experience working together, making it easier to rapidly develop designs for the next model. When the model change occurs, suppliers continue to move down the experience curve.

In contrast, US auto manufacturers have attempted to keep input prices low by maintaining size and bargaining power over suppliers. By splitting their business among many suppliers and rotating them frequently, US manufacturers have repeatedly destroyed the experience curves of suppliers by ensuring that no one supplier could accelerate down the experience curve to accumulate decisive cost advantages. The US suppliers in our sample claimed that they typically have only a 69 percent chance of rewinning the business at a model change. Thus, at each model change, the experience of the previous supplier is destroyed and a new supplier must incur start-up costs. Supplier engineers typically do not develop long-term relationships and experience with automaker engineers.

A 1989 survey found that the average length of the contract between US suppliers and automakers was only 2.5 years, up from 1.3 years in 1984.[10] The survey also found that, as the length of the contract between the supplier and automaker increased, so did the supplier's investments in CNC machine tools, CAD/CAM systems, robotics and manufacturing cells. Without long-term commitments, US suppliers rationally refuse to make long-term investments in capital equipment. Moreover, without the ability to make long-term forecasts, it is very difficult to make maximum use of capacity and capital equipment.

A final benefit of having fewer suppliers is the positive effect on quality. When more suppliers are used for a given part, variation increases and reliability goes down. As quality guru W. Edwards Deming notes: 'Even with a single supplier, there is substantial variation lot-to-lot and within lots.'[11] Using multiple suppliers only increases the variation of parts that causes production problems and poor quality.

Customized investments

Developing a Japanese-style partnership is much more complex than simply reducing the number of suppliers you use. The differences between JSPs and more traditional supplier relationships are illustrated by the following questions. How often do supplier–purchaser agreements in the United States involve:

- Building a supplier plant within 15 miles of the customer plant to reduce transportation costs, improve delivery and generally improve co-ordination?
- Allowing supplier engineers to work daily at customer technical centres with customer engineers in designing new products?
- Transferring the purchaser's executives or employees to the supplier to work on a temporary (one to two years) or permanent basis?
- Sending in consultants (paid by the purchaser) to work with the supplier (often for months) to improve production methods, implement just-in-time delivery systems or assist in solving other problems?

The answer to all four questions is 'rarely'. Most US companies are simply not willing to take the risk in making customized investments. Consequently, they forgo the value that these investments can create.

JSPs generally require various types of investment in customized assets (investments specifically related to the relationship) by one or both firms in order to optimize the production and flow of goods and services. Three types of customized investment are employed:

1 Site-specific investments – plants are located so that they are dedicated largely to a particular customer in order to improve co-ordination and economize on inventory and transportation expenses.
2 Physical investments – manufacturing equipment such as tools, dies, moulds, jigs, machinery and so on is customized.
3 Human capital investments – dedicated design or manufacturing engineers develop significant partner-specific knowledge.

These partner-specific investments create substantial buyer and supplier switching costs and, once made, make the two parties highly interdependent. This interdependence can create potential contracting problems if the parties do not completely trust each other. (Contracting problems may arise because these investments are not marketable or redeployable; thus one party may act opportunistically since it, in effect, has a monopoly on the customized investments.) However, the investments also create value substantially beyond what could have been achieved without them.

Toyota's just-in-time (JIT) systems are a good example of how customized investments can create value. JIT was designed to reduce complexity and costs by eliminating inventories and work in process and to ensure that there were no redundant buffer stocks, distribution facilities or quality inspections. However, to implement JIT effectively, Toyota and its partner suppliers had to make customized investments in information systems, plants and flexible manufacturing systems that created mutual dependency. For example, in our survey of 25 Toyota partner–suppliers, we found that the average (median) distance from the supplier's manufacturing plant to the Toyota assembly plant was only 17 miles. The close proximity of these plants makes it economical for suppliers to make an average of 7.4 deliveries each day (over 20 percent of Toyota suppliers make hourly deliveries) and keep minimal inventories.[12] Naturally, this site-specific plant investment, more than 75 percent of which is dedicated to Toyota, keeps inventories extremely low. In a comparison of the now-closed GM (Framingham) plant and the Toyota (Takaoka) plant, Womack et al. found that, while the GM plant had an average of two weeks of inventory, the average buffer inventory at the Toyota plant would last only two hours.[13] Thus, in this particular case, GM and its suppliers needed to invest in and store as much as 200 times the inventory, on average, as Toyota and its suppliers (assuming the plants operate 16 hours a day). While this may be an extreme example, clearly the savings from Toyota's supplier investments in customized assets (i.e. site-specific investments in plants) can be substantial.

Of course, one must remember that these investments tend to bind suppliers to customers. However, JSPs work because these partner-specific investments that reduce costs and increase quality outweigh the costs (risks) associated with being dependent on outside parties. Thus, these investments expand the pie for both parties. As Deming notes: 'A supplier assured of long-term contracts is more likely to risk being innovative and modify production processes than a supplier with a short-term contract who cannot afford to tailor a product to the needs of a buyer.'[14]

Developing partnerships rather than huge bureaucracies enables the Japanese to maintain a decentralized economy in which two-thirds of the Japanese labour force are in establishments with under 300 workers, while in the United States, two-thirds are in establishments with over 300 workers.[15] Moreover, as Friedman observes: 'From 1954 to 1977, the contribution of small and medium-sized firms to Japan's manufacturing value-added rose from about 49 percent to 58 percent of total manufacturing. In contrast, small and medium firms accounted for approximately 35 percent of American value-added in manufacturing, a share that remained steady throughout the post-war era.'[16] In short, during the past 40 years, small manufacturers have become markedly more important throughout the Japanese economy. Perhaps this explains why Japanese firms are so good at rapid incremental innovation – there are thousands of entrepreneurs trying to make rapid, albeit minor, improvements to their products as they try to stay one step ahead of their roughly equal competitors.

Why are Japanese companies more cooperative?

The Japanese have recognized the need to be *inter*dependent (especially on highly complex tasks) and have responded by developing bonding mechanisms that build trust and goal congruence between companies. There are numerous competing theories on why the Japanese have developed networks of partnership firms. Perhaps the lack of an open market for corporate control in Japan explains why firms have not attempted to integrate more frequently. This suggests that the Japanese were forced to develop new organizational arrangements because of constraints on mergers and acquisitions. Also, the Japanese government has provided protection and financial support for small companies, thereby making it easier for small firms to be competitive.[17] And finally, cultural reasons may explain the relationships among firms – they are simply an anomaly of a homogeneous and unique culture.[18]

The Japanese do not rely on legal contracts to protect their interests in exchange relationships. Indeed, Asanuma describes how Japanese firms use a flexible legal contract that is a very general 'constitution' for a relationship and can be constantly adjusted and renegotiated.[19] However, the key issue is understanding *why* Japanese companies can use such a flexible agreement. Next we discuss some of the most important Japanese practices in developing intercompany trust.

Career paths between firms

[One] way Japanese firms build trust is by requiring career paths in which employees transfer from firm to firm (or simply work at partner firm facilities). Employee transfers, both temporary (usually two years) and permanent, are common among business partners, particularly between large manufacturers and their subcontractors.[20] Asanuma describes how executive transfers were particularly important in the auto industry because they 'usually preceded technical assistance, loans or exclusive procurement contracts'.[21] He found that employee transfers *preceded* additional partner-specific investments by the automakers. Toyota is more likely to make investments in partners when it trusts the individuals it is dealing with – and who better to trust than former employees or people you've worked with for years? Our own study indicates that almost 30 percent of the top management teams at Nissan's *kankei-gaisha* are former Nissan employees. Clearly, this innovative practice helps Nissan and its suppliers work cooperatively.

In addition to permanent and temporary employee swaps, suppliers often send guest engineers to work at their customer technical centres on an ongoing basis. For example, Toyota currently has almost 350 guest engineers (mostly from supplier partners) at its main technical centre in Japan. These engineers become a part of the design team and are given desks next to the Toyota engineers. Not only do these career path practices help build trust between firms, but also transferred and guest employees are better able to understand how to optimize the efficiency of the value chain because they know both customer and supplier operations.

Face-to-face contact

Direct contact is much more important than other forms of contact in developing ways for employees to know and trust each other. *Kankei-gaisha* and automakers encourage a tremendous amount of face-to-face contact between supplier salespeople and engineers and between automaker purchasing agents and engineers. *Kankei-gaisha* have almost seven times the direct contact with automakers (than US automakers do), even when one does not include employee transfers.

Minority ownership

Japanese firms like Nissan will, instead of vertically integrating, either swap stock or take significant minority ownership positions in many key suppliers. Nissan owns 33 percent (on average) of the shares of its major supplier partners. This ownership stake builds trust and goal congruence between Nissan and its supplier partners. Interlocking stock ownership represents a commitment to the supplier that needs an incentive to make the customized investments Nissan requires.

Specialized investments

As previously mentioned, Japanese auto suppliers develop more unique parts for their customers and make greater investments in specialized assets than do US suppliers. A *kankei-gaisha* does *not* receive a separate payment for the investment in tools, dies, moulds and jigs that are highly customized (because they 'touch the part') and would need to be scrapped if the automaker cut off orders to the supplier. (In contrast, US suppliers require that US automakers buy the customized tools, dies and moulds that the supplier uses to make the product.)

As previously mentioned, *kankei-gaisha* manufacturing plants are built close to the customer and are largely dedicated to a specific customer. Clearly, the suppliers' specialized capital investments make them highly dependent on the automakers, with the real possibility of opportunistic exploitation.

However, automakers are also significantly dependent on *kankei-gaisha*. Most *kankei-gaisha* parts are 'black box', meaning that the automaker provides only very general specifications while the supplier does all the detailed functional specifications and blueprints. Consequently, suppliers have significantly more knowledge about the design and manufacture of the part than does the automaker. Because *kankei-gaish* black-box parts are customized to a specific model, the automaker is highly dependent on the supplier. If the supplier did not perform as desired, the automaker would have difficulty simply shifting business to another supplier, given the product's customized nature. One *kankei-gaisha* executive states: 'They can't really move business away from us very easily. They need us for our skills, just as we need them.'[22]

Under these conditions, each party makes substantial specialized investments, which creates a composite profit stream only if the transactors continue working together. If the relationship is terminated, each party loses some portion of the rent. Thus these specialized investments create interdependence, which in turn creates incentives to cooperate.

What are the implications for US businesses?

The question is whether the Japanese partnership approach is adaptable to US companies or is uniquely 'Japanese'. The answer is that we can adapt the partnership approach to our environment in the same way that we are learning Japanese production practices. For example, Toyota has worked successfully as a partner with Flex-N-Gate, a bumper maker, and Johnson Controls Inc. (JCI), a seat maker. Both US companies have allowed Toyota consultants to spend weeks with their organizations teaching them how to improve their operations and work closely with Toyota. Both have made significant changes in their production systems. Both have incorporated Toyota's just-in-time system. And both claim that the Toyota model of working with suppliers is far superior.

The results speak for themselves: Flex-N-Gate has reduced die-change time from 47 minutes to 22 minutes and a bumper that used to take three days to produce now takes only 42 minutes. Overall, Flex-N-Gate has more than doubled productivity while cutting lead times 94 percent, inventories 98 percent and defects 91 percent.[23] JCI's Georgetown plant (just down the road from Toyota's Georgetown assembly plant) operates at almost one half-hour of inventory. The entire process of ordering, seat assembly, shipping and installation into the Camry takes a little over three hours. JCI makes complete seats only for Toyota. According to JCI general manager Don Buchenberger: 'Toyota took a close look at our metals operation, and we began making changes. At one time, we had a thirty-two-day inventory in metals. Now it's seven days. The Toyota supplier technical support group taught us about quick dies change. The savings over the old way are immeasurable.'[24] Perhaps most important is the trust and cooperation building between Toyota and these suppliers. According to Jeffrey Smith, JCI's Toyota account executive, this kind of cooperation has built a depth of trust he has not seen anywhere else: 'We've spent $10 million preparing for the 1992 Camry model change, without a single purchase order. I don't know that we'd do that with any other customer.'[25]

Other US firms are making progress. Xerox has lowered costs and increased quality by reducing its suppliers from 4000 to 500, while imitating many features of the Japanese approach. Chrysler, Ford, Boeing and other US companies are starting to do the same. However to effectively utilize partnerships, US managers must learn the following lessons:

1   Don't over-integrate. In cases where all things appear equal, you should probably show a preference for outside production. Extensive vertical integration often leads to less innovation and world-class underperformance. In short, US managers must recognize their dependence on those individuals and companies outside their organization who have the ability to supply key inputs and perform key tasks more efficiently and effectively than they do.
2   Reduce the number of direct suppliers to reduce costs and increase quality through greater economies of scale and less variation in inputs.
3   Make customized investments to optimize the value chain and tailor the system to meet customer and supplier needs. Investments in customized assets can create significant economic value when information is openly shared, problems are continuously identified and solved and a see-through value chain is created.
4   Force suppliers to compete and reward superior performance. Moreover, help your weaker suppliers improve so that they will continue to provide competition to your stronger suppliers. Work with partners as a consultant to solve problems jointly and improve productivity.
5   Protect investments by building trust. Whether it be through stock swaps, interfirm employee transfers, flexible contracts or other mechanisms, find ways to trust each other while making customized investments to reduce costs and improve quality.

Of course, many will argue that these practices simply won't work in the United States because we're 'different'. But much of what has made Japanese corporations successful is transferable to US companies. Indeed, Japanese firms operating outside Japan have been able to achieve roughly equivalent productivity in their US plants. The challenge for US firms is to learn from the Japanese in order to gain the advantages of Japanese-style partnerships. But we must adapt them – as the Japanese have adapted our best practices – to fit the requirements of our environment.

References

1   Ministry of International Trade and Industry, *White Paper on Small and Medium Enterprises in Japan* (Tokyo: MITIT, 1987), pp. 36–37.
2   *World Motor Vehicle Data* (Detroit, Michigan: Motor Vehicle Manufacturers Association of the US, Inc., 1991), p. 14.

3 A. B. Fisher, 'Behind the hype at GM's Saturn', *Fortune*, 11 November 1985, pp. 34–46.

4 'Shaking up Detroit', *Business Week*, 14 August 1989, pp. 74–79.

5 K. B. Clark and T. Fujimoto, *Product Development Performance* (Boston: Harvard Business School Press, 1991), p. 40.

6 K. B. Clark, 'Project scope and project performance: the effect of parts strategy and supplier involvement on product development', *Management Science* 35 (1989): pp. 1247–1263.

7 Bain & Company, unpublished automotive study, January 1985.

8 J. McMillan, 'Managing suppliers: incentive systems in the Japanese and US industry', *California Management Review*, Summer 1990, p. 51.

9 Author interview with GM executive, 23 March 1991.

10 P. Ghemawar, 'Sustainable advantage', *Harvard Business Review*, September–October 1986, p. 53.

11 Author interview with the sales vice president of a Toyota supplier, 9 September 1992.

12 S. Helper, 'Automotive supplier relations: results of 1989 survey', IMVP International Policy Forum, May 1989.

13 M. Walton, *The Deming Management Method* (New York: Perigee Publishing Group, 1986), p. 62. From Dr Deming's diary, 'Travel Logs, Around the World by Air', 1946–1947, p. 88.

14 J. P. Womack, D. T. Jones, and D. Roos, *The Machine That Changed the World* (New York: Harper Perennial, 1990), p. 160.

15 Ibid.

16 Walton (1986), p. 64.

17 T. J. Pempel, *Policy and Politics in Japan – Creative Conservatism* (Philadelphia: Temple University Press, 1982), p. 20; and M. J. Smitka, *Competitive Ties: Subcontracting in the Japanese Automotive Industry* (New York: Columbia University Press, 1991), p. 206.

18 D. Friedman, *The Misunderstood Miracle: Industrial Development and Political Change in Japan* (Ithaca, New York: Cornell University Press, 1988), p. 35.

19 T. Nishiguchi (1989), 'Strategic dualism: an alternative in industrial societies' (Oxford, England: Oxford University, Nuffield College, Ph.D. thesis, 1989), pp. 154–227.

20 R. Dore, 'Goodwill and the spirit of market capitalism', *British Journal of Sociology* 34 (1983): 459–482; and McMillan, (1990), p. 40.

21 B. Asanuma, 'The contractual framework for parts supply in the Japanese automotive industry' and 'The organization of parts supply in the Japanese Automotive Industry', *Japanese Economic Studies* 15 (1985a&b): 32–78; and S. Kawasaki and J. McMillan, 'The design of contracts: evidence from Japanese subcontracting', *Journal of the Japanese and International Economies* 1 (1987): pp. 327–349.

22 Author interview with Mitsubishi manager, 14 October 1990.

23 J.B. Treece, 'The lessons GM could learn for its supplier shakeup', *Business Week*, 31 August 1992, p. 29; and M. Blake, 'The evolution of an American business', *Synergy*, a publication of Toyota Motor Sales, 1991, p. 13.

24 'Sitting pretty', *Synergy*, 1991, p. 13.

25 Ibid.

17 The Way Forward: Partnership Sourcing

Ken Lewis and Steve Lytton

Partnership sourcing – a commitment by both customers and suppliers, regardless of size, to a long-term relationship based on clear, mutually agreed objectives to strive for world-class capability and competitiveness – has been around for a good many years. Some areas of the automobile industry, for example, have been operating it since the early 1980s, but unfortunately it has been very slow to catch on with the rest of British industry. True, it can be very hard to move from the established way of doing things (purchasing on basis of the invoice price) to the more sensible, new way of purchasing (on the basis of the total cost of the acquisition of the products and services), but the benefits are clear. First, you know what the products or services really cost and, second, you can then focus your activities on specific areas with a view to eradicating waste and getting your costs down.

All this, however, requires systems of measurement and few companies and organizations are willing or able to set up the correct monitoring systems. They therefore continue to plough on in their old sweet way, usually at the behest of the chief executive, believing, or electing to believe, that the price they are paying on their invoice is, and should be, the main supply criterion. Where such an approach prevails – and sadly, this is almost everywhere in the UK – suppliers tend to be seen as a constraining source causing lots of problems and having very little to add to the party.

At Dutton, we see the relationship with our suppliers somewhat differently. We consider our suppliers to be a valuable resource, with specialist knowledge, skills and equipment, which, if properly focused, will help improve our company's competitive performance. Our view is that our suppliers, as an integral part of our supply chain, must by definition play an integral part in our success. All chains are only as strong as their weakest link and the same goes for supply chains. Unless you, your suppliers and your customers are all pulling in the same direction, none of you will ever succeed in turning in a world-class performance.

The definition of partnership sourcing just cited is a wonderful motherhood statement, pointing out, in my view, in a handful of words the way forward to achieving your goals and objectives. Many representatives who visit or telephone our company still find it difficult to understand what we mean by long-term relationships. They often ask if they can tender when we review our present arrangements and seem to expect this to be every 12 months. This is not what we mean by a long-term relationship. We mean that our relationships are ongoing and are based on quality performance backed by confidence and trust.

Our confidence exists because we maintain very close links with the companies in our supply chain. For example, our suppliers each have an electronic pass allowing them free access to any part of our company during our normal business hours. This means that, as they fill our kanban bins, often on a daily basis, they can, and do, meet our management and team members as they wish to. It also allows us to meet them and maintain links, while at the same time providing an early warning signal, should one be needed, of any deterioration in their performance.

Once a year we have a suppliers' day, when we take all our suppliers out to lunch, explain what we have been up to in the previous year and outline our strategy for the next three years. By knowing where we are going, our suppliers are able then to plan confidently their own investments to meet our future needs. Each year we award our most outstanding supplier a 'Supplier of the Year' trophy, which suppliers go all out to win. This helps build up the rapport that is so essential for a strong and effective supply chain.

The key objectives of partnership sourcing are:

- *Minimizing total costs.* As mentioned already, in reality invoice prices do not indicate the full cost of getting goods or services to where they are required in your organization. When company executives believe that their purchasing departments have successfully completed their task if they have negotiated the lowest available price, they are neglecting whole areas of additional costs. What about rejects, rework and the other areas of the company affected by poor supplier performance? These should also be brought into the cost equation.
- *Maximizing product and service development.* We, along with many other companies, have found that by working together with our customers we have been able to reduce significantly the time to market of our (and hence their) products. In addition, with fewer changes required, as production levels ramp up, a noticeable competitive advantage has been gained.
- *Obtaining competitive advantage.* At Dutton, we have found that joint activities between us and our suppliers has helped us to keep prices down and stable for four years – and this despite the world-wide increase in raw materials!

However, to get to this position requires very considerable trust, which can take many years to develop. In my view, when approaching the issue of partnerships the lead should always come from the customers. Our experience has shown that our suppliers have been much more willing to participate in partnering than many of our customers. Customers tend to be sceptical about the free flow of information that is required. All this is perhaps understandable, because it changes the status of the 'expendable' supplier into a fully fledged contributor to the overall product process. Once customers have had a taste of the opportunities and benefits of the new relationship, however, they slowly start to inch their way down the road to closer relations with ever increasing confidence.

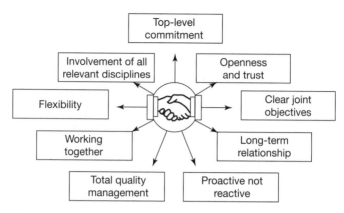

Figure 17.1

As always in business, for new paths to be successfully explored the determining factor is genuine commitment from top-level management (Figure 17.1). Half-hearted and anodyne statements will not achieve anything. Building trust is neither a smooth process nor a quick fix. It really needs time, perhaps even years, to establish itself firmly. After all, it might involve throwing over perhaps a lifetime of alternative practices.

One major requisite for developing openness and trust, for example, involves *open-book accounting*, in which companies exchange accounts. The first time we did this our suppliers were completely dumbfounded. They had never previously received a set of accounts from any of their customers. Such an action indicates to the suppliers that what they are about to receive really is going to be different. It clearly displays your confidence in them as partners.

You will also need to set clearly understood, joint, long-term objectives and agree which lines of communication are to be used. At Dutton, over the years, we have adhered strictly to the long-term nature of these partnerships, only changing suppliers when they have proved incapable of making the quantum leap forward that both we and partnership sourcing required.

As the years have gone by, however, things have not stood still; and, in the same way as our customers' demands have grown, so have ours, regarding suppliers' performance. Some of our suppliers have not lived up to their promise. One company that won our Supplier of the Year Award in the first year is no longer with us. Unfortunately, they were unable to bring themselves into line with the same performance standards as the rest of the companies in our supply chain.

Such relationships need to be highly proactive, as opposed to being merely reactive. We are not experts in banking, insurance, vehicle maintenance or many of the other spheres required to keep an engineering company functioning effectively. Therefore, we look to our suppliers, as the specialists, and expect them to bring along with them the latest technology, equipment and techniques in their industry, so that we can integrate all this top-notch expertise into our supply chain and pass on the benefits accrued. For us to succeed, it is vitally important for our suppliers to have their own top-quality management who have a sense of vision and are sincere.

Another equally vital aspect for partnerships to be effective is that all departments of the various companies must work together, with all barriers broken down and all preconceived ideas shed. Attitudes in each of the companies must be flexible and sympathetic. There must be a strong will to win. The defending of empires, which is so common in industry, and its replacement by such departmental cooperation may involve some difficult decisions and may take a long time to achieve; but the old-style methods of purchasing (whereby both the buyer and the salesman each try to concede as little as possible) is definitely steadily on its way out as far as the best and most highly respected companies are concerned.

Today, purchasing needs to be a team effort and this realization might come to help soften some of the hard-bitten attitudes held by so many for so long.

Advantages for purchasers

So, what are the advantages for purchasers in going down this route?

Security of supply

Partnerships should help ensure your company security of supply. No longer should it happen that your turn comes after that of more powerful purchasers. Also, your needs should soon come to be understood along the whole length of your supply chain.

But how do you get to this position and what steps need to be taken? Since you already have a supply chain, it is highly likely that you know who the good and bad suppliers are currently. I would recommend, if you have not already begun to do this, that you start to drop your poor suppliers and start developing your good ones. As your level of business increases with these good suppliers, you will generally start to become a more valued customer. You can then work towards the situation in which, when they deliver their products to you, if the first one is right then the last one will be right, too.

You should also seek to understand what your suppliers' plans are when faced by a disaster scenario. I am constantly amazed how often this information is not sought out by even the largest UK companies, despite the fact that they often do not carry stock themselves to cover such eventualities.

Partnership sourcing should also bring you on-time deliveries, because the supplier can now plan longer term to meet your requirements, knowing that renegotiation will not get in the way. He will often be able to buy at better prices from his own sources of supply and this should also be reflected both in the price and in his delivery performance. The quality of the products being supplied should steadily improve, as your suppliers are now confidently assured of your business. You should also find that they will begin investing in the right tools and equipment to satisfy your quality needs.

In our company, we have taken a policy decision to single source, i.e. to use just one supplier for particular product lines. This has added even greater advantages, particularly in terms of the amount of administrative controls we require to manage the process. Such a small basket of suppliers has meant that we could reduce the controls to an absolute minimum.

In our experience, once all-round confidence has been achieved and suppliers really understand (perhaps for the first time ever) where you are going and their place in this, you will see them exceeding all your expectations.

Reduced paperwork

One of our trading conditions is that our suppliers are only allowed to send in one invoice each month. Since they are only going to get one payment per month, why do we need all those individual invoices flooding in? We receive a one-sheet summary and they receive one payment. Actually, we have now taken this even further now. The monthly invoice now comes in on computer disk, coded accordingly to our cost centres, which are entered by the supplier.

Each supplier has only one purchase order, which he retains forever. The supplier of our admin. materials, for example, has an order that states: 'To supply material for the administrative functions as required.' Only once did a supplier try to pull a fast one. Our system of controls picked it up immediately. This broke the previous relationship of trust and we found an alternative source of supply.

Working closely with your suppliers, as the specialists in their own field, you should also see a reduction in your time to market performance, as well as a substantial reduction in the stocks you need to hold and a reduction in your total cost of acquisitions.

Simpler delivery systems

At Dutton, some 90 per cent of raw materials and consumables are now delivered on a kanban system. This is a very simple and effective supply technique, generally based on a two-box system with one week's supply of components held in each box. When the first box is emptied, the operator places in a central position on the component rack a component-specific ticket detailing the component part number, description and quantity. The team operator then starts using the second week's box of components. In the meantime, the ticket and empty box is collected by the supplier and refilled with one week's supply of components. The replenished box is replaced on the supplier's next visit and the next set of tickets and empty boxes is collected.

In the four to five years that we have been operating this Kanban system, we have never yet run out of a component.

It is up to our suppliers to decide what batch sizes they can most efficiently manufacture or buy in and buffer stock for us. This simple system has saved us all unimaginable amounts of time. A Dutton operator assembling an enclosure can confidently put out his hand, time after time, every time, to pick up nuts, bolts, hinges, locks etc., all the while knowing that there will be a quality product there waiting for him. And all this without a special purchase order, or a goods received or inspection department, etc. Neither do we need to make a telephone call, send a fax or do anything else to get that product there. It is where it should be when we want it, with the minimum of administrative control.

Improved quality and cost savings

The entry point for anyone wishing to be a world-class manufacturer is quality products and service quality. Our experience of partnership sourcing has shown that our suppliers have both sharpened their standards and continually improved their performance quality. This has meant that our products and service levels have also improved and we have been able to pass on the cost savings to our customers. By eliminating the goods-inwards inspection, for example, we made major cost savings and it has become clear that if you share the right kind of quality culture with your suppliers many such costly and unnecessary expenses can be saved.

Faster product development

If you, the purchaser, can tap into the skills and strengths of your suppliers, you will be able to get into the marketplace a lot quicker with your products. Enormous competitive advantage can be achieved when your designers, drawing offices and purchasing departments are all working closely with your suppliers.

Lower stocks and smaller overdrafts

Lower stocks are another feature of partnerships, particularly if you adopt a kanban system. Many companies should be looking at a minimum of 25 stock turns per year and could aim to set their sights at 50. With such reduced stock and reduced work in progress, your overdraft should shrink dramatically.

Reduced total cost

With the old-style adversarial relations, costs are often kept high because of the perpetual telephoning, contacting, cajoling, pushing and shoving that is necessary to remedy supply problems. Under these circumstances Murphy's Law seems always to prevail and the cost of rectifying the problem is always very high. The truth is, however, that very few companies actually measure their remedial, cost-of-quality expenditure, most of which is built in through outmoded and outdated systems of control.

With developed partnerships, by working together to introduce new-style collaborative systems, you should find the cost of running your business falling considerably and continuing to decline.

Advantages for suppliers

Partnerships, by definition, are not there just for the customers. Suppliers, too, must see a range of significant benefits if they are to play ball.

Forward planning

For your suppliers, having long-term agreements will boost their confidence in terms of their ability to plan their own businesses.

Where long-term agreements are in place, your suppliers will be able, perhaps for the first time, to study your company's requirements and make their own forward plans regarding acquisitions of plant, equipment, premises and other developments that will enhance your business.

My view is that in the UK in the past (and for many companies this is still the case) we never really gave our suppliers the opportunity to perform to the best of their ability. Here, and in much of the West, we are much more used to the old supply methods and to short-termism. We are used to denying suppliers access to our design and development people and yet it is precisely these people who generally appreciate the valuable input that suppliers can give. This has tended to act against product quality and has helped build in costs.

Over time, partnerships push suppliers into performing to their best ability and often bring the suppliers renewed vigour and an enhanced sense of satisfaction. 'Win/win' moves from mere verbiage into reality. There is, moreover, another major upside. Such relationships encourage innovation and development, because suppliers no longer tend to feel that they are only being paid for what the customer has specified. They often start to look ahead to see what they can do to improve the customer's product.

Financial stability and payment on time

Partnerships depend on trust and there can be no real partnership unless customers guarantee to pay their suppliers on time. There should also be plenty of scope for mutually beneficial financial arrangements, resulting in better cash flows and the effective pooling of resources.

Virtually all companies experience cash flow problems at some time or other; but where regular payments have become the norm in your supply chain much more help and support tends to be provided by both your customers and suppliers. After all, it is in everyone's interest that such temporary setbacks are resolved.

Reduced total costs

Suppliers can enjoy the benefit of seeing reduced total costs if they themselves adopt the somewhat radical ideas put forward here. Figure 17.2 shows the steamship of cost sailing along captained by a traditional purchasing department that focuses on price.

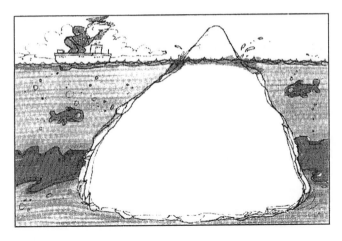

Figure 17.2

To be fair to the crew, this is probably exactly what the managing director of the shipping line has commanded them to do. But below the water line are many hidden costs that are not generally measured by companies.

Besides the cost of internal inspection discussed earlier, there are many other costs that should be identified: reject-processing costs, just-in-case inventories (because you are never sure if your supplier is going to supply a quality product on time), associated lost production time, purchasing costs, progress costs, accounts administration costs and so on, including the very high cost of remedial action when things have gone wrong.

Unfortunately, I have seen too many purchasing departments in British industry where the people appear to have an inadequate training in such basic requirements as cost accountancy. They are often unfamiliar with statistical process control and with many other tools of total quality management. They certainly tend to have little understanding of the cost of quality.

The good news is that things are changing. Much more effort is being made by the professional bodies to raise quality standards within the field of purchasing, which has now finally been allowed to emerge from the backroom and been acknowledged as one of the most vital areas within any organization.

Finding and keeping top-class suppliers

So, how do we go about finding all these wonderful new suppliers that are out there? First we conduct some trial business with suppliers using ISO 9000 or similar vendor rating-assessment techniques. If the trial is successful, we then assemble a multifunctional team to assess the new supplier. The team reviews all aspects of the company's performance: Is the paperwork neat and tidily presented? Does it arrive on time? Is it understandable? Is it accurate? What is the supplier like on the telephone? How well do they respond to problems?

The team members also review the technical aspects of the supplier's products and the supplier's attitude to the team itself – how cooperative and proactive they are. We have a weighted factor of 30 per cent of the results of the assessment associated with the culture of the company. We want suppliers who are like Dutton Engineering. It is no good working with suppliers whose culture is out of line with our own.

Quality and on-time delivery are rated at 25 per cent each. Price is rated at only 20 per cent. This often amazes other business people, but our experience has shown that if any of the other elements are not in line, the apparent price benefits are illusory, because working with such companies always costs us more anyway.

PARTNERSHIP SOURCING
TRADITIONAL PRACTICE v PARTNERSHIP SOURCING
OLD

- Price is dominant
- Check product quality
- Poor performance, change supplier
- Renegotiate at regular intervals
- Win/lose relationship

Figure 17.3

PARTNERSHIP SOURCING
TRADITIONAL PRACTICE v PARTNERSHIP SOURCING
NEW

- Total cost is dominant
- Assured quality
- Offer preventive help, pool resources
- Build firm relationship
- Teamwork to improve competitiveness
- Win/win relationship
- Mutual profitability

Figure 17.4

Figure 17.3 contrasts traditional practice (where lowest price is dominant) with partnership sourcing in Figure 17.4. If you go down the former route you have to have inspection in place to check on product quality. With the traditional route, if suppliers perform badly, you just change them and continue to change them. Often, however, the new ones prove to be even worse than the previous ones. In addition, you must ensure that you renegotiate at regular intervals with a view to seeing if you can screw the supplier down even more or kick up a fuss about his quality and delivery performance.

Other key aspects of such a relationship are that you keep the supplier at arm's length telling them very little and holding all your cards to your chest. Confidentiality is the watchword. Such relationships are win/lose – either you win and they lose or vice versa.

Partnership sourcing marks a totally different way of doing things. Here, the dominant criterion is total cost. Our measurements have proved indisputably that it makes financial sense. Now, even our accountants are convinced! Quality becomes assured. Preventive help becomes part of the norm and resources are pooled. Firm and lasting relationships are created and the developing team work will act to improve both companies' competitiveness. Such a relationship is win/win, with both companies benefiting both financially and socially.

All these changes of attitude towards trading with your suppliers can only be based on trust and developing this can sometimes take a long time for both parties. Once the process is under way, however, and the relationship starts to develop, the benefits to both companies soon start to flow. Confidence grows and bolder and bolder steps are taken. The competitive force thus unleashed is very powerful indeed. It will engender an atmosphere in which both supplier and customer will be able to eliminate the massive amounts of wasted time and resources bound up in traditional processes – processes once considered absolutely fundamental for running any business.

Figure 17.5

An important improvement will be your just-in-case stockpile (Figure 17.5), which is in truth just a comfort factor that you will no longer require. On my journeys around British industry, I am truly staggered at the amount of stores and stock items that are still retained – often only because they make the balance sheet look healthy. Goods are *only* of value if you can sell them. If you cannot sell them, they are a liability. They take up very valuable space and, moreover, when you want that left-hand widget you bought two years ago, you generally cannot even find it among all the stock. You waste lots of time looking and eventually still end up having to go out and buy another one.

Much of this stock has probably come from that 'wonderful' minimum order charge, which obliges you to buy 20 times more than you really need. In my company, I adopt the principle that, if we cannot sell it within four weeks, we ought to throw it away. This I often do, to the dismay of some of my 'magpie' colleagues.

As I mentioned earlier, paying your suppliers on time is fundamental to partnership sourcing. If you do not pay on time, you will never develop the right kind of relationship with your suppliers. We always agree on terms with our suppliers from the outset. Then we adhere religiously to those terms of trading. It is particularly important for larger companies to ensure that they pay their smaller suppliers on time, since a two-to-three-month wait for payment can often plunge small companies into a very difficult financial position.

Traditional methods of purchasing and supply often create that terrifying character, the paper monster. Our experience at Dutton is that paper is simply a comfort factor that adds nothing of any value to the business. Most of it comes from outdated systems that should have been changed years ago.

Partnership sourcing will eliminate a large number of these wasteful paper documents. We, for example, have managed to reduce the number of purchase invoices processed by our company each month from nearly 200 to 60 (Figure 17.6). The beauty of our situation is that even if we double or treble the amount of business with these suppliers, we still will not have more than approximately 60 invoices a

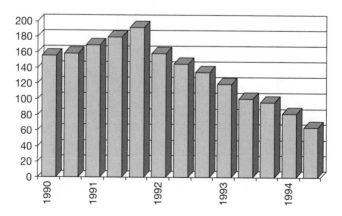

Figure 17.6 Purchase invoice processing

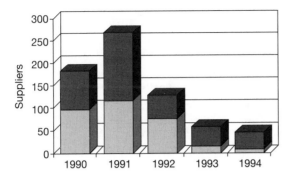

Figure 17.7 Single sourcing in action

month. This means that we will not need to employ additional staff to shuffle the additional paper around.

Our single-sourcing policy has streamlined our activities very considerably (Figure 17.7). In 1991, we saw a substantial growth in the company and had more than 250 suppliers. In 1992, we thought we had reduced our supply chain to the optimum level when we hit the 100 mark. However, we reduced the number still further by looking at our best suppliers.

For example, our nut and bolt supplier was so good that we asked him if he could supply our polishing consumables. This represented a whole new business area for him to set up; but he did it and he has now expanded the range he can offer to the rest of his customer base. It helped him and it helped us to condense our range of suppliers still further.

We have now just under 50 suppliers, with a core of ten. I doubt if we shall be able to reduce it much more: it is, after all, highly unlikely that our stationery supplier will be able to supply us with our steel.

Partnership sourcing and kanbans had a dramatic effect on our stock and work in progress (Figure 17.8). This declined from the 1991 level of over £250,000 to the 1992 level of £150,000. In 1993, we reduced it to just over £100,000

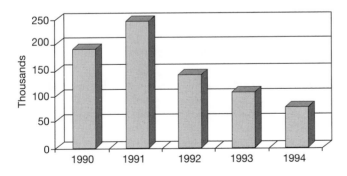

Figure 17.8 Impact on stocks/work in progress

by the introduction of lean manufacture, whereby we make one when we have sold one. Annual hours brought us a great surprise when the figure fell one month to £89,000. And all this despite the fact that, over those four years, our sales had increased by 50 per cent. The secret was that we pulled material in only when we needed it.

We are still continuing to develop and improve our supply chain. At present we are working with our suppliers to introduce computers and information technology with a view to becoming a paperless business within three years. What is clear is that we need our suppliers on board with us, thinking the same way we do. At Dutton, if our suppliers continue to demonstrate the same commitment to our company as they do at present, they will be on board for life.

Partnership sourcing can and should have an enormous impact on your company; but it needs some brave decisions to be taken, as well as absolute support from top management to see the whole project through.

Part 3

Change

Section E Organizational Restructuring

The last 30 years have seen a succession of management fads. Three key ones were continuous improvement, empowerment and reengineering – advocating incremental, bottom-up and a radical top-down approach respectively. Here Schroeder and Robinson describe the history of continuous improvement, Bowen and Lawler describe various degrees of empowerment and Hammer outlines the principles behind reengineering.

Schroeder and Robinson trace the development of continuous improvement programmes, from early attempts at suggestion schemes and incentive management, through Japanese refinements of these ideas into quality circles, zero defects and kaizen programmes. They also emphasize factors that are critical to the successful implementation of continuous improvement programmes, including facilitating the free flow of ideas, sustaining an efficient system of idea management, continuously training and developing staff and appreciating that payback will be achieved over a long rather than a short period.

Bowen and Lawler consider the benefits and costs of empowerment. Are you better off limiting empowerment and predetermining service as UPS and Disney do, or are you better allowing staff a measure of freedom, the route taken by Federal Express and Club Med? While staff often like the control empowerment affords them, Bowen and Lawler caution that empowerment also costs, for example through additional training. They conclude that different degrees of empowerment are appropriate in different situations – basically less empowerment where speed and cost are critical and more empowerment where service and care are more important, there is a long-term relationship with the client and/or the environment is changeable.

In his classic contribution Hammer describes the benefits of reengineering. Although now much vilified since it became synonymous with downsizing, the increased use of IT and structural changes means there can be a case for reengineering certain procedures from first principles, for example jobs that have been computerized piecemeal and are still modelled on manual procedures. Hammer suggests that any reorganization should be around outcomes, performed by the person who uses the output and data should be input once. He is less explicit about the potential loss of trust and tacit knowledge that can easily accompany wholesale change. The lessons of the 1990s suggest that one needs to watch one is not throwing the baby out with the bathwater and make a point of involving the workforce at every stage in any major change programme.

18 America's Most Successful Export to Japan: Continuous Improvement Programmes

Dean M. Schroeder and Alan G. Robinson

Continuous improvement programmes (CIPs) unleash employee experience and creativity to improve both products and processes. They are often cited as the most important difference between the Japanese and Western management styles and as a major factor in Japan's economic success.[1] Yet the CIP was conceived, developed and brought to maturation in the United States. After World War II, the US government helped to export it to Japan, where it was well received and promptly flourished.

Japanese companies have put almost 40 years into the development and refinement of CIPs, or kaizen programmes as they are known in Japan, and have brought the art and science of managing them to new levels of sophistication. The aim of these programmes is precisely to design and implement a system whose natural equilibrium is constant improvement and change.

The Industrial Revolution

For most of its history, manufacturing was a craft performed by skilled artisans. Apprenticeships were used to pass production methods and skills onto the next generation. The artisans or workers largely determined how work was to be done.

Two important developments during the 19th century altered this state of affairs. The first was the increasing standardization of parts to make them interchangeable, championed in particular by Eli Whitney, then a successful rifle manufacturer. The tightly controlled uniformity necessary to make interchangeable components required manufacturing to measurements and standards, which naturally led to a reduction in the artisan's latitude and authority. The second development was the increased mechanization of skills and division of labour begun during the Industrial Revolution. Tasks that had required highly trained artisans could now be performed on machines by workers with little training or education.

The tradition of the worker determining the method of production remained largely in place, however, even though the workforce was now less skilled and trained. As the pace of change quickened, the level of industrialization rose and production methods became more complex, the limitations of this state of affairs soon became painfully apparent.

To correct this problem, Frederick Taylor and Frank Gilbreth advocated that the 'one best way' to produce should be found through the application of an objective 'scientific' method; they placed responsibility for this search firmly on management.

Despite offering a powerful method to production mangers, scientific management, as practised, did not slow the established trend toward disenfranchisement and deskilling of the worker begun by standardization and the Industrial Revolution.[2] The disenfranchisement continued because the source of methods improvement and cost reduction was now (quasi-officially) restricted to management. Those performing the work were told what to do and, often, not to think; the jobs requiring 'thinking' were separated from those requiring 'doing'. Unfortunately, much of the direct knowledge of the process and shop floor was thus eliminated from decision making.

Henry Gantt, a protégé of Frederick Taylor, noticed this shortcoming. In a 1901 paper Gantt concluded with some thoughts about reintroducing the worker into the improvement process:

> The system is one of education, with prizes for those who learn; but the prizes have so far been awarded for learning and doing only what our experts already knew. The next and most obvious step is to make it to the interest of the men to learn more than their cards can teach them. So far nothing has been done in this line, not because the need for some such provision has not been felt, but for the reason that no entirely satisfactory method has suggested itself.
>
> The writer believes in paying a liberal compensation for improved methods of work, and in offering special inducements to a workman to make out instruction cards, by which others are enabled to carry out these methods. The compensation should be sufficiently liberal not only to induce him to part with what information he may have, but to use his ingenuity to devise better methods.[3]

The reintroduction of the worker into the improvement process marked the beginning of modern CIP management.

Early continuous improvement programmes

Denny of Dumbarton

One early system was the 'awards scheme' started in 1871 by Denny of Dumbarton, a Scottish shipbuilder.[4] He claimed it was the first industrial suggestion system in Great Britain.

All claims were evaluated by a two-person committee consisting of a member of the engineering department and a person from outside the company. In addition to the cash awards for each suggestion, a premium of ten pounds (then a substantial sum) was awarded for every fifth suggestion a worker contributed. (In 1921, this scheme was made even more generous.)

National Cash Register

One of the earliest examples of a CIP in the United States was that of the National Cash Register Company (NCR) in Dayton, Ohio, under the leadership of its legendary founder, John H. Patterson.[5] In 1894, a large shipment of defective cash registers was returned to the company from England. When Patterson, who until then had been almost entirely involved in sales, found that acid had been poured into the mechanisms (obviously by his own employees), he moved his desk onto the factory floor to find the problem. He quickly discovered that the working conditions were unsafe, dark, dingy and unpleasant and had lowered morale to the point of hostility. It didn't take him long to determine what had to be done.

From this experience, he pioneered the 'daylight' factory – a well-lit and pleasant facility whose walls and ceiling were 80 percent glass. He installed safety devices, ventilation, bathrooms for use on company time, lounges and individual lockers. He also kept doctors and nurses on the premises and started a laundry service in the plant to provide clean towels and aprons for employees. A subsidized hot meals programme reduced absenteeism enough to pay for itself. A period of mandatory daily exercise was instituted long before this became a fashionable trademark of a 'team-oriented' company.

At the same time, Patterson set up a programme aimed at soliciting written suggestions for improvement from the factory workers. His idea was that the company pyramid should be supported by the base, not the top, in which case it could be viewed as having a 'hundred-headed brain'. In 1894, prizes of $30 were awarded for the best ideas and the factory magazine published the names and photos of the winners. Award amounts grew rapidly in size, reaching $500 in gold by 1897. By the 1940s, the company was receiving an average of 3000 suggestions each year. Patterson had discovered that by recognizing and rewarding improvement suggestions, many problems were resolved with minimal intervention by top management. Some, in fact, were resolved even before management became aware of them.

But NCR's continuous improvement programme was more comprehensive than a good work environment and a suggestion system. Extensive evening ('owl') classes were offered, for one dollar each, to further the education and development of employees. Subjects included mathematics, blueprint reading, accounting, dressmaking, public speaking, home economics, mechanical drawing, salesmanship, shorthand, typing, machine-shop training and tool design. As employees learned, they became more eligible for advancement.

Lincoln Electric Company

James T. Lincoln of Lincoln Electric Company (the world's largest manufacturer of arc-welding supplies and equipment) also understood the value of the 'hundred-headed brain'. To harness this 'collective intelligence', Lincoln designed an 'incentive management' system to promote continuous improvement. Lincoln achieved this through company policies and operating procedures that rewarded workers with compensation in proportion to output and gave them increased status for achievement and publicity for contribution.

In 1915, Lincoln began a piece-rate system. In 1929 the company implemented a suggestion system that remunerated employees with half of the savings resulting from any improvement idea during the first year of its implementation. This programme was later subsumed by a profit-based employee bonus system begun in 1934. Employee bonuses often approximated the worker's annual wages.

Despite his belief in management's ultimate authority, Lincoln succeeded in creating a climate of openness and respect between workers and managers. Workers had full responsibility for their workstations and were held accountable for the quality of their output. Open communication between management and workers was encouraged by managerial open-door policies and an employee advisory board elected by the workforce, which met twice-monthly with top management to pass on ideas and to identify problems.

Another way Lincoln tried to lower barriers between management and workers was through uniform treatment of *all* employees. Management had no special benefits such as assigned parking spaces or an executive dining room. Fifty percent of the company's stock was owned by 70 percent of its employees through a special programme. Management offices were intended to be strictly functional and only the president and CEO had private offices, which also doubled as conference rooms. All promotions came from within the company; any employee was entitled to apply for an open job and jobs were posted on employee bulletin boards. Employees understood that increased productivity would not result in their termination, for Lincoln Electric assured lifetime employment.[6]

Lincoln also had a unique view on how profits should be distributed. He believed that the people responsible for creating profits should receive the largest share of them. Since customers, more than absentee stockholders, provided funds for company growth and profitability, they were rewarded with low prices and high quality. Because productive workers created products and profits, employees were rewarded with compensation that was often twice that of workers performing similar operations at other companies . . . Even with such highly paid workers, Lincoln Electric's high productivity resulted in lower labour costs per dollar of sales than any other company in the electric equipment manufacturing industry.

The export and foreign development of CIPs

Employee suggestion programmes have become a mainstay of many corporate kaizen programmes in Japan. Prior to World War II, Japanese suggestion systems mostly took input from a handful of elite workers thought to have the capability to offer ideas. After the war, however, suggestion systems proliferated rapidly; they expanded to include the entire workforce and were integrated closely with broader continuous improvement efforts. There were two reasons for this surge in popularity. First, they proved an inexpensive means to improve production and reduce costs during a time of severe resource shortages. Eiji Toyoda, the long-serving CEO of

Toyota Motor Corporation, explains how his company adopted such a system after his 1950 visit to the United States:

> Soon after my return to Japan, payment for the procurements had not come in yet, so management got together and discussed what internal changes the company should be making that didn't require an input of cash. We decided then and there that we could streamline operations and cut transportation costs. Both could be accomplished without further expenditures. All we had to do was use our know-how. While at Ford, I had seen how considerable savings in manpower could be had in materials handling by judiciously making even minor changes, so we decided to begin there. That's how Toyota's suggestion system got started.[7]

The second reason for the surge in popularity was that the US military occupation authorities, fearing widespread starvation and unrest in Japan if industry was not rebuilt quickly, contracted with TWI Inc. to run programmes in Japan using ex-instructors from the wartime US TWI service.[8] It was hoped that TWI could successfully boost Japanese industry from within.

The suggestion system and the drive for continuous improvement grew naturally out of the TWI programmes, which consisted of three ten-hour courses (JIT, JMT and JRT).

JIT (job instruction training) taught supervisors the value of good training and how to provide it. TWI was able to reduce the time to train lens grinders from *five years* to *two months*, thus eliminating the shortage. JMT (job methods training) taught supervisors how to generate methods improvement ideas and how to make sure they were implemented. TWI taught managers to write up improvement proposals with expected cost reductions, improved quality, and increased safety all clearly presented. The JRT (job relations training) course taught supervisors both how to deal with job relations problems and how to prevent them from arising in the first place. It is estimated that, in 1952, over one million Japanese supervisors were actively undergoing TWI training.[9]

The exposure of Japanese management to TWI, the low cost of CIPs and the experiences Japanese executives brought home from US tours combined to give kaizen programmes a good start. Companies that adopted such programmes early included Toshiba in 1946, Matsushita Electric in 1950 and, as mentioned earlier, Toyota in 1951.

Although suggestion systems and boxes became widespread in Japanese companies during the 1950s, at first they achieved only moderate success because of the difficulty in getting group-oriented Japanese workers to contribute individual ideas. Furthermore, many workers had neither the time nor the inclination to write up their suggestions. However, quality control circles, a group based *oral* forum for suggestions, began to appear in Japan in the early 1960s. Indeed, QC circles are credited with starting the zero defects (ZD) movement at NEC in 1965, where workers were required to make contracts agreeing to produce no defects whatsoever.

During the 1973 oil crisis, kaizen programmes again proliferated as companies looked for proven methods to reduce costs without making new investment. The experience of Canon Inc. is evidence of this trend.[10] There was great consternation when, in 1975, the company posted its first loss since 1949. A full-blown kaizen programme was started as a component of a long-range strategic plan to make Canon a world-class company. Over the next ten years the company saved an estimated $200 million in direct costs from employee-generated ideas, for a paltry corporate investment of $2.2 million, of which 96% was prize money.[11] The indirect benefits of such a programme are difficult to assess, but are probably much greater. It would be hard to put a value on reduced defects, higher morale and a workforce alert for opportunities to improve production methods and eliminate waste.

CIPs return to the United States

In 1984 General Motors and Toyota established NUMMI, a joint venture, to produce the Chevrolet Nova and Toyota Corolla. GM wished to gain experience with the Japanese management style; Toyota wanted an introduction to US workers, suppliers and management. The CEO of the new company was Tatsuro Toyoda, son of the founder of Toyota. The plant was to be operated in the Toyota style.

The chosen facility was an old GM plant in Fremont, California, which had been closed in 1982 in no small part because of its history of labour–management conflict, poor quality, low productivity and high absenteeism. At the time of plant shutdown, absenteeism exceeded 20 percent, over 60 firings were in dispute and there were more than 1000 unresolved grievances.

By agreement with the United Auto Workers Union (UAW), the workforce was to comprise as many members as possible of the original 5000 workers laid off in 1982. NUMMI was able to hire over 80 percent of its workforce from the ranks of former GM employees. In addition, the 1987 NUMMI–UAW contract specifies that: 'Together we are committed to building and maintaining the most innovative and harmonious labour–management relationship in America. The parties are committed to . . . constantly seek improvement in quality, efficiency, and work environment through *kaizen*, QC circles, and suggestion programmes.'[12]

With this emphasis on kaizen and continuous improvement, the contract also stipulates that it be difficult to lay off workers – it even forbids layoffs owing to productivity increases. Participation in the employee suggestion scheme grew rapidly, from 26 percent to 71 percent over two years.

Dale Buss, an auto industry reporter for the *Wall Street Journal*, summarized the results in 1986: NUMMI 'has managed to convert a crew of largely middle-aged, rabble-rousing former GM workers into a crack force that is beating the bumpers off the Big Three plants in efficiency and product quality.'[13]

Successful CIP management

We now go on to identify some of the requirements for successful CIP management and also discuss why the CIP has not been deployed as successfully over the last 40 years in the United States as it has in Japan.

Improvements at first cause dislocation and almost always require time before they prove worthwhile

It is not always easy to link the positive impact of minor improvements to the bottom line. Shigeo Shingo, one of Japan's foremost manufacturing experts, explains the problem:

> Since improvement to a greater or lesser extent demands new procedures, a certain amount of difficulty will be encountered 99 percent of all improvement plans would vanish without a trace if they were to be abandoned after only a brief trial. People in charge of plant improvement must grasp this fact.[14]

The experience of Kobayashi Kose, the fourth largest cosmetics manufacturer in Japan, reflects this productivity-reducing initial effect of change.[15] In January 1977 the company introduced a total quality control programme that, naturally, included continuous improvement. In the first year costs *rose* by 7 percent and the number of customer complaints *rose* by almost 25 percent. Three years later, however, costs were *down* by 12 percent and complaints by 60 percent.

During the window of learning time, managing the process will require both the ability to look beyond the costs that increase in the short term and sufficient technical manufacturing knowledge to lead the changes in the proper direction. These two requisites for success are not always present when they are needed.

It is unfortunate that current standard accounting methods, while well suited to measuring the tangible direct costs of improvement, fail to reflect less tangible (but often more significant) benefits such as better quality, higher morale, lower inventories and shorter lead times.

The wrong signals sent by accounting methods can pose a problem if the company is led by 'generic' managers.[16] Generic managers are people with 'managerial' skills that supposedly enable them to run any company well, regardless of its line of business. Since their expertise is industry and product independent, such managers obviously must get their signals from financial and accounting data to a much greater extent than if they had a solid technical understanding of the process.

Strong pressure to produce, when combined with the short-term downturn in performance that any improvement brings, can induce a bias to seek immediate and dramatic improvements, rather than the stream of small improvements that can result from a CIP. The effect of a major innovation, after all, can be more cleanly and directly measured than the effects of a large number of incremental improvements. According to Masaaki Imai, a leading Japanese improvement expert, these pressures have led to considerable differences in the way change is managed in the United States and Japan:

> Western managers worship at the altar of innovation. Innovation is dramatic, a real attention-getter. *Kaizen*, on the other hand, is often undramatic and subtle, and its results are seldom immediately visible. While *kaizen* is a continuous process, innovation is generally a one-shot phenomenon.
>
> In the West, for example, a middle manager can usually obtain top management support for such projects as CAD (computer-aided design), CAM (computer-aided

manufacture), and MRP (materials requirements planning), since these are innovative projects that have a way of revolutionizing existing systems. As such, they offer ROI (return on investment) benefits that managers can hardly resist.

However, when a factory manager wishes, for example, to make small changes in the way workers use the machinery, such as working on multiple job assignments or realigning production processes (both of which may require lengthy discussions with the union as well as re-education and retraining of workers), obtaining management support can be difficult indeed.[17]

While major innovations can improve performance dramatically, they offer little opportunity for sustained competitive advantage. Their visibility and rapid commercialization by vendors often allow them to be quickly copied by rivals. The incremental improvements of a CIP, however, originate and remain within a company and can thus develop into a considerable cumulative advantage that remains safely proprietary.[18]

Operating practices that restrict the flow of ideas must be eliminated

One of the aims of a CIP is to allow ideas to flow freely and to make everyone, regardless of level or function, into a 'thinker'. Any corporate scheme or management behaviour that divides people into 'thinkers' (such as top management) and 'doers' (such as workers) will therefore undermine improvement efforts. Although initiatives to bring workers and managers closer together often use words like 'trust', 'respect', 'teamwork' and 'worker empowerment', some of the most prized perquisites and trappings of managerial power have the opposite effect. Imai explains:

> The typical Western manager's behaviour is every cultural anthropologist's nightmare. His behaviour is just the opposite of everything a person wishing to establish rapport with strangers is supposed to do. Since the manager views the workplace as a hostile jungle, his office is a well-fortified, plush outpost where he entrenches himself and shuns communication. If communication exists at all, it is at best one way. The manager feels protected by walls he builds between himself and the workers. He often flaunts his status and power in the face of the less privileged workers.
>
> From the colour of the shirts they wear to the separate dining rooms they use, workers are constantly reminded that they are a different breed of animal. And yet, management today loves to talk about such ideals as personal fulfilment and the quality of the work environment.[19]

Compensation practices can also create barriers. One of the clearest ways to communicate the value placed on employees is through the relative size of their pay packets. Excessive disparity in wages and benefits between workers and managers has long been recognized to be counterproductive. In Book 744 of *The Laws*, Plato proposes that the wealth disparity between the top and bottom layers be no more than five to one, as a means to avoid discontent.

It is unfortunate that the trend among US firms is one of increasing wage disparity. A recent study by Sibson & Company shows that while the average compensation for hourly production workers has grown 57 percent (in nominal terms) between 1979 and 1988, the average compensation of their top managers has grown by 179 percent.

The trend in Japan has been in the opposite direction. In the last 60 years, the disparity between the average compensation of the company president and the lowest paid employee has been steadily decreasing. In 1927, the corporate president earned, on average, over 100 times the total compensation of an entry-level college graduate. By 1980, this ratio had dropped to less than eight to one.[20]

The way in which management captures the benefits from improvement can also separate workers and managers and reduce the flow of ideas. This can happen in two ways. First, a company can cash in on productivity gains by decreasing the number of its employees. Why should workers make improvement suggestions when these may make their lives harder, or even, in extreme cases, cost them their jobs? Successful CIPs are often found where some form of employment guarantee is in place. This guarantee ensures that employees do not feel that their job security is based on their continued inefficiency.

The second practice common in large organizations is for a company to reward improvement efforts by reducing allocated resources. For example, by basing next year's budget upon the resources consumed this year, a company rewards increased efficiency with a lower budget. The message for those who would implement improvements is clear – it may well cost them resources.

Employees must be continuously trained and developed, particularly in techniques of methods improvement

Even companies that consider their employees to be their greatest asset often give more care to the improvement and maintenance of equipment than to the development and training of their workers. The workforce, if not constantly upgraded and improved, can become a company's greatest liability.

Unfortunately, we often think of training as teaching people to perform a particular job in a prescribed way. Employee development, however, involves much more than this. Employees need to be able to improve the methods by which their work is done. This requires that they learn problem-solving techniques that distinguish among goals, means and ends.[21] The end is the important thing; goals help achieve ends and means help achieve goals.

Extensive training in job methods alone can make employees resistant to methods improvements for fear of making their skills obsolete. There is a name for people who use their knowledge and experience to shut down valid improvement proposals:

Nyet is the Russian word for 'no'. In any plant there are usually several *nyet*-sayers who always have their reasons for claiming that things will not work. *Nyet* engineers tend to be well-educated and to hold relatively high positions, which makes the problem all the thornier. Any proposed improvement is bound to entail problems, some minor, some major. But saying 'this won't work' all the time will never lead to progress.[22]

It is no simple task to overcome either entrenched patterns of thinking or the natural tendency to resist change. It is possible, however, to *facilitate* change through structured group problem-solving techniques (such as brainstorming) and other mechanisms to generate new ideas and give them a fair hearing. This was done, for example, by Shin-To Plastics in Japan, where a special brainstorming room was set up with procedures and rules for idea generation posted on the walls. Included is a notice that a fine of 100 yen (80c) is due for each criticism levied in the room, since fear of criticism lowers the willingness to share even the most creative ideas.

Continuous improvement needs an efficient mechanism to handle improvement ideas

Without a well-planned means to gather, evaluate, implement and reward improve-ment ideas, no CIP will succeed. Many companies operationalize their CIPs using some form of employee written suggestion system.

Several characteristics seem to be common to effective suggestion systems. They are simple to participate in and workers are actively encouraged to submit suggestions. All ideas, no matter how trivial they appear, are subjected to a structured evaluation by technically knowledgeable judges who then give employees rapid feedback. Accepted ideas are implemented as quickly as possible. Rewards, whether in the form of recognition or merit, are clearly linked to the quality of ideas. Ideas that are not accepted are used as opportunities to develop employees by explaining why in a manner than expands the contributor's knowledge of the operation. This last point, unfortunately, is often forgotten.

Canon's kaizen programme includes an exemplary employee suggestion system. Worker-submitted proposals are initially judged by a factory committee that immediately determines whether or not they merit a participation award (75 yen or 50c) or one of the first four levels of awards (ranging from 150 yen to 3000 yen or $20). Suggestions deemed worthy of higher ratings are then forwarded to a higher committee that grants awards ranging from 5000 yen ($33) to 50,000 yen ($330) or even, in special cases, air tickets to travel abroad. At the end of each week, the supervisors pass down the production lines distributing cheques for the previous week's suggestions. In addition to cash, each proposal is awarded points that apply toward awards for annual and lifetime point totals. Each year the 20 people with the highest lifetime totals receive 300,000 yen ($2000) and the 20 people with the highest annual totals receive 100,000 yen ($660). Over 90 percent of the Canon proposals are implemented; indeed, most are not formally proposed until they prove successful.

Offering monetary rewards is not the only way to elicit suggestions from employees, of course. In fact, some argue that it is not appropriate to offer extra money for suggestions. Almost 50 years ago, the TWI service argued that written suggestions should be part of the job, and not something voluntary that management should wait for and be grateful for.

Conclusion

Without some form of CIP, it is hard for a company to keep up with a competitor that has one. We have recently observed CIPs that were implemented at great expense, with extensive retraining, and accompanied by much fanfare, only to wither into perfunctory exercises as soon as it became obvious to the workers and lower management that an uncommitted upper management was merely introducing the programme to be fashionable or in response to corporate or customer pressures. Frederick Taylor understood the reasons behind this type of failure:

> The mechanism of management must not be mistaken for its essence, or underlying philosophy. Precisely the same mechanism will in one case produce disastrous results and in another the most beneficent. The same mechanism that will produce the finest results when made to service the underlying principles will lead to failure and disaster if accompanied by the wrong spirit in those who are using it.[23]

A strong CIP is a key component for the long-term competitiveness of a company. Lincoln Electric Company, for example, remains the dominant manufacturer of electric arc-welding equipment, with a 40 percent US market share. The incentive management system, with its important component of continuous improvement, has changed little over the years. The company still considers its employees to be the highest paid production workers in the world. Yet its high productivity has enabled it to prevent some very aggressive Japanese competitors from gaining significant market share. In fact, Lincoln recently opened a cored welding wire manufacturing plant in Japan.

Although the nature of continuous improvement is to be patiently incremental, a company need not have a long-established programme such as Lincoln's to notice the resulting benefits. The turnaround of the Harley Davidson Company is largely the story of a group of managers who, upon competitive benchmarking of their production facilities against those of Japanese competitors (who were driving them out of business), realized that they needed to install a CIP immediately.[24] In 1984 Harley Davidson came *four minutes* away from bankruptcy. Today, it is again the dominant manufacturer of large motorcycles in the world. The power of a successful CIP is, almost, as simple as that.

Apart from the fact that it is voluntary, and therefore immune to management by objective, the written suggestion system has one other obvious weakness. This weakness is the overhead it generates – paperwork, committees and the administration of the reward scheme. There are ways to eliminate such overhead and still retain a viable and vigorous atmosphere of continuous improvement. For example, National Cash Register dropped its written suggestion system in 1974 when the company went through a serious crisis because its electromechanical technology became outdated. The speed of change demanded by the new environment required faster and more directed continuous improvement efforts. As the company rapidly globalized and decentralized to restructure its technological base, NCR pushed operating decisions down to the shop floor by giving increasing authority to its workforce. Cells of workers were made responsible for their tasks, including the continuous improvement of products and processes. With this responsibility and power now well in place, work cells generate, evaluate and implement ideas rapidly. A large part of each worker's compensation depends on the productivity of the process he or she is in charge of or 'owns'.

References

1 See for example: M. Imai, *Kaizen: The Key to Japan's Competitive Success* (New York: Random House, 1986); Japan Human Relations Association, *The Idea Book: Improvement Through Total Employee Involvement* (Cambridge, Massachusetts: Productivity Press, 1988); MIT Commission on Industrial Productivity (1989); and S. Shingo, *Non-Stock Production: The Shingo System for Continuous Improvement* (Cambridge, Massachusetts: Productivity Press, 1988).
2 For an extensive and thorough analysis of the early history of this phenomenon, see R. C. Tucker, *The Marx–Engels Reader* (New York: W.W. Norton and Company, 1972), pp. 277–303.
3 H. L.Gantt, 'A bonus system of rewarding labor', *Transactions of the American Society of Mechanical Engineers* (1901), pp. 341–360. Reprinted in *Classics in Management*, ed. H. F. Merill (New York: American Management Association, 1960).
4 See W. Denny and Bros. Ltd, *Denny Dumbarton* (London: E. J. Burrow and Company, 1932); and Japan Human Relations Association (1988).
5 See I. F. Marcosson, *Wherever Men Trade: The Romance of the Cash Register* (New York: Dodd, Mead, and Company, 1945).
6 During the industry recession of 1982–1983, for example, company sales dropped 42 percent. No employees were involuntarily laid off and bonuses, although much smaller, were still paid. The excess workforce on the shop floor was reduced when 50 shop floor workers volunteered to become sales representatives to help introduce a new welder. Lincoln stayed profitable through the recession and even emerged with an increased market share.
7 E. Toyoda, *Fifty Years in Motion* (New York: Kodansha International/USA Ltd, 1987).
8 See International Economic Services, Ltd., *Report on Training Within Industry in Japan* (Tokyo: 1951); and A. R. Zipser, 'Japan's feudalism yields in industry', *Wall Street Journal*, 23 September 1951.
9 L. O. Mellen, personal communication.
10 Japan Management Association and C. E. Dyer, *Canon Production System: Creative Involvement of the Total Workforce* (Cambridge, Massachusetts: Productivity Press, 1987).
11 Canon employees submitted a total of 893,301 suggestions in 1985 or an average of 70.2 per employee. Even this proposal rate, unheard of in any US company, left Canon 13th out of all Japanese companies with kaizen programmes. First place went to Matsushita Electric Industries with 6.5 million proposals. Matsushita was also the first Japanese company to successfully achieve zero defect manufacturing, a feat accomplished in 1977 at one of its washing machine division plants, which produced no defects for a seven-month period.
12 NUMMI-UAW Contract, 1987, pp. 1–2.
13 D. Buss, 'Gung ho to repeat assembly-line errors', *Wall Street Journal*, 27 March 1986.
14 S. Shingo, *The Sayings of Shigeo Shingo: Key Strategies for Plant Improvement* (Cambridge, Massachusetts: Productivity Press, 1987), p. 152.
15 Imai (1986).

16   See R. H. Hayes and W. J. Abernathy, 'Managing our way to economic decline', *Harvard Business Review*, July–August 1980, pp. 67–87.

17   Imai (1986), p. 23.

18   M. E. Porter, 'The technological dimension of competitive strategy', in *Research on Technological Innovation, Management and Policy*, ed. R. S. Rosenbloom (Greenwich, Connecticut: JAI Press, 1983).

19   Imai (1986), p. 174.

20   J. C. Abegglen and G. Stalk, *Kaisba: The Japanese Corporation* (New York: Basic Books, 1985).

21   See Shingo (1987); and Shingo (1988).

22   Shingo (1988), p. 193.

23   F. W. Taylor, *The Principles of Scientific Management* (New York: Harper and Brothers, 1911) p. 129.

24   P. C. Reid, *Well Made in America: Lessons from Harley Davidson on being the Best* (New York: McGraw-Hill, 1990).

19 The Empowerment of Service Workers: What, Why, How, and When

David E. Bowen and Edward E. Lawler III

In recent years, businesses have rushed to adopt an empowerment approach to service delivery in which employees face customers 'free of rulebooks', encouraged to do whatever is necessary to satisfy them, but that approach may not be right for everyone. Managers need to make sure that there is a good fit between their organizational needs and their approach to front-line employees.

Empowering service workers has acquired almost a 'born again' religious fervour. Tom Peters calls it 'purposeful chaos'. Robert Waterman dubs it 'directed autonomy'. It has also been called the 'art of improvisation'.

Yet in the mid-1970s, the production line approach to service was the darling child of service gurus. They advocated facing the customer with standardized, procedurally driven operations. Should we now abandon this approach in favour of empowerment?

Unfortunately, there is no simple, clear-cut answer. In this article we try to help managers think about the question of whether to empower by clarifying its advantages and disadvantages, describing three forms that empower employees to different degrees and presenting five contingencies that managers can use to determine which approach best fits their situation. We do not intend to debunk empowerment, rather we hope to clarify why to empower (there are costs, as well as benefits), how to empower (there are alternatives) and when to empower (it really does depend on the situation).

The production line approach

In two classic articles, the 'Production-line approach to service' and the 'Industrialization of service', Theodore Levitt described how service operations can be made more efficient by applying manufacturing logic and tactics.[1] He argued:

> Manufacturing thinks technocratically, and that explains its success. By contrast, service looks for solutions in the performer of the task. This is the paralyzing legacy

of our inherited attitudes: the solution to improved service is viewed as being dependent on improvements in the skills and attitudes of the performers of that service.

While it may pain and offend us to say so, thinking in humanistic rather than technocratic terms ensures that the service sector will be forever inefficient and that our satisfactions will be forever marginal.[2]

He recommended (1) simplification of tasks, (2) clear division of labour, (3) substitution of equipment and systems for employees and (4) little decision-making discretion afforded to employees. In short, management designs the system, and employees execute it.

McDonald's is a good example. Workers are taught how to greet customers and ask for their order, including a script for suggesting additional items. They learn a set procedure for assembling the order (for example, cold drinks first, then hot ones), placing items on the tray and placing the tray where customers need not reach for it. There is a script and a procedure for collecting money and giving change. Finally, there is a script for saying thank you and asking the customer to come again.[3] This production line approach makes customer service interactions uniform and gives the organization control over them. It is easily learned; workers can be quickly trained and put to work.

What are the gains from a production line approach? Efficient, low-cost, high-volume service operations, with satisfied customers.

The empowerment approach

Ron Zemke and Dick Schaaf, in *The Service Edge: 101 Companies that Profit from Customer Care*, note that empowerment is a common theme running through many, even most, of their excellent service businesses, such as American Airlines, Marriott, American Express and Federal Express. To Zemke and Schaaf, empowerment means 'turning the front line loose', encouraging and rewarding employees to exercise initiative and imagination: 'Empowerment in many ways is the reverse of doing things by the book'.[4]

The humanistic flavour of empowerment pervades the words of advocates such as Tom Peters:

> It is necessary to 'dehumiliate' work by eliminating the policies and procedures (almost always tiny) of the organization that demean and belittle human dignity. It is impossible to get people's best efforts, involvement, and caring concern for things you believe important to your customers and the long-term interests of your organization when we write policies and procedures that treat them like thieves and bandits.[5]

And from Jan Carlzon, CEO of Scandinavian Airlines Systems (SAS):

> To free someone from rigorous control by instructions, policies, and orders, and to give that person freedom to take responsibility for his ideas, decisions and actions is to release hidden resources that would otherwise remain inaccessible to both the individual and the organization.[6]

In contrast to the industrialization of service, empowerment very much looks to the 'performer of the tasks' for solutions to service problems. Workers are asked to suggest new services and products and to solve problems creatively and effectively.

What, then, does it really mean – beyond the catchy slogans – to empower employees? We define empowerment as sharing with front-line employees four organizational ingredients: (1) information about the organization's performance, (2) rewards based on the organization's performance, (3) knowledge that enables employees to understand and contribute to organizational performance and (4) power to make decisions that influence organizational direction and performance. We will say more about these features later. For now, we can say that with a production line approach, these features tend to be concentrated in the hands of senior management; with an empowerment approach, they tend to be moved downward to frontline employees.

Which approach is better?

In 1990, Federal Express became the first service organization to win the Malcolm Baldrige National Quality Award. The company's motto is 'people, service, and profits'. Behind its blue, white and red planes and uniforms are self-managing work teams, gainsharing plans and empowered employees seemingly consumed with providing flexible and creative service to customers with varying needs.

At UPS, referred to as 'Big Brown' by its employees, the philosophy was stated by founder Jim Casey: 'Best service at low rates.' Here, too, we find turned-on people and profits. But we do not find empowerment. Instead we find controls, rules, a detailed union contract and carefully studied work methods. Neither do we find a promise to do all things for customers, such as handling off-schedule pickups and packages that don't fit size and weight limitations. In fact, rigid operational guide-lines help guarantee the customer reliable, low-cost service.

Federal Express and UPS present two different faces to the customer and behind these faces are different management philosophies and organizational cultures. Federal Express is a high-involvement, horizontally co-ordinated organization that encourages employees to use their judgement above and beyond the rulebook. UPS is a top-down, traditionally controlled organization, in which employees are directed by policies and procedures based on industrial engineering studies of how all service delivery aspects should be carried out and how long they should take.

Similarly, at Disney theme parks, ride operators are thoroughly scripted on what to say to 'guests', including a list of pre-approved 'ad libs'! At Club Med, however, CEO Jacques Giraud fervently believes that guests must experience real magic and the resorts' GOs (*gentils organisateurs*, 'congenial hosts') are set free spontaneously to create this feeling for their guests. Which is the better approach? Federal Express or UPS? Club Med or Disney?

At a recent executive education seminar on customer service, one of us asked, 'Who thinks that it is important for their business to empower their service personnel as a tool for improving customer service?' All 27 participants enthusiastically raised their hands. Although they represented diverse services – banking, travel, utilities, airlines and shipping – and they disagreed on most points, they all agreed that empowerment is key to customer satisfaction. But is it?

Empowering service employees: Why, how, and when

Why empower: The benefits

What gains are possible from empowering service employees?

Quicker on-line responses to customer needs during service delivery

Check-in time at the hotel begins at 2pm, but a guest asks the desk clerk if she may check in at 1.30pm. An airline passenger arrives at the gate at 7.30am, Friday, for a 7.45am departure and wants to board the plane with a travel coupon good Monday through Thursday and there are empty seats on the plane. The waitress is taking an order in a modestly priced family restaurant; the menu says no substitutions, but the customer requests one anyway.

The customer wants a quick response. And the employee would often like to be able to respond with something other than: 'No, it is against our rules' or 'I will have to check with my supervisor.' Empowering employees in these situations can lead to the sort of spontaneous, creative rule breaking that can turn a potentially frustrated or angry customer into a satisfied one. This is particularly valuable when there is little time to refer to a higher authority, as when the plane is leaving in 15 minutes. Even before greeting customers, empowered employees are confident that they have all the necessary resources at their command to provide customers with what they need.

Quicker on-line responses to dissatisfied customers during service recovery

Customer service involves both delivering the service, such as checking a guest into a hotel room and recovering from poor service, such as relocating him from a smoking floor to the non-smoking room he originally requested. Although delivering good service may mean different things to different customers, all customers feel that service businesses ought to fix things when service is delivered improperly. Figure 19.1 depicts the relationships among service delivery, recovery and customer satisfaction.

Fixing something after doing it wrong the first time can turn a dissatisfied customer into a satisfied, even loyal, customer. But service businesses frequently fail in the act of recovery because service employees are not empowered to make the necessary amends with customers. Instead, customers hear employees saying, 'Gee. I wish there was something I could do, but I can't', 'It's not my fault', or 'I could check with my boss, but she's not here today.' These employees lack the power and knowledge to recover, and customers remain dissatisfied.

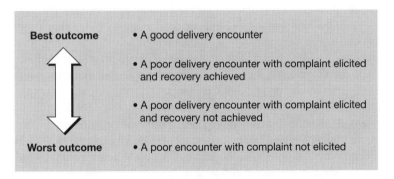

Figure 19.1 Possible outcomes during service delivery and recovery

Source: Service Breakthroughs: Changing the Rules of the Game by James L. Heskett, W. Earl Sasser, Jr., and Christopher W. L. Hart. Copyright © 1990 by James L. Heskett, W. Earl Sasser, Jr., and Christopher W. L. Hart. Adapted with permission of The Free Press, a Division of Macmillan, Inc.

Employees feel better about their jobs and themselves

Earlier we mentioned Tom Peters' thinking on how strict rules can belittle human dignity. Letting employees call the shots allows them to feel 'ownership' of the job; they feel responsible for it and find the work meaningful. Think of how you treat your car as opposed to a rented one. Have you ever washed a rental car? Decades of job design research show that when employees have a sense of control and of doing meaningful work they are more satisfied. This leads to lower turnover, less absenteeism and fewer union organizing drives.

Employees will interact with customers with more warmth and enthusiasm

Research now supports our long-standing intuition that customers' perceptions of service quality are shaped by the courtesy, empathy and responsiveness of service employees.[7] Customers want employees to appear concerned about their needs. Can empowerment help create this? One of us has done customer service research in branch banks that showed that when the tellers reported feeling good about how they were supervised, trained and rewarded, customers thought more highly of the service they received.[8] In short, when employees felt that management was looking after their needs, they took better care of the customer.

In service encounters, employees' feelings about their jobs will spill over to affect how customers feel about the service they get. This is particularly important when employee attitudes are a key part of the service package. In banking, where the customer receives no tangible benefits in the exchange other than a savings deposit slip, a sour teller can really blemish a customer's feelings about the encounter.

Empowered employees can be a great source of service ideas

Giving front-line employees a voice in 'how we do things around here' can lead to improved service delivery and ideas for new services. The bank study showed that the tellers could accurately report how customers viewed overall service quality and how they saw the branches' service climate (e.g. adequacy of staff and appearance of facilities).[9]

Front-line employees are often ready and willing to offer their opinion. When it comes to market research, imagine the difference in response rates from surveying your employees and surveying your customers.

Great word-of-mouth advertising and customer retention

Nordstrom's advertising budget is 1.5 percent of sales, whereas the industry average is 5 percent. Why? Their satisfied-no-matter-what customers spread the word about their service and become repeat customers.

The costs

What are the costs of empowerment?

A greater dollar investment in selection and training

You cannot hire effective, creative problem solvers on the basis of chance or mere intuition. Too bad, because the systematic methods necessary to screen out those who are not good candidates for empowerment are expensive. For example, Federal Express selects customer agents and couriers on the basis of well-researched profiles of successful performers in those jobs.

Training is an even greater cost. The production line approach trains workers easily and puts them right to work. In contrast, new hires at SAS are formally assigned a mentor to help them learn the ropes; Nordstrom department managers take responsibility for orienting and training new members of the sales team; customer service representatives at Lands' End and L. L. Bean spend a week in training before handling their first call. They receive far more information and knowledge about their company and its products than is the norm.

The more labour intensive the service, the higher these costs. Retail banking, department stores and convenience stores are labour intensive and their training and selection costs can run high. Utilities and airlines are far less labour intensive.

Higher labour costs

Many consumer service organizations, such as department stores, convenience stores, restaurants and banks, rely on large numbers of part-time and seasonal workers to meet their highly variable staffing needs. These employees typically work for short periods of time at low wages. To empower these workers, a company would have to invest heavily in training to try to quickly inculcate the organization's culture and values. This training would probably be unsuccessful and the employees wouldn't be around long enough to provide a return on the investment. Alternatively, the organization could pay higher wages to full-time, permanent employees, but they would be idle when business was slow.

Slower or inconsistent service delivery

Remember the hotel guest wanting to check in early and the airline passenger requesting special treatment at the gate? True, there is a benefit to empowering the employee to bend the rules, but only for the person at the front of the line! Customers at the back of the line are grumbling and checking their watches. They may have the satisfaction of knowing that they too may receive creative problem solving when and if they reach the counter, but it is small consolation if the plane has already left.

Based on our experiences as both researchers and customers, we believe that customers will increasingly value speed in service delivery. Purposeful chaos may work against this. We also believe that many customers value 'no surprises' in service delivery. They like to know what to expect when they revisit a service business or patronize different outlets of a franchise. When service delivery is left to employee discretion, it may be inconsistent.

The research data show that customers perceive reliability – 'doing it right the first time' – as the most important dimension of service quality. It matters more than employees' responsiveness, courtesy or competency or the attractiveness of the service setting.[10] Unfortunately, in the same research, a sample of large, well-known firms was more deficient on reliability than on these other dimensions. Much of the touted appeal of the production line approach was that procedurally and technocratically driven operations could deliver service more reliably and consistently than service operations heavily dependent upon the skills and attitudes of employees. The production line approach was intended to routinize service so that customers would receive the 'best outcome' possible from their service encounters – service delivery with no glitches in the first place.

We feel that service managers need to guard against being seduced into too great a focus on recovery, at the expense of service delivery reliability. We say 'seduced' because it is possible to confuse good service with inspiring stories about empowered employees excelling at the art of recovery. Recovery has more sex appeal than the nitty-gritty detail of building quality into every seemingly mundane aspect of the service delivery system, but an organization that relies on recovery may end up losing out to firms that do it right the first time.

Violations of 'fair play'

A recent study of how service businesses handle customer complaints revealed that customers associate sticking to procedures with being treated fairly.[11] Customers may be more likely to return to a business if they believe that their complaint was handled effectively because of company policies rather than because they were lucky enough to get a particular employee. In other words, customers may prefer procedurally driven acts of recovery. We suspect that customers' notions of fairness may be violated when they see employees cutting special deals with other customers.

Giveaways and bad decisions

Managers are often reluctant to empower their employees for fear they will give too much away to the customer. Perhaps they have heard the story of Willie, the doorman at a Four Seasons Hotel, who left work and took a flight to return a briefcase left behind by a guest. Or they have heard of too many giveaways by empowered

Nordstrom employees. For some services, the costs of giveaways are far outweighed by enhanced customer loyalty, but not for others.

Sometimes creative rule breaking can cause a major problem for an organization. There may be a good reason why no substitutions are allowed or why a coupon cannot be used on a certain day (e.g. an international airfare agreement). If so, having an empowered employee break a rule may cause the organization serious problems, of which the employee may not even be aware.

These are some of the costs and benefits of empowerment. We hope this discussion will help service businesses use empowerment knowledgeably, not just because it is a fad. But we must add one more caveat: there is still precious little research on the consequences of empowerment. We have used anecdotal evidence, related research (e.g. in job design) and our work on service. More systematic research must assess whether this array of costs and benefits fully captures the 'whys' (and 'why nots') of empowerment.

How to empower: Three options

Empowering service employees is less understood than industrializing service delivery. This is largely because the production line approach is an example of the well-developed control model of organization design and management, whereas empowerment is part of the still evolving 'commitment' or 'involvement' model. The latter assumes that most employees can make good decisions if they are properly socialized, trained and informed. They can be internally motivated to perform effectively and they are capable of self-control and self-direction. This approach also assumes that most employees can produce good ideas for operating the business.[12]

The control and involvement models differ in that four key features are concentrated at the top of the organization in the former and pushed down in the organization in the latter. As we discussed earlier, these features are the following: (1) information about organizational performance (e.g. operating results and competitor performance); (2) rewards based on organizational performance (e.g. profit sharing and stock ownership); (3) knowledge that enables employees to understand and contribute to organizational performance (e.g. problem-solving skills); and (4) power to make decisions that influence work procedures and organizational direction (e.g. through quality circles and self-managing teams).

Three approaches to empowering employees can be identified (see Figure 19.2).[13] They represent increasing degrees of empowerment as additional knowledge, information, power, and rewards are pushed down to the front line.

Empowerment, then, is not an either/or alternative, but rather a choice of three options:

1   *Suggestion involvement* represents a small shift away from the control model. Employees are encouraged to contribute ideas through formal suggestion programmes or quality circles, but their day-to-day work activities do not really change. Also, they are only empowered to recommend; management typically retains the power to decide whether or not to implement.

Suggestion involvement can produce some empowerment without altering the basic production line approach. McDonald's, for example, listens closely to the front line. The Big Mac, Egg McMuffin and McDLT were all invented by employees, as was the system of wrapping burgers that avoids leaving a thumb-print in the bun. As another example, Florida Power and Light, which won the Deming quality award, defines empowerment in suggestion involvement terms.

2   *Job involvement* represents a significant departure from the control model because of its dramatic 'opening up' of job content. Jobs are redesigned so that employees use a variety of skills. Employees believe their tasks are significant, they have considerable freedom in deciding how to do the work, they get more feedback and they handle a whole identifiable piece of work. Research shows that many employees find enriched work more motivating and satisfying and they do higher quality work.[14]

Often job involvement is accomplished through extensive use of teams. Teams are often appropriate in complex service organizations such as hospitals and airlines because individuals cannot offer a whole service or handle a customer from beginning to end of service delivery. Teams can empower back-office workers in banks and insurance companies as well.

Employees in this environment require training to deal with the added complexity. Supervisors, who now have fewer shots to call, need to be reoriented toward supporting the front line, rather than directing it. Despite the heightened level of empowerment it brings, the job involvement approach does not change higher level strategic decisions concerning organization structure, power and the allocation of rewards. These remain the responsibility of senior management.

3   *High-involvement organizations* give their lowest level employees a sense of involvement not just in how they do their jobs or how effectively their group performs, but in the total organization's performance. Virtually every aspect of the organization is different from that of a control-oriented organization. Business performance information is shared. Employees develop skills in teamwork, problem solving and business operations. They participate in work unit management decisions. There is profit sharing and employee ownership.

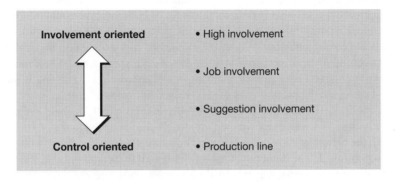

Figure 19.2 Levels of empowerment

High-involvement designs may be expensive to implement. Perhaps most troublesome is that these management techniques are relatively undeveloped and untested. People Express tried to operate as a high-involvement airline and the ongoing struggle to learn and develop this new organizational design contributed to its operating problems.

Today, America West is trying to make the high-involvement design work. New hires spend 25 percent of their first year's salary on company stock. All employees receive annual stock options. Flight attendants and pilots develop their own work procedures and schedules. Employees are extensively cross-trained to work where they are needed. Only time will tell if America West can make high-involvement work as it struggles with its financial crisis stemming from high fuel costs and rapid growth.

Federal Express displays many high-involvement features. A couple of years ago, it began a company-wide push to convert to teams, including the back office. It organized its 1000 clerical workers in Memphis into superteams of five to ten people and gave them the authority and training to manage themselves. These terms helped the company cut customer service problems, such as incorrect bills and lost packages, by 13 percent in 1989.

When to empower: A contingency approach

Management thought and practice frequently have been seduced by the search for the 'one best way to manage'. Unfortunately, business does not lend itself to universal truths, only to 'contingency theories' of management. For example, early job enrichment efforts in the 1960s assumed that all employees would prefer more challenging work and more autonomy. By the 1970s it was clear that only those employees who felt the need to grow at work responded positively to job enrichment.[15] As the research on it is still thin, it is at least possible that empowerment is a universal truth, but historical evidence weighs against its being the best way to manage in all situations.

We believe that both the empowerment and production line approaches have their advantages and that each fits certain situations. The key is to choose the management approach that best meets the needs of both employees and customers.

Table 19.1 presents five contingencies that determine which approach to adopt. Each contingency can be rated on a scale of 1 to 5 to diagnose the quality of fit between the overall situation and the alternative approaches. The following propositions suggest how to match situations and approaches. Matching is not an exact science, but the propositions suggest reasonable rules of thumb.

Proposition 1: The higher the rating of each contingency (5 being the highest), the better the fit with an empowerment approach; the lower the rating (1 being the lowest), the better the fit with a production line approach.

Proposition 2: The higher the total score from all five contingencies, the better the fit with an empowerment approach; the lower the total score, the better the fit with a production line approach. A production line approach is a good fit with situations

Table 19.1 The contingencies of empowerment

Contingency	Production line approach						Empowerment
Basic business strategy	Low cost, high volume	1	2	3	4	5	Differentiation, customized, personalized
Tie to customer	Transaction short time period	1	2	3	4	5	Relationship, long time period
Technology	Routine, simple	1	2	3	4	5	Non-routine, complex
Business environment	Predictable, few surprises	1	2	3	4	5	Unpredictable, many surprises
Types of people	Theory X managers, employees with low growth needs, low social needs and weak interpersonal skills	1	2	3	4	5	Theory Y managers, employees with high growth needs, high social needs, and strong interpersonal skills

that score in the range of 5 to 10. For empowerment approaches, suggestion involvement is a good fit with situations that score in the range of 11 to 15, job involvement; with scores that range from 16 to 20 and high involvement with scores that range from 21 to 25.

Proposition 3: The higher the total score, the more the benefits of increasing empowerment will outweigh the costs.

We now describe each contingency's implications for a production line or empowerment approach.

Basic business strategy

A production line approach makes the most sense if your core mission is to offer high-volume service at the lowest cost. 'Industrializing' service certainly leverages volume. The question is what is the value-added from spending the additional dollars on employee selection, training and retention necessary for empowerment? This question is especially compelling in labour-intensive services (e.g. fast food, grocery stores and convenience stores) and those that require part-time or temporary employees.

The answer depends on what customers want from the service firm and what they are willing to pay for. Certain customer segments are just looking for cheap, quick and reliable service. They do want quality – a warm hamburger rather than a cold one. But they are not necessarily expecting tender loving care. Even if they wanted it, they wouldn't pay for it.

These customers prefer a production line approach. A recent study of convenience stores actually found a negative relationship between store sales clerks being friendly with customers.[16] Customers wanted speed and friendly clerks slowed things down. The point is that customers themselves may prefer to be served by a non-empowered employee.

At Taco Bell, counter attendants are expected to be civil but they are not expected or encouraged to be creative problem solvers. Taco Bell wants to serve customers who want low-cost, good-quality, fast food. Interestingly, the company believes that as more chains move to customized, service-oriented operations, it has more opportunities in the fast, low-price market niche.

The production line approach does not rule out suggestion involvement. As mentioned earlier, employees often have ideas even when much of their work is routinized. Quality circles and other approaches can capture and develop them.

An empowerment approach works best with a market segment that wants the tender loving care dimension more than speed and cost. For example, SAS targets frequent business travellers (who do not pay their own way). The SAS strategy was to differentiate itself from other airlines on the basis of personalized service. Consequently, the company looked at every ingredient of its service package to see if it fitted this segment's definition of service quality and, if so, whether or not customers would pay for it.

Tie to customer

Empowerment is the best approach when service delivery involves managing a relationship, as opposed to simply performing a transaction. The service firm may want to establish relationships with customers to build loyalty or to get ideas for improving the service delivery system or offering new services. A flexible, customized approach can help establish the relationship and get the ideas flowing.

The returns on empowerment and relationship building are higher with more sophisticated services and delivery systems. An employee in the international air freight industry is more likely to learn from a customer relationship than is a gasoline station attendant.

The relationship itself can be the principle valued commodity that is delivered in many services. When no tangibles are delivered, as in estate planning or management consulting, the service provider often is the service to the customer and empowerment allows the employee to customize the service to fit the customer's needs.

The more enduring the relationship and the more important it is in the service package, the stronger the case for empowerment. Remember the earlier comparison between Disney, which tightly scripts its ride operators, and Club Med, which encourages its GOs to be spontaneous? Giraud, Club Med's CEO, explains that Disney employees relate to their guests in thousands of brief encounters; GOs have week-long close relationships with a limited number of guests. The valuable service they sell is 'time'.

Technology

It is very difficult to build challenge, feedback and autonomy into a telephone operator's job, given the way the delivery technology has been designed. The same is true of many fast food operations.

In these situations, the technology limits empowerment to only suggestion involvement and ultimately may almost completely remove individuals from the service delivery process, as has happened with ATMs.

When technology constrains empowerment, service managers can still support front-line employees in ways that enhance their satisfaction and the service quality they provide. For example, managers can show employees how much their jobs matter to the organization's success and express more appreciation for the work they do. In other words, managers can do a better job of making the old management model work!

Routine work can be engaging if employees are convinced that it matters. Volunteers will spend hours licking envelopes in a fundraising campaign for their favourite charity. Disney theme park employees do an admirable job of performing repetitive work, partly because they believe in the values, mission and show business magic of Disney.

Business environment

Businesses that operate in unpredictable environments benefit from empowerment. Airlines face many challenges to their operations: bad weather, mechanical breakdowns and competitors' actions. They serve passengers who make a wide variety of special requests. It is simply impossible to anticipate many of the situations that will arise and to 'programme' employees to respond to them. Employees trained in purposeful chaos are appropriate for unpredictable environments.

Fast food restaurants, however, operate in stable environments. Operations are fairly fail-safe; customer expectations are simple and predictable. In this environment, the service business can use a production line approach. The stability allows, even encourages, management with policies and procedures, because managers can predict most events and identify the best responses.

Types of people

Empowerment and production line approaches demand different types of managers and employees. For empowerment to work, particularly in the high-involvement form, the company needs to have Theory Y managers who believe that their employees can act independently to benefit both the organization and its customers. If the management ranks are filled with Theory X types who believe that employees only do their best work when closely supervised, then the production line approach may be the only feasible option unless the organization changes its managers. Good service can still be the outcome. For example, most industry observers would agree that Delta and American Airlines are managed with a control orientation rather than a strong empowerment approach.

Employees will respond positively to empowerment only if they have strong needs to grow and to deepen and test their abilities – at work. Again, a checkered history of job enrichment efforts has taught us not to assume that everyone wants more autonomy, challenge and responsibility at work. Some employees simply prefer a production line approach.

Lastly, empowerment that involves teamwork requires employees who are interested in meeting their social and affiliative needs at work. It also requires that employees have good interpersonal and group process skills.

The future of service world

How likely is it that more and more service businesses will choose to face the customer with empowered employees? We would guess that far more service organizations operate at the production line end of our continuum than their business situations call for. A 1989 survey of companies in the Fortune 1000 offers some support for this view.[17] This survey revealed that manufacturing firms tend to use significantly more employee-involvement practices than do service firms. Manufacturing firms use quality circles, participation groups and self-managing work teams far more than service firms.

The intense pressure on the manufacturing sector from global competition has created more dissatisfaction with the old control-oriented way of doing things. Also, it can be easier to see the payoffs from different management practices in manufacturing than in service. Objective measures of productivity can more clearly show profitability than can measures of customer perceptions of service quality. However, these differences are now blurring as service competition increases and service companies become more sophisticated in tracking the benefits of customer service quality.

As service businesses consider empowerment, they can look at high-involvement manufacturing organizations as labs in which the various empowerment approaches have been tested and developed. Many lessons have been learned in manufacturing about how to best use quality circles, enriched jobs and so on. And the added good news is that many service businesses are ideally suited to applying and refining these lessons. Multisite, relatively autonomous service operations afford their managers an opportunity to customize empowerment programmes and then evaluate them.

In summary, the newest approaches to managing the production line can serve as role models for many service businesses, but perhaps not all. Before service organizations rush into empowerment programmes, they need to determine whether and how empowerment fits their situation.

References

1   T. Levitt, 'Production-line approach to service', *Harvard Business Review*, September–October 1972, pp. 41–52; and T. Levitt, 'Industrialization of service', *Harvard Business Review*, September–October 1976, pp. 63–74.
2   Levitt (1972), op.cit.
3   D. Tansik, 'Managing human resource issues for high-contact service personnel', in *Service Management Effectiveness*, eds D. Bowen, R. Chase and T. Cummings (San Francisco: Jossey-Bass, 1990). [Note: McDonald's staff are now allowed to improvise their greeting.]
4   R. Zemke and D. Schaaf, *The Service Edge: 101 Companies that Profit from Customer Care* (New York: New American Library, 1989), p. 68.
5   As quoted in Zemke and Schaaf (1989), p. 68.
6   J. Carlzon, *Moments of Truth* (New York: Ballinger, 1987).
7   V. Zeithaml, A. Parasuraman and L. L. Berry, *Delivering Quality Service: Balancing Customer Perceptions and Expectations* (New York: Free Press. 1990). See also B.

Schneider and D. Bowen, 'Employee and customer perceptions of service in banks: replication and extension', *Journal of Applied Psychology*, 70, 1985, pp. 423–433.

8   Schneider and Bowen (1985).

9   Ibid.

10 Zeithaml, Parasuramany and Berry (1990), op.cit.

11 C. Goodwin and I. Ross, 'Consumer evaluations of responses to complaints: what's fair and why', *Journal of Services Marketing*, 4, 1990, pp. 53–61.

12 See E. E. Lawler III, *High-Involvement Management* (San Francisco: Jossey-Bass, 1986).

13 See E. E. Lawler III, 'Choosing an involvement strategy', *Academy of Management Executive*, 2, 1988, pp. 197–204.

14 See for example J. R. Hackman and G. R. Oldham, *Work Redesign* (Reading, Massachusetts: Addison-Wesley, 1980).

15 Ibid.

16 R. J. Sutton and A. Rafaeli, 'Untangling the relationship between displayed emotions and organizational sales: the case of convenience stores', *Academy of Management Journal*, 31, 1988, pp. 461–468.

17 E. E. Lawler III, G. E. Ledford Jr. and S. A. Mohrman, *Employee Involvement in America. A Study of Contemporary Practice* (Houston: American Productivity & Quality Center, 1989).

20 Reengineering: Don't Automate, Obliterate

Michael Hammer

The essence of reengineering

At the heart of reengineering is the notion of discontinuous thinking – of recognizing and breaking away from the outdated rules and fundamental assumptions that underlie operations. Unless we change these rules, we are merely rearranging the deck chairs on the *Titanic*. We cannot achieve breakthroughs in performance by cutting fat or automating existing processes. Rather, we must challenge old assumptions and shed the old rules that made the business underperform in the first place.

Every business is replete with implicit rules left over from earlier decades. 'Customers don't repair their own equipment.' 'Local warehouses are necessary for good service.' 'Merchandising decisions are made at headquarters.' These rules of work design are based on assumptions about technology, people and organizational goals that no longer hold. The contemporary repertoire of available information technologies is vast and quickly expanding. Quality, innovation and service are now more important than cost, growth and control. A large portion of the population is educated and capable of assuming responsibility and workers cherish their autonomy and expect to have a say in how the business is run.

It should come as no surprise that our business processes and structures are outmoded and obsolete: our work structures and processes have not kept pace with the changes in technology, demographics and business objectives. For the most part, we have organized work as a sequence of separate tasks and employed complex mechanisms to track its progress. This arrangement can be traced to the Industrial Revolution, when specialization of labour and economies of scale promised to overcome the inefficiencies of cottage industries. Businesses desegregated work into narrowly defined tasks, reaggregated the people performing those tasks into departments and installed managers to administer them.

Our elaborate systems for imposing control and discipline on those who actually do the work stem from the post-war period. In that halcyon period of expansion, the main concern was growing fast without going broke, so businesses focused on cost, growth and control. And since literate, entry-level people were abundant but well-educated professionals hard to come by, the control systems funnelled information up the hierarchy to the few who presumably knew what to do with it.

These patterns of organizing work have become so ingrained that, despite their serious drawbacks, it's hard to conceive of work being accomplished any other way. Conventional process structures are fragmented and piecemeal and they lack integration necessary to maintain quality and service. They are breeding grounds for tunnel vision, as people tend to substitute the narrow goals of the particular department for the larger goals of the process as a whole. When work is handed off from person to person and unit to unit, delays and errors are inevitable. Accountability blurs and critical issues fall between the cracks. Moreover, no one sees enough of the big picture to be able to respond quickly to new situations. Managers desperately try, like all the king's horses and all the king's men, to piece together the fragmented pieces of business processes.

Managers have tried to adapt their processes to new circumstances, but usually in ways that just create more problems. If, say, customer service is poor, they create a mechanism to deliver service but overlay it on the existing organization. Bureaucracy thickens, costs rise and enterprising competitors gain market share.

In reengineering, managers break loose from outmoded business processes and the design principles underlying them and create new ones. Ford had operated under the old rule that 'we pay when we receive the invoice'. While no one had ever articulated or recorded it, that rule determined how the accounts payable process was organized. Ford's reengineering effort challenged and ultimately replaced the rule with a new one: 'We pay when we receive the *goods*.'

Reengineering requires looking at the fundamental processes of the business from a cross-functional perspective. Ford discovered that reengineering only the accounts payable department was futile. The appropriate focus of the effort was what might be called the goods acquisition process, which included purchasing and receiving as well as accounts payable.

One way to ensure that reengineering has a cross-functional perspective is to assemble a team that represents the functional units involved in the process being reengineered and all the units that depend on it. The team must analyze and scrutinize the existing process until it really understands what the process is trying to accomplish. The point is not to learn what happens to form 73B in its peregrinations through the company but to understand the purpose of having form 73B in the first place. Rather than looking for opportunities to improve the current process, the team should determine which of its steps really add value and search for new ways to achieve the result.

The reengineering team must keep asking Why? and What if? Why do we need to get a manager's signature on a requisition? Is it a control mechanism or a decision point? What if the manager reviews only requisitions above $500? What if he or she doesn't see them all? Raising and resolving heretical questions can separate what is fundamental to the process from what is superficial. The regional offices of an East Coast insurance company had long produced a series of reports that they regularly sent to the home office. No one in the field realized that these reports were simply filed and never used. The process outlasted the circumstances that had created the need for it. The reengineering study team should push to discover situations like this. In short, a reengineering effort strives for dramatic levels of improvement. It must break away from conventional wisdom and the constraints of organizational boundaries and should be broad and cross-functional in scope. It should use information technology not to automate an existing process but to enable a new one.

Principles of reengineering

Creating new rules tailored to the modern environment ultimately requires a new conceptualization of the business process – which comes down to someone having a great idea. But reengineering need not be haphazard. In fact, some of the principles that companies have already discovered while reengineering their business processes can help jump-start the effort for others.

Organize around outcomes, not tasks

This principle says to have one person perform all the steps in a process. Design that person's job around an objective or outcome instead of a single task. The redesign at Mutual Benefit Life, where individual case managers perform the entire application approval process, is the quintessential example of this.

The redesign of an electronics company is another example. It had separate organizations performing each of the five steps between selling and installing the equipment. One group determined customer requirements, another translated those requirements into internal product codes, a third conveyed that information to various plants and warehouses, a fourth received and assembled the components and a fifth delivered and installed the equipment. The process was based on the centuries-old notion of specialized labour and on the limitations inherent in paper files. The departments each possessed a specific set of skills and only one department at a time could do its work.

The customer order moved systematically from step to step. But this sequential processing caused problems. The people getting the information from the customer in step one had to get all the data anyone would need throughout the process, even if it wasn't needed until step five. In addition, the many handoffs were responsible for numerous errors and misunderstandings. Finally, any questions about customer requirements that arose late in the process had to be referred back to the people doing step one, resulting in delay and rework.

When the company reengineered, it eliminated the assembly line approach. It compressed responsibility for the various steps and assigned it to one person, the 'customer service representative'. That person now oversees the whole process – taking the order, translating it into product codes, getting the components assembled and seeing the product delivered and installed. The customer service rep expedites and coordinates the process, much like a general contractor. And the customer has just one contact, who always knows the status of the order.

Have those who use the output of the process perform the process

In an effort to capitalize on the benefits of specialization and scale, many organizations established specialized departments to handle specialized processes. Each department does only one type of work and is a 'customer' of other groups' processes. Accounting does only accounting. If it needs new pencils, it goes to the purchasing department, the group specially equipped with the information and expertise to perform that role. Purchasing finds vendors, negotiates price, places the order, inspects the goods and pays the invoice and eventually the accountants get their pencils. The process works (after a fashion), but it's slow and bureaucratic.

Now that computer-based data and expertise are more readily available, departments, units and individuals can do more for themselves. Opportunities exist to reengineer processes so that the individuals who need the result of a process can do it themselves. For example, by using expert systems and databases, departments can make their own purchases without sacrificing the benefits of specialized purchasers. One manufacturer has reengineered its purchasing process along just these lines. The company's old system, whereby the operating departments submitted requisitions and let purchasing do the rest, worked well for controlling expensive and important items like raw materials and capital equipment. But for inexpensive and non-strategic purchases, which constituted some 35% of total orders, the system was slow and cumbersome; it was not uncommon for the cost of the purchasing process to exceed the cost of the goods being purchased.

The new process compresses the purchase of sundry items and pushes it on to the customers of the process. Using a database of approved vendors, an operating unit can directly place an order with a vendor and charge it on a bank credit card. At the end of the month, the bank gives the manufacturer a tape of all credit card transactions, which the company runs against its internal accounting system.

When an electronics equipment manufacturer reengineered its field service process, it pushed some of the steps of the process on to its customers. The manufacturer's field service had been plagued by the usual problems: technicians were often unable to do a particular repair because the right part wasn't on the van, response to customer calls was slow and spare-parts inventory was excessive.

Now customers make simple repairs themselves. Spare parts are stored at each customer's site and managed through a computerized inventory-management system. When a problem arises, the customer calls the manufacturer's fieldservice hotline and describes the symptoms to a diagnostician, who accesses a diagnosis support system. If the problem appears to be something the customer can fix, the diagnostician tells the customer what part to replace and how to install it. The old part is picked up and a new part left in its place at a later time. Only for complex problems is a service technician despatched to the site, this time without having to make a stop at the warehouse to pick up parts.

When the people closest to the process perform it, there is little need for the overhead associated with managing it. Interfaces and liaisons can be eliminated, as can the mechanisms used to coordinate those who perform the process with those who use it. Moreover, the problem of capacity planning for the process performers is greatly reduced.

Subsume information-processing work into the real work that produces the information

The previous two principles say to compress linear processes. This principle suggests moving work from one person or department to another. Why doesn't an organization that produces information also process it? In the past, people didn't have the time or weren't trusted to do both. Most companies established units to do nothing but collect and process information that other departments created. This arrangement reflects the old rule about specialized labour and the belief that people at lower organizational levels are incapable of acting on information they generate. An accounts payable department collects information from purchasing and receiving and reconciles it with data that the vendor provides. Quality assurance gathers and analyses information it gets from production.

Ford's redesigned accounts payable process embodies the new rule. With the new system, receiving, which produces the information about the goods received, processes this information instead of sending it to accounts payable. The new computer system can easily compare the delivery with the order and trigger the appropriate action.

Treat geographically dispersed resources as though they were centralized

The conflict between centralization and decentralization is a classic one. Decentralizing a resource (whether people, equipment or inventory) gives better service to those who use it, but at the cost of redundancy, bureaucracy and missed economies of scale. Companies no longer have to make such trade-offs. They can use databases, telecommunications networks and standardized processing systems to get the benefits of scale and coordinations while maintaining the benefits of flexibility and service.

At Hewlett-Packard, for instance, each of the more than 50 manufacturing units had its own separate purchasing department. While this arrangement provided excellent responsiveness and service to the plants, it prevented H-P from realizing the benefits of its scale, particularly with regard to quantity discounts. H-P's solution is to maintain the divisional purchasing organizations and to introduce a corporate unit to coordinate them. Each purchasing unit has access to a shared database on vendors and their performance and issues its own purchase orders. Corporate purchasing maintains this database and uses it to negotiate contracts for the corporation and to monitor the units. The payoffs have come in a 150 percent improvement in on-time deliveries, 50 percent reduction in lead times, 75 percent reductions in failure rates, and a significantly lower cost of goods purchased.

Link parallel activities instead of integrating their results

H-P's decentralized purchasing operations represent one kind of parallel processing in which separate units perform the same function. Another common kind of parallel processing is when separate units perform different activities that must eventually come together. Product development typically operates this way. In the development of a photocopier, for example, independent units develop the various subsystems of the copier. One group works on the optics, another on the mechanical paper-handling device, another on the power supply and so on. Having people do development work simultaneously saves time, but at the dreaded integration and testing phase, the pieces often fail to work together. Then the costly redesign begins.

Or consider a bank that sells different kinds of credit – loans, letters of credit, asset-based financing – through separate units. These groups may have no way of knowing whether another group has already extended credit to a particular customer. Each unit could extend the full $10 million credit limit.

The new principle says to forge links between parallel functions and to coordinate them while their activities are in process rather than after they are completed. Communications networks, shared databases and teleconferencing can bring the independent groups together so that coordination is ongoing. One large electronics company has cut its product development cycle by more than 50 percent by implementing this principle.

Put the decision point where the work is performed and build control into the process

In most organizations, those who do the work are distinguished from those who monitor the work and make decisions about it. The tacit assumption is that the people actually doing the work have neither the time nor the inclination to monitor and control it and that they lack the knowledge and scope to make decisions about it. The entire hierarchical management structure is built on this assumption. Accountants, auditors and supervisors check, record and monitor work. Managers handle any exceptions.

The new principle suggests that the people who do the work should make the decisions and that the process itself can have built-in controls. Pyramidal management layers can therefore be compressed and the organization flattened.

Information technology can capture and process data and expert systems can to some extent supply knowledge, enabling people to make their own decisions. As the doers become self-managing and self-controlling, hierarchy – and the slowness and bureaucracy associated with it – disappears.

When Mutual Benefit Life reengineered the insurance application process, it not only compressed the linear sequence but also eliminated the need for layers of managers. These two kinds of compression – vertical and horizontal – often go together; the very fact that a worker sees only one piece of the process calls for a manager with a broader vision. The case managers at MBL provide end-to-end management of the process, reducing the need for traditional managers. The managerial role is changing from one of controller and supervisor to one of supporter and facilitator.

Capture information once and at the source

This last rule is simple. When information was difficult to transmit, it made sense to collect information repeatedly. Each person, department or unit had its own requirements and forms. Companies simply had to live with the associated delays, entry errors and costly overhead. But why do we have to live with those problems now? Today when we collect a piece of information, we can store it in an on-line database for all who need it. Bar coding, relational databases and electronic data interchange (EDI) make it easy to collect, store and transmit information. One insurance company found that its application review process required that certain items be entered into 'stovepipe' computer systems supporting different functions as many as five times. By integrating and connecting these systems, the company was able to eliminate this redundant data entry along with the attendant checking functions and inevitable errors.

Section F   Impact of Technology

One of the major changes in our lifetime is the increasingly ubiquitous presence of information and communications technology. The last three chapters address the impact of these technologies on business organization. Apgar describes the shift out of the office. Mulgan and Briscoe describe the network structure of some of the most successful technology-based enterprises. Hof et al. speculate on the prospects for e-commerce.

Apgar explains how technology is facilitating a shift to home-based working. Technology has facilitated flexitime, mobile workstations, telecommuting, home-based and remote working. The impetus may be cost savings: ATT for example, reckon they save about $2000 per employee through the use of shared office space (where staff share PCs and a desk rather than having dedicated space). But this is not the only benefit, these alternative work arrangements often seem to improve customer and employee satisfaction.

Mulgan and Briscoe draw our attention to the fact that two of the most successful enterprises of the information age – the Internet and Visa – employ a network structure that is at odds with the standard organization with its single chain of command and emphasis on control. The Internet is owned by no one and operates on leased lines, it is a bottom-up organization that gets its innovations from users. Similarly Linux the operating system developed by a Finnish student, debugged and improved by about 10,000 net enthusiasts. Visa is an open organization. Anyone meeting certain criteria can join and 20,000 organizations have; these members jointly own Visa. The head office comprises a skeletal staff, yet it does business of over $650 billion a year. Regulation is built in rather than having to be imposed, as to increase market share Visa members need to offer a better service at a cheaper price. Mulgan and Briscoe suggest that this form of network organization seems to thrive on diversity and multiple lines of power rather the uniformity and single power line associated with industrial-age organizations. They also argue that a version of the network society approach could usefully be applied to the telecommunications industry.

No book on innovation and change in the 21st century would be complete without something on e-commerce. Here Hof et al. outline some of the ways in which e-commerce is changing the way we do business. A proportion of the travel and car-buying public have already switched to using the Internet. Of course, like all overly hyped phenomena some claims are exaggerated and in early 2000, many dot.com stockholders paid the price. Nevertheless, e-commerce offers a radically new approach to business and is ignored by any organization at its peril.

21 The Alternative Workplace: Changing Where and How People Work

Mahlon Apgar IV

A spectrum of options

Different companies use different variations on the alternative work (AW) theme to tailor new work arrangements to their own needs. To one company, for example, establishing an alternative workplace may mean simply having some workers on different shifts or travel schedules, share desks and office space. AT&T determined that for some groups of employees, up to six people could use the same desk and equipment formerly assigned to one. The company now has 14,000 employees in shared-desk arrangements.

Replacing traditional private offices with open-plan space is another option. In such arrangements, a company typically provides team rooms and workstations in open areas. Free address facilities are a variation on that format. As Jill M. James, director of AT&T's Creative Workplace Solutions initiative, describes them:

> You are assigned to one facility, but you can move around and choose a variety of work settings during the day. You don't have to log in or put your name tag on a specific work space. And everyone can find you because your phone, pager, and PC go with you.

Some companies have embraced the concept of '*hoteling*'. As in the other shared-office options, 'hotel' work spaces are furnished, equipped and supported with typical office services. Employees may have mobile cubbies, file cabinets or lockers for personal storage; and a computer system routes phone calls and E-mail as necessary. But 'hotel' work spaces are reserved by the hour, by the day or by the week instead of being permanently assigned. In addition, a 'concierge' may provide employees with travel and logistical support. At its most advanced, 'hotel' work space is customized with individuals' personal photos and memorabilia, which are stored electronically, retrieved and 'placed' on occupants' desktops just before they arrive and then removed as soon as they leave.

Satellite offices are another form of alternative workplace. Such offices break up large, centralized facilities into a network of smaller workplaces that can be located close to customers or to employees' homes. Satellites can save a company up to 50% in real estate costs, diversify the risk of overconcentration in a single location and broaden the pool of potential employees. Some are shells – sparsely furnished and equipped with only basic technology; others are fully equipped and serviced. Satellites are generally located in comparatively inexpensive cities and suburban areas. Most often, they have simpler and less costly furnishings and fixtures than their downtown counterparts.

Telecommuting is one of the most commonly recognized forms of alternative workplace. Telecommuting – that is, performing work electronically wherever the worker chooses – generally supplements the traditional workplace rather than replacing it. At IBM, however, telecommuters comprise an entire business unit. And at PeopleSoft, telecommuting is the dominant style of work throughout the entire company.

General Dennis J. Reimer, the US Army's Chief of Staff, offers compelling insight into what an executive can do from a remote location. Reimer travels with a laptop and routinely communicates by E-mail with 350 general officers and 150 garrison commanders around the world. Using a web-based network called America's Army On-line, which also includes an intranet chat room similar to those offered through commercial providers, Reimer can raise issues with his officers and receive advice on key decisions, often within hours. 'The network allows me to be productive and to maintain a pulse on what is happening whether I'm in Washington or overseas,' Reimer says. It not only saves travel costs but also enables collaborative teamwork across organizational and geographic boundaries around the globe.

Gradually, this is changing the culture from one in which 'my information is power' to one in which 'sharing is power'.

Home offices complete the spectrum of AW operations. Companies vary widely in their approaches to home offices. Some simply allow certain employees to work at home at their own discretion and at their own expense. Others – such as AT&T, IBM, and Lucent Technologies – provide laptops, dedicated phonelines, software support, fax-printer units, helplines and full technical backup at the nearest corporate facility. One major company goes still further by providing employees who work at home with a $1000 allowance for furnishings and equipment to be used at their discretion.

Most organizations find that a mix of AW options is better than a one-size-fits-all approach. Indeed, the very concept of the alternative workplace means tailoring the programme to an organization's specific needs. AT&T's Creative Workplace Solutions strategy, for example, combines three options: shared offices, telecommuting and virtual offices. These options can accommodate nearly all AT&T's office-based functions.

Is the alternative workplace right for your organization?

The first step toward determining whether any or all of the AW options could work for your organization is to answer a few basic questions.

Are you committed to new ways of operating?

For example, are you prepared to overhaul performance measures as necessary to align them with the new ways in which employees work? Are you braced for a cultural tailspin as your employees learn new ways of connecting with one another from afar? Are you committed to examining your incentives and rewards policies in light of the different ways in which work maybe completed? Consider what Kevin Rirey, an IBM marketing manager, said about performance measurement and rewards in his unit after the mobility initiative was put in place: 'We've always rewarded for results, but when you are in a traditional office environment and see the effort that people put into a job, it's very difficult not to reward them at least partly for that effort. We don't tend to do that anymore. We focus a lot more on results than on effort. But it's a difficult transition.'

Is your organization informational rather than industrial?

This distinction refers to a management philosophy and style rather than to an economic sector or customer base. *Industrial* in this context means that the organization's structure, systems and management processes are designed for intensive face-to-face interaction and that employees remain rooted to specific workplaces. In such an environment, the potential for AW arrangements are limited.

Informational organizations, by contrast, operate mainly through voice and data communications when it comes to both their employees and their customers. Informational, as used here, does not necessarily mean high-tech. But it does mean that managers and employees are moving up the curve toward information-age literacy, which is characterized by flexibility, informality, the ability to change when necessary, respect for personal time and priorities and a commitment to using technology for improving performance.

Until recently AT&T and IBM were among the many companies perceived by customers and analysts as industrial organizations; that is, they were seen as tradition bound, formal, bureaucratic and slow to change. As former AT&T chairman Robert Allen noted on the company's Telecommuting Day in 1994, 'Work is where the phone is and it's logical that we should work like a phone-based organization. When our initiative began, however, AT&T looked like an antiquated company, with fixed schedules, expensive space and a heavy hierarchy.' When the two companies launched their AW programmes nearly ten years ago, top-level managers had already begun to reposition their organizations as informational.

Do you have an open culture and proactive managers?

A dynamic, hierarchical, technologically advanced organization is more likely than a highly structured, command-driven one to implement an AW programme successfully. That's why so many newer and smaller companies – particularly those that are heavily involved in the business of information or in electronic commerce – are using AW techniques with great success and with few transition pains. Yet as we've seen, even tradition-conscious organizations can use such techniques to eliminate fixed costs and facilitate performance improvements. The key is whether managers at all levels are open to change.

Richard Karl Goeltz, vice-chairman and CEO of American Express, comments:

> It's important to have a multifunction team of senior managers promoting and supporting a virtual-office initiative right from the start. We had three departments involved in our effort: HR, technology, and real estate. The individuals on the team must be enthusiastic and not unnecessarily fettered by traditional approaches. And they must be made knowledgeable about all the key issues – from the ways in which corporate policies may be redefined to deal with various types of problems and opportunities to the different options for providing furniture or allowances to employees. Still, I would be skeptical about whether management by fiat would work very well. It's better to be able to say, 'Here's an opportunity to enable you to do your job better, more efficiently, and more economically. You don't have to use it, but it's here.' What I've seen happen elsewhere – and we're beginning to see it in our own initiatives – is that once a fairly large department takes the first step, others are quick to follow.

Can you establish clear links between staff, functions and time?

AW programmes assume that certain jobs either do not depend on specific locations and types of facilities or depend on them only part of the time. To analyze whether an AW programme can work in your company, you must understand in detail the parameters of each job you are considering for the programme. What function does the job serve? Is the work performed over the phone? In person? Via computer? All of the above? How much time does the employee need to spend in direct contact with other employees, customers and business contacts? Is the location of the office critical to performance? Does it matter whether the job is 9 to 5? Is it important for others to be able to reach the employee immediately?

If a critical mass of corporate functions cannot work in an AW environment, the potential benefits may be too marginal relative to the required investment and effort. But managers who assume intuitively that an AW initiative is limited only to road warriors on the salesforce may be surprised; often, more jobs are suited to a different way of working than at first seems possible. Executives at Dun and Bradstreet, for example, initially thought that only 5% of their global workforce could be involved in an AW programme but learned that two-fifths of the company's functions – involving half their employees – could adapt with only minor adjustments in work practices.

Are you prepared for some 'push back'?

As Lorraine Fenton, vice-president of information technology for IBM North America observes, most 'twenty-somethings' entering the workforce have never had a private office, so to begin their work life without one is not a traumatic change. But for many employees, the transition from conventional to alternative workplaces is not as easy. Employees who are accustomed to a structured office environment may find it hard to adjust to a largely self-directed schedule and those who are used to working within earshot of many colleagues may be lonely in a remote setting. Moreover, middle managers, who lose their visual and verbal proximity to their direct reports, have to change the way in which they relate to those employees. In fact, middle managers usually put up the strongest resistance to the alternative workplace, in large part because they feel as though the very foundations of their roles are being pulled out from under them.

Can you overcome the external barriers to an AW programme?

Even if the work is suited to an AW format and managers and employees alike are amenable to change, physical and logistical barriers may exist. If space is at a premium in employees' homes – for example, if many employees live in small apartments – then an AW initiative that calls for people to work at home may not be feasible. This is a key consideration in US cities and in most countries abroad. In Japan, for instance, there simply is no 'swing' space in most employees' homes that could be used as office space; to accommodate a home–office initiative there, employees would have to sacrifice living space. Conducting employee focus groups at the exploratory and planning stages of an AW initiative can uncover such concerns effectively.

Will you invest in the tools, training and techniques that make AW initiatives work?

To improve the chances of an AW programme's success, all who are involved must be armed with a full set of tools: relevant training and appropriate, flexible administrative support. Are you committed, for example, to providing standardized computer software for people working in all locations? Accessible, qualified technical assistance? Do you have the financial resources to provide all this?

Too many AW programmes are undertaken with only partial support from the organization. Confusion and frustration inevitably ensue, not to mention drops in productivity. These programmes are only marginally successful and might ultimately fail. When an employee at home can't communicate with other employees or clients, access the right information, or easily reach a help desk to solve a technology problem, the initiative is destined to fail. As AT&T's James puts it: 'The technology has to work from the start. When you're asking people to give up their space and all that goes with it, you owe it to them to make sure that the systems are flawless. Because employees are mobile, the tools they use are their lifeline. They can't survive without them.'

If you have answered 'yes' to the foregoing questions, you could seriously consider an AW programme. The next step is to drill down into the economics of AW initiatives.

Tangible and intangible economics

As I suggested earlier, the main reason for AW programmes is to reduce current costs and avoid future ones. For established organizations that are pressed for cash, the savings from relinquishing space and making better use of what remains can dwarf the necessary investment in equipment and training. For young organizations, an AW programme can give managers a viable alternative to expensive, long-term lease commitments.

But for the typical enterprise, the economics of the alternative workplace are more complex and the decision to adopt an AW programme rests as much – or more – on intangibles as it does on simple financials. Jerome T. Roath, IBM's manager of infrastructure expense, says: 'The obvious savings from real-estate cost reduction may hide qualitative improvements in employee satisfaction and customer service that are less measurable but no less important and in the end might justify an [AW] program.' On the flip side, AmEx's Goeltz comments on how a business might think about satellite locations:

> Instead of 2,000 people concentrated in one place, one could consider 100 sites of 20 people each around the country. That might cut real estate costs tremendously. But there would be other critical issues to address. For example, would the company provide cafeteria and health club facilities or instead provide allowances to help people pay for their own? And how does one coordinate HR activities across a dispersed group?

Managers should look at the economics of a potential AW programme from three perspectives – the company's, the employee's and the customer's – and weigh the tangible and intangible costs against the respective benefits. Tangible set-up costs for the company include hardware, software, training and any equipment or furniture the company provides; ongoing costs include allowances, phone charges and technical support. In home offices, employees provide their own space and some, if not all, of the furnishings and equipment. Intangible costs for the company and its employees include the time spent learning new work habits and ways of communicating with colleagues and customers.

Aside from real estate savings, the organization benefits from increased employee productivity, recruiting and retention – usually because AW employees have both more professional and more personal time. In one AT&T unit, for example, the average AW participant gained almost five weeks per year by eliminating a 50-minute daily commute. Employees in home offices and other remote locations also can be more efficient during the workday because they have fewer distractions and less down-time. As AT&T's James notes: 'When I have 30 minutes between meetings, I can load in my disk and be productive on the spot.' Customer satisfaction also improves: as customers become comfortable communicating with the organization electronically, they can reach employees more quickly and receive more direct, personal attention.

Intangible benefits include closer teamwork and greater flexibility. The simple act of removing the walls that separate people in traditional private offices often fosters teamwork. Stephen M. Brazzell, AT&T's vice-president for global real estate, says: 'Connectivity between individuals and groups comes in many forms, both physical and electronic. Those in shared offices tell us, "The new arrangement works. It really helps us communicate quickly and effectively because we're all together." There is a definite improvement in communication, and communication means productivity.' What's more, meetings in the alternative workplace take less time because participants manage their time better; they meet not just to discuss issues but to resolve them.

US Army's Reimer highlights the importance of intangible benefits in his widely dispersed organization:

> The biggest benefit I have found is that leaders who are 'far from the flagpole' in places like Bosnia and Korea have direct access to me and to my latest thoughts on many issues. In turn, I receive feedback from the field army as quickly as I would from my staff at the Pentagon. This empowers our leadership team, and it allows the army to speak and act with one voice on rapidly changing situations.

A crucial intangible benefit of an AW programme is the value that employees place on increased personal time and control. Although they tend to work longer hours and may even have difficulty leaving their home offices, AW employees find the promise of flexibility attractive, so they are easier to recruit and retain. As Reimer says: 'We are now training soldiers when and where it is needed. This not only reduces costs and improves readiness, but it also reduces the time soldiers spend away from home and family – an ever-increasing burden with our intensive training and operational requirements. This helps us retain quality soldiers and their families.'

Box 21.1 illustrates one company's assessment of its tangible economics. Over five years, AT&T's initiative is expected to generate annual savings of nearly $50 million as people become accustomed to and take full advantage of the new style of working. This will be a substantial contribution to AT&T's overall aim of reducing annual occupancy costs by $200 million. The plan begins by defining the ratio of occupants to work space for each type of office, the square feet and cost per person and the expected savings and payback. Shared-office and virtual-office workers use one-third to one-tenth as much corporate space as they do in traditional offices. Over time, these changes could yield annual savings of $5000 to $10,000 per person. For a group of 100 employees occupying space that costs $24 per square foot, the savings range from $200,000 to $600,000 and payback ranges from one to three years. AT&T's James, who authored the plan, estimates that some 34,000, employees – one-quarter of the total – could be accommodated in AW settings by 2003.

IBM's experience in the alternative workplace provides another good example of well-balanced cost-benefit ratios. IBM began piloting various AW options in 1989 to reduce real-estate-related costs and to explore the use of technology to support sales. But by 1993, the company's profitability and competitiveness had declined to the point that more fundamental changes in corporate strategy were called for. In that context, the early pilot projects were transformed into a mainstream initiative in the North America sales and service organization – an initiative designed to improve customer responsiveness, reduce costs and increase productivity.

Box 21.1 AT&T's creative workplace plan

AW's five-year plan reflects the significant impact of creative workplace initiatives on reducing total occupancy costs. The financial benefits result from four interrelated factors to be implemented over time: shifting from traditional to shared and virtual offices, adopting more efficient individual workspace – designs, improving office utilization – reducing total company space and adjusting the number of occupants using company space. The plan's current benchmarks can be summarized as follows.

Benchmarks

			Costs		Savings	
Office type	Utilization ratio	Square foot per person	$ per person (setup)	$ per person (annual)	$ per unit (annual)	Payback (years)
Traditional	1:1	225	12,000	12,000	NA	NA
Shared	3:1	125	7,500	9,000	450,000	1.4
Virtual	10:1	30	5,000	6,000	600,000	0.8

$ per person (annual) includes real estate, voice and data communication costs
$ per unit is based on a 100-person unit occupying leased space at $24 per sq foot

---

Lee A. Dayton, IBM's vice-president for corporate development and real estate, recalls:

Two principles were – and are – at the heart of the initiative. First, we want to reduce our employees' travel time. When they are travelling from one customer to another, or from the IBM office to the customer, they're not productive. Second, if employees are at home or at a customer's office, we want to eliminate the need to travel to an IBM office. And if they're not going to work in an IBM office, we want to eliminate the dedicated space with all of its overhead and services.

Currently, IBM's entire US salesforce can operate independently of a traditional workplace. More than 12,000 employees have given up their dedicated work spaces and another 13,000 are capable of mobile operation. IBM also has implemented mobility initiatives, involving some 15,000 employees in Asia, Europe and Latin America. Thus, approximately 17% of IBM's total worldwide workforce is sufficiently equipped and trained to work in AW formats and one-third of all the company's departments have at least some mobile employees.

The results? In 1992, worldwide occupancy and voice-IT expenses (that is, phone-based communication charges) totalled $5.7 billion. By 1997, the total had dropped 42% to $3.3 billion. During that period, real estate savings totalled $1 billion from mobility initiatives alone. Even more telling, worldwide costs per person declined 38% from $15,900 to $9800 and the combined ratio of occupancy and voice-IT expenses to revenues dropped from 8.8% to 4.2% – a 52% improvement. (See Box 21.2.)

Box 21.2 Economics of mobility at IBM North America

IBM's entire US salesforce can operate independently of a traditional office. More than 12,500 employees have given up their dedicated work spaces and another 13,000 are capable of mobile operation. Managers monitor the performance of the company's mobility initiative in several ways, including those illustrated in Figure 21.1.

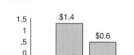

Total occupancy and voice-IT costs
$ billion

Occupancy and voice-IT costs per person
$ thousand

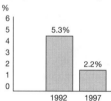

Occupany and IT-costs as a percentage of revenue

Figure 21.1

    The top chart shows the total occupancy and voice-IT costs for IBM North America. The middle chart, which breaks down those costs by employee, helps managers assess whether the mobility initiative is using space, information and communications efficiently. The bottom chart, which shows total occupancy and voice-IT costs as a percentage of IBM North America's revenue, helps managers assess the productivity and efficiency of the mobility initiative.

    As Roath comments, IBM must keep close watch over voice-IT charges. They are still small compared with occupancy costs and other IT expenses, but they could explode as more people go mobile. Still, Dayton says: 'The costs you incur with mobility – IT technology, communications, wireless costs – are all going down, while the relative costs of real estate continue to rise.'

    Dayton also notes that the key to success is evaluating and managing the initiative with the ultimate business goal in mind:

We cost-justified our program based on reductions in spending, primarily from real estate. From the start, we allowed business managers to make the trade-off between real estate savings and investments in technology. And we insisted on saving more than we spent. Every laptop and cellular phone we bought for the initiative was cost-justified. We also introduced an annual worldwide scorecard that tallied cost and square feet per person. The scorecard applied to manufacturing and development departments as well as to sales and distribution. We published the results internally, and, of course, nobody wanted to be last.

Looking ahead, John Newton, IBM's manager of IT plans and measurements, believes that the company's extraordinary cost savings will plateau: 'The main short-term problem in mobility economics is that as more people go mobile, we still need a support structure for them. We are reaching a point of diminishing returns, because we can't keep pulling people out of offices forever. There will be productivity benefits but not occupancy cost savings!'

Indeed, any organization adopting an AW initiative can be expected to reach a new plateau – with lower fixed costs, higher productivity and greater employee and customer satisfaction than it previously experienced. But by redeploying some of the savings into better equipment, technical support, even the company picnic, the organization that benefits from AW initiatives can realize further dividends in employee commitment and loyalty.

22 The Society of Networks

Geoff Mulgan and Ivan Briscoe

Technologies transform the nature of forms. Sometimes they make new organizational forms necessary. The car, for example, a new infrastructure of garages and service stations and, as Alfred Chandler wrote brilliantly in *The Visible Hand*, the railways impelled the invention of the modern corporation to keep track of a far more complex logistical system. At other times technologies make new organizational forms possible: the telephone, for example, made it possible to manage dispersed operations in real time, while the car made possible the suburb and the supermarket.

Today a new wave of technologies is once again transforming the nature of organizations. Virtual companies are being established without an office and in some cases without even any staff. Small software companies are emerging as if from nowhere to become corporate titans. Traders are now dealing on world markets from remote cottages.

Given the remarkable level of innovation in organizational forms it is surprising that most commentators take it for granted that the age of cyberspace will be based on the classic organizational models of the 20th century. There is no shortage of imagination about the technologies and uses of the superhighway, but it is still widely assumed that the networks of the 21st century will be organized in the same way as the infrastructures of the past, either as publicly owned corporations or as regulated private ones.

The organizational forms which have dominated this century were designed for an age of materially based industry, for economics based on hardware and for relatively uneducated workforces. Their characteristics have tended to be uniformity, standardization, clear and pyramidal lines of management and unified ownership. Within the organization the norm has been to have hierarchical command structures exercising control over dispersed production processes, flows of goods and over labour, much of which has been devoted precisely definable repetitive tasks, whether in the factory or the classroom, the government office or the hospital.

The information age has posed fundamental challenges to these models of behaviour and production in two ways. The first is that it tends to favour difference rather than uniformity. Employees in classic industrial occupations have to perform their tasks consistently and predictably. Autonomy and variation threaten the smooth running of the machine. Where information and knowledge are concerned, by contrast, the value the employee adds is less predictable, concerned with creativity, with reshaping information for new uses. The second major difference is that far faster flows of information make it possible to organize in far more complex ways, with networks or flotillas of organizations joined together loosely, rather than depending on integrated command structures.

These differences are particularly evident in the case of infrastructures. Where the classic infrastructure provided a largely undifferentiated product (such as gas, electricity or water) or an undifferentiated carrying capacity (like a motorway), in the information age what is required is a far more varied set of services, ranging from mobile communications to databases. And where the classic firm and the classic infrastructure could be vertically integrated, those of the information age seem to work best by articulating diverse types of service supply and diverse types of use.

Unfortunately, few of the key organizations in the information industry reflect this new reality. The great majority are organized on traditional principles and are little different from firms in manufacturing or retailing. Yet it is a striking fact that those which have designed their organizational shape to reflect the nature of information have, on the whole, proven far more successful than those which have stuck to older models.

One of these is the Internet, the fastest growing medium in human history. The Internet is not owned by anyone, but makes use of leased lines to interconnect different public and private networks. There is no substantial physical body underlying the whole operation – which is why the term 'cyberspace' was coined to describe the virtual by net surfers. Central to the popularity of this 'network of networks' is its distribution of intelligence and innovative capacity throughout the system. The Internet is essentially a 'bottom-up' structure. Innovations on the net have generally come from users and niche software companies: the world wide web, for instance, was invented by a computer scientist in Switzerland, while the companies which provide connection to the Net are small operations, almost all under five years old.

From complexity and network chaos has emerged something like order and a slow but very useful system of knowledge and communication. While large telecom companies have lumbered into broadband technology, this initially low-key and highly technical medium for communication has become an extraordinary success. This performance has owed nothing to advertising or corporate brainstorming; it has been the system's adaptability, the freedom it gives users, which have given it its edge.

The second model of an information age organization is Visa, in financial services. Instead of offering a credit card supported by the resources of one bank or a consortium of banks – like the failed experiments of American banks in the 1960s – Visa operates a credit card service which is owned by the large number of financial institutions (over 20,000) which offer its cards and services. Visa itself is only a skeletal overseeing administrative organization linking the operations of its members into a cohesive and efficient whole. It is, in short, an organization which enables. By doing this, it has succeeded in managing seven billion transactions per annum, worth over $650 billion. This is, according to Visa's founding chief executive Dee Hock, 'the largest single block of consumer purchasing power in the world economy'.

What is interesting about both these new forms of organization is the way in which they operate broad infrastructures incorporating diversity, competition and multiple lines of power. It is no coincidence that the areas in which they have thrived are markets for information – markets in which the number of transactions, exchanges and communications handled would bemuse many more centrally directed organizations. Instead of being paralyzed by this complexity, they have flourished on it. Consumers have been drawn to Visa by the ease of using the card anywhere in the world; constant innovations, like cheap voice transmission, broaden the appeal of the Internet each year.

New theoretical accounts of the organization have trailed in the wake of the information age. Dee Hock has advocated the development of more 'chaordic' organizations such as Visa, which would avoid the institutional sclerosis experienced by hierarchical 'command-and-control' organizations. By distributing ownership and power, according to Hock, an organization or infrastructure can embrace huge complexity and, like the human mind, evolve into an extremely effective organism able to withstand shocks and incorporate new ideas. This biological motif is also prominent in the work of Internet expert Kevin Kelly, who champions evolutionary models for complex systems of information exchange (and many other types of co-ordinated networks or systems). He argues that our fixation with mechanical design is damaging – and likely to retard innovations in a huge number of scientific and informational fields: a neo-biological technology is far more rewarding than a world of clocks, gears and predictable simplicity.

Many organizations are ill suited to this type of organic structure: the form of their product or the nature of their markers make evolutionary, fragmented designs inappropriate. Railway networks would fall apart in such a loosely co-ordinated, haphazard environment (although the most imaginative thinking in transport is concentrating on how information and connections between different forms of transport can reduce journey times and waiting times, in contrast with the traditional emphasis on capacity – such as high-speed rail links or new roads).

The new systems also have their faults. The Internet is currently plagued by public concerns about the on-line distribution of pornography and racist or even terrorist propaganda. Freedom for users does not always translate into moral rectitude. And so far it has proven hard to adapt the Internet into a genuine market, able to sustain financial transactions.

But there are important lessons to be drawn about how the infrastructures of the next century might be better organized. The current debate sees the choice as one between monopolistic public utilities and competitive (large) private firms. The wider public interest is conceived in terms of a set of social obligations to be imposed on these firms by a regulator – such as the obligation to connect schools and hospitals or externally imposed controls on pricing.

This faith in regulation as the key to a successful information society rests on the successes of the 1980s. Pricing controls and regulatory rules encouraged greater competition, lower prices and a wider range of services. Regulated competitive markets proved more innovative and more efficient than earlier models of state monopoly. But recent developments have shown up the limits of regulated competition. Regulators have found it hard to understand the technological trends and cost structures of the firms they are regulating. Despite competition, erstwhile monopolists remain overwhelmingly dominant and, more importantly, it has proven far harder than many expected to open up networks to a multiplicity of service providers. In part this is because of conflicts of interest: vertically integrated dominant companies, like BT in Britain and Deutsche Telekom in Germany, are involved both in providing services themselves and the services of others. Moreover because these large telecom companies have their origins in an engineering-based culture and the more traditional job of providing an undifferentiated service, their cultures may be ill suited to the far more customer-oriented task of cultivating a myriad of new services, ranging from teleshopping to education, video-on-demand to home alarm systems.

If the information superhighway is to become anything like a supermarket of options, then something has to be done to guarantee open access and diverse content.

The alternative model, what we call a 'society of networks', draws on the approach taken by Visa and is deliberately designed to suit the nature of an informational infrastructure. Instead of having the superhighway run either by a single network operator or by a small group of competing private companies, all service providers (including, in the British case, BT and Mercury, Ionica and Energis) would have a share of ownership in an open profit-making association governing the main network infrastructure. As with Visa, membership would be open to any service provider able to meet set criteria, rather than being a closed cartel.

There would still be strong incentives to improve the network and the technology used. But unlike current models, there would also be an incentive to minimize the cost of access, since service providers will naturally want to maximize the market for their services. This would not be a model of monopoly. Indeed it should have, and would need, no formal privileges. Any competing network provider would be free to set up in competition. But the odds are that most service providers would want to remain part of the 'society'.

This vision of the broadband network would achieve many of the goals that liberalization and deregulation have found elusive. It would ensure open access to the core network, incentives to maximize usage and keep prices low and provide permanent competitive pressures. By building both competition and cooperation into the very heart of the organization, it would enable regulation to be more focused and more effective. Complexity could be managed in something resembling the 'distributed control' of Kelly's predictions.

Looking further ahead, the society of networks model suggests how businesses could evolve in the future. Instead of developing internally, either through growth or acquisition by a single organizational entity, the key issues in the future business environment may come to concern what we might call the interfaces: the means by which different units interconnect. In the case of the Internet and Visa these are clear-cut rules governing such things as transactions and technical standards. In other types of organization they might include shared commitments to principles or rules governing the exchange of knowledge. These would become the glues of federations that both compete and cooperate. Whose elements are both autonomous and interdependent.

Structures of this kind seem to defy the logic of organizations in the industrial age. Whereas industrial-age organizations were defined by their boundaries, in this new model the key characteristic of an organization is the range and number of connections to the outside environment – its connectivity. This is the virtue of the society of networks model. The fact that the Internet is the fastest growing medium and Visa the highest turnover business enterprise the world has ever seen, is proof that these models are more than an abstract idea. They have a capacity to grow and to adapt that no other organizational form can match.

23   The 'Click Here' Economy

Robert D. Hof with Gary McWilliams and Gabrielle Saveri

Mike Dobres knew something was up a few years ago, when prospective buyers started walking into his car dealership with printouts of dealer invoice prices. Dobres, general sales manager of Royal Motor Sales in San Francisco, quickly realized that car-buying services on the Internet, such as Auto-By-Tel Corp., were giving customers a frightening new edge on his salespeople. Since then, his profits have sunk by as much as 25%. 'People know what you pay for your car,' he sighs, 'and they don't let you make the big profits.'

Some 2000 miles east, car dealer Jeff Peters is downright chipper about the Internet. The sales manager of Byers Chrysler Plymouth Dodge in Columbus, Ohio, hooked up four months ago with Autoweb.com, a net car-buying service and is now selling 12 additional cars per month on top of his usual 160 – and paying just $29 per Internet referral. His biggest surprise: a wired buyer in Kentucky, hundreds of miles away, struck a deal with him. Says Peters: 'There's no way I could've gotten that guy without the Internet.'

Big threats and fresh opportunities – that's the web. The companies embracing the web and weaving it to their own ends – whether they're using it to sell products, streamline operations or automate customer service – are thriving. For the rest, blithely buzzing along in real space, things are getting very sticky very fast. 'This is fundamentally a new economy that will displace and rebuild the existing economy,' says analyst Clay Ryder of Zona Research Inc. in Redwood City, California.

Without a doubt, the Internet is ushering in an era of sweeping change that will leave no business or industry untouched. In just three years, the net has gone from a playground for nerds into a vast communications and trading centre where some 90 million people swap information or do deals around the world. Imagine: It took radio more than 30 years to reach 60 million people and television 15 years. Never has a technology caught fire so fast.

Selling everywhere

But then, few have made this much sense. Like a central nervous system, the information highway courses around the globe, making all manner of commerce instantly possible. More than 400,000 companies have hung www.————-.com atop their digital doorways with the notion that being anywhere on the net means they can sell virtually everywhere. And sure enough, sales are picking up: goods and services sold online to US and European consumers topped $5.1 billion – more than double the 1997 figure, according to Forrester Research Inc.

While that's still small in the grand scheme of business, the numbers don't come close to capturing the real wallop of the net. Beyond the glitzy websites and chatrooms, businesses are adopting the Internet to get serious work done. By using the Internet to link directly to suppliers, factories, distributors and customers, these companies are electrifying their usually time-consuming and tedious tasks.

It is nothing less than the collapse of time and space between partners. With the help of the web, businesses are wringing time out of product design, speeding up the order and delivery of components, tracking sales by the hour and getting instant feedback from customers – all the while keeping inventories to a bare minimum. It is reengineering all over again, only this time geared to getting every nanosecond of advantage out of the Internet. 'If companies can learn to get the slop out of the system – and the Internet is absolutely crucial for this – prices come down,' says Bryan Stolle, chief executive officer at Agile Software Corp. in San Jose, California.

Savings and speed

Indeed, behind this blinding speed shimmers the promise of incredible efficiency. Companies have barely begun to realize how potent the net can be. But consider the vanguard already wired. At Boeing Co., there are 75 projects for using the net to connect to contractors and customers – everything from zapping documents to the government to tracking the history of every plane Boeing sells. The expected savings will reach into the millions of dollars. And at Adaptec Inc. in Milpitas, California, the maker of computer storage products has sped up communications with its Taiwanese chip suppliers by way of links over the net. The results have been marked: Adaptec has reduced its time from order to delivery by more than half, to just 55 days, and the company has saved more than $1 million in costs.

Saving money is just the start. The ultimate prize is the creation of new wealth: as the net tears down the walls of geography, companies are creating entirely new businesses and tapping markets they never could have reached before. Network

ONLINE SALES ARE SOARING

FINANCIAL SERVICES
1997: $1.2 billion
2001: $5 billion*

APPAREL AND FOOTWARE
1997: $92 million
2001: $514 million*

PC HARDWARE AND SOFTWARE
1997: $863 million
2001: $8.8 billion*

TICKET EVENT SALES
1997: $79 million
2001: $2 billion*

ENTERTAINMENT
1997: $298 million
2001: $2.7 billion*

TRAVEL
1997: $654 million
2001: $7.4 billion*

BOOKS AND MUSIC
1997: $156 million
2001: $1.1 billion*

BUSINESS-TO-BUSINESS SALES
1997: $8 billion
2001: $183 billion*

Figure 23.1

Associates in Santa Clara, California, for instance, doesn't market its anti-virus software in many countries outside the United States because it's too expensive. But recently its first sale of a new help-desk software product came from a bank in Spain, which downloaded it and ordered a 30-seat license. 'That's the marketing power you get online,' says division manager Zach Nelson. 'Instant sale. No cost.' (See Figure 23.1.)

Kitty Hawk era

It's the promise of frictionless capitalism. And there are signs that it is gaining speed. US businesses will exchange an estimated $17 billion in goods and services over the net, more than double the amount in 1997, according to Forrester. By 2002, that's expected to explode to $327 billion. Combine that with cost savings to business and online consumer buying and the Internet could add an estimated $10 billion to $20 billion to gross domestic product in four years, *Business Week* estimates. Says Jeff Bezos, chief executive of web bookseller Amazon.com: 'This is the Kitty Hawk era of electronic commerce.'

That's the upside. With the emergence of a new era also comes upheaval across nearly every industry, often with frightening results. The flip side of squeezing inefficiencies out of business transactions, after all, is that it sometimes squeezes out entire businesses along the way. In coming years, thousands of employees could find their jobs turned topsy-turvy as human tasks, such as selling airline tickets or tending to customer complaints over the phone, are taken over by the one-to-one, buyer-to-seller, nature of the net.

One of the first to feel the pinch: the travel industry. When you can bone up on vacation destinations, compare flights and purchase an airline ticket on the net, what's left for the travel agent? Some travel sites offer an option to have an agent issue the ticket, but 'customers see no added value' in that, says Rich Barton, general manager of Microsoft Travel Services, which runs the Expedia travel website. Just ask Vanita Louie, president of San Francisco-based South Pacific Express Travels, a $25 million agency. 'We've lost at least 10% to 15% of our sales to the Internet over the past year,' she laments.

From travel agents to stockbrokers to retailers, businesses are feeling the force of the net. The threat goes by the unwieldy name disintermediation – the process of cutting out middlemen. But whatever you call it, it's already taking a big bite out of companies that have been slow to adapt to the massive changes the net has wrought. Online brokerages, for example, are quickly gaining converts, with more than 5 million accounts. E*Trade Group Inc. trumpets savings over traditional brokers in TV ads and billboards that declare: 'Someday, everyone will trade this way.' It also offers a free book punningly titled *Boot Your Broker*. Cracks E*Trade CEO Christos M. Cotsakos: 'The brokerage branch network will be a great place to have fast food franchises.'

Blurring roles

Indeed, the net is deconstructing the fundamental nature of business transactions. As every link in the supply chain is wired, the traditional roles of manufacturers, distributors and suppliers are blurring – and buyers will be the ultimate winners. Why? Because on the web, buyers can quickly compare products and prices from a wide range of suppliers faster and more easily than ever before – putting them in a better bargaining position. They can even share information among themselves. 'The balance of power shifts away from business and to the consumer,' says Amazon.com's Bezos.

The same goes for corporate buyers. The web makes it easier to deal with multiple suppliers, which is often too cumbersome and time consuming to do offline. Wired corporations find themselves armed to play suppliers off one another and get lower prices or better service. General Electric Co. bought $1 billion worth of supplies via the net last year. That saved the company 20% on materials costs because its divisions were able to reach a wider base of suppliers to hammer out better deals. By 2000, GE expects to be buying $5 billion over the net.

Profitable websites

The upshot: 'It's a huge sea change for all businesses,' says Tim Koogle, CEO of Internet portal Yahoo! Inc. Koogle should know: Yahoo! started as a commercial operation in 1995 with a simple, if humongous, list of websites to help people navigate the web. But like the web itself, Yahoo! is changing fast. The once amazing ability to search the entire world wide web became prosaic in a net instant, so Yahoo!, at the tender age of two years, began reinventing itself as a place to trade stocks, make travel reservations and conduct commerce. It's even profitable, valued by investors at an almost unthinkable $5.5 billion – more than Apple, Circuit City, Dow Jones or Maytag.

Yahoo! isn't the only net pioneer taking wing. From stodgy industries such as utilities and insurance to fast-moving businesses such as computers and stock trading, companies are taking advantage of the net to revamp their businesses or build brand-new ones.

And they're no longer black holes for investment. By the close of 1997, the number of profitable websites – both for consumers and for inter-business transactions – jumped to 46%, ending three years of stagnation at 30%, according to a survey by market researcher ActivMedia of Peterborough, NH. And some 81% of the remainder expect to be profitable in a year or two. 'We're being transformed into a "click here" economy,' says Renee Cantu, marketing promotions programme manager for SportsSite.com, an online sports equipment retailer.

No company has grasped that better than Dell Computer, a direct seller of personal computers. Its famed build-to-order model was initially based on telephone orders by customers and on the weekly blizzards of purchase orders it faxed to parts suppliers. Even before the birth of the public Internet, Dell's supply chain was efficient, its inventories lean and its profits lush.

Cloning

Then the Internet happened, and Dell began minting money. Today, instead of daily fax alerts to warehouses telling everyone what supplies are needed, Dell sends messages out every two hours over the net. Dell's suppliers also get an inside view of the company's inventories and production plans and they receive constant feedback on how well they are meeting shipping criteria. Now, its speed in customizing and delivering products is unmatched. Inventory on hand is down to eight days – vs. Compaq's 26 – and revenue growth is about 55%.

The Internet, is helping Dell shatter conventional wisdom about how computers are best bought and sold. Compaq, HP and IBM have tried to clone Dell's direct-sales

Figure 23.2 How the Internet changes (almost) everything

Businesses are ahead of consumers in embracing the Internet. Even the slow-growing business markets are bigger than fast-growing consumer sectors.

Business purchases

Early adoption
Durable goods:
Led by makers of computers and other high-tech hardware, more than 43% of durable-goods manufacturers will conduct business-to-business commerce over the Internet by 2001, with sales reaching $99 billion, says Forrester Research.
Wholesaling:
Companies that wholesale office supplies, electronics goods and scientific equipment are embracing the net. Projected sales by 2001: $89 billion.

Later adoption
Services:
Doctors, lawyers and accountants generally provide their services in person – one reason the sector will be slower to adopt e-commerce. Projected sales by 2001: $19 billion.
Transportation:
Most transportation companies are already committed to the alternative known as electronic data interchange (EDI), so Forrester says Internet sales by 2001 might be only $300 million.

Consumer purchases

Early adoption
Travel:
Flyers are bedeviling agents by browsing the Internet for bargain fares. Sales in 2001: $7.4 billion.
Computer software and hardware:
It's an ideal sector for e-commerce. Buyers tend to be net-savvy, and you don't need to sniff, squeeze, or try on the merchandise. Forrester projects 2001 sales of $3.8 billion.
Books, music and entertainment: This is a sector where online purchases may raise total spending, not just cannibalize sales from brick-and-mortar merchants. Forrester's 2001 forecast is $3.8 billion.

Later adoption
Housing:
The Internet is a great place to browse for houses, apartments and mortgage loans, but transactions are still being done the old-fashioned way.
Food and beverages:
Supermarkets won't be closing their doors anytime soon. Forrester pegs 2001 sales at $460 million – less than for gifts, flowers and greetings.
Services:
Telemedicine notwithstanding, healthcare is still a face-to-face business. Same goes for most other services – except computer updates and fixes, which are an online natural.

Data: Forrester Research Inc. Business Week

model. And they've all snatched up similar electronic tools to streamline dealings with retailers. But the new supply chain logic demands revolutionary tactics and a rethinking of every business process, which for now elude Dell's competitors, who still rely heavily on dealers. The PC prices you will find on IBM's direct-to-consumer web pages aren't any lower than what's already available in retail stores and they don't match Dell's.

For all the ruckus net-age wizards like Dell may be causing, the result long-term likely will be an explosion of brand-new business. Even as some businesses see their prospects dim, new digital middlemen – call them cybermediaries – are cropping up to fill opportunities spawned by e-commerce (see Figure 23.2).

New wave

Experts see a big role for sites that bring together buyers and sellers and provide value by offering trusted advice, personal service or other benefits. This, says Zona's Ryder, is the start of the third wave of Internet commerce: not just saving money, not just selling existing products online, but generating new wealth. Says Paul Saffo, director of the Institute for the Future, a think tank in Menlo Park, California: 'At the end of the day, you end up with more intermediaries, not fewer.'

These new cybermediaries range from portals such as Yahoo! to net start-ups that are creating unique markets on the net – such as FastParts Inc., a site where electronics companies around the world buy and sell surplus parts. 'If the Internet hadn't come along,' says FastParts chairman Gerry Haller, 'this business wouldn't have worked.'

The business models these upstarts are employing are as diverse as they are inventive. Some, such as Instill Corp. – which serves as a virtual order desk for restaurants and food service operators – streamline an inefficient buying process. Others are consumer magnets, drawing buyers with useful info or services and steering them to manufacturers and service providers in return for a fee or a cut of transactions. These services include sites such as Auto-By-Tel and Autoweb.com, credit companies such as Get-Smart.com and E-Loan and insurance services such as InsWeb Corp.

Some of the greatest opportunities lie in using the net to simplify complex and costly transactions. Realtor.com, a site for home buyers, is streamlining the harrowing task of purchasing a home. Stuart Wolff, CEO of the start-up in Westlake Village, California, figures there are up to a dozen middlemen involved in a typical home sale, from realtors to title agents. Realtor.com, which is affiliated with the National Association of Realtors, directs shoppers to one of its realtors – no surprise. But it hopes to automate many other aspects of home sales, such as loans and title searches.

These digital middlemen aim to be the nexus of large numbers of buyers and sellers. The key dynamic: once the cybermediary gathers a critical mass of buyers and sellers, more keep flocking there, because that's where the action is. 'Do you want to be where there're 800 Beanie Babies or 8000 Beanie Babies?' asks Meg Whitman, CEO of eBay, a website that lets individuals auction off products to each other.

By continuing to gather buying power, digital go-betweens will soon be able to flex some muscle up the supply chain. Ask Payam Zamani, co-founder and executive vice-president of Autoweb.com. He believes his site offers such an economical way to reach car buyers that it will spur consolidation among dealers and Autoweb will take on more of the customer relationship. 'The business model is not complete until we control 100% of the buying process,' says Zamani. What does the auto-sales business of the future look like? 'Ultimately, there will be virtual dealerships. It will be more cost-effective to send cars to homes to test-drive than to have 300 cars sitting in a lot.'

Naturally, traditional dealers and manufacturers don't relish the idea of these upstarts gaining all the clout, so they, too, are jockeying for position. Early starters such as Cisco are already selling $11 million in networking gear a day on the net, and Dell is selling $5 million a day in PCs.

Yet most existing businesses must walk a fine line on the net. They risk upsetting partnerships with distributors and retailers. Conflict with an existing sales channel was the biggest impediment to selling online cited by respondents to a recent *Business Week*/Harris poll. That's hard to justify when net commerce is still so small relative to their overall businesses and returns far from certain.

And it explains why firms such as Goldman, Sachs & Co. and Merrill Lynch & Co. are deliberating over how to go online, where discount brokers proliferate. 'On the Internet, there's no shortage of information, but wisdom is a valued commodity,' says Randal Langdon, director of interactive sales technologies for Merrill Lynch, which is cautiously moving its business – and its 14,000 financial consultants – onto the net.

No wonder the net is keeping a lot of executives and business owners up at night. Liz Heller, executive vice-president at Capitol Records Inc., for instance, is worried that unauthorized net-based music sites could soon take a big bite out of CD sales. 'It's all happening faster than we thought,' she frets. 'How do you stop a moving train?'

Make that a speeding bullet.

Index